Management for Professionals

The Springer series "Management for Professionals" comprises high-level business and management books for executives, MBA students, and practice-oriented business researchers. The topics cover all themes relevant to businesses and the business ecosystem. The authors are experienced business professionals and renowned professors who combine scientific backgrounds, best practices, and entrepreneurial vision to provide powerful insights into achieving business excellence.

The Series is SCOPUS-indexed.

Philip Bauer

A Comprehensive Project Management Guide

Quality Management, Integrated Six-Sigma and Change Management Compilation

Springer

Philip Bauer
Six Sigma Management Academy
Köln, Nordrhein-Westfalen, Germany

ISSN 2192-8096 ISSN 2192-810X (electronic)
Management for Professionals
ISBN 978-3-031-68251-3 ISBN 978-3-031-68252-0 (eBook)
https://doi.org/10.1007/978-3-031-68252-0

This Springer imprint is published by the registered company Springer Nature Switzerland AG
The registered company address is: Gewerbestrasse 11, 6330 Cham, Switzerland

Preamble

The **Project Management Compilation** is based on the IPMA® competence baseline (ICB) version 3.0, which itself is also heavily related to the project management standards: PMBOK Guide (official ANSI Norm) and DIN. Purpose of this workbook is to provide supporting self-study material to complement the daily project management needs. It offers:

- A reliable basis for theoretical and practical work
- A reference and a comprehensive overview of the current state of development of project management and adjacent disciplines
- A tailored working basis for master's studies on "project management"
- A compilation of knowledge from experienced industry experts from around the world

Innovative problem-solving in interdisciplinary project groups is an essential characteristic of successful, flexible companies. The field of possible assignments can be very broad, ranging from a short-term solution of an economic organizational problem to the implementation of long-term, complex investment projects.

Project management is a cross-disciplinary method and is now the standard—for the planning and control purposes. The individual techniques and tools are not the key elements, but rather the focus on the successful resolution of the project task. The use of appropriate computer applications also belongs to the tools of the project manager, as well as modern methods of project and process control.

This and several other aspects—including an in-depth look at the Six Sigma philosophy of project management with practical examples for the industry—are covered in this workbook.

Contents

List of Abbreviations

ETC	Estimated time to completion
AC	Actual cost
ACWP	Actual cost of work performed
ANSI	American National Standards Institute6
APM	Agile project management
BAC	Budget at Completion
BCWP	Budgeted cost of work performed
BCWS	Cost of work scheduled
BIC	Best-in-class
BOM	Bill of material
CEO	Chief executive officer
CPI	Cost performance index
CPM	Critical path method
CTQ	Critical to quality
CTS	Critical to satisfaction
CV	Cost variance
D	Duration
DCOV	Define, characterize, optimize, verify
DFMEA	Design failure mode and effects analysis
DFSS	Design for Six Sigma
DIN	Deutsche Institut für Normung e. V.
DMAIC	Define, measure, analyse, improve, and control
DPCI	Rating
EAC	Estimate at completion
EET	Earliest end time
EPC	Engineering procurement construction
EQ	Emotional quotient
EST	Earliest start time
ETC	Estimate to complete
ETC	Estimated total cost
EV	Earned value
EVA	Earned value analysis
EVM	Earned value management
FB	Float buffer

FBB	Free float buffer
FEED	Front-end engineering design
FMEA	Failure mode and effects analysis
FPDS	Ford Production Development System
GPD	Global production system
HOAI	Honorarordnung für Architekten und Ingenieure
HOQ	House of Quality
IB	Independent buffer
ICB	International Competence Baseline
IPMA	International Project Management Association
IRR	Internal rate of return
ISO	International Organization for Standardization
IT	Information technology
JIT	Just in time
KAIZEN	Change for better
KANBAN	Signboard
KIV	Key input variables
KLT	Key life tests
KOV	Key output variable
KPIV	Key process input variable
LET	Latest end time
LST	Latest start time
MSA	Measurement system analysis
MTA	Milestone trend analysis
NASA	National Aeronautics and Space Administration.
NIST	National Institute of Standards
PDM	Precedence diagram method
PERT	Project (or program) evaluation and review technique
PFMEA	Process failure mode and effects analysis
PM	Project management
PMBOK	Project Management Body of Knowledge
PMO	Project management office
POC	Point of closure
PRINCE2	Projects IN Controlled Environments
PV	Planned value
Q1	First quarter
Q3	Third quarter
QFD	Quality functional deployment
QM	Quality management
R	Responsible
R&R	Repeatability and reproducibility
RFP	Request for proposal
RFQ	Request for quote
SAC	Schedule at completion
SCRUM	Scrummage

Serum	Crowd
SMART	Specific, measurable, achievable, relevant, and time-bound
SPI	Schedule performance index
SV	Schedule variance
TFB	Total float buffer
TOC	Theory of constraints
TQM	Total quality management
V. Nr	Node number
VAC	Variance of completion
V-Modell XT	Extreme tailoring
VOC	Voice of the customer
WBS	Work breakdown structure
WP	Work package

List of Figures

List of Tables

Project, Project Management, and PM Process

1

1.1 Project and Project Management

The first rudimentary elements of the project management were developed at the time of the construction of the pyramids (e.g., documentation of salary, documentation of the construction progress and crisis management at the premature death of a Pharaoh) and at the time of the construction of the Great Wall of China. The Romans military engineers drove the construction of their forts by planning them systematically so they could build faster and efficiently. Systematic planning to reduce complexity was applied to the building of forts, ecclesiastical and secular construction projects, and the planning of warfare. Even in modern times project management has not ceased to develop. The most prominent project management improvement actions required were for the NASA Apollo program after the near disaster that befell Apollo 13.

A few years ago, continuity and stability were the bywords of corporate operations. Now, with companies facing ever more demanding customers and tougher competition, on-going operational performance improvement has become a strategic essential. Executives are constantly trying to wring improved performance from their operations by following Yellow-Brick Roads, Balanced Scorecard, Supply-Chain Integration—or with any of a dozen other popular programs, including today's favourite, Six Sigma.

But although each of these performance-improving initiatives can generate operating results, they need to be positioned under a process management that if they are to be successfully integrated. Otherwise, companies face the risk of program abundance, of being burdened with disconnected improvement efforts. Program abundance is dangerous: It dissipates resources and creates confusion as people try to understand how each effort relates to the others. It creates harmful competition among specialists, with each group promoting its program as the worthiest of resources. It also fosters suspicion; employees believe that management cannot be serious about so many programs and hence think the company is serious about none.

P. Bauer, *A Comprehensive Project Management Guide*, Management for Professionals, https://doi.org/10.1007/978-3-031-68252-0_1

Companies such as Ford, ThyssenKrupp, Bombardier, Air Products, and Johnson & Johnson avoid the dangers of program abundance by integrating their performance improvement initiatives under the banner of process management. Doing so, they ensure that these efforts match rather than compete with one another and are able to manage their collection of initiatives in an organized way. In particular, positioning Six Sigma under the process management umbrella ensures that a company benefits from this important tool while avoiding the trap of applying it where it does not fit.

Nowadays projects are a common phenomenon. We find projects in all areas in industry, in administration, in teaching, or even in leisure activates. Projects are seen as a challenge that need a special approach, namely project management.

Projects are always goal oriented, i.e., each project should have a defined measurable objective connected to the customer and to a business objective and there is a high degree of complexity according to kind and extent. Large size projects require the division of the project task into subtasks. These interdependent subtasks can even compete with each other as well as with non-project tasks for the allocation of resources.

The project is therefore content and time-limited. The task to be solved is extraordinary in a sense and is normally located outside the operational routine (daily work). Due to the different nature of the project tasks, it is necessary to structure plan and control the tasks. For this reason, methods and techniques are applied to master the complexity such as Six Sigma, Kaizen, and Lean management and project management that requires clear structures and discipline. This principle also follows the philosophy of Six Sigma.

In addition, projects require an interdisciplinary cooperation of specialists from various fields, who support with their relevant expertise, and working together with various outside vendors is often required.

1.2 Definition of Project

A project is often connected with a high degree of innovation because a project is usually located outside the routine process area. A project is always a temporary activity or task dependent on limited resources, time, and organizational structures it emerges from a product, a service, an event, or a change. A project is unique and has a start and end date.

> 🕮 Definition: "A *Project* is innovative complex, has a goal, timing, and financial oriented organized and structured work process, which requires the interdisciplinary cooperation of all professionals and different levels of management".

☞ Example: For a small handcraft company, the building of a car would be a big project, as it would take a year or more, whereas for an automotive company that builds cars in series is just daily work. For the automotive company the development process would then only be identified as a project.

A main criterion is that the project is "unique", which does not mean that you cannot use standardized parts of the project/process for future projects. Example: The development of a new car can be a project even if the industry uses of a cross-platform carryover segment based on the current car in the market. The newly developed elements then account for the "uniqueness".

The project "goal" is mainly related to the objective settings and the expected results in the project and furthermore to meet the project framework of timing, resources, and cost.

A project is normally characterized by dedicated project organization. This organization works for the project period and is usually released from the daily work organization. Unfortunately, today because of the lack of resources, it is not unusual to work on projects in parallel to the main job. In addition, the lack of resources can also affect the workload if a project is led by a "one man band" there is a big risk of not meeting the framework objective. Even so you can still use all the project management tools available.

The key is to define what is the project goal and what is the project framework (*Timing, Cost, Quality*) to then be aware if the project is feasible for a "one man project" or if not feasible then to define the project as a "work task".

Projects differ from the daily routine work and need to be handled under different aspects:

Routine processes are typically structured permanently by organizational actions and mastered by the employees of an organization without any major problems. However, in projects associated with a high degree of innovation, the novelty can relate to the approach to problem-solving method and the desired results. Taking this into account at project execution you can only partially use existing planning. A clear plan on manageable steps, on-going control, and possible intervention if there is some sort of deviation can then significantly reduce the risk of a project failure.

1.3 Definition of Project Management

Project management is a special concept designed to tackle complex tasks, whereas the management proportion has a functional (control of the system, e.g., project planning, control communication, conflict resolution) and intuitional (management tasks such as project participation task and competence) split. What is or is not project management can be is seen in Table 1.1.

Table 1.1 Project management is/is not

Is	Is not
• A steering/running of quality costs and time	• A rough estimate when the project phases are finished
• Structured approach (e.g., DMAIC)	• Static, one-time estimate of the end date
• Dynamic—Changes happen	• Automated or controlled by software (MS project)
• The anticipating and troubleshooting work in a dedicated team	• The effort of an individual
• Passionate execution of the task	• Externally controlled by projects

A project is in terms of content time-limited; it has a defined start and end date. Because a project normally has time and resource restrictions the project must be planned very carefully.

It can be difficult to integrate time-limited projects into a traditional company's existing organizational structure, as the quality and speed of the information exchange can be restricted by the formal hierarchical communication. A poor coordination can extend the timing of the project; increase the project costs and the subsequent risk of failure. To prevent this, organizational measures must be taken. This is what project management is all about and it is about controlling the process, the functions, and the people involved.

🕮 Definition: "Project management is according to DIN 69901-5 the whole population of management tasks, management organization, technical management processes, and management resources that are used for the initialization, definition, planning, control, and the closure of projects".

The term "Management" used in the definition is not to be understood as to "lead" but more related to "execute". The execution is related to the organization, planning, control, and coordination of the project and not related to the value-added chain of the product itself.

The two main aspects of project management clearly can be identified "Institutional Project Management" (management tasks such as project participation task and competence) and the instrumental implementation "Functional Project Management" (control of the system, e.g., project planning, control communication, conflict resolution).

☞ Example: In most automotive companies around the world a project management office is established, led by an experienced project manager expert who consolidates all the project managers and the whole team are responsible for the product planning and product control. The office will run and control all projects/programs in the company professionally, using internal company project management standards (Checklists, Methods, and Tools).

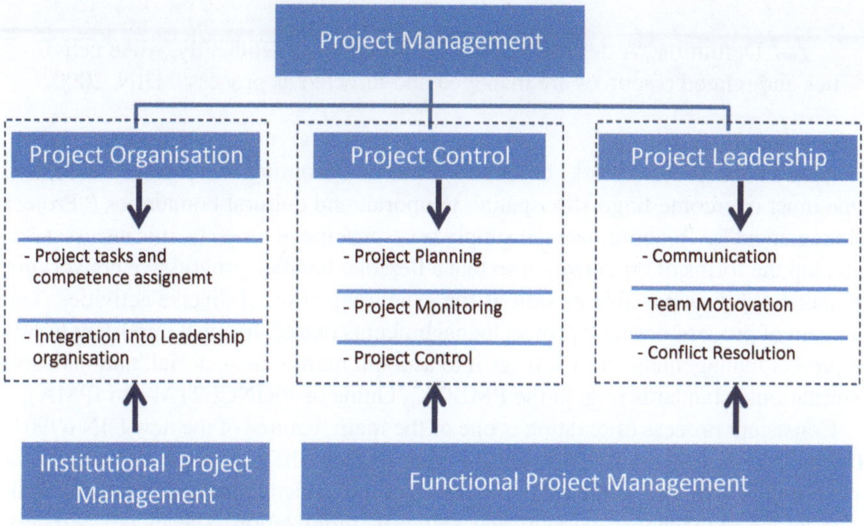

Fig. 1.1 Project management components

The project management has three features of project processing (Fig. 1.1), this is the

- *Organization function*: Who is involved in the project
- *Control function:* Planning, monitoring, and control (Process model).
- *Leadership function*: Team leadership, motivation, and conflict management.

One main element of project control is the "Process Model" which will be explained in detail in the next chapters. All of these functions can be controlled through a structured team management.

1.4 Project Management Processes

Similar to the overall quality management restructure a few years ago there has been a change in orientation in project management towards structured process models. Project management processes are understood as all tasks with manifold interactions driven by the project management goal to transfer input into a meaningful output. Usually, the project tasks are split into different logical repeatable and capsulated segments to help the team to orientate on which phase to work on step by step.

Our professional everyday life is now strongly influenced by processes. A process is a set of activities that transform inputs into results. The use of resources, which is necessary for this transformation, should be as effective and efficient. These tasks are often difficult due to the wide variety of internal and external stakeholders and often parallel activities. ISO 9000 strongly contributed the process orientation approach to the spread of the concept.

Definition "A desired result is achieved more efficiently, when activities and related resources are managed and directed as process". DIN, 2000.

Also in the project work, communication is becoming increasingly complex. One must overcome linguistic, spatial, temporal, and cultural boundaries ("Project Management"). To coordinate the supply relationships in projects, it is necessary to develop the forms of organization so that a flexible, boarder-progressive networking of stakeholders is possible as well as the synchronization of diverse activities. The concept of process-oriented project management is one of the most important trends in project management. Now it takes into account numerous sectorial, national, and international standards (e.g. in the PMBOK® Guide or PRINCE2TM and IPMA).

Consistent process orientation is one of the main features of the new DIN 69901. The project management processes are mapped from the beginning to the end of a project and correlated to the other processes of any added value and organizational, such as the management support and value of initialization. The model "Process House" (Fig. 1.2) in the style of the "house of quality" used in the DIN 69901 is as follows.

It is a framework for the synchronization-diversified processes in organizations. Given that project management here fulfils an integrative role and serves as an interface between the internal stakeholders as well as to external partners (cross-cutting function). The new standard is only a frame, but does not have detailed methods and structure. The model is therefore very flexible and can be designed by the respective organizational or to the project-specific requirements.

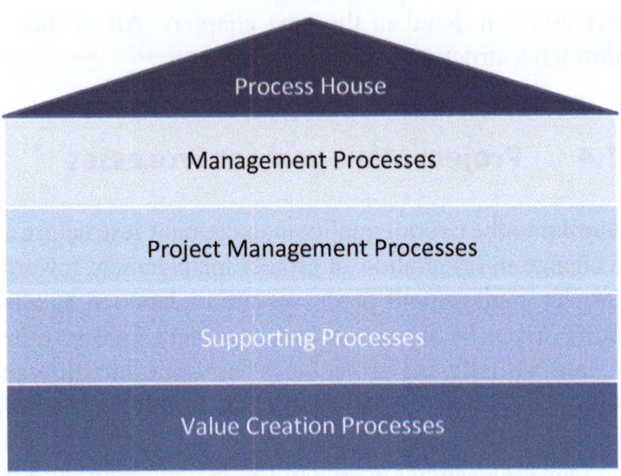

Fig. 1.2 Process House DIN 69901:2009

☞Example: The automotive industry uses the project management process phases based on the VDA 1998 standards, which are *Initiate, Define, Plan, Control,* and *Closure*. The project management phases refer to logical project management sequence through the whole project lifecycle. The synchronization between the project management phases/processes and the project phases and the value add chain is the task of the project organization and reflects the difference between a project and project management.

Project management process can be split into different phases/tasks: Initiate, Define, Plan, Control, and Closure.

These phases are related to project management and not the project phases. The task of a project is to develop one or several solutions for a concrete problem. A number of so-called process models have been designed specifically for different industry-related functions. The main properties of these process models are to develop the projects step by step by following a pre-defined phase. These steps are arranged in a chronological and logical order and all steps can be repeated in exceptional cases if necessary (Fig. 1.3).

☞Example: Listed are some familiar projects phased models:

- Solving process for Architects by the HOAI (Fee Structure for Architects and Engineers).
- In the quality function Six Sigma: DMAIC, DFSS (DCOV).
- In manufacturing KAIZEN (continuous improvement), LEAN,
- KANBAN.
- In Production FPDS
- In Product Developer GPDS
- The concept phases of systems engineering: (1) From the "Rough to Detail", (2) system design in stages, (3) Progressive alternative development and deletion. (4) The phase development for the process.

This process model must always be adapted to the current tasks of the project (*Tailoring*).

The main advantages of focusing on process-oriented project management are the possibility of adaption to industry-, project-, or organizational needs, to be compatible with QM concepts like ISO 9000:2000, SIX SIGMA and the advantage of being open for continuous improvement and enhancement.

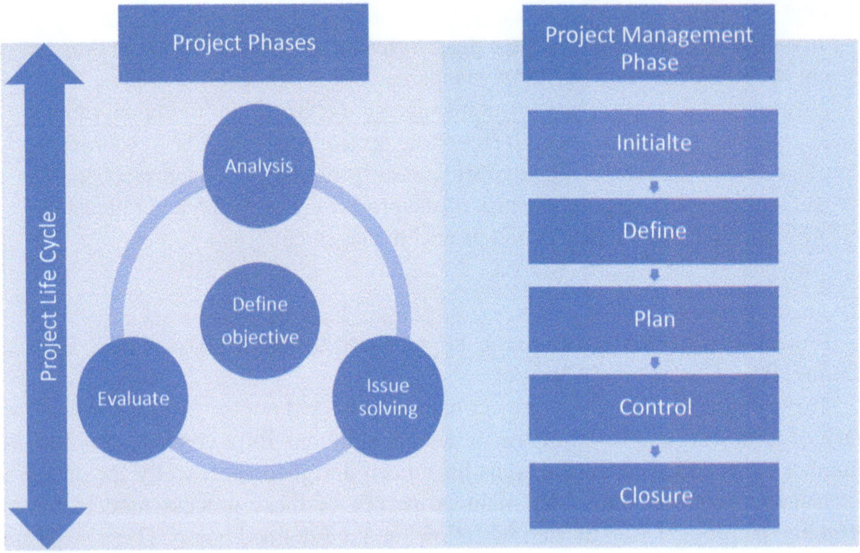

Fig. 1.3 Steps and phases of projects

1.5 Process Model DIN 69901

Let us look at the process model defined by DIN 69901 and DIN 2009b (Fig. 1.4). The model was designed taking a process-orientated project management into account. The norm basically was carved out of a process model, split into the project management phases: *Initiate, Define, Plan, Control,* and *Closure* and all project management processes were visualized showing all dependences and interactions with each "*input*" and "*output*" process steps.

The structure of the process model follows the five-project management phases and arranges every single process into sub-groups. This results in a total of 59 project management processes. These are then segmented in the five horizontal phases of project management and vertically into one of the eleven process sub-groups (Fig. 1.5).

The processes can be flexibly adapted as only 14 process steps are mandatory and set as a "minimum standard" but these processes are relevant for all projects. An individual solution for project management can be found and therefore reduce costs for the project management significantly.

Each process step (milestone) is described with a fix process number, a successor and predecessor process steps, purpose and background, process description for each milestone including timing and the "Input–Method–Output" sequence.

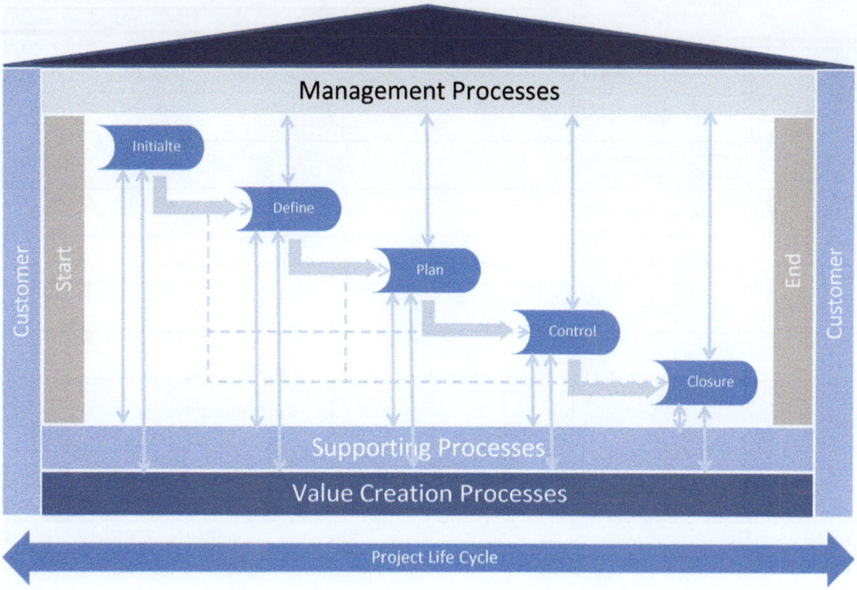

Fig. 1.4 PM phases according to DIN 69901: 2009

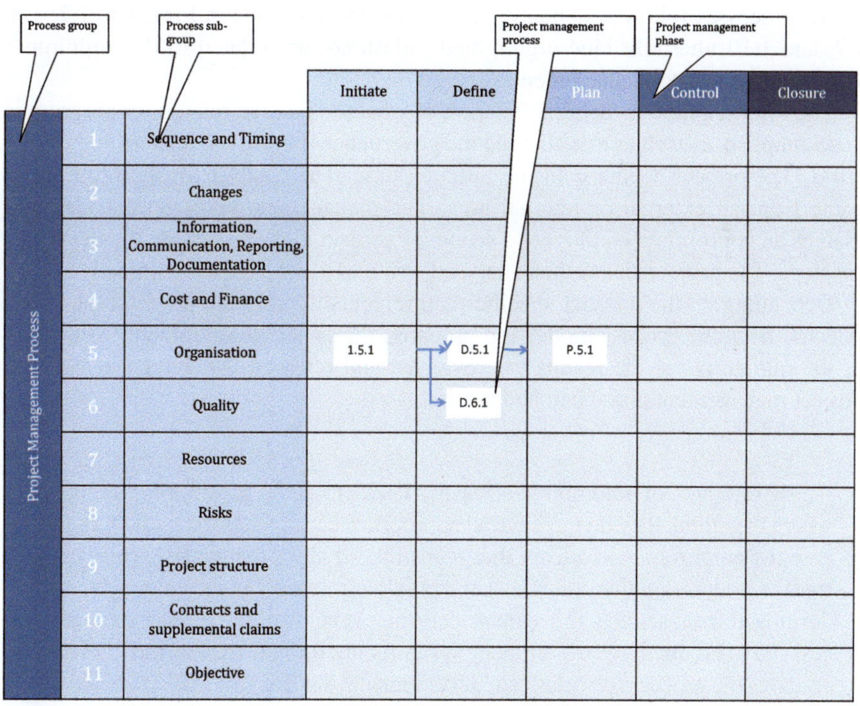

Fig. 1.5 PM process model according to DIN 69901: 2009

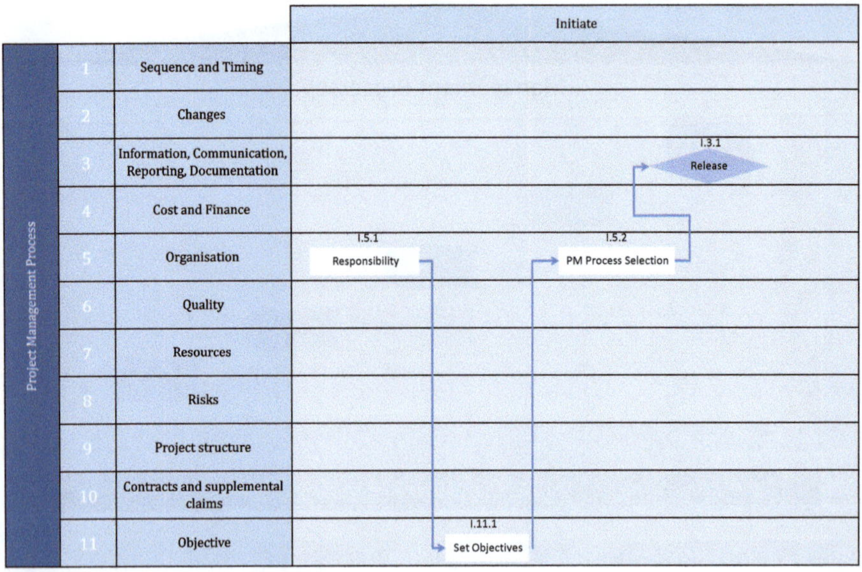

Fig. 1.6 PM process initialize according to DIN 69901: 2009

All processes follow a standard pattern and are described in Figs. 1.6, 1.7, 1.8, 1.9, and 1.10, the light blue highlighted milestones are related to the "minimum standard" for project management.

The *Initiate* phase is the identification of what the project, release, or program is to accomplish, as well as establishing the governance that will be responsible for the effort. The project begins with the initiate phase. The catalyst for the project can come from an external or internal area. The management takes on the idea and assigns an appropriate employee to scope the project idea and initiate the next logical steps. The project idea is then analysed, evaluated and a business objective is set.

Depending on the product-specific requirements the relevant processes are then selected from the process model and prepared for project development. At the end of the initiate phase the results are reviewed and released. After release the next project management phase can be launched.

☞Example: An automotive company needs to close gap in a car segment where they think they do not have an appropriate car to cover the market. In this case the employee is in a team that scans first of all of the market needs (customer surveys) and then calculates the possible revenue. As the car needs to be developed from scratch, the team selects the elements of the development process PDS (Production Development System) only for new cars, as the PDS also contains the process for "platform development" and for "*Mid Cycle Actions*".

Proper project selection is one of the most critical success factors influencing the outcome of the project. Selecting a project that is too large will cause valuable time to be lost during the *Define* Phase as project teams struggle to scope their projects and develop "*Problem Statements*".

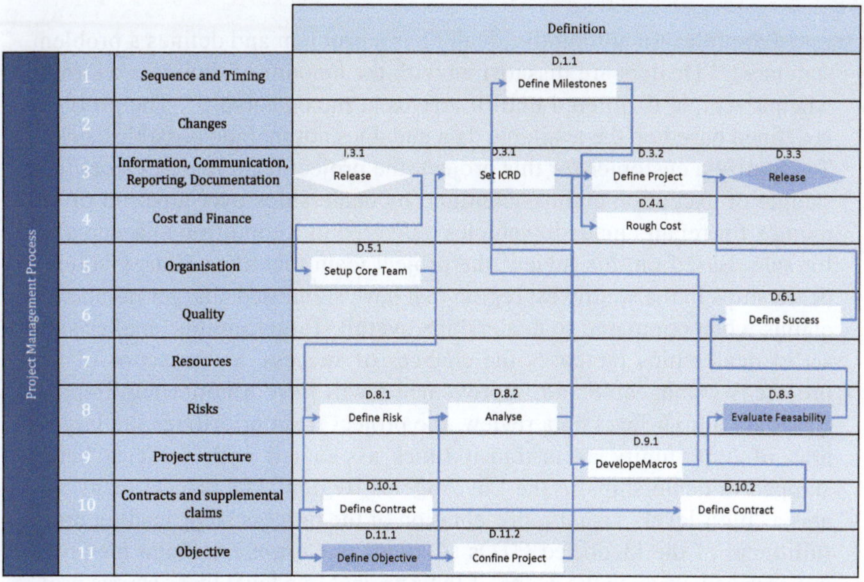

Fig. 1.7 PM process definition according to DIN 69901: 2009

In the *Define* phase the project should largely be outlined. First, we create the project definition that includes the problem/opportunity statement, the objective of the project, the expected benefits, what items are in scope and what items are out of scope, the team and the team structure, and the project timeline. The scope will include details such as resources, boundaries, customer segments, milestones, and timing.

The next step is to determine and define the customer requirements. Customers can be both external consumers and internal stakeholders. At the end of this step, you should have a clear operational definition of the project metrics and their linkage to critical business levers as well as the objective for improving the measurable metrics. Business levers can consist of:

- Return on invested capital.
- Profit.
- Customer Satisfaction.
- Responsiveness.

The last step in this phase is to define the process boundaries and high-level inputs and outputs.

☞Example: An automotive dealer has a problem and defines a problem statement: "Dealers are dissatisfied with the amount of time it takes from when a vehicle is ordered until it arrives at the dealership". The problem is defined based on the available data and does not include possible causes. To identify a customer for this project, the project team reviews a random sample of exception claims submitted by dealerships over a period of six months for repairs made to vehicles delivered in a condition unacceptable for sale. Based on this review, the project team identifies 5 large-volume dealerships in the southwest region that have submitted a larger number of claims when compared to dealerships overall. Targeting this smaller subset of dealerships increases the chances of success, as the scope of the project is manageable and improvements will have a noticeable impact. Based on a high-level data review, the project team prioritizes the largest area of opportunity as in-transit times associated with vehicles being shipped to dealerships in the Los Angeles Region. The project team creates a "high-level" visual representation of the process steps leading up to fulfilment of the identified CTQs (*Critical to Customer*). Team members must strive to reduce the scope of their project to a level that ensures project feasibility. A refined problem statement is a highly defined description of the problem. Beginning with the general problem statement, and applying what has been learned through further scoping the project team refined the problem statement:

"Delivery times for Explorers assembled at the Louisville Assembly plant and shipped to Los Angeles region dealerships are on average in excess of 35 days".

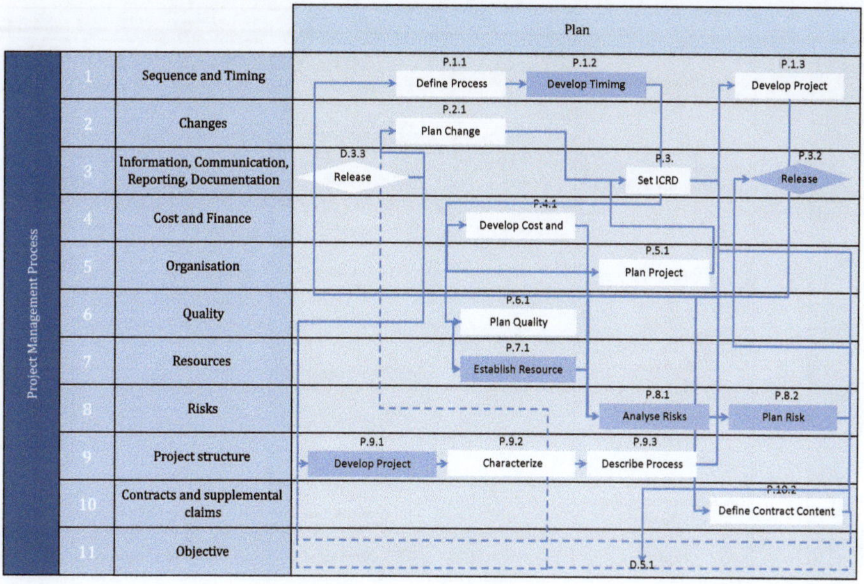

Fig. 1.8 PM process plan according to DIN 69901: 2009

The *Plan* phase is both the concentrated planning of the later work and the re-planning during later phases, as scope changes are evaluated and accepted. Planning is the rigorous evaluation of what the project, release, or program is to accomplish, and the development of all controlling processes to determine how the effort will be accomplished. This includes estimating work effort, planning all resource needs and allocating budget to segments, etc.

The planning begins with the creation of a project structure plan cascaded down to the detailed work packages and the work tasks. Based on these work tasks the timing, resources, and costs are planned. This is an iterative loop as in the practical world the detected risks will need countermeasures that then need to be adjusted in the define phase. At the end of this iterative loop the project plan can be created/published. The project plan is a compilation of all timing's resources, costs, and quality plans. In a further step the contracts with the suppliers are negotiated. The last step is to get a final "*ok to go*" release from the stakeholder, which is vital, as from now the resources and cost will rise considerably.

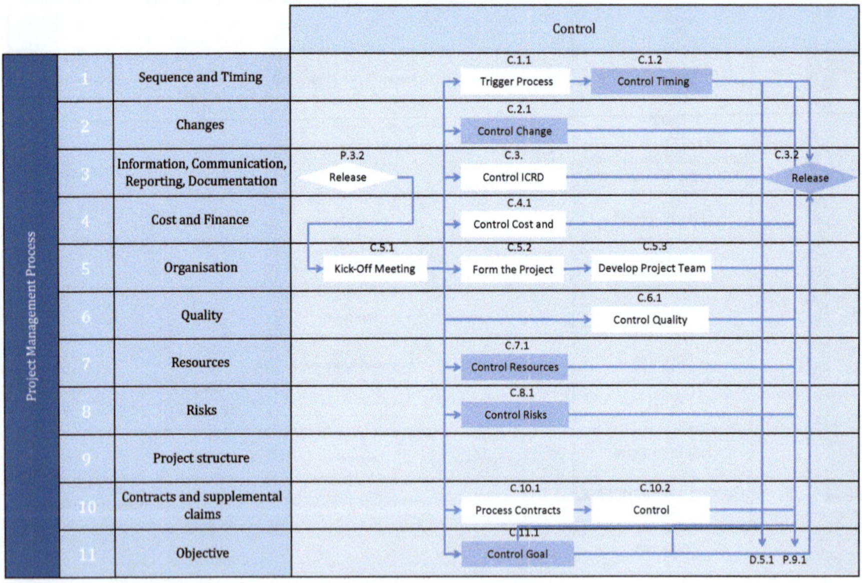

Fig. 1.9 PM process control according to DIN 69901: 2009

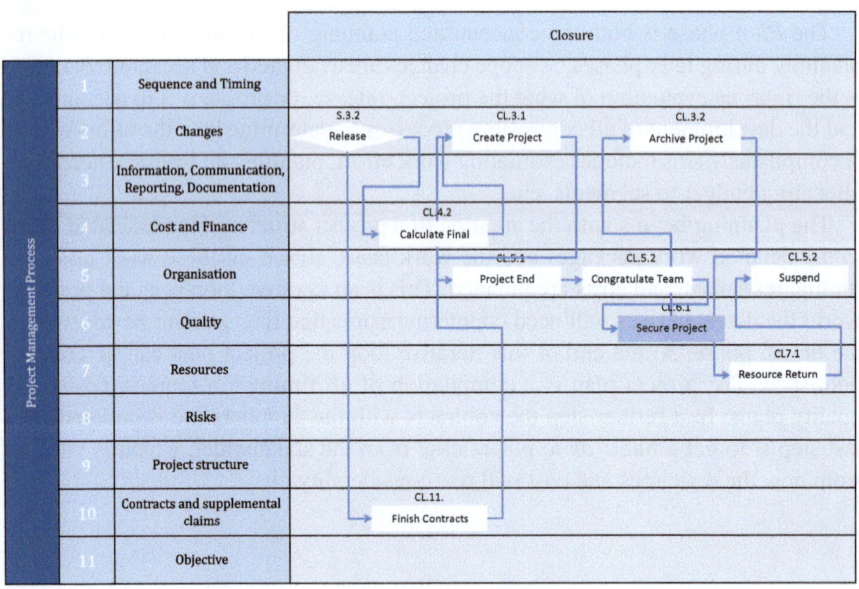

Fig. 1.10 PM process closure according to DIN 69901: 2009

The Execute and *Control* phases occur roughly in parallel. The Execute phase involves the careful implementation of the project, release, or program's plans. The control phase involves monitoring the execution, the measurement of progress, and all the communication needed to stakeholders of that progress at all levels. As noted in the phase illustration, the plan phase continues during this time frame, as scope changes require revisiting the plans to be executed and controlled.

The start of a project is often not transparent, even though it has been characterized as a project with a defined beginning and end that are often unrecognizable. But when does a project start? Frequently this question cannot be generally answered because the project has historic related studies and insights that could already be seen as a starting point.

In the beginning there is an idea, a proposal from the functional departments or from the executive board. Then someone is selected to be responsible; they then get the job to define the goals, resources, and utilization aspects of the project. From the outcome of this study a project letter draft is developed. Now "*Politics*" are made! The start date will be moved continuously because you have already collected insights that you do not need to replicate; then, suddenly, the project is approved. The end date has however remained and not moved anywhere. This is when you ask yourself: "How to achieve that timing?" and "Do I really need to have time for this project". This causes a diminishing of the qualified resources in the team and unnecessary confusion.

It must be clear to all team members what objectives, timings, costs, resources, and risks the project has and what is the current status compared to the objectives all the time. Every single change or deviation from nominal has to be controlled and if necessary adjusted and documented. In addition, the project plan has to be updated if the changes have an effect on the project outcome.

> ☞Example: A quality issue in manufacturing caused a big recall. A project to optimize the part design uses this issue to prevent the future design from failing and to be more robust. They changed design, the control plan, the testing in the plant and changed the project plan to reflect the timing for the changes.

The *Closure* phase is the formal set of activities involved in shutting down the project, release, or program. This includes the analytical work of identifying, documenting, and sharing *lessons learned,* the final reporting of the project, release, or program, the archiving of all material consistent with corporate recordkeeping requirements, and the release of all resources. This phase is conducted at either the natural lifecycle end or for an activity that is ended early for whatever reason.

1.6 Project Type

Next to the definitional characteristics of a project (goal-oriented, time-limited, relatively new, complex, interdisciplinary) additional project properties allow a classification of the various types of projects, which are Table 1.2*:*

- *Internal* projects: An internal project contractor belongs to same organization.
- *External* projects: Are dependent on the market demand and executed by an external service supplier.
- *Program*-oriented: It inevitably has no impact on the organizational structure after project implementation. (E.g., quality improvement of a car air conditioning).
- *Process* orientation: The project has an impact on the organizational structure after the introduction. (E.g., The Ford strategy "One Ford" has a significant influence on the organization.)

The wide variety of projects can be differentiated according to how they were initiated; this results into sub-dividing the projects into internal or external projects:

For *internal projects* staff is assigned to the project within the company; the client and contractor belong to the same organization. The internal client normally only outlines the objective settings; the more detailed objective settings of the project represent its own project task. The creation of standards for project work and the quality of the project results depend mainly on how the people involved think it is important. This creates a high degree of flexibility in the project execution but can also cause a project to fail because of missing liability or lacking regress demands.

☞Example: An internal project could be a Six Sigma project that is started to improve product quality in a plant. The plant own Black Belt is assigned as project leader and assigns the internal plant project team consisting out of manufacturing experts, quality experts, machining operators, and a product development engineer for the component from the development office.

External projects however are triggered by market demand and accomplished by an external customer; for these external companies a clearly defined project contract in terms of a legally secured service contract is agreed. The project partners must guarantee fulfilment of the promised task. An unclear definition of the work tasks in the contract can easily lead to misunderstandings and in extreme cases to legal suites.

☞Example: A company sources a quality team at an engineering service agency to reduce resource budget and therefore cost. An external supervisor who makes sure the agreed work tasks are distributed and solved at a timely and qualified manner controls the project interface.

A further distinction can be made according to the orientation of the project. Either a project is aimed to change the production and marketing programs or a structural change of performance and management processes:

Program-oriented projects are typically completed after their implementation and are then closed for the company; there are no inevitable implications for the organizational structure. The *Process-oriented* projects have an impact on the handling of the company's internal processes and therefore also on the organizational structure. It is of particular importance to consider people that are affected by the project results as it can often lead to subsequent corrections and adjustments based on different viewpoints and requirements.

Table 1.2 Project type examples

		Project Orientation	
		Progamm Orientation	Process Orientation
Project Type	Internal Projects	Develpe a new "Focus"	Develpe a new company strategie "One Ford"
	External Projects	Develop a subsystem of the car by an external engineering supplier	Business consultancy

Another distinguishing feature is on how the employees are assigned to the project. According to the definition above, projects require an interdisciplinary cooperation of specialists from various fields, to consolidate their relevant expertise. However, while the actual execution of the project can be done by a single staff member or by a project group, but there are also a number of important reasons for not assigning a single person to lead and execute a project.

The project takes too long due to low staffing; therefore, the project solution will be available too late. Because projects affect different areas, a qualified professional is not always available ad hoc for a "one-on-one" meeting. The project risk through personnel shortfall of a "*One Man Band*" is much higher usually resulting in misaligned of timing performance and the project solution is influenced far more by subjective decisions than in a team and the teamwork is usually assessed to be more creative and effective.

Therefore, you will find only small projects that are led by a single employee. The rule is the use of a wide variety of employees for a project. These teams are referred to differently. E.g., As a *project group, project team* or *work group.*

Based on the scale of the project work the projects are distinguished as "*Full-Time*" and "*Part-Time*" projects. Part-time projects are worked on only with a fraction of the person's regular working time. The remaining time is used for regular daily work. Often, we find a combination of single project work and project teamwork. A "hard core" of the project group works full-time on the project, while involved specialists support the team only by the hour. This is also called "*Agenda-Driven*" project work. This type of project work model is very common in the automotive business.

With regard to the participation of third parties (such as Service Engineering Companies, Management Consultancies, Freelancer, Project Management Companies) for projects, three types of projects can be distinguished:

For an *External Project* the overall project will be assigned to a foreign agency. This can be done, for example, by transferring the general responsibility to the agency. The contractor then works on the desired project solution without the company's direct involvement. The payments can then be regulated in different ways.

In *Mixed Projects*, the project team consists of company employees and external experts. The project manager does not even need to be an internal employee and in this case the project responsibility must be specified separately.

Running "One *Man Band*" projects, all project staff including project manager are employees of the company and the project responsibilities can only be in the own company.

The involvement of external resources can occur for various reasons:a one is the lack of own experts or the lack of staff capacity or to acquire project experienced resources. Unfortunately, external project staff costs are almost always higher compared with own employees but on the other side usually external resources work on the basis of a "*contract for services*" with a looser legal binding to the company more beneficial than the extensive cost.

Reference

Deutscher Normenausschuß (Hrsg.): D1N 69901: Projektmanagement. (2009). Berlin.

2 Project Management Success

Process management is a systematic approach to achieving performance improvements by meticulously designing and executing a company's end-to-end processes. Essentially, a business process comprises a structured series of related activities that collectively generate valuable outcomes for customers, such as order fulfilment, product development, and post-sales support. The emphasis here is on the terms "structured" and "collectively".

In a business process, every activity must function cohesively, aligned towards the common objective of meeting customer needs. Employees should work collaboratively as a unified team, rather than concentrating solely on individual tasks or safeguarding their specific areas of responsibility. Additionally, each activity within the process should follow a clearly defined design that outlines what needs to be done, when it should be done, and who is responsible for doing it. This process design is crucial for ensuring that activities are repeatable and consistent, leading to reliable and efficient operations.

Companies typically find it effective to identify five to ten major business processes. Take order fulfilment, for instance: this process encompasses all activities from when a customer places an order to when the customer receives the shipment and makes the payment. This order-to-cash process crosses functional boundaries, integrating customer service, logistics, finance, and even manufacturing to achieve a common goal. Other top-level processes are similarly broad in scope.

In a functionally organized company, while all activities required to convert an order into payment are performed, they are not executed as a cohesive process. Different departments, often unaware of each other's activities and pursuing different performance objectives, handle these tasks. This leads to conflict, suboptimization, increased overhead, and non-value-adding work. Additionally, without someone overseeing the entire process from start to finish, there is no one to enforce a consistent and repeatable overall design, resulting in variation and improvisation.

Process management ensures that activities are conceived, designed, and performed within a process context. When employees understand that their tasks are

P. Bauer, *A Comprehensive Project Management Guide*, Management for Professionals, https://doi.org/10.1007/978-3-031-68252-0_2

part of a larger whole, they align their efforts with customer needs and common goals. An explicit end-to-end process design allows for consistent execution and enables managers to make disciplined improvements. Process management ensures that business processes are well designed, adhered to, and regularly updated.

The central figure in process management is the process owner. The process owner ensures that those performing the process understand it, are trained in it, have the necessary tools, and follow the specified design. The process owner makes minor adjustments to the process design to fix flaws or address new issues. If there is a significant gap between the current performance and the desired performance, the process owner leads an effort to create a completely new process design, known as a reengineering project.

The benefits of successful process management are substantial. A rigorous process design enhances performance by eliminating wasted resources and time, ensuring that projects do not fall through the cracks.

☞ Example: In the mid-1990s, Caterpillar introduced a four-stage process for creating and launching new models. This innovation reduced the cycle time for a new product development from up to 10 years to as little as 3 years. A second example of a manufacturer that built two-way radio systems implemented a detailed 25-step sales process, focusing resources on profitable sales opportunities, resulting in a 500% increase in EBIT.

Process management also benefits by aligning everyone around a customer-oriented goal. In the early 1990s, a semiconductor manufacturer faced a challenge where customer orders took up to 180 days to deliver. Responsibility for order completion was spread across x-functional departments and locations, each with different performance goals and no overall accountability for the order. By fostering universal awareness of the entire process and introducing cycle time as a shared metric, the manufacturer eliminated suboptimizations, arguments, and buck-passing, ultimately reducing cycle time by up to 75%.

Process management provides a structured framework for reengineering the intentional and comprehensive redesign of workflows. The success of an enterprise relies on the effective performance of well-crafted processes. Regardless of effort, employees cannot exceed the limitations of an inadequately designed process. Continuous improvement thus requires an enhanced design.

Take, for instance, Progressive Casualty Insurance Company's dramatic improvement in claims-handling performance. Initially, a claimant would report an accident to an agent, who would then pass the information to a customer service representative. This representative would route it to a claims manager, who then would group the claim with others in the same terrain and assign it to a claims adjuster. The claims adjuster would then schedule a time to inspect the vehicle, typically taking seven to ten days from the accident to inspection, realizing that quick claim initiation is vital for customer satisfaction. Progressive sought improvement. Recognizing that pushing employees harder or fixing execution flaws wouldn't suffice, the company decided in 1992 to overhaul the entire process.

Today, Progressive's adjusters work in teams, with one member handling claimant calls while others operate in the field. When a call comes in, the adjuster manages as much as possible over the phone. If an inspection is required, a field team member is contacted to schedule the visit promptly. Progressive now measures the time from call to inspection in hours rather than days.

Diverse companies such as Ford, IBM Corp., Duke Power Co., United Parcel Service, and Cadbury Schweppes have adopted process management as a central theme in their operational performance improvement programs. However, process management extends beyond improving individual processes; it is a holistic approach to running and managing a business.

Traditional management systems, which focus on measurement, compensation, organizational structure, and managerial roles, are often misaligned with process-centric approaches, as they cater to functionally-centred organizations. As process management becomes ingrained, all organizational management systems shift to support processes. Employees work in teams rather than departments, with compensation linked to results instead of activities or seniority. Managers serve as coaches rather than supervisors. Computer systems are integrated to support end-to-end processes, not just individual departments, and the company culture promotes both individual accountability and collective responsibility. An enterprise that has embedded process management and aligned its management systems accordingly transforms into a process enterprise, centred on its customers and managed around its processes.

2.1 What Is Project Success

The magic triangle (Fig. 2.1) represents the three main project parameters in their context: *Scope, Timing*, and *Cost*. Both qualitative and quantitative activates are included in the scope parameter. Often the factor quality is added separately to the triangle, although quality is only an attribute of scope. The wording "*Magically*" derives from the fact that the three parameters have competitive relationships and interact with each other in the entire course of the project. While the scope is to be maximized, cost (budget) and the time (periods) should be minimized Compliance with the contractually set parameters of the magic triangle is the basis for project success. However, there are additional other factors affecting the success of projects.

Fig. 2.1 Magical triangle

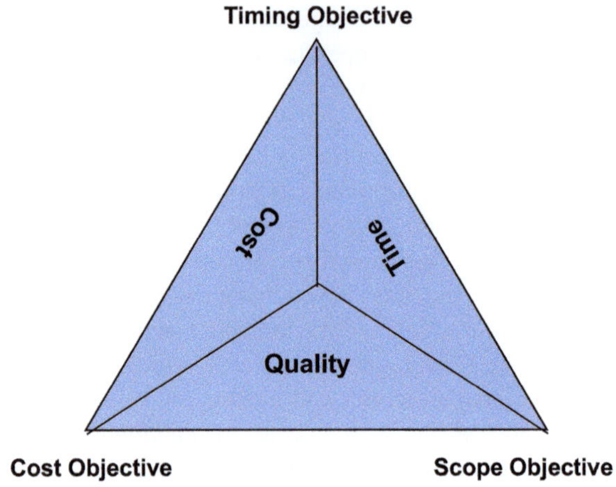

The success of projects is the recognition of the project results through the relevant stakeholders. A basic prerequisite is to know the expectations of the relevant stakeholders on the results of the project and to take them into account. In conflict target situations appropriate solutions must be created to create a win–win situation and if necessary, develop a strategy for dealing with the conflicts that you expect.

If a parameter is changed, the others change as well. The higher the requirements are on the *Scope* objectives; the more necessary number of resources and time are required. Raising the scope objectives content and quality normally extends the duration of the project and increases the costs on human and financial resources. This situation is not unusual in itself; in managing projects, typically innovative solutions are required, so that interaction between these three targets only can be very vaguely defined.

The objectives of the magic triangle should be planned holistically in the framework of project planning, so that they can be achieved under normal circumstances. The task of project management is then to ensure compliance with these targets through appropriate measures at the end of the project. It is essential that project control is not only an on-going assessment "*Timing*" and "*Cost*", but also includes the assessment or projects progress.

☞Example: *Costs*—You have a budget for the development of a website for your department. The specifications are available and you accepted the offer of € 3500.00. *Time*—The development time has been set to 30 days, by the customer based on their resource and timing calculations. *Quality*—The specification essentially describes base functionality on text (html) and graphics for a home page with five pages. But this is what normally happens: the customer wants that the home page to open with a "Flash movie", and he shortens the development time to 15 days, in addition the budget will be cut by 10%. Changing all the parameters in all dimensions does not work you can only change in 2 levels at a time. The volume of the pyramid is fixed, so there is only 1 degree of freedom for the change.

Definition: Project success is the performance of the contracted services in required quality and quantity, as well as in the context of the financial and time frame, taking into account the approved supplements (claims). The priorities and the relationship of each parameter to each other are only project-related and therefore situational outlined. In addition, stakeholders of the project, in particular, the contractors, the customers project team, and affected employees must be satisfied with the implementation and the results and evaluate the project as successful.

2.2 What Is Project Management Success

Project management success starts with the selection of projects. It is particularly important and part of strategic project management, to select the right projects for the company, to set priorities, and to initiate. One must avoid unnecessary projects and not oversee important projects.

In the definition and planning phases the selection of appropriate instruments, team development, team building, and the internal and external communication are of particular importance for the success of the project management. Experts repeatedly pointed out that the focus on the importance of the early-stage processes pays off. This so-called "*Front Loading*" creates a higher timing and financial investment but this will compensate quickly by using a more consistent approach, avoiding risks, etc. The implementation phase of a project requires good project controlling, stakeholder and team management as well as risk management.

Definition: Project management success is the effective and efficient usage of methods and project management instruments to improve the business success and the stakeholder satisfaction of individual projects, the project portfolio as a whole, and the success across the organization. The essential project management activities must be defined and implemented. In principle the process approach in project management should be standardized introduced and the "mindset" adopted.

3 Project Requirements and Objectives

Objectives are the quantifiable high-level goals of the company. They are the statements of how you will determine and measure your success. They must be statements of what you are striving to achieve. Objectives might look like this:

- Increase market share
- Reduce manufacturing costs
- Increase new product introductions
- Reduce cycle times for product delivery and service response
- Zero safety incidents
- Reduce water and air emissions
- Improve profit

In business economics-related terms, objective is understood to be a state of the real environment (target state), which is considered by the economic, political decision maker as desirable. In terms of this definition the result of the project would merely be the objective and the implementation framework and the conditions of implementation would only be observable constraints (restrictions). In accordance with the project management literature, the statements "not to produce more than x €" or "not to finish the project later than …" should be spelt out as objectives and not restrictions.

The objectives Scope/Performance, *Schedule*, and *Cost* are often illustrated in the "*Magic Triangle of Project Management*" (Fig. 2.1). Usually, they form the core of the customer (internal or external customer, etc.) requests. This diagram makes it clear that all three objectives cannot be achieved at the same time. If you add the further important factor "operating resource", it becomes the magic square; expanded it again with the factor *Satisfaction* (stakeholders: clients, team), it develops to the magical hexagon.

In any undertaking that is going to place demands on time, budgets, and other resources, we need to begin with a definition of the perceived benefits we hope to

P. Bauer, *A Comprehensive Project Management Guide*, Management for Professionals, https://doi.org/10.1007/978-3-031-68252-0_3

derive. In the case of a corporate-wide Six Sigma program, the intention is to change the entire corporate culture for the better.

Beginning with the traditional customer—the receiver or products or services that we provide—it is apparent that the best internal systems cannot be developed in isolation. In some respects, we learn from our mistakes so that an exceptional system is the result of trial and error; however, such a system may also be developed by just listening to the customer. If customer satisfaction is the primary focus of a Six Sigma program, we cannot ignore the customer's expectations, because that set of expectations defines quality and enables us to spot defects.

The questions that every corporate leader and employee should be asking are based on acknowledging that the customer defines quality itself. The best projects begin not inside the business but outside it, focused on answering the question. How can we make the customer more competitive? What is critical to the customer's success?

Customer satisfaction is the essential and defining objectives for all projects. If we also extend this definition so that all of us deal with a "customer" in some manner, then the smart theories of improved customer relations can be applied across the entire organization. One of the beliefs that harm morale among non-marketing employees is the polarizing observation that they never see or speak to a customer. So, an elite subculture arises, in which marketing employees bring in the profits while non-marketing people merely shuffle paper. This is one of the most damaging themes seen in corporations, and it is most pronounced in companies involved with marketing directly to customers.

So as a goal, it is not enough to define the program as aimed towards improving customer service; it should also extend that definition so that everyone, even those who merely shuffling papers, can adopt the same attitude focused on improved customer service. This brings us to a second goal of any project: employee involvement. As a member of a department, an employee is likely to be expected to focus very narrowly on specific functions, deadlines, and procedures. These processes are often best performed in an isolated manner, while a supervisor or manager worries about interaction with other departments or with management. Depending on the type of department, the limitation of processes often makes sense. When it comes to broader involvement in and participation in quality control, that same employee is given a different type of incentive.

This ownership over processes derived from developing improved, more creative, more efficient, or more profitable methodology—is satisfying and rewarding and may give the employee a sense of real participation. This satisfaction may be lacking in the departmental routines and attendant deadlines. So quality participation can do a lot to improve employee morale. Allowing people to define how processes can be improved is perhaps the single most important step a company can take to improve morale among its employees.

Any project that improves service to customers or vendors has to also improve the quality of corporate life for employees. Positive change invariably has that effect, but we have to be aware that we need to change a cultural attitude. Project participation is intended to help employees—whether marketing or administrative—to move beyond the demoralizing characterization of some employees as having no customer contact.

The focus on achieving results with projects often leads to that only the expected results (deliverables) are defined and verified. Generally we speak about "result deliverables/objectives". But also, for the project management actions/process steps in the course of the project (project scope, project implementation) you should agree objectives—the so-called "*Procedure Objectives*" (Fig. 3.1).

> ☞Example: A part of the "*Procedure Objectives*" may be to include a certain persons or groups (organization). Typically, members could be members of the work council, customers, sales representatives, etc.

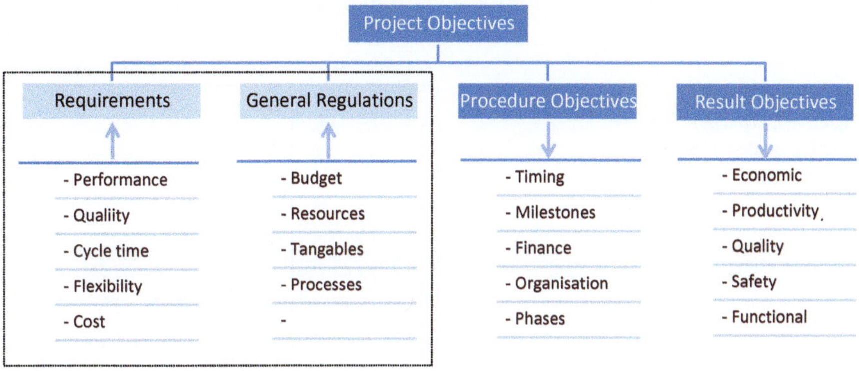

Fig. 3.1 Objective setting content

Without a clear objective a realistic project plan and even final sustainable assessment of the project success is not possible. For this reason, we need to define specifically the released objectives. This is where the project management becomes involved into an intensive dialogue with the contracting authority or the other stakeholders and defines action-oriented objectives, as far as possible using all three dimensions of the magic triangle, namely taking into account project results by scope and quality, time and cost. It must be ensured that individual targets do not contradict to each other. If necessary, mutual interactions need to be compensated, to avoid that high performance targets are set without having appropriate resources.

3.1 SMART Objectives

To set effective goals, their definition should be guided by the SMART scheme (Fig. 3.2), you can resolve the SMART acronym in being Specific, Measurable, Aligned, Realistic, and Timed-Targeted, depending on the organisation production - and in particular project culture. Individual letters can be changed in the respective authority alternatively for example, attractive (in the sense of motivating), appropriately (agreeable), accountable (to), achievable/attainable (accessible)or relevant (of importance for the achievement of agency goals).

Fig. 3.2 SMART objectives; criteria for an effective goal setting

S	tretch pecific
M	easurable
A	ligned
R	ealistic
T	ime argeted

Stretched, Specific, requested: The objectives apply to the respective area. They are clear and unambiguous, but also compatible with other objectives. Objectives should be challenging and state exactly what will be achieved. Question you should answer:

- How does the objective challenge you?
- Does the objective address more than just the daily running of the business?
- Will achieving the objective result in a competitive advantage?
- Is it clear exactly what you will have achieved once the objective has been met?

Measurable: Objectives must be quantifiable so that you will know if you have met the requirements. Quantity: How many? How often? Quality: How good? How successful? Question you should answer:

- How will someone else know you have achieved the objective?
- What metrics will tell you that you have achieved the objective?

Aligned: Achievement of objectives requires a certain effort or is challenging. There must be a clear link between the objective and the Business Plan/Balanced Scorecard. Question you should answer:

- Is the objective aligned with organizational objectives?
- Does the objective support the team's objectives?

Realistic: The objectives can be influenced actively within the framework of the project and not lie outside the area of competences. While objectives should be challenging, they should be achievable. Question you should answer:

- Data needs to be reviewed:
  - Current figures vs. desired result
  - Benchmark—with different units, with competitors
- Given the current environment, is the objective realistic?
- What capability you need to have to achieve the objective?
- Make the work objectives challenging but not impossible.

Time-Targeted: The objectives are defined where appropriate, also by intermediate dates/milestones at least by a finish date. Objectives should specify a completion date and milestones.

- When will this objective be met? Weekly, Monthly, Every Quarter, at the end of the Year 20xx, on the 1st of every month, etc.
- Are there significant timing milestones that should be tracked along the way?

The objectives need to be reviewed based on completeness and solution independency. This means that all objectives are weighted and allow different solutions. The objective setting must allow more than one possible solution (Fig. 3.3), because possible solution alternatives would be excluded in the project preparation. The objectives need to adapt permanently to the current situation and the current state of knowledge in the further advancement of the project. To be able to dynamically update the objectives the documents with the objective framework definitions in the project documentation need to remain to any project team member. An upcoming target discussion process (e.g., by changing framework conditions) can then be clearly traced.

Smart Objectives				
Key Objective	**Performance to Objectives/Accomplishments**	**Start Date**	**Due Date**	**Status**
Deliver Process Excellence 1. Support Product Development capability study 2. Communicate and follow Annual Spend reduction plan 3. Roll out Initiative (Dealer visits) 4. Continue "Sticker Events" 5. Support Body Six-Sigma Process needs. 6. Support functional led process and continue the worksteams established (Weekly meeting reviews, Quality reviews, Report outs, Special attention reviews with CEO)	1. Two new sticker events planned in March and September	01.01.20XX	12/31/20XX	20% Accomplished
Achieve Quality Objectives per scorecard For Body Exterior and supporthings Things gone wrong , Repairs/1000 and Cost Per Units targets. 1. Spend: Body Exterior xx.x mil $ incl. Supplier Recovery 2. Supplier Recovery x.xx mil $ 3. Generate addition x.xx mil $ by supplier recovery dedicated head 4. Demonstrate quality execution 4. Implement a closed loop Failure Mode Analysis Process 5. Re-energize targeted prevent recurrence projects - and support FER process with dedicated resources for whole Body Exterior 6. Coordinate and lead the introduction of Quality metric reporting.		01.01.20XX	12/31/20XX	None
People & Safety: 1. Integrate new spend team into mechansim team and live ONE FORD behavior 2. Allign with quality supervisors. 3. Define R&R's between Body Exterior functional areas and the warranty spend reduction process and support proactivly. 4. Clean Desk policy adherence 5. Be evacuation leader for ME3		01.01.20XX	12/31/20xx	None
Six Sigma 1. Support active Six-Sigma Projects. 2. Train 50 new Black Belts	1. Closed one Prjoect worth x.xx mil $	01.01.20XX	12/31/20XX	55% Accomplished
Improve Organizational Health & Pulse: 1. Drive and support continues improvement of tools and processes		01-01-2015	12/31/2015	None

Fig. 3.3 Industry example of SMART objectives

There are different methods you can follow to create your objectives two (Top-Down and Bottom-Up) are to show and described here.

With the retrograde/progressive method sub-objectives are derived so that they correspond to the hierarchical levels of the organizational structure (objective cascading). This has the advantage that the key points of contact are automatically known.

☞Example: In a project, where the turnover of the company is to be increased for by €1 million per month, by implementing special sales enhancing initiatives. The objectives could now be: the North region increases revenue to €200,000, the region Midway around €300,000, the region service East €200,000, and the region South €300,000.

You would then split the increase of the sales force North to €200,000 into the target for the sales district Louisville with €50,000 and for the remaining five service districts North to €30,000 each. You could continue further and cascade down to the objectives for each individual service employee.

In a *Top-Down* (Table 3.1) process the targets are cascaded downwards step by step. Starting from the upmost functional level the objectives are forwarded to the next lower level and adjusted to fit the resources performance ability. The top-down method is used in the Automotive Industry as a standard.

With the *Bottom-up method* (Table 3.1) single objective proposals are collected, at each hierarchal level to gain more sub-objectives. These are then condensed from level to level upwards and included into the corporate target setting.

Table 3.1 Pro/contra for objective setting methods

		Pro/Con	
		Advantage	Disadvantage
Method	Top-Down	• Consistent. • Taking future aspects into account.	• Low motivation of employees. • Neglection of knowledge of staff resulting in lack of realism.
	Bottom-up	• Taking emploee knowledge into account, resulting in realistic targets. • High motivation.	• Divergent opinions • Somewhat low level of quality • Past orientation

3.2 Milestones and Functional Target Setting

Milestones are defined events of particular importance. In particular (1) *Delivery* items or intermediate results (2) *Checks* (such as approvals, reviews), (3) *Decisions* (such as go), and (4) *Phase Transitions*. Deliverables and intermediate results, audits, and decisions are derived from the result objectives; Phase transitions are deducible from procedure objectives. In short: Milestones are materialized result and process goals! Milestones have a supporting role in the project planning; they have the following characteristics:

- The contents of the milestone represent an intermediate result that allows an assessment of project progress; it is set in advance, clearly defined and is able to be reviewed qualitatively. This can be, for example, a completed situation analysis or a full-featured system concept.
- The intermediate result is to be reached to a specific milestone-date; this date is determined in the context of forward planning and set.
- The milestone decision involves reporting to the project leader for the decision about the further execution. At the end of a process, the decision for the release triggers the next process step or the possible looping and repeating of the process step to achieve a result that is different or better, the even stopping the whole project.

> 🕮 Definition: Milestones are essential project intermediate results, resulting from the sequence of project execution.

Each stage of the project execution begins after a milestone and ends with a milestone. These milestones are used for reporting to the steering committee and the decision on the further execution of the project, simply the management of the overall project. The setting of milestones is an effective process for monitoring the project progress and project results. It aims to switch between a relatively autonomous work of the project group to a pre-defined, measurable subtotal and the control and the decision by the internal stakeholder. The stakeholder is given the opportunity to influence on the further processing of the project.

In addition, further milestones can be set also to ensure control of the project flow during a process step. These milestones relate to intermediate results within a process step of the project that are critical for the further flow of the project. The kind and the number of such additional milestones largely depend on the scope and the level of project risk; they are usually defined in the risk analysis as early warnings and reporting points.

The risk of cancelling a project is far greater than in the later improve and transformation phases. However, you cannot end a project in all phases and at all times easily. There is a project *point of no return*, after passing this milestone the project abortion does simply no longer make sense, is impractical, or even impossible (driven by investments, legal contract commitments, etc.). This is why there should be early warning points implemented to check periodically when the point of no return will be achieved, so that if the project deviates seriously from the objectives, the project can be cancelled without too much risk.

The timely illustration of the execution of the work packages and the milestone dates is shown with the help of horizontal +-bar charts (*Gantt charts*). Milestones can be summarized to milestone plans. These provide a quick overview of the essential steps of the project planning and are therefore ideal for the stakeholder. In addition, the milestones and trend analysis are the basis for the structure of project control. The most important documents for milestone decisions are listed in Table 3.2.

Table 3.2 The most important milestone setting documents

#	Documents for Milestone Setting
1	Project contract (possibly revised)
2	Objective phrasing and revised objectives
3	Work breakdown structure and responsibilities within the project group
4	Activity list with dates or revised list of reasons for deviations between target and curremt status
5	Resource and cost plan respectively revised planning (Ressource strain, resource and cost accrued obligations and budgeted cost of the work packages, annual cost and total project cost, may be divided into types of costs) with justification for deviations between target and current performance.
6	Brief reports of investigated solution variants, assessment results and proposal for a possible solution.
7	Profitability calculations (Operating cost, Manufacuturing cost, costsavings, profits, pay-back time, ROI, internal interest rate, cost/benefit comparisons,...)
8	Notes on specific Problems, risks...
9	Experiences from the previous project work and any result of any success or quality control.

The goal of functional and reliability target setting is to enable the improvement of product quality and reliability. Functional and reliability target setting should serve as a catalyst for achieving improved, robust, and defect-free designs.

Functional result targets set the criteria to determine if the performance of the component (subsystem, or system) meets the customer expectation as shown in the upper portion of Fig. 3.4. The reliability is the percentage of the product whose performance is always higher than the customer expectation over time as shown in the lower portion of the chart. Determining the functional and reliability target setting process involves establishing:

- Detailed engineering functional metrics and their values which correlate with customer expected performance for 10 years/150 K miles.
- A reliability level, which sets the minimum requirement for the percentage of product, which must meet the functional requirement over a 10 years/150 K miles life.

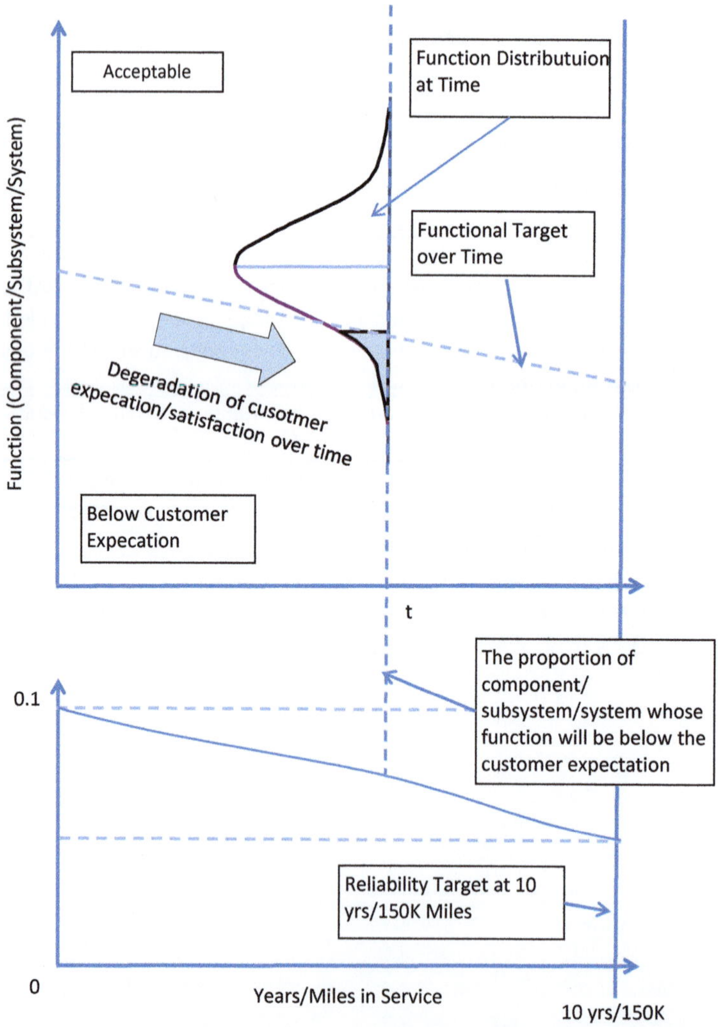

Fig. 3.4 Functional and reliability targets for a car over lifetime

The functional target setting process requires one to utilize marketing research information to understand what the customer wants, to conduct robustness analysis, system engineering, and reliability analysis of the systems and components to optimize their functions. The target values are based on knowledge of customer expectation, or from performing Key Life Tests (KLT) on Best-in-Class (BIC) products.

If design improvement actions are required and have been incorporated, the design is subjected to appropriate tests during the design verification phase to demonstrate that the functional and reliability targets have been achieved.

Functional targets can be established through simulation, or bench and rig tests. If physical tests are applied to set the target, they should focus on tracking functional degradation levels, and failure times. This permits reliability measurement during the product development process. The objective is to establish component performance levels that will deliver customer satisfaction with the system and vehicle, and then evaluate design alternatives based on the probability of meeting those performance levels and cost.

The functional target setting process is based on:

- Understanding what the customer wants and what is the corresponding engineering attribute.
- Knowledge of the system's external and internal relationships.
- The availability of a generic or program-specific test (KLT), which is designed to generate the degradation of the functional performance or failure of interest.
- Knowledge of how results on these tests are correlated to customer expectations, or BIC performance on such tests.

Functional and reliability targets should be broken down from system level to the lowest possible component levels. At this level, tests can be conducted on reasonable sample sizes to empirically investigate improvement opportunities, and to measure whether the target (functional and reliability) has been met or preferably exceeded. Success at this level should provide high confidence that the system and vehicle will deliver the expected function to the customer.

The benefits of target setting are that the primary role of functional and reliability target setting is to serve as a catalyst for continuous improvement and defect-prevention actions, so as to meet customer expectations or BIC performance. The targets provide important functional and reliability measures for optimizing trade-off with cost/weight decisions, and other requirements which need to be satisfied on vehicle programs. The target setting process drives a determination of competitive and customer expectation levels.

The major assumptions and limitations for functional objective setting are that the degradation of the performance and/or failure is known and that the noise and their extent can be estimated for our product as well as the competition's. Failure modes of the product are understood through the selection of the appropriate noise factors. The effect of these noise factors can be effectively applied to our product and the competition's. The customer expectation and the BIC targets are always changing; therefore, affordable targets can never be absolute and are regarded as the minimum requirements. The goal should always be to exceed the affordable target at the lowest cost.

Preliminary targets should be established in the product-planning phase before product development phase. An estimate of capability should be reconciled with requirements via value management. Final affordable targets must be established before product development. The input required for functional objective setting is the so-called Program Description Book (PDB)—Markets and hardware assumptions and information. Relevant failure modes/degradation events and *Key Life Test* (KLT), which generates the failure modes and customer expectations at the end of product lifetime, e.g. 10 years/150 K miles or at benchmarked performance.

Risks and Opportunities 4

Only if it is known what the risks can occur in a project, can you deal with possible effects of the project and prevent damage or at least mitigate the damage. The function of risk analysis is to identify factors hazardous to the project success (in terms of performance, cost, and schedule), using defined criteria to evaluate in to picture in a risk portfolio and to set appropriate countermeasures.

The identification of project risks is normally done by using brainstorming events supported by a diverse team with a high expertise. In addition, "lessons learned" documentation from other projects should also be used. Experience has shown that the relevant risk factors include:

- Resource constraints (availability of material resources and personnel) lead to delays, if necessary, to failure of a measure.
- Inadequate or unsound financial planning for all phases of the project may lead to stop a project.
- Insufficient support by the authority line (missing promo gate) and resistance of the affected stakeholders delay the implementation of a project.
- Early fixation on a particular system/procedure or insufficient consideration of alternative solutions leads to an implementation/application deadlock.
- To ambitious scheduling and over-optimistic resource planning led to delays and cost explosions of the project.
- Missing or inadequate control leads to uncontrolled matter outflow and thus a cost of the project.
- The absence of concrete measures for the success of the project does not allow an assessment of the efficiency and effectiveness of the project and its implementation.

All collected risks are then uniquely named, described, and recorded in a risk list. The captured risks are evaluated in terms of their probability of occurrence and their damages and prioritized.

P. Bauer, *A Comprehensive Project Management Guide*, Management for Professionals, https://doi.org/10.1007/978-3-031-68252-0_4

4.1 The Purpose of Risk Management

Risk is inherent in any project/program. A risk is an uncertain event, threat, or condition that has the potential to adversely impact the program's ability to meet its chartered objectives. This impact can manifest into some level of failure within a project and reduce the overall probability of successful completion. Failure is defined as anything accomplished in a less than acceptable manner or delivering a less than acceptable result (e.g., not achieving the business case, increased costs, schedule slippage, diminished quality, and technical non-performance).

All projects have some degree of uncertainty due to related assumptions. Size and complexity factors, as well as, the development approach and/or technological environment selected can create risk conditions that can jeopardize program success. Risk cannot be eliminated entirely, but must be anticipated in order to reduce its potential for negative impact.

Risk conditions are identified and analysed in the very early stages of a project or program and need to be continuously managed in a disciplined manner throughout all program life cycle phases. To effectively manage the quality and performance of the program, risk is one of the most important areas to be regularly monitored by the program manager.

The primary consequence of not performing risk management is that management will not have insight into what could go wrong accordingly.

- More resources are spent correcting problems (exhibited as issues) that may occur without warning and could have been avoided sooner,
- Decisions are made without complete information or adequate knowledge of future consequences, and
- The program operates in a "crisis management" or "fire-fighting" mode.

In summary, risk management forces a forward-looking approach—thinking about tomorrow and beyond, identifying uncertainties, and anticipating potential outcomes.

> 📖 Definition: The difference between a risk and an issue is:
>
> - Risk management is anticipating what can go wrong and based on the expected level of negative impact, either executing actions that prevent problems from occurring or reducing the severity of the consequences.
> - Issues are problems that have already occurred. The presence of many issues may indicate risk management is either not present or not effective. Therefore, since risks may produce issues, re-evaluate the risk management plan in the areas where frequent issues are occurring to understand the source of the real problem.

4.2 The Results of Risk Management

Risk management systematically identifies the areas of risk that may impact a particular program and then establishes an explicit program risk management plan (Table 4.1) to manage these risks. The risk management plan describes the risk, severity, corresponding mitigation strategy, and where necessary, an associated contingency plan.

Severity is evaluated in terms of its level of negative impact across multiple dimensions that can affect the success of a program.

Mitigation strategies are proactive actions put in place to minimize the probability that certain risks will cause or contribute to a failure within a program. Taking early action is more effective and less costly than trying to rectify the consequences after some failure has occurred.

Contingency plans are planned responses to react to (minimize or eliminate the impact) or recover from actual failures occurring in the program. They are implemented when the mitigation strategy has not been effective and the risk is threatening program success.

Table 4.1 Examples of a program risk management plan

RISK ASSESSMENT	**Amount of Program Risk Impact**	(Total negative severity impact across all program dimensions) (Sort in descending sequence)
	Severity of Program Risk Impact	(HIGH - at least one program dimension is rated a 3; MEDIUM - no program dimensions are rated a 3, and at least one is 2; LOW - no program dimension is higher than 1)
	Risk Condition Statement	RISK = Characteristics of the program or feature of the environment recognized to have a potential adverse effect on the program. (Write in terms of a "condition - impact" format "given the <condition> there is a possibility that <impact> will occur".
MITIGATION RISK RESPONSE	**Mitigation Strategy**	(Preventive, proactive actions to minimize the impact of a known risk to the program)
	Planned Mitigation Cost	(Expected dollar cost to implement, and if applicable, any expected impact to schedule
	Actual Mitigation Cost	(Once implemented, the actual dollar cost to mitigate, and if applicable, the actual impact to schedule
CONTINGENT RISK RESPONSE	**Contingency Plan**	(A pre-planned response to a risk, invoked when the mitigation strategy is not effective; if applicable, indicate any reserves to support this contingency plan)
	Planned Contingency Cost	(Planned dollar cost to implement, and if applicable, any expected impact to schedule
	Actual Contingency Cost	(If invoked, the actual contingency dollars spent, and if applicable, the actual impact to schedule
	Date Identified	(Date documented as a risk)
	Assigned To	(Who is responsible for evaluating the EFFECTIVENESS of the mitigation strategy and, if applicable, contingency plan)

4.3 The Process of Risk Management

Risk management is a continuous process that occurs throughout the project and is an integral part of project management decision-making at all levels. Since program risks apply to a broader scope than a single project or release, they have the potential to impact the entire program and therefore cannot be managed only by project and release managers. Given that a program's view is across all releases/projects, it is critical to be aware of and plan for; overall risk conditions and any associated events that the program team anticipates may affect the success of the program. Effective risk management is organized and systematic and encompasses the following (Fig. 4.1):

- Risk management planning
- Risk identification
- Risk analysis and evaluation
- Risk response planning and implementation
- Risk monitoring and control

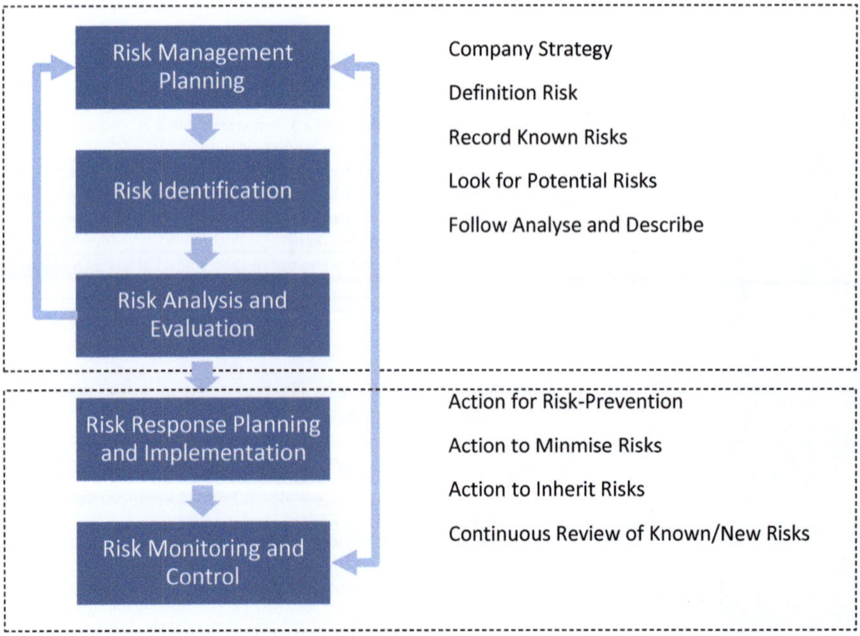

Fig. 4.1 Workflow structured risk management

4.4 Risk Management Planning

Risk management planning (performed during the Initiate phase of a program) addresses structuring the risk management activities of the entire program such that they will be executed in a consistent and high-quality manner. This includes, but is not limited to, identifying and establishing the risk management structure such as common templates, sources of risk information, roles and responsibilities, timing, reporting, and tracking. Risk management planning does NOT address the actual risks of the program, which occurs later during the activity of risk Response Planning.

4.5 Identify Risk Conditions

The next activity of risk management, performed during the Initiate and plan phases of a program, is to identify all potential risk conditions (e.g., degree of sponsorship commitment, extent of user knowledge, newness of technology to the company) that can adversely affect a program. It is important to perform this during the early phases so that managing risk is planned for and proactive, rather than reactive. As part of this exercise, identify anticipated events and warning signs to the program.

There are two types of program risk to consider. Those risk conditions inherent to the mission of the program that would be risky no matter who would undertake them (e.g. a global solution, complex solution, brand new technology in the marketplace) and those that are dependent upon the environment which an organization is more able to manage and control (e.g. skill gaps, sponsorship, resource availability). Questions to ask are:

- What conditions can negatively impact this program?
- What are the indicators (e.g., symptoms, warning signs) that a risk may be negatively impacting the success of the program?

Multiple idea generation techniques such as *Brainstorming*, *Affinity Analysis*, *Delphi*, *Cause-and-Effect Diagrams*, and use of *Checklists* support the risk identification. Input to produce the results of this exercise can be the team members' previous experiences (*Lessons Learned*), risk analyses from other programs, industry expert data, and the analyses of external factors upon the program. This process should be both intuitive and analytical.

Once all the program risk conditions (Table 4.2) are identified it is advisable to categorize them, since many risk conditions may be interrelated. An example is shown in the chart below:

Table 4.2 Categorized risks

Category: Sponsorship	Category: Software Package	Category: User Participation
Risk Conditions: • Multiple Sponsors • Degree of Sponsor Commitment • Sponsorship Span of Control • Commitment of User management • Commitment of User quality planning	Risk Conditions: • Potential Functional Match to Requirements • IT's Involvement in Package Selection • Team's Knowledge of Package	Risk Conditions: • Decision-Making Authority • Extent of User Knowledge • Sufficient Time Allocation

4.6 Risk Analysis and Evaluation

During the *Initiate* and *Plan* phases of a program/project, the identified risk conditions are evaluated to determine the potential extent of negative impact to the entire program. This can be performed qualitatively and/or quantitatively.

Qualitative risk analysis determines the importance of the identified risk by analysing its expected impact and probability (likelihood) and then prioritizing these risks according to level of severity. To be consistent across the program, this should be performed using pre-determined rating systems, which are usually stated in generic qualitative terms of "Low", "Medium", and "High" (Table 4.3). When the two factors, expected impact and probability (of the risk condition) are jointly evaluated, the result denotes the relative level of severity of a negative impact to the program (Table 4.4).

Table 4.3 Example of a pre-determined rating system for probability analysis

Probability Of Occurrence	Probability Assessment
Low	• The condition will probably not exist OR • Historical evidence, suggests this to be an Unlikely condition OR • Has not happened in other programs of this size, in this organization, etc.
Medium	• This condition has a reasonable likelihood of occurrence OR • Historical evidence, suggests this may exist
High	• This condition is very likely to exist OR • Historical evidence, suggests this to be a very likely condition OR • Has happened in other programs of this size, in this organization, etc.

Table 4.4 Example of qualitative analysis

Risk Condition	Expected Impact	Probability	Level of Severity of Impact
Nonstandard Hardware	Medium	High	High
Software Package's Functional Match to Requests	High	Medium	High

Table 4.5 Table to evaluate the severity of impact

If Expected Impact equals	And Probability equals			= Then Severity of Impact is
High	&	High	=	High
High	&	Medium	=	High
High	&	Low	=	Medium
Medium	&	High	=	High
Medium	&	Medium	=	Medium
Medium	&	Low	=	Medium
Low	&	High	=	Low
Low	&	Medium	=	Low
Low	&	Low	=	Low

Use a table, such as the one presented in Table 4.5), to evaluate the relative severity of the expected impact and the probability of occurrence.

4.7 Evaluating Program Impact

While significant activity occurs within the many projects of a program, it is the responsibility of the program manager to ensure that the program successfully achieves its overall goals and objectives. To accomplish this, the program manager should focus on several high-level areas or program dimensions:

- *Mission/Solution*—ability to support the customer's vision with the solution.
- *Governance*—ability to manage the performance of the program.
- *Schedule*—ability to meet major milestones.
- *Cost*—ability to meet the planned budget (including planned contingencies).
- *Technical/Supportability*—performance capability of the solution, and over time the cost to operate and maintain.

Each dimension can be severely affected by risk but in varying degrees. That is to say, there are stronger relationships of negative impact between specific categories of risk and specific dimensions of a program (Fig. 4.2). For example, sponsorship problems will most likely impact the effectiveness of decision-making (governance); a new software package due to many unknowns has the potential for severe budget overruns.

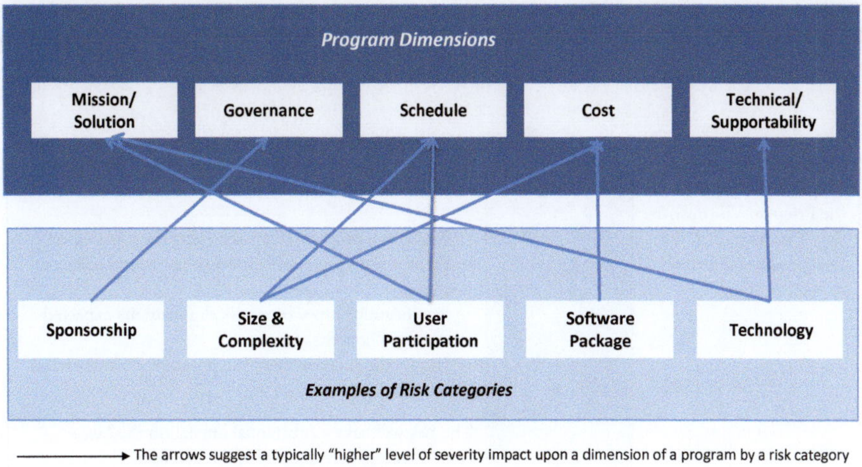

Fig. 4.2 Example of the relationships of severity and of risk impact upon program dimensions

Since it is important for the program manager to effectively manage all dimensions of the program, it is important therefore for the program manager to be aware of these relationships. To conduct a more comprehensive risk analysis, the level of severity of impact of each risk condition against each dimension of a program needs to be evaluated. In order to consistently perform this evaluation, a pre-determined rating system is utilized, as illustrated in Table 4.6), to evaluate the impact of each risk condition and to refer as an example of a pre-determined rating system for all program dimensions.

Table 4.6 Example of a pre-determined rating system to evaluate the impact of risk upon a program's "mission"

Dimension	Impact Level	Description of Impact
Mission / Solution The ability to support the Program Vision with the IT solution (e.g. the final products delivered to the customer)	High	The risk will have a severe impact on the Mission/Solution. The impact of the risk will: · Inhibit the program from achieving the mission, or · Prevent the program from delivering a workable solution, or · Significantly reduce or totally eliminate the expected value and benefits, or · Hinder the acceptance of the program in all impacted organisations
	Medium	The risk will have a substantial impact on the Mission/Solution. The impact of the risk will: · Limit the program from achieving the full mission, or · Result in the loss of key functionality in the program solution, or · Diminish the expected value and benefits, or · Postpone the acceptance of the program in some of the impacted organisations
	Low	The risk will have a minor impact on the Mission/Solution. The impact of the risk will: · Have a negligible effect on the ability to achieve the program mission, or · Cause some loss of non-vital functionality in the program solution, or · Affect the expected value and benefits, but will likely be acceptable), or · Require the program to be re-sold to some of the impacted organizations
	No Impact	The risk will have no impact on the Mission / Solution.

Quantitative risk analysis also analyses probability (likelihood) and impact and then prioritizes according to their potential effect—but does so numerically. The probability of a risk would be assigned a value between 0.0 and 1.0 and the impact could be measured in dollars. When the two factors, probability and impact, are multiplied together the result denotes the cost of the risk condition to the program. Since this exercise requires considerable effort, consider performing quantitative evaluation only when the data is available to conduct the analyses. Use the results of quantitative risk analysis when obtaining approval for mitigation and contingency dollars by comparing the impact of mitigation/contingency spending versus accepting the risk.

4.8 Risk Response Planning and Implementation

Risk response planning is the process of developing actions, called mitigation strategies to minimize the likelihood and impact of a known risk to a program. They are intended to be preventive and proactive. A question to ask during this exercise is "What can be done to prevent it from going wrong, or at least reduce the severity of its consequences?"

Risk response planning also includes identifying and planning contingent actions. These are reactive responses or fallback plans normally invoked if a risk condition has occurred and is contributing to a failure within the program. This generally happens when the mitigation strategy has not produced successful results. Risk response planning includes determining when mitigation strategy and contingency plans are required. The following chart (Table 4.7) provides a general "rule of thumb" for making this decision.

Table 4.7 Risk decisions table

Severity of Negative Impact	Mitigation Strategy Required	Contingency Plan Required
High	✓	✓
Medium	✓	*
Low	-	-

[a] All "Medium" severity impact risks should have an approach to contingency, but do not require a complete contingency plan

Both “Medium” and “Low” risks should be continually monitored to determine if their impact has changed to a higher level of severity.

Next, strategies are formulated to determine options to respond. Responding to risk comes at a cost, either in time and/or money. This is due to adding processes, applying methods, proposing alternative approaches, and adding resources that are not directly associated with creating program deliverables.

Mitigation costs should be appropriate relative to the likely probability and associated consequences. For example, if the mitigation strategy seems costly, is the cost of ignoring or accepting the risk more expensive? The selection of strategy should be based on the question “Will it control the expected outcome?”

Once risk responses are decided, it should be planned how mitigation strategies will be implemented, who will be assigned responsibility to monitor effectiveness, and estimate any additional costs. Estimate, separately, the costs to implement the “High” severity risk contingency plans and obtain approval for any incremental costs.

> 🕮 Tip: Hold contingency funds in reserve and explicitly describe under what conditions they can be spent. These are often called a “contingency allowance” and can include time, money, or resources to cover contingent plans. It is important to note that these funds should not be used by default to cover changes in scope and cost overruns due to poor estimating, unless a risk (e.g. new technology) had been identified and planned for and funds were specifically approved to contain scope and estimating problems. Otherwise, should the risk that the contingency was originally planned for, occur, the funds would not be available and would produce an over-budget condition. Had the contingent funds been available to address the risk, the program’s budget condition might not have changed. Therefore, while it might be tempting to use these contingencies on some other unplanned event, this is not an acceptable risk management practice. And, if at the end of the program, these reserves are not spent, they become additional funds available to the customer.

When formulating a response, also examine the relationship and dependencies among the risks should be examined. On the positive side, a strategy may mitigate multiple risks. On the negative side, a strategy may reduce risk in one area, but increase risk in another.

> 🕮 Tip: Programs can have “unknown” risks that cannot be predicted or planned for and therefore cannot be proactively managed. If there is a concern that this program may be subject to “unknown” risks, an acceptable practice is to reserve a general contingency fund ONLY to be used for these unplanned risk conditions.

4.9 Risk Monitoring and Control

Since risk can rarely be eliminated, it must be continuously monitored and controlled. A specific risk condition may disappear if, for example, a significant change in approach is decided during the life of the program, but new conditions may also emerge. Formal risk reviews of the risk management plan should occur:

- At pre-determined review points.
- When there is a change in program scope, structure, or approach, and
- Immediately when a significant risk exposure is detected.

For example, with large programs mitigation strategies should be monitored monthly by the program manager to determine their effectiveness, to look for signs of failure and, if necessary, to re-evaluate the risk severity level. The program manager should also review the effectiveness of any contingency actions in effect.

Effectiveness is defined as the following:

- Mitigation strategies that:
  - Prevent "High" and "Medium" risk consequences from actually occurring.
  - Control "High" and "Medium" risk consequences that are occurring.
  - Reduce risk severity levels, where possible.

- Contingency actions that:
  - Reduce or eliminate the impact of some level of program failure.

The program manager should also monitor if negative impact levels have changed (e.g., medium to high; low to medium). Should more stringent mitigation strategies be desired, additional or alternate mitigation strategies may be introduced. Should a risk materialize into a problem (failure), invoke the contingency plan.

As part of Monitor and Control, it should also be verified monthly, whether new risks in the risk management plan have surfaced.

> 🕮 Tip: Due to the nature of risk that is inherent to the mission of the program (e.g. a global solution, complex solution, brand new technology in the marketplace), it is very difficult to reduce the severity level of the impact; therefore, the primary focus of risk management is to ensure that mitigation strategies are working. Those risks that are dependent upon the environment (e.g., skill gaps, sponsorship, resource availability), however, have more options for mitigation since more is within control of the organization, therefore the focus should be to try, if possible, to reduce the level of negative impact.

4.10 An Illustration of a Risk Management Process

The following is an example of one approach to demonstrate how all the elements of managing risk integrate into a complete risk management process. The purpose is to facilitate an understanding of risk management and to help a program manager to evaluate an approach that will be thorough. Program managers should choose the best risk management approach for their program. The illustration in (Fig. 4.3) depicts the risk management components of "Identify, Evaluate and Plan" for risks.

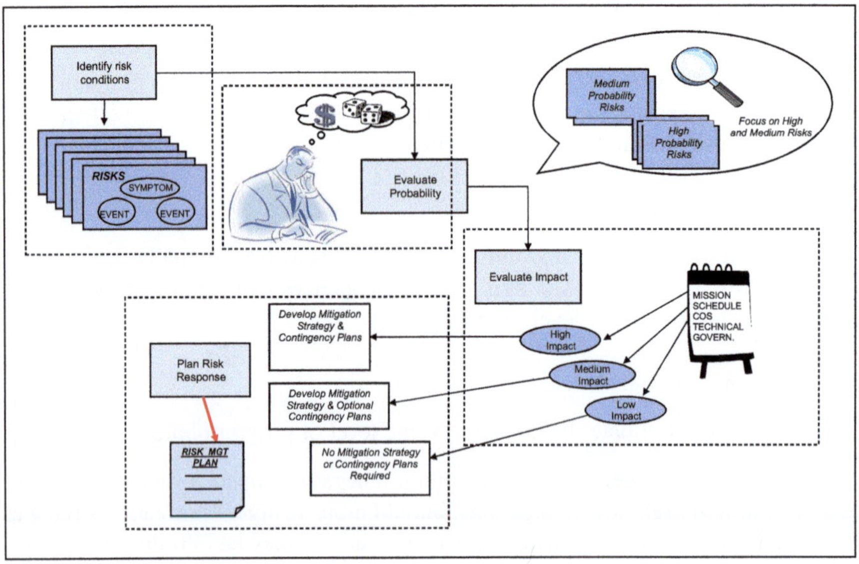

Fig. 4.3 "Identify, evaluate, and plan" for risk

4.11 Risk Identification

Identifying risk entails understanding conditions that will threaten a program success. Using the "List of Common Program risks" job aid as a thought starter, choose those risks that seem to be problematic on this project (Table 4.13). Exclude those risks that appear to be negligible.

The program manager leads a team to identify if there are other additional risks that need to be managed, using multiple idea generation techniques, such as Brainstorming, Affinity Analysis, Delphi, and Cause-and-Effect Diagrams. Input to produce the results of this exercise can be the team members' previous experiences (lessons learned), risk analysis from other programs, industry expert data, and analysis of external factors upon the program. This process should be both intuitive and analytical. Any newly identified risks are then added to the original list generated from the "*List of Common Program Risks*".

For each risk condition, the example events and symptoms are reviewed. These are indicators to signal how a risk may trigger a failure condition and to alert the program team to the occurrence of risk. The events and symptoms from the "List of Common Program risks" are modified, added, or deleted as necessary. For new risks events and symptoms need to be identified (Table 4.8).

Table 4.8 Example of program X's risk conditions and events/symptoms

PROGRAM 'X'		
POTENTIAL RISKS Risk Categories and Conditions		APPEARANCE OF RISK Examples of Events or Symptoms Describing the Risk Occurrence
SPONSORSHIP	Multiple Sponsors	The sponsors have divergent views on objectives, benefits and direction.
		The sponsors have conflicts on objectives, benefits and direction.
	Extent of Sponsor Commitment	The sponsor is unwilling to make decisions.
		The sponsor is not involved as required.
		The sponsor does not support the development team.
USER PARTICIPATION	Extent of User Knowledge	Key user participants are not able to provide the required details to complete the program deliverables.
		Input from key users is inconsistent relative to the mission direction.
		Content of deliverables requiring user input is not completed in a timely or quality manner.
		Test participants indicate that the solution is not meeting their needs.
SIZE and COMPLEXITY	Number of Organizations to Coordinate	Affected organizations cannot reach consensus in all required aspects of the program.
		All affected organizations are not participating in all required aspects of the program.
		The coordination of input from all organizations is difficult or unmanageable.
		Affected organizations are late approving formal documentation.
		The program team does not understand the various organizations in order to determine each's required level of participation.
TECHNOLOGY	Newness of Technology to Company	The program team is having difficulty obtaining support within IT for the planned technology.
		The program team is having difficulty finding qualified personnel for the planned technology.
		The delivery of technology tasks are late and/or over budget.
		The program team can find qualified personnel for the planned technology, but not at the hoped-for cost.
		The program team is having difficulty creating a solution that performs as expected by the users.
SOFTWARE PACKAGE	Functional Match of Package to Requirements	During development, the vendor announces a shift in package direction that conflicts with the customizations in process.
		Significant gaps (more than planned) exist between requirements and the package.
		Performance and usability are degrading the system due to the changes made.
		Requirements are revised because of limitations of the selected package.
		Key user personnel are not providing their acceptance of the deliverables related to the package.

4.12 Risk Assessment

From the list of identified risks, the program should focus on those presenting the most threat and having the most potential to adversely impact the program's ability to meet its chartered objectives. To accomplish this, evaluate the probability of the prior identified conditions and associated events to identify those with "High" and "Medium" likelihoods of occurrence.

The example in Table 4.9) provides suggested interpretations of probability. For those risks where these interpretations are not helpful, the prior (Table 4.3) can also be used as a guide.

Table 4.9 Example of program X's probability assessment

POTENTIAL RISKS		APPEARANCE OF RISK	PROBABILITY ASSESSMENT Likelihood the Risk will Occur			
	Risk Categories and Conditions	Examples of Events or Symptoms Describing a Risk Occurrence	Low (e.g. Condition will probably not exist; historical evidence suggests this to be an unlikely condition)	Medium (e.g. Condition has reasonable likelihood of occurrence; historical evidence suggests this may exist)	High (e.g. Condition is very likely to exist; historical evidence suggests this to be a very likely condition)	PROGRAM 'X'
SPONSORSHIP	*Multiple Sponsors*	The sponsors have divergent views on objectives, benefits and direction. The sponsors have conflicts on objectives, benefits and direction.	The program has one sponsor.	The program has two sponsors.	The program has more than two sponsors.	Low
SPONSORSHIP	*Extent of Sponsor Commitment*	The sponsor is unwilling to make decisions. The sponsor is not involved as required. The sponsor does not support the development team.	The sponsor is identified, enthusiastic, and	The sponsor is identified but passive.	The sponsor is unknown.	Medium
USER PARTICIPATION	*Extent of User Knowledge*	Key user participants are not able to provide the required details to complete the program deliverables. Input from key user participants is inconsistent relative to the mission direction. Content of deliverables requiring user input is not completed in a timely or quality manner. Test participants indicate that the solution is not meeting their needs.	Key user participants are fully knowledgeable in the subject matter required to meet their roles and responsibilities to the program.	Key user participants are somewhat knowledgeable in the subject matter required.	Key user participants are not knowledgeable in the subject matter required.	Medium
SIZE and COMPLEXITY	*Number of Organizations to Coordinate*	Affected organizations cannot reach consensus in all required aspects of the program. All affected organizations are not participating in all required aspects of the program. The coordination of input from all organizations is difficult or unmanageable. Affected organizations are late approving formal documentation. The program team does not understand the various organizations in order to determine each's required level of participation.	This program includes coordinating between two closely related organizations.	This program includes coordinating between two organizations that are not closely related.	This program includes coordinating among three or more organizations.	Low
TECHNOLOGY	*Newness of Technology*	The program team is having difficulty obtaining support within companys IT for development using the planned technology. The program team is having difficulty finding qualified personnel for the planned technology. The delivery of technology tasks are late and/or over budget. The program team can find qualified personnel for the planned technology, but not at the hoped-for cost. The program team is having difficulty creating a solution that performs as expected by the users.	The program is using technology that is a fully supported corporate standard within Ford IT.	The program is using technology that is known to Ford IT, but is either no longer or not yet a fully supported corporate standard.	The program is using technology that is completely new to the companys IT.	High
SOFTWARE PACKAGE	*Functional Match to Requirements*	During development, the vendor announces a shift in package direction that conflicts with the customizations in process. Significant gaps (more than planned) exist between requirements and the package. Performance and usability are degrading the system due to the changes made. Requirements are revised because of limitations of the selected package. Key user personnel are not providing their acceptance of the deliverables related to the package.	The program team plans to use a package that matches the system requirements well (minimal modification required).	The program team plans to use a package that matches the system requirements fairly well (moderate modification required).	The program team plans to use a package that does not match the system requirements well (major modification required).	High

Once the probability assessment is complete, analysis will continue with only the "High" and "Medium" probability risk conditions. Continue to evaluate program risk by assessing how these remaining risk conditions could negatively affect program success in the following important dimensions of program impact:

- *Mission/Solution*—ability to support the customer's vision with the solution
- *Governance*—ability to manage the performance of the program
- *Schedule*—ability to meet major milestones
- *Cost*—ability to meet the planned budget (including planned contingencies)
- *Technical/Supportability*—performance capability of the solution, and over time the cost to operate and maintain.

A risk can impact one or more program dimensions, therefore evaluate each risk condition against each of the dimensions to understand the full extent of impact to the program (Table 4.10). Obtaining this view of impact across multiple dimensions of the program is important in order to design a comprehensive mitigation strategy and to provide a better comparison of severity of all risks relative to each other. The "Instrument to Evaluate Large Program Impact" job aid was used to conduct this evaluation.

Table 4.10 Example of program X's evaluation of impact against all program dimensions

PROGRAM 'X'	IMPACT OF RISK ON PROGRAM DIMENSIONS				
RISK CONDITIONS	Mission/ Solution	Gover-nance	Schedule	Cost	Technical/ Supportabi-lity
Extent of Sponsor Commit-ment	Medium	High	Medium	Medium	No
Extent of User Knowledge	Medium	No	Medium	Medium	No
Newness of Technology to Company	High	No	Medium	Medium	High
Degree of Sponsorship and Commitment	NA	NA	NA	NA	NA
Functional match to Require-ments	Medium	No	Medium	High	Medium

Continue the evaluation (Table 4.11) for each risk condition by:

- Totalling all the dimensions and record as "Dimension Severity Amount"
- Recording the "Dimension Severity" by choosing the highest rating the risk condition has across all dimensions
  - "High" denotes the highest rating in any dimension was "High"
  - "Medium" denotes the highest rating was a "Medium"
  - "Low" denotes the highest rating was "Low"

Table 4.11 Example of program X's determination of dimension severity

PROGRAM 'X'							
	IMPACT OF RISK ON PROGRAM DIMENSIONS						
RISK CONDITIONS	Mission/ Solution	Governance	Schedule	Cost	Technical/ Supportability	# Dimension Impact	Dimension Severity
Extent of Sponsor Commitment	Medium	High	Medium	Medium	No	9	High
Extent of User Knowledge	Medium	No	Medium	Medium	No	6	Medium
Newness of Technology to Company	High	No	Medium	Medium	High	10	High
Functional Match to Requirements	Medium	No	Medium	High	Medium	9	High

The final step of risk Analysis and Evaluation is to determine TOTAL Program risk Impact (Tables 4.12 and 4.13) by revisiting the probability from an earlier step and applying the results against the Dimension Impact. To do this, for each risk:

- Evaluate the Level of Program risk Impact using the table below (Table 4.5).
- Calculate the Amount of Program risk Impact by multiplying the Amount of Dimension Impact by the Probability.

Table 4.12 Example—Table to evaluate the level of program risk impact

If Expected Impact equals	And	Probability equals		#NAME? of Impact is
High	&	High	=	High
High	&	Medium	=	High
High	&	Low	=	Medium
Medium	&	High	=	High
Medium	&	Medium	=	Medium
Medium	&	Low	=	Medium
Low	&	High	=	Low
Low	&	Medium	=	Low
Low	&	Low	=	Low

Flows into Table 17: Column PROGRAM SEVERITY

Table 4.13 Example of program X's determination of TOTAL program risk impact

PROGRAM 'X'										
	IMPACT OF RISK ON PROGRAM DIMENSIONS								PROGRAM SEVERITY	
RISK CONDITIONS	Mission/ Solution	Governance	Schedule	Cost	Technical/ Supportability	Amount of Dimension Impact	Dimension Severity	Probability	Severity of Program Risk Impact (see table)	Amount of Program Risk Impact
Extent of Sponsor Commitment	Medium	High	Medium	Medium	No	9	High	Medium	High	18
Extent of User Knowledge	Medium	No	Medium	Medium	No	6	Medium	Medium	Medium	12
Newness of Technology to Ford	High	No	Medium	Medium	High	10	High	High	High	30
Functional Match to Requirements	Medium	No	Medium	High	Medium	9	High	High	High	27

Again, obtaining this view of impact across multiple dimensions of the program is important in order to design a comprehensive mitigation strategy as well as to compare the severity of all risk conditions relative to each other.

4.13 Risk Response Planning

Recording into the risk management plan, the statements of risk and their corresponding severity from the prior risk analysis and evaluation activities make the beginning. The risk statement is comprised of the category, condition(s), and consequences. The impact is derived from the analysis that occurs as each risk condition was evaluated against each program dimension. It is organized from the highest total severity amount to the lowest (Table 4.14).

Table 4.14 Example of program X's documented risk assessment

RISK ASSESSMENT			
Amount of Program Risk Impact	Severity of Program Risk Impact	Risk Condition Statement	Tracking #
30	High	CATEGORY: TECHNOLOGY CONDITION: *Newness of Technology - The program is implementing technology completely new IT.* IMPACT: If not properly managed, the solution delivered may miss the goal and objectives of the Business Case. Therefore, schedule and cost may be substantially impacted. Additionally, since technology chosen is not currently standard, ability of the company's IT to maintain the implemented solution long-term is not present.	1
27	High	CATEGORY: SOFTWARE PACKAGE CONDITION: *Functional Match to Requirements - In order to meet the business requirements, major modifications required to the selected package.* IMPACT: If not properly managed, there could be significant cost overruns. Secondarily, key functionality could be subjected to quality problems, schedules may slip, and long-term support could be very complex.	2
18	High	CATEGORY: SPONSORSHIP CONDITION: *Extent of Sponsor Commitment - Historically this business sponsor has not always been actively engaged in the program.* IMPACT: As a result, effective governance will be at risk. Delayed decision making can negatively affect the cost and schedule of the program.	3
12	Medium	CATEGORY: USER PARTICIPATION CONDITION: *Extent of User Knowledge - Not all key users have the subject matter required.* IMPACT: Key users assigned do not have the knowledge to adequately define the requirements for the software package. There is a risk relative to all key functionality being defined properly without a need for rework. This has the potential to negatively affect the cost and schedule.	4

> 🕮 Tip: It is important that the risk Statement be specific as it relates to the program, so that the original characterization can be understood over time.

According to the rule of thumb described in a prior section, (Fig. 4.4) depicts for Program "X", in order of importance, when to develop mitigation strategies and contingency plans. For each risk condition, formulate strategies to respond proactively and, for those determined to have contingency plans, reactively.

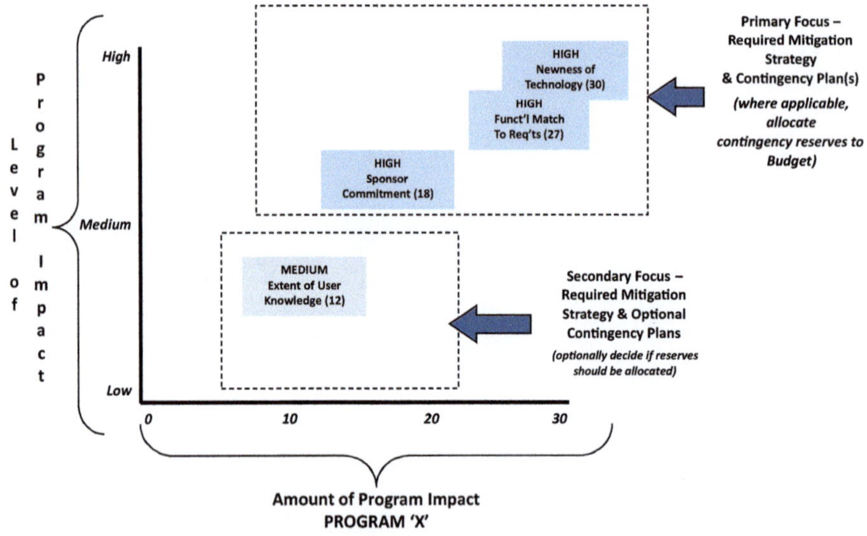

Fig. 4.4 Example—Charting the risk assessment

Additionally, it should be determined who is responsible for evaluating the effectiveness of the mitigation strategy and, if applicable, contingency plan. These should be the same individuals who planned the mitigation strategy and contingency plan. Table 4.15 depicts the risk management plan for program "X".

Table 4.15 Example of program X's risk management plan

PROGRAM 'X' RISK MANAGEMENT PLAN									
RISK ASSESSMENT			MITIGATION RISK RESPONSE			CONTINGENT RISK RESPONSE			
30	High	**CATEGORY: TECHNOLOGY** **CONDITION: Newness of Technology - The program is implementing technology completely new to the companys IT.** **IMPACT:** If not properly managed, the solution delivered may miss the goal and objectives of the Business Case. Therefore, schedule and cost may be substantially impacted. Additionally, since technology chosen is not currently a companys standard, ability of companys IT to maintain the implemented solution long-term is not present.	Contacted outside company, provided as a reference from technology vendor, with similar problem (no experience in technology) for their approach and lessons learned. Include in plan, technology vendor's phased training to program/project personnel and support personnel on the new technology. Added 4 technology consultants to work with analysis and design project teams. Added time into implementation for potential technology problems. Actively involve personnel from Technology organization in key activities to garner sponsorship and support.	$5M over the life of the program	$800K spent to date	Stop progress and evaluate user expectations and scope, should there be major concerns about the cost or ability to create a solution that meets their needs. Engage IT executive management for internal IT sponsorship issues.	$150K to stop and evaluate	Program Manager and Principal Information Architect	1
12	Medium	**CATEGORY: USER PARTICIPATION** **CONDITION: Extent of User Knowledge - Not all key users have the subject matter required.** **IMPACT:** Key users assigned do not have the knowledge to adequately define the requirements for the software package. There is a risk relative to all key functionality being defined properly without a need for rework. This has the potential to negatively affect the cost and schedule.	Multiple quality checkpoints built into plan to verify and communicate to Business Sponsors the quality of business information being provided into the analysis and design deliverables. Time built into plans for these reviews.	$50K		**Enlist users with subject matter knowledge and rework.**	$250K	Program Manager and Business Program Sponsor	4

The risk management plan (Table 4.15) becomes the working document that is used throughout the program to document the results of monitoring and controlling risks.

4.14 Alignment

In the IPMA Competence Baseline Version 3.0 guide, risk management is basically comprised of the following processes:

- Risk management planning
- Risk Identification
- Qualitative risk analysis
- Quantitative risk analysis
- Risk Response planning, and
- Risk Monitoring and control

The IPMA processes are specific to releases and projects, while chapter targets the approach to risk management across an entire program. The processes in this technique are very similar to the IPMA guide; however, there are two visible differences:

- IPMA *Qualitative* and *Quantitative* analysis processes are combined into risk analysis and evaluation.
- Risks are evaluated against the major dimensions of a program to ensure that the full impact of the risk across the entire program is understood and that the mitigation strategies and contingency plans address the full impact. These dimensions are:
  - *Mission/Solution*
  - *Governance*
  - *Schedule*
  - *Cost*
  - *Technology/Supportability*

4.15 Projects Within a Program

The purpose of risk management at the program level is to identify and manage conditions of risk to the entire program. Since risk conditions, characteristically, exist for the life of a program they will often affect many projects in a similar way. Successful methods to manage risk at its first occurrence should, if possible, be used throughout the program. It is critical to ensure that these risks do not allow the program to fail. These are all the responsibility of the program manager.

While evidence of risk can be confirmed at the program level, most actual events or symptoms will occur within and/or across multiple projects. Therefore, the incidence of risk should be communicated from the Release and project Managers upward; but it is from the program manager's vantage point that the true impact to the program can be discerned. Similarly, downward communication to the various projects should come from the program manager's insight as to how risk has affected projects within the program, in order to create advanced awareness of potential future conditions and the successful experiences to address it.

Although projects and releases can have risk(s) that are distinctive to it, it is still important to evaluate and review all risks at the program level since potential failure will be elevated to the program and the program manager will ultimately be held accountable.

References

Michael Gessler. (2011). Kompetenzbasiertes Projektmanagement (PM3) Handbuch für die Projektarbeit, Qualifizierung und Zertifizierung auf Basis der IPMA Competence Baseline Version 3.0 / unter Mitwirkung der spm swiss project management association (4. Auflage ed., Vol. 1). Nürnberg: GPM Deutsche Gesellschaft für Projektmanagement.

http://www.brighthubpm.com/project-planning/. (n.d.). BRIGHT HUB PROJECT MANAGEMENT. New York.

5 Quality

If you were to ask quality experts to define "quality", you would likely receive a variety of answers. However, common themes would emerge, such as "Fitness for purpose", "Right first time", "Meeting customer needs", "Conformance to standards", "Value for money", and "Delivering the right thing at the right time". The diversity in definitions stems from individual preferences and perspectives. The meaning of quality often depends on context and application. Here are several possible interpretations:

One definition of quality is fitness for use. A product or service is considered of poor quality if it fails to perform its intended function, thus costing users. Another definition is meeting customer expectations. Quality, in this sense, involves satisfying the customer, who ultimately defines and perceives the quality of a product or service. A third perspective views quality as exceeding customer expectations, meaning the product or service surpasses the needs and expectations of the customer or user. Lastly, quality can be seen as superiority to competitors, indicating how a company's offerings compare to those of its rivals or to its own past products.

Additionally, quality is the characteristic of a unit in terms of its ability to satisfy stated and implied requirements. Achieving quality involves the entire organization and every department working together towards this common goal.

People constantly make judgements about what constitutes good quality and what does not, in both everyday life and business. These opinions can range from the taste of sandwiches to whether Apple or Microsoft produces the best cell phones, or how the experience of driving a particular car is perceived. Despite these varied opinions, everyone seeks to use products and services of the highest quality, whether in their professional endeavours or daily routines.

For companies, their service and quality departments, the customer's point of view is one of the major factors the former work on. People are analysing this to find out how the customer drives quality, what the customer expects, what quality should

P. Bauer, *A Comprehensive Project Management Guide*, Management for Professionals, https://doi.org/10.1007/978-3-031-68252-0_5

look like, and of course how to satisfy the customer the best. The most important thing is to cover what the customer expects of the product or service that will be offered. That means every organization wants to detect and meet the voice of the customer. When you buy a Coca-Cola, you expect a consistent experience every time you open a can. If the drink tasted overly sweet one time and lacked the signature secret ingredient the next, you would notice the difference and feel dissatisfied. The Coca-Cola Company understands this expectation and meticulously controls the quantity and composition of each ingredient in its drinks. They achieve this consistency through precise specifications, which are designed to meet customer expectations and ensure satisfaction.

In fact, cultural influences and circumstances depend on the respective country, industry, and organization. If the cultural influences have an effect on the organization of a company, they also have an effect on their project and quality behaviour.

Germany, for example, differs with Spain because of different cultures. Cultural influences can be variables like history, education, expectation, location, weather, environment, and work style. As a result, there are different ways of running project management within a company. To ensure best results working with quality it is important to understand how other cultures behave and think. Also, products should be checked to see if they suit to the selected country to avoid loss of intended message and to ensure correct placement of the right statement.

Our understanding of quality in projects has evolved significantly in recent years, aligning more closely with the overall concept of quality within a company. In the past, the focus on quality in projects was primarily product-oriented. However, since around 1996, this focus has expanded to include project management processes. Today, considerations of project quality encompass both the quality of the project outcomes and the quality of project management itself.

The growing emphasis on quality management in projects correlates with the increasing reliance on project management. A decade ago, only 5–10% of a company's workload was managed through assigned projects, but this proportion has now risen to approximately 30%. Consequently, the success of project-based work has become a more critical factor in a company's operational performance and overall success. Implementing systematic quality management practices helps ensure project success.

As quality-conscious companies adopt project management, synergies between quality management in the line organization and in projects become more pronounced. Project-oriented companies integrate project management into their overall quality management systems. These companies are evolving from purely product-based quality control to a more comprehensive approach, focusing on both product and process quality management, ultimately aiming for a holistic Total Quality Management (TQM) system.

It is not surprising that this trend is also evident in project management. Today, organizations employ both line-oriented and project-oriented quality management systems, each at varying levels of maturity.

5.1 Terms and Definitions

This chapter presents the modern understanding of quality and quality management in regard to projects, programs, and project portfolios, and is used in reference to the company-wide total quality management concept. Quality belongs to the core competence elements of the project manager. All phases and all components of the project, its leadership, and its results are considered in the framework of quality management. This will be shown in depth with help of the Six Sigma quality management system.

In particular, the planning and steering of the quality of the project management processes requires profound knowledge. The methods and instruments presented here are closely related to the project planning and control processes; they can strongly influence the success of the project. Therefore, the requirements for quality management are ever more frequently contractually set in projects.

One of the most influential figures in industrial quality is the American W. Edwards Deming. His quality cycle (Fig. 5.1), known as "Plan-Do-Check-Act" (PDCA), illustrates the model for continuous improvement and is widely referenced globally. Deming is often called the "Father of the quality movement" in Japan, where he did most of his work. This movement played a crucial role in Japan's economic recovery, helping Japanese products gain major market shares worldwide. In recognition of his contributions, the Union of Japanese Scientists and Engineers (JUSE) established the "Deming Prize" in 1951, which is awarded annually to companies with outstanding quality management systems.

Fig. 5.1 Deming's quality circle

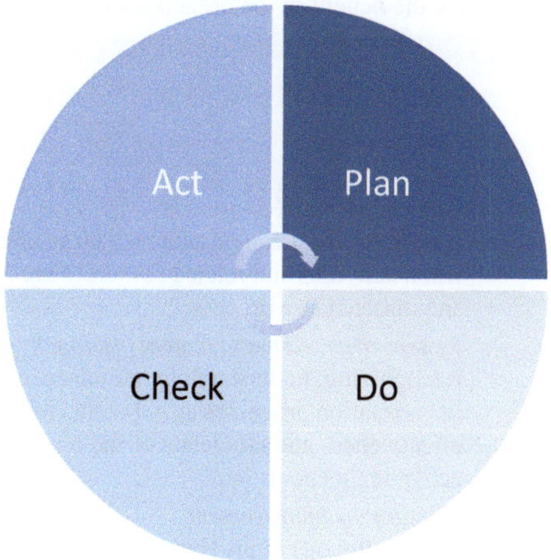

To guide organizations toward sustainable success, ISO 9000:2000 outlines eight fundamental principles of quality management. These principles align closely with modern project management standards and can be directly applied to project management. Conversely, contemporary project management practices inherently incorporate quality management activities. (Table 5.1).

Table 5.1 Comparison of the QM-Fundamentals EN ISO 9000:2000 and their relevance for the PM-Elements based on ICB Version 3 (IPMA, 2006)

Index	Quality management fundamentals	Main project management Elements based on ICB
1	*Customer orientation*: Organizations depend on their customers and should understand therefore present and future requirements of the customers and to meet their requirements and strive to exceed their expectations.	1.01 project management success 1.02 Interested parties 1.03 project requirements & objectives 1.14 Procurement & contract 1.18 Communication 1.19 Start-up 1.20 Close 2.14 Values appreciation
2	*Leadership*: Leaders create compliance of purpose and orientation in the organization. They should create and preserve the internal environment, in which people can fully comply with achieving company objectives.	Qualification and certification project manager IPMA 4LQ & 4LC (IPMA, 2006: Section 1.6 and 3) Professional Project Management (IPMA, 2006:2)
3	*Involvement of individuals*: People are the essence of an organization at all levels and their full involvement enables to use their skills for the benefit of the organization.	1.06 project organization 1.07 Teamwork 1.12 Resources 1.18 Communication 1.19 Start-up 1.20 Close 4.20 Social and personal competence 3.08 Personal Management
4	*Process-oriented approach*: A desired result can be achieved more efficiently when activities and related resources are managed and directed as a process.	Compare section 2.2 and 2.3
5	*System-oriented management approach*: Recognizing, understanding, guidance, and steering in correlation processes as a system contribute to the effectiveness and efficiency of the organization in achieving its goals.	4.3 PM-Context competence
6	*Continuous improvement*: The continuous improvement of the overall performance of the organization represents a permanent objective of the organization.	1.11 Time & project phases 1.20 Close- 3.05 Base organization (organizational training)

(continued)

Table 5.1 (continued)

Index	Quality management fundamentals	Main project management Elements based on ICB
7	*Objective approach to decision-making*: Effective decisions are based on the analysis of data and information.	1.03 Project requirements and objectives 1.10 Scope and deliverables 1.15 Changes 1.16 Control and reports 1.17 Information and documentation
8	*Supplier relations for mutual benefit*: An organization and its suppliers are interdependent. The mutual beneficial relationships increase the value creation capability of both sides.	1.02 Interested parties 1.14 Procurement and contract 1.18 Communication 1.19 Start-up 1.20 Close 2.14 Reward and Recognition

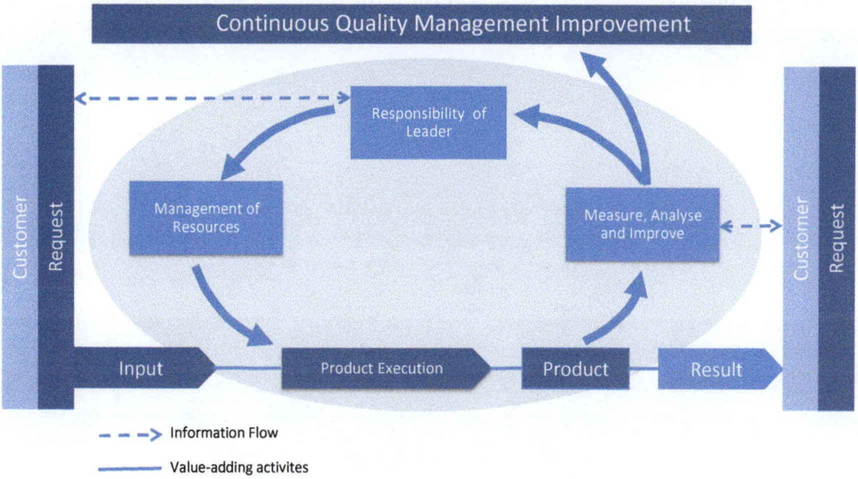

Fig. 5.2 Structure of a process-oriented QM-System according to ISO 9000:2000

Figure 5.2 represents the process orientation quality management system. The model shows a customer to the customer interacting system. The value chain (product realization) is determined by the needs and the satisfaction of our customers, the arrows visualize the process of continuous improvement.

Ultimately the client (project client, stakeholder) defines what a good quality product is. The customer acceptance and wishes (as specifications or rough concept) should be available in the first phases of the project or already before the project initiation.

A popular and effective method to translate customer requirements, "the voice of the customer", into specific product characteristics, is the quality function deployment (QFD) method that was developed in Japan at the end of the 1960s. Typical tools of this method are the so-called quality panels, which consist of a matrix with several fields. It is called "House of Quality" (Fig. 5.3) because of their combined outer shape. Both internal customers and external customers are understood as stakeholders that will have something to do with the product after the completion (such as Marketing, Sales, Data centre for IT projects or Production, Assembly, Service for construction projects), the quality panels are updated and completed throughout the project phases and are used in the implementation phase of the project management and quality assurance. Meanwhile, there are further developments of the QFD method. These are used not only for product features, but also for the processes and systems can.

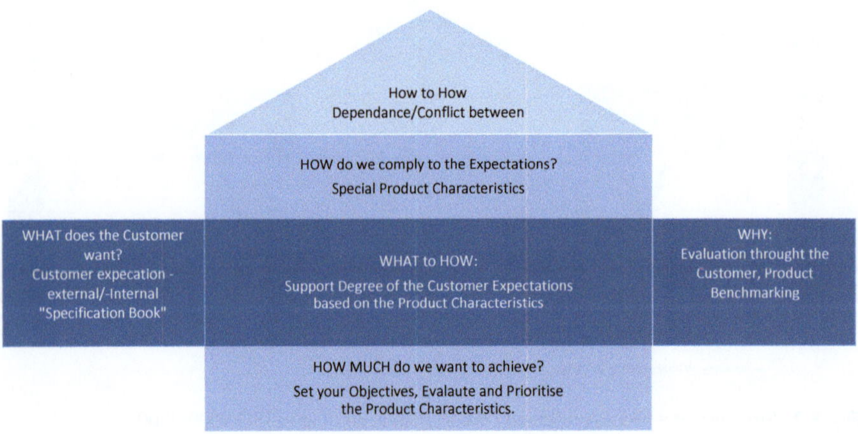

Fig. 5.3 QFD house of quality

The best method to achieve a successful project is dependent on its variables like team, application, time, and capabilities and on the strategic way of handling management forces. There are qualitative as well as quantitative techniques to select a certain project. Qualitative techniques can be benchmarking and the balanced scorecard. The Q7 tools, which include, e.g., brainstorming, histogram, Pareto, and Ishikawa diagram are relevant. Quantitative techniques can be Failure Mode and Effects Analysis (FMEA), Statistical Process Control (SPC), Design of Experiments (DoE), Quality Function Deployment (QFD), or Define, Measure, Analyse, Improve, and Control (DMAIC) through Six Sigma.

5.2 Quality Function Deployment (QFD)

Quality Function Deployment (QFD) is a strategic planning tool designed to translate high-level customer needs and desires into specific design parameters and process variables critical to meeting those needs. Through the QFD methodology, relationships are identified between the quality characteristics valued by customers and the corresponding technical requirements defined by engineers (Cohen 1988). These technical requirements are referred to as "critical-to" characteristics.

In QFD, customers articulate their needs and desires in their own terms, which typically lack technical specificity. This customer input, known as the "voice of the customer", is refined into a comprehensive list of needs and wants. This list is then used to populate a relationship matrix, known as the "House of Quality" (HOQ), with the help of an affinity diagram. This structured approach ensures that customer requirements are systematically translated into actionable engineering specifications.

Understanding customer needs and desires is crucial for designing effective products and services efficiently. By using the QFD methodology, developers can achieve the shortest development cycles while ensuring customer requirements are met.

QFD excels at linking and prioritizing requirements, helping the design team concentrate their efforts and resources with remarkable precision. In this chapter, we will outline the detailed methodology for creating and evaluating the four QFD "houses" for completeness and quality. Additionally, we will introduce the Kano model to better capture and interpret the voice of the customer.

5.3 History of QFD

The history of QFD traces back to Japan in the late 1960s and has since evolved into a widely adopted practice across various industries worldwide. QFD was first conceptualized by Dr. Yoji Akao and Shigeru Mizuno in Japan during the late 1960s. Their goal was to create a systematic process that would ensure that customer needs and desires were effectively integrated into product design and development. The first practical application of QFD occurred at the Mitsubishi Heavy Industries Kobe Shipyard in 1972. The company used QFD to improve the quality of its large-scale shipbuilding projects, which led to significant enhancements in both product quality and customer satisfaction.

The success of QFD in the shipbuilding industry caught the attention of other Japanese companies, particularly in the automotive sector. Toyota, one of the earliest adopters, implemented QFD in the mid-1970s to streamline its product development processes. Toyota's use of QFD contributed to its reputation for high-quality vehicles and efficient manufacturing practices. QFD began to gain recognition outside of Japan in the 1980s. The method was introduced to the Western world through academic publications and conferences. One of the pivotal moments in its international adoption was the publication of the book "Quality Function Deployment: How to Make QFD Work for You" by Dr. Yoji Akao in 1990, which provided comprehensive insights into QFD principles and applications.

Over the years, QFD has evolved and expanded beyond its initial focus on product design. It is now used in various industries, including manufacturing, healthcare, software development, and service sectors. The methodology has also been integrated with other quality management and improvement frameworks, such as Six Sigma and Lean manufacturing, to enhance overall organizational performance.

The QFD process typically involves creating a series of matrices, often referred to as the "House of Quality", to systematically link customer requirements to specific engineering and operational parameters. This structured approach helps organizations prioritize customer needs, allocate resources effectively, and ensure that all aspects of the product or service align with customer expectations.

5.4 QFD Methodology

Quality Function Deployment (QFD) is a structured methodology designed to transform customer needs and desires into specific engineering and operational requirements. This systematic approach ensures that the voice of the customer is consistently translated into high-quality products and services. The QFD methodology involves several key steps and tools, most notably the creation of the "House of Quality" (HOQ), which serves as the cornerstone of the process. The QFD methodology is deployed through a four-phase sequence shown in Fig. 5.4.

The first step in the QFD process is to gather and identify the needs and requirements of the customers. This is often referred to as the "voice of the customer"

(VOC). Techniques such as surveys, interviews, focus groups, and market research are used to collect this information. The goal is to understand what customers value most in a product or service.

Once customer needs are identified, they are translated into specific design requirements. This step involves converting qualitative customer desires into quantitative technical specifications. This translation is crucial for ensuring that the design team can address these needs in measurable terms.

The House of Quality is the primary tool used in QFD to relate customer requirements to the company's capabilities. It is a matrix that captures the relationships between customer needs and the design requirements.

The four phases are: (McKay 2001)

- House 1: Critical to satisfaction planning
- House 2: Functional requirements planning
- House 3: Design parameters planning
- House 4: Process variable planning

In each of these four phases, the House of Quality (HOQ) is utilized, with variations occurring primarily in Rooms 1 and 3. Figure 5.4 illustrates the generic structure of the HOQ. Let's explore each room sequentially:

Starting with Room 1, the focus is on answering the question "What?" These "What's" correspond to the "How's" rotated from Room 3. Each "What" is evaluated based on its overall importance and is placed in the Importance column.

Moving to Room 2, the comparison involves assessing our performance and that of competitors against the identified "What's" from the customer's perspective. This evaluation is typically subjective and rated on a scale from 1 to 5. Different symbols are used to represent various providers, creating a graphical representation within Room 2.

Room 3 is then populated with the "How's". For each "What" identified in Room 1, the question asked is "How can we achieve this?" Additionally, the direction of improvement required to satisfy each "What" is specified—whether it involves maximizing, minimizing, or targeting specific criteria.

Lastly, in Room 4, the relationship strength between each "What" and "How" is determined. This relationship is assigned a weight using a scale of 9 for strong, 3 for moderate, and 1 for weak. In the actual HOQ, these weights are depicted graphically, commonly represented by symbols such as a solid circle for strong relationships, an open circle for moderate ones, and a triangle for weak connections (Fig. 5.4).

This structured approach within the House of Quality ensures that customer requirements are systematically linked to actionable design and improvement strategies, facilitating the development of products and services that meet or exceed customer expectations.

Once the relationship assignments are finalized, the next step involves deriving key metrics and assessments across the remaining rooms of the House of Quality (HOQ). Here's how each room is typically addressed:

In Room 5, the calculated importance of each "how" is determined by multiplying the weight of its relationship with the importance of the corresponding "what", summing these values for each "how".

Room 6 focuses on quantifiable benchmarks for both competitive and internal performance metrics. This provides a clear comparison in the eyes of industry experts.

Room 7 outlines specific targets and constraints for each "how", establishing clear objectives for improvement or maintenance.

Room 8, often referred to as the roof, evaluates the interdependencies (correlations) among the "how's". This involves assessing how maximizing one aspect might affect others. Achieving synergy indicates beneficial outcomes, while compromises suggest trade-offs.

Where relationships are absent, these spaces remain blank. For instance, aiming to enhance customer intimacy by reducing call handlers might inadvertently increase wait times—a clear compromise scenario. While ideally supported by correlation and regression data, such assessments often rely on practical experience and business principles.

Once all eight rooms of the HOQ are completed, the next step involves sorting based on importance from Rooms 1 and 5. This process ensures that the most critical "what's" and corresponding "how's" receive appropriate attention. Finally, the entire HOQ is evaluated for completeness and balance, ensuring that all aspects of customer requirements and improvement strategies are adequately addressed.

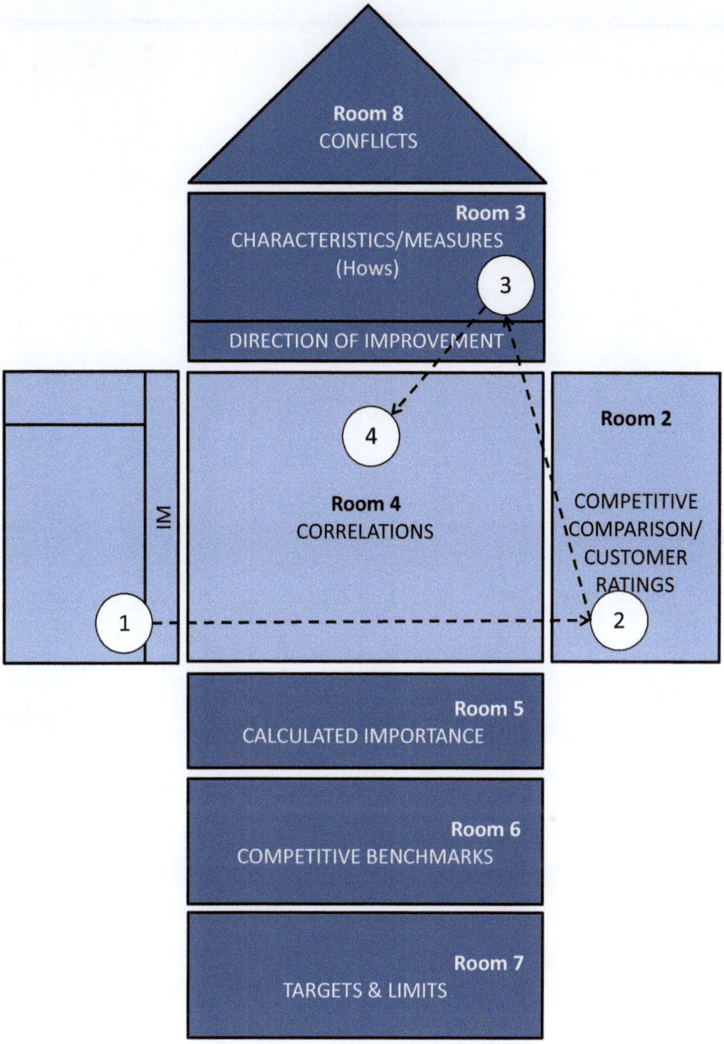

Fig. 5.4 Quality functional deployment

5.5 HOQ Evaluation

After completing the House of Quality (HOQ), the next crucial step is to conduct a thorough review to ensure quality, checks, and balances, and alignment of design resource priorities. Several diagnostic checks can be performed to validate the effectiveness of the HOQ:

- Diagonal Pattern in Room 4: Check for a diagonal pattern of strong correlations. This indicates that the design parameters ("how's" in Room 3) align well with

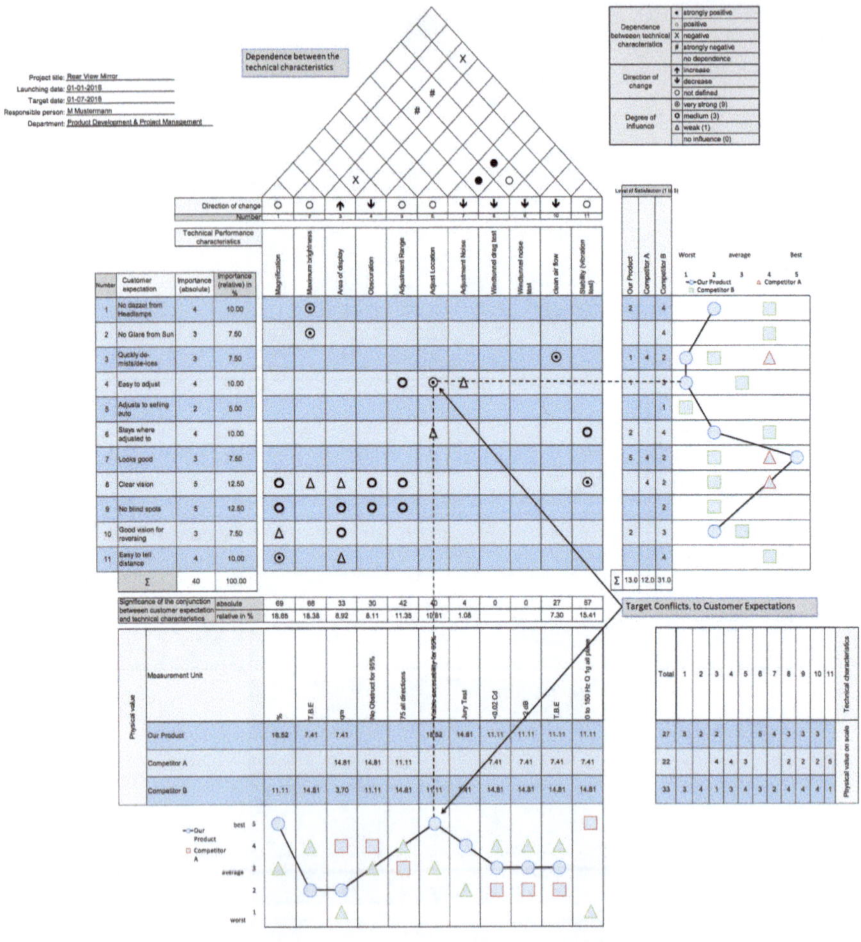

Fig. 5.5 Example-QFD rear-view mirror

customer requirements ("what's" in Room 1), reflecting a good alignment between customer needs and design specifications.

- Coverage of "How's" in Room 3: Ensure that each design parameter ("how" in Room 3) has at least one strong correlation with a customer requirement ("what" in Room 1). This ensures comprehensive coverage of all identified customer needs.
- Empty or Weak Rows in Room 4: Identify any empty or weak rows in Room 4, as these indicate unaddressed customer requirements ("what's"). Addressing these gaps is crucial to ensuring that all customer wants and needs are adequately addressed in the design process.
- Empty Columns in Room 4: Evaluate Room 4 for empty columns, which indicate design parameters ("how's") that do not contribute to fulfilling any customer requirements ("what's"). These redundant design elements should be reassessed or eliminated to streamline the design focus.

- Highest Score in Room 2: Review the highest score in Room 2 to determine the primary design target. This score reflects the most critical customer requirement that should guide design and development efforts.
- Customer Rankings vs. Technical Benchmarks (Room 2 vs. Room 6): Compare customer rankings in Room 2 with technical benchmarks in Room 6. If Room 2 values are lower than those in Room 6, it may indicate discrepancies between customer perceptions and technical capabilities. Addressing these gaps is essential to meeting customer expectations effectively.
- Trade-offs in Room 8: Evaluate Room 8 for trade-offs and conflicting correlations among design parameters (Room 3). Identify strong conflicts or synergies that could impact other characteristics if changes are made to one parameter. This analysis helps in managing trade-offs effectively during the design process.

By conducting these diagnostics, project teams can ensure that the HOQ is robust, aligned with customer needs, and optimized to deliver products or services that meet or exceed customer expectations. Continuous refinement based on these evaluations enhances the overall effectiveness and reliability of the HOQ as a strategic tool in quality management and product development.

☞ Example: A car company needs to be optimized its rear-view mirror in a new car based on the historical customer feedback given by their customers (VOC). The HOQ analysis shows that there is conflict between "Easy to adjust" and "Adjust Location", as the customer evaluates this as being unsatisfactory and as this attribute has a strong interaction with the targets, this is a key contributor to focus on (Fig. 5.5).

5.6 Kano Model

Manufacturing companies are increasingly focusing on meeting the unique needs of individual customers in a fiercely competitive global market. When planning a product or service, it's essential to ask: "What do customers need, and how should this technology fulfil those needs?" This can be determined through customer surveys and consumer insight methods. A constant challenge for manufacturers is managing customer satisfaction, which significantly influences their willingness to purchase. Understanding and addressing customer needs are widely recognized as critical factors for successful product design and market success (McKay 2001). Kano's model (McKay 2001) identifies three types of product requirements that impact customer satisfaction in different ways when met:

Must-be requirements (Basic Quality): These are the essential criteria of a product. If these requirements are not met, customers will be extremely dissatisfied.

However, because customers take these requirements for granted, meeting them does not increase satisfaction. Fulfilment of must-be requirements leads only to a state of "not dissatisfied". Customers see these as prerequisites and do not explicitly demand them. Despite being unspoken needs, they are crucial; if unmet, customers will lose interest in the product entirely. These needs are best summarized as "Just prevent it, and I won't be unhappy".

One-dimensional requirements (Performance Quality): Satisfaction with these requirements is directly proportional to their level of fulfilment the more they are fulfilled, the higher the customer's satisfaction, and vice versa. Customers explicitly demand these requirements, making them spoken wants. Satisfaction grows proportionally with performance, leading to the sentiment "I want more". These are measured with variable data.

Attractive requirements (Excitement Quality): These criteria have the greatest impact on customer satisfaction. They are neither explicitly expressed nor expected by the customer. Meeting these requirements leads to disproportionately high satisfaction, but their absence does not cause dissatisfaction. These unspoken wants are often difficult to articulate until experienced and produce a "Wow!" effect. The advantages of classifying customer requirements using the Kano method are clear: it helps prioritize product features, ensuring basic needs are met, performance requirements are optimized, and opportunities for delighting customers are identified:

- Focus on Product Development Priorities: Instead of investing in must-be requirements that are already satisfactory, it is more effective to enhance one-dimensional or attractive requirements, which significantly impact perceived product quality and customer satisfaction levels.
- Enhanced Understanding of Product Requirements: Identifying the product criteria that most influence customer satisfaction allows for a focused approach. Classifying requirements into must-be, one-dimensional, and attractive dimensions helps prioritize development efforts.
- Optimal Integration of Kano's Model with QFD: Kano's model, integrated with Quality Function Deployment (QFD), requires understanding customer needs, hierarchy, and priorities (Griffin 1993). This approach establishes the importance of product features for customer satisfaction, facilitating process-oriented product development activities.
- Guidance in Trade-off Situations: Kano's method aids in navigating trade-offs during product development. When technical or financial constraints prevent meeting all requirements simultaneously, prioritizing criteria that most enhance customer satisfaction becomes crucial.
- Segment-Specific Requirements: Must-be, one-dimensional, and attractive requirements vary in utility across customer segments. This insight enables the development of tailored solutions that ensure optimal satisfaction in diverse customer groups.
- Creating Differentiation Opportunities: Fulfilling attractive requirements opens avenues for differentiation (Cohen 1988). Products that merely meet must-be and

one-dimensional requirements are perceived as average and interchangeable (Lobenwein 1994).

The traditional method for conducting the Kano model (Fig. 5.6) is to ask functional and dysfunctional questions around known wants/needs or CTSs. Functional questions take the form of "How do you feel if the CTS is present in the product/service?" Dysfunctional questions take the form of "How do you feel if the CTS is not present in the product/service?"

Collection of this information is the first step, and then detailed analysis is required, which is beyond the scope of this book. For a good reference on processing the voice of the customer, see Qianli Xu & Roger J. Jiao (2008).

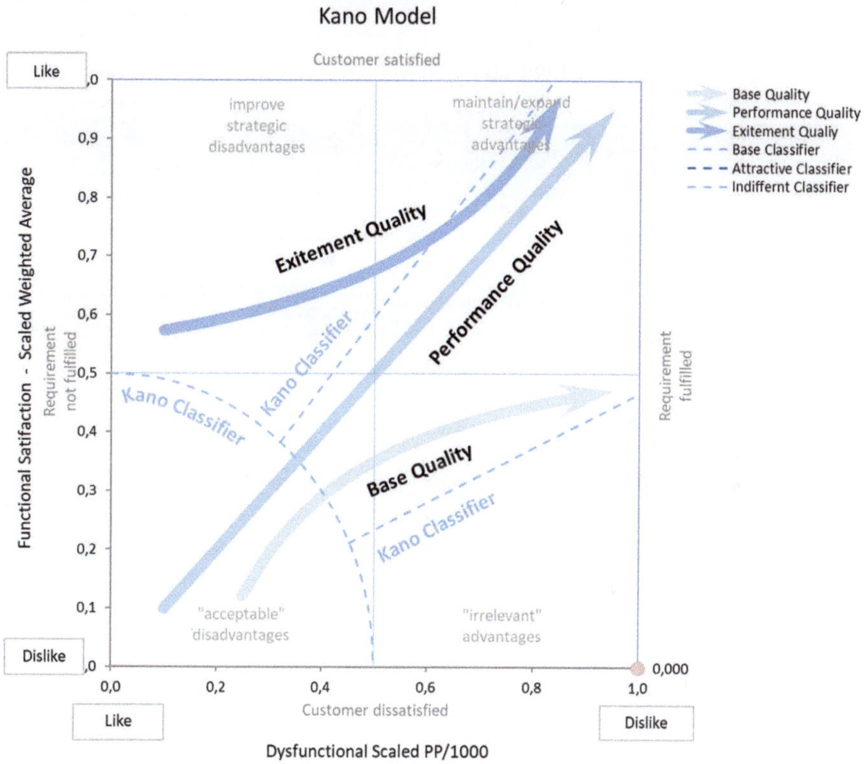

Fig. 5.6 Kano model

When planning a product or service and how to manage the project, you must ask the question: "What customer needs should this technology/project satisfy?". The answer can be found in: Customer surveys, Consumer Insight methods, and historical projects.

☞Example: A car company wants to know which cars from different car companies meet the customer satisfaction for the car's interior the most. A Kano model shows that 2 cars from VW are on the upper right quarter, which shows clear excitement quality. Ford is also showing excitement quality but has room for improvement. Ford needs to move to the upper right quarter to be more competitive versus VW on Interior customer satisfaction (Fig. 5.7).

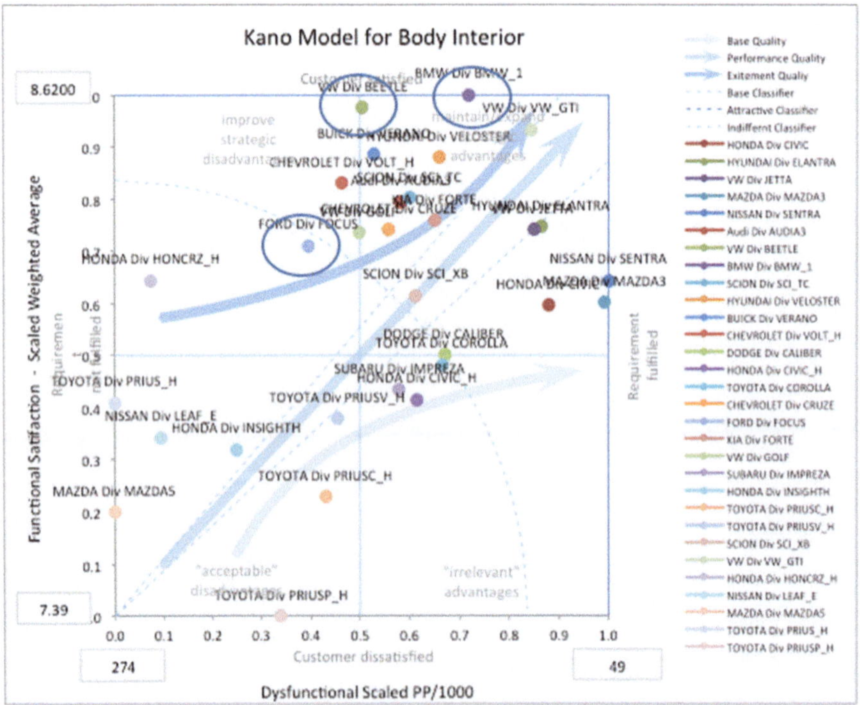

Fig. 5.7 Kano model example automotive interior customer satisfaction

5.7 Implementation of QM Tools

In the following sections the QM tools will be described with the help of the Six Sigma QM-Methodology. Technically, Six Sigma is a specific measure of quality—namely, 3.4 defects per million opportunities. Most companies operate at a much lower level of quality (typically in the two-to-three-Sigma range, from 45,500 to 2700 defects per million opportunities). But the technical definition is irrelevant. Some companies don't need to reach that level, whereas others need to go even higher (Table 5.2).

Table 5.2 The sigma scale

Sigma (σ) Long Term	Defects per Million Opportunities (DPMO)	Percentage of defects (%)	Percent Success (Yield %)
1	691,462	69	31
2	308,538	31	69
3	66,807	6.7	93.3
4	6210	0.62	99.38
5	233	0.023	99.977
6	3.4	0.00034	99.99966

In the industrial sector, Six Sigma has established itself as a hallmark of methodologies and techniques aimed at enhancing quality and cutting costs. Among these, the DMAIC methodology stands out as the most widely adopted approach, prominently featured in best-selling literature. DMAIC, which stands for Define, Measure, Analyse, Improve, and Control (Fig. 5.8), provides a systematic and rigorous framework for addressing business challenges.

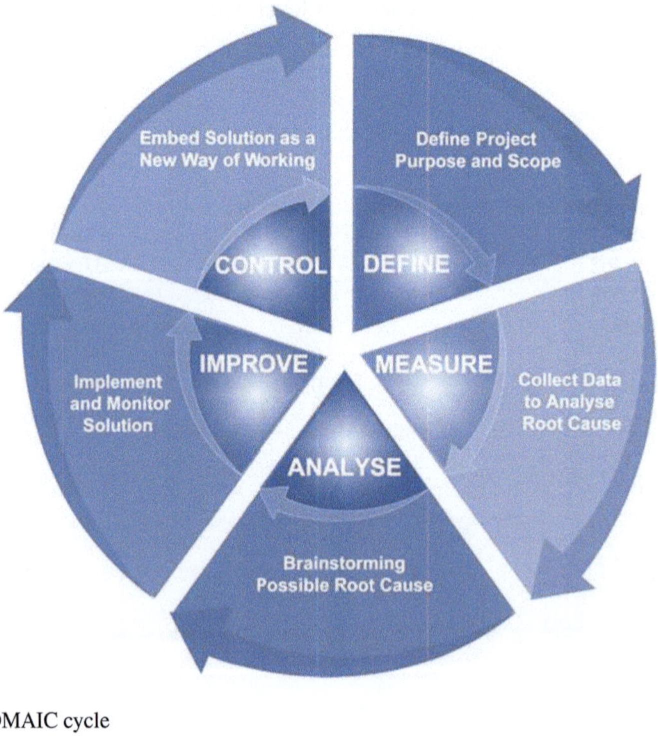

Fig. 5.8 DMAIC cycle

Six Sigma is built on the premise that companies require consistently higher levels of quality and lower costs, achieved through a disciplined and systematic approach that targets variance, waste, and errors deeply ingrained in operations. Unlike superficial fixes, Six Sigma addresses issues at their root causes. For instance, if defects are excessive, the solution isn't merely to identify and discard faulty items; instead, it involves meticulous measurement and analysis to understand precisely how and why defects occur, followed by strategic interventions to address these underlying causes.

The DMAIC methodology within Six Sigma outlines a structured path: defining and quantifying the problem, gathering precise measurement data to clarify its scope, using analytical tools to trace the problem to its core, implementing solutions at the root cause, and establishing on-going controls to prevent recurrence. Six Sigma employs a toolkit rich in techniques, primarily rooted in statistical data analysis and quality improvement practices, drawing from both traditional Total Quality Management (TQM) methods and more advanced, contemporary approaches.

Central to Six Sigma is its project-based approach, where teams led by Six Sigma Black Belts—a title denoting expert practitioners—tackle specific performance issues identified by the organization. Projects typically span 3 to *6 months* and are expected to yield significant savings, ranging from €150,000 to €500,000 per project. A proficient Black Belt can lead multiple projects annually, leveraging the methodology's structured rigour to address complex operational challenges efficiently.

The strength of Six Sigma lies in its disciplined methodology for navigating the intricacies of business operations. Rather than relying on guesswork, organizations employing Six Sigma methodically pinpoint the root causes of quality issues, ensuring that solutions are targeted and effective. Often likened to detective work, Six Sigma involves methodically sifting through evidence to unravel problems and implement sustainable improvements.

☞Example: Consider a pharmaceutical company facing surging demand for a critical compound, yet grappling with low production yields on its assembly line. Initially attributing the issue to subpar raw materials from a supplier, the company turned to Six Sigma for deeper analysis. Through meticulous Six Sigma scrutiny, the root cause was pinpointed: inconsistent temperature variations across different zones of the production facility. By optimizing the HVAC system to maintain uniform temperatures, production yields surged by a remarkable 60%. This enhancement not only directly saved the company over €17 million but also alleviated the need for a planned €500 million investment in expanding production capacity.

Six Sigma, originally pioneered by Motorola in the 1980s and later popularized by General Electric in 1996 under CEO Jack Welch, has garnered widespread attention as a methodological approach to enhancing quality and curbing costs within industries. It operates on the premise that sustained high quality and reduced costs can be achieved through systematic elimination of variation, waste, and errors inherent in operational processes. Unlike superficial fixes, Six Sigma delves into root causes, aiming not just to detect defects but to comprehensively understand why they occur and devise targeted solutions.

Following GE's widely celebrated success, Six Sigma gained immense popularity, spreading like wildfire across corporate America. By the early 2000s, approximately 25% of Fortune 200 companies had embraced Six Sigma as a cornerstone of their operational strategy. Prominent organizations such as Ford Motor Co., Bank of America Corp., Eastman Kodak Co., DuPont, and American Express Go were among those with robust Six Sigma programs in place.

A survey conducted at a 2001 conference on process-based performance improvement underscored the rapid adoption of Six Sigma. Out of 65 participating companies, 40 reported already implementing Six Sigma, while the remainder expressed intentions to do so imminently. These figures highlight the substantial commitment companies were making to Six Sigma initiatives. Ford, for example, had dedicated significant resources, training 2500 black belts and initiating nearly 2000 projects aimed at leveraging Six Sigma's methodologies for operational enhancement and cost savings.

Despite the bold assertions of its proponents (such as one widely cited book claiming Six Sigma as "the most important breakthrough management tool ever devised"), achieving success with Six Sigma does not guarantee overall business success. Several early adopters, including Kodak, Xerox Corp., and Polaroid Corp., have encountered significant business setbacks despite their initial enthusiasm for Six Sigma. Even Motorola, a pioneer in Six Sigma, has experienced fluctuations in performance over the years.

General Electric (GE) stands out as a rare example of sustained success among Six Sigma practitioners, consistently demonstrating superior performance. However, it's noteworthy that many companies have achieved operational improvements and financial success without adopting Six Sigma. For instance, IBM's resurgence in the mid-1990s came after experimenting with and subsequently moving away from Six Sigma methodologies.

Even successful companies that have embraced Six Sigma have come to recognize its limitations. Bombardier, a prominent Canadian corporation involved in aerospace, rail transportation, recreational products, and financial services, provides an instructive case study. By the year 2000, Bombardier boasted over 80,000 employees and generated revenues exceeding €16 billion (Canadian). Building on its positive experiences with Total Quality Management (TQM) in the early 1990s and subsequent exposure to Six Sigma, Bombardier's leadership made a commitment to the methodology in 1996. They trained 200 black belts in the DMAIC methodology and initiated more than 300 projects. Over a 5-year period, Bombardier achieved net cash-flow savings totalling €137 million (Canadian), having invested €21 million in Six Sigma.

In 1999, Bombardier conducted a comprehensive evaluation of its Six Sigma initiatives and identified significant shortcomings despite its accomplishments:

- Most Six Sigma initiatives were narrowly targeted, focusing on small-scale activities within specific departments. Attempts to scale these projects to larger initiatives often resulted in unsatisfactory outcomes until the scope was appropriately adjusted.
- Six Sigma implementation lacked alignment with the organization's overall strategy. While individual projects yielded benefits, they did not collectively contribute to broader corporate objectives.
- The Six Sigma efforts did not challenge the company's foundational assumptions or its functional organizational structure. Achieving transformative improvements in performance necessitates addressing these fundamental aspects, limiting Six Sigma's overall impact.

In essence, while DMAIC-based Six Sigma can enhance quality and reduce costs, it falls short in driving significant business performance improvements. Over the past decade, companies such as IBM and Allmerica Financial Corp. have achieved substantial cost reductions totalling hundreds of millions, alongside significant boosts in customer satisfaction. They accomplished this through comprehensive transformation programs, not solely relying on DMAIC. Bombardier's management similarly found DMAIC insufficient for transformative change. Early adopters such as American Express, Merck, Motorola, and Air Products and Chemicals have echoed these sentiments.

The inherent limitations of Six Sigma lie in its project-focused, problem-solving approach. It employs statistical tools to identify flaws in current processes but does not challenge whether these processes fundamentally need rethinking. Six Sigma assumes that existing processes are fundamentally sound and merely require minor adjustments for efficiency gains, which may not lead to dramatic improvements.

Moreover, Six Sigma's project orientation, while manageable, also constrains its impact. Companies deploy numerous independent project teams addressing discrete issues, often resulting in successful outcomes and favourable returns on investment. However, this approach lacks the capacity for a holistic, systemic attack on a company's core challenges.

Integration with other performance improvement initiatives is critical. Is Six Sigma standalone or part of a broader strategy? Effective process management is key here. Companies best leverage Six Sigma as a component within a comprehensive toolkit of *process management* strategies rather than relying on it alone.

5.8 Fitting Six Sigma into Process Management

In the field of modern process management, where efficiency dominates continuous improvement is the slogan, Six Sigma stands as a beacon of excellence. Its methodologies have become synonymous with quality and optimization, making it a natural fit within the framework of process management. However, integrating Six Sigma into existing processes is not a task to be taken lightly. It requires a careful balance of strategy, implementation, and organizational alignment. In this chapter, we delve into the nuances of fitting Six Sigma into process management seamlessly.

At its core understanding the essence of Six Sigma, Six Sigma is a disciplined, data-driven approach aimed at reducing defects and variation in processes. It emphasizes the importance of statistical analysis, rigorous problem-solving methodologies, and a relentless pursuit of perfection. Six Sigma operates on the principle of DMAIC (Define, Measure, Analyse, Improve, Control), providing a structured roadmap for process improvement. Each phase of DMAIC plays a vital role in identifying opportunities, analysing root causes, implementing solutions, and ensuring sustained results.

To effectively integrate Six Sigma into process management, organizations must first align their goals and objectives. Process management focuses on enhancing efficiency, minimizing waste, and delivering value to customers. Similarly, Six Sigma aims to streamline processes, eliminate defects, and enhance overall quality. By aligning these complementary objectives, organizations can create a unified approach to continuous improvement.

Successful integration of Six Sigma requires more than just implementing tools and methodologies—it necessitates a cultural shift within the organization. A culture of continuous improvement, where employees are empowered to identify problems, propose solutions, and drive change, is essential. Leadership plays a crucial role in fostering this culture by promoting transparency, encouraging innovation, and recognizing achievements. When employees embrace the principles of Six Sigma as part of their daily work, it becomes ingrained in the fabric of the organization.

Six Sigma offers a diverse toolkit of statistical methods, process mapping techniques, and problem-solving frameworks. Organizations can leverage these tools to identify inefficiencies, analyse root causes, and implement targeted solutions. From Pareto charts and fishbone diagrams to control charts and regression analysis, Six Sigma provides a comprehensive suite of resources for process improvement. By equipping employees with the necessary skills and training, organizations can harness the full potential of Six Sigma to drive meaningful change.

Metrics are the lifeblood of Six Sigma, providing sensible evidence of improvement and guiding decision-making. Key performance indicators (KPIs) such as defect rates, cycle times, and customer satisfaction scores enable organizations to track progress and measure success. Equally important is the concept of sustainability—ensuring that improvements are integrated into standard operating procedures and maintained over time. Through on-going monitoring, feedback loops, and continuous refinement, organizations can ensure that the benefits of Six Sigma endure in the long term.

Six Sigma is a powerful methodology for process improvement, aiming to reduce defects and enhance quality across various business operations. To harness the full potential of Six Sigma, effective project management is essential. This chapter explores how project management principles and practices can be integrated with Six Sigma to maximize its benefits.

To maximizing Six Sigma using effective project management, establish a strong foundation by leadership and commitment to ensure that top-level executives are committed to Six Sigma and provide the necessary support and resources.

Their involvement is crucial for driving the initiative and overcoming resistance. The Six Sigma Champions need to be appointed dedicated Six Sigma champions who are responsible for overseeing projects and ensuring alignment with strategic objectives.

To clear vision and objectives, you need to define clear, measurable goals that align with the organization's strategic objectives. These goals should be specific, achievable, and relevant to the business context. Develop a project charter for each Six Sigma project. The charter should include the problem statement, project scope, objectives, timelines, and key stakeholders.

In addition, implement structured training programs for different Six Sigma roles, such as Yellow Belts, Green Belts, Black Belts, and Master Black Belts. Ensure that the training covers both Six Sigma tools and project management techniques and encourage practical application of Six Sigma concepts through hands-on projects and case studies during training.

Select projects that align with the organization's strategic goals and have a significant impact on performance. This ensures that Six Sigma efforts contribute to broader business objectives and evaluate potential projects based on their expected benefits, feasibility, and alignment with strategic priorities. The next step is to develop a framework for prioritizing projects based on factors such as potential cost savings, impact on customer satisfaction, and alignment with strategic goals. Allocate resources strategically to high-priority projects, ensuring that they receive the necessary support and attention.

Maximizing the benefits of Six Sigma requires a comprehensive approach that integrates project management principles with Six Sigma methodologies. By establishing strong leadership, providing comprehensive training, selecting and prioritizing strategic projects, emphasizing data-driven decision-making, managing change effectively, integrating Six Sigma with existing processes, continuously monitoring and controlling improvements, celebrating successes, and fostering a culture of continuous improvement, organizations can achieve significant and sustainable improvements in quality, efficiency, and overall business performance.

Integrating Six Sigma into process management is not a one-time endeavour but an on-going journey towards operational excellence. By aligning goals, fostering a culture of continuous improvement, leveraging tools and techniques, and measuring success, organizations can realize the full potential of Six Sigma in driving efficiency, quality, and customer satisfaction. In doing so, they unlock the power of process management to achieve sustainable competitive advantage in today's dynamic business environment.

5.9 QM Toolbox Usage

There are a variety of statistical tools, which support the quality control of products and processes. The following "seven basic Quality Tools" highlighted in Table 5.3 were collected in the 1960s in Japan by Mr. Ishikawa and were composed as a central toolbox of quality management. They are relatively easy-to-use methods of continuous improvement process. These include:

Table 5.3 QM toolbox

Project Phase	Candidate Six Sigma Tools
Define	• VOC Tools (Surveys, Focus Groups, Letters, Comment Cards) • *Process Map* • *Cause-and-Effect Diagrams (Ishikawa)* • QFD, SIPOC • Project Charter • Benchmarking • *Histogram*
Measure	• Measurement Systems Analysis • Exploratory Data Analysis • Descriptive Statistics • Data Mining *Run charts* • *Pareto analysis*
Analyse	• *Histogram* • *Cause-and-Effect Diagrams (Ishikawa)* • Tree Diagrams • Brainstorming • *Quality Run Charts* • Design of Experiments • Enumerative Statistics (Hypothesis Tests) Inferential Statistics (X's and Y's) • *Box Plots & Scatter-Plots* • Simulation
Improve	• Force Field Diagrams • 7M Tools • Project Planning and management Tools Prototype and Pilot Studies
Control	• SPC • *FMEA* • ISO 9000 • Change Budgets, Bid Models, Cost Estimating Models Reporting System

Based on the five steps of the Six Sigma process methods DMAIC, the tools that are related to each phase support the analysis and knowledge transfer step by step. To communicate Six Sigma fundamental tools one example from the automotive industry will be used. This example is hypothetical in nature but has benefited from work performed in conjunction with Six Sigma projects. This example is a straightforward approach to a typical project and can be used as guides in the application of Six Sigma tools within real-world projects.

After project selection, the purpose of the Define phase is to further refine the Six Sigma project team's understanding of the problem to be addressed. In addition, the project team will use the Define phase to get organized, determine roles and responsibilities, establish goals and milestones, and review process steps.

The outcomes at the completion of the Define phase, the project team will have:

- Defined the problem with a problem statement.
- Specifically identified the process or product's customer.
- Defined CTQs (Critical-to-Quality Characteristics) from the customer's viewpoint.

- Scoped the project.
- Produced a refined problem statement.

The key concepts and tools used are:

- Voice of Customer
- Project Scoping
- Cause-and-Effect prioritization
- Project Planning

Because subsequent Six Sigma process steps build upon work completed during the define phase, project team members should ensure that the customer and CTQs have been accurately identified. Likewise, the project team should ensure that the current process has been accurately mapped, the project has been narrowly scoped, and a descriptive problem statement has been written.

Example: Delivery Timing

☞Example: An Automobile Company's dealers are dissatisfied with the amount of time it takes from when a vehicle is ordered until it arrives at the dealership. This is the step 1:

☞Example: Delivery Timing

Problem Statement

Dealers are dissatisfied with the condition of vehicles when they are delivered to the dealership.

The next step is to identify customer, in this step, the project team will determine who is directly impacted by the problem and what costs can be associated with that impact.

☞Example: Delivery Timing

Identify Customer

The delivery timing project team will compare existing "order and build" data against dealership delivery records to determine which dealerships are experiencing the longest average delivery times.

Based on this high-level data review, the project team prioritizes the largest area of opportunity as in-transit times associated with vehicles being shipped to dealerships in the Louisville Region.

Cost of Poor Quality

The project team identifies potential costs associated with the problem, including:

- Costs associated with longer inventory turnover
- Costs of managing consumer waiting periods
- Costs of lost sales

Once a customer is identified, the project team will need to determine what is important to that customer from the customer's point of view. In Six Sigma terminology this process is referred to as identifying the Critical-To-Quality characteristics (CTQs). Identification of CTQs ascertains how the particular characteristics appear when meeting customer expectations. For example:
What is "*good condition*"
No preparation required, wash and deliver only?
Without need for mechanical or body repair?
What is "*on time*"?
On time measured in days?
On time measured in weeks?—Starting when, stopping when?

After CTQs are identified, the project Team must develop *Operational Definitions* for each CTQ. Effective Operational Definitions are accurately describing the Critical-To-Quality characteristic, specifically annotate what is considered meeting the customer expectation and are written to ensure consistent interpretation and measurement by multiple people.

Commonly used tools of identifying CTQs include:
Focus Groups
Surveys
Interviews

☞Example: Delivery Timing

To determine CTQs, the project team issues a survey to general managers and sales managers for dealerships in the Louisville region.

CTQ

Vehicles will arrive at the dealership within 35 days of date of order.

Operational Definition

Vehicles ordered to fulfil consumer requests, or as part of standard stock replenishment, will be received into dealership inventory on or earlier than the 35th day subsequent to the date registered as part of online order submission. All days, except those recognized as holidays in the union contract, will be included in the count.

5.10 The Process Map

The project Team creates a "*High-Level*" visual representation (Fig. 5.9) of the process steps leading up to fulfilment of the identified CTQ. This "as is" process map will be useful throughout the process as a:

- Method for segmenting complex processes into manageable portions
- Way to identify process inputs and outputs
- Technique to identify areas of rework

- Way to identify bottlenecks, breakdowns, and non-value-added steps
- Benchmark against which future improvements can be compared with the original process

Process mapping, also called flowcharting, is a technique to visualize the tasks, activities, and steps necessary to produce a product or a service. The preferred method for describing a process is to identify it with a generic name, show the workflow with a process Map, and describe its purpose with an operational description.

Remember that a process is a blending of inputs to produce some desired output. The intent of each task, activity, and step is to add value, as perceived by the customer, to the product or service we are producing. You cannot discover if this is the case until you have adequately mapped the process.

There are many reasons for creating a process map: It helps all process members understand their part in the process and how their process fits into the bigger picture, it describes how activities are performed and how the work effort flows, it is a visual

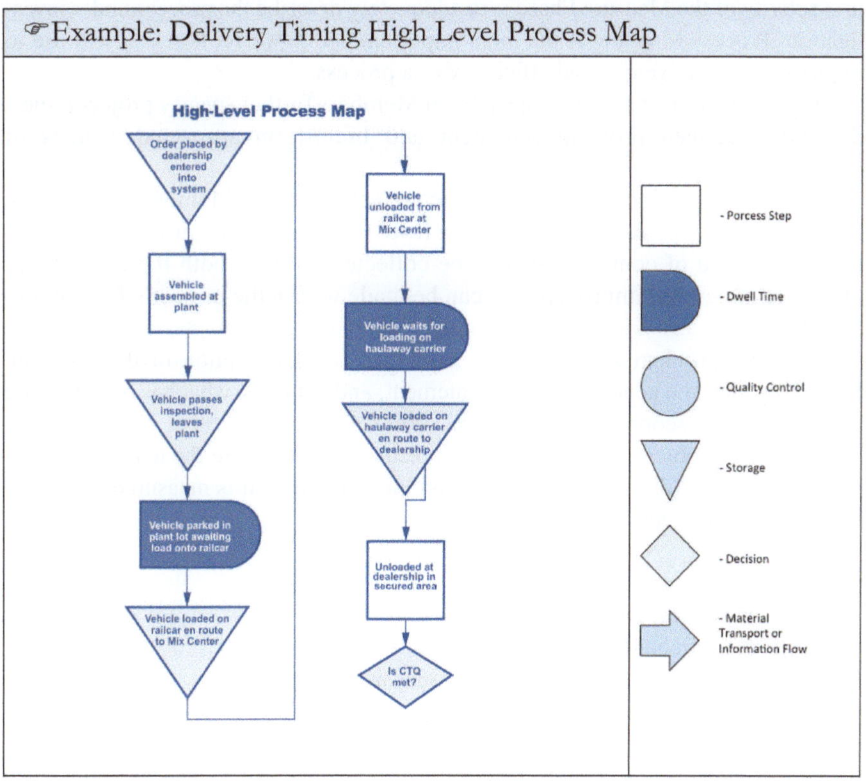

Fig. 5.9 High-level process map

way of standing above the process and watching how work is done. In fact, process maps can be easily uploaded into model and simulation software where computers allow you to simulate the process and visually see how it works.

- It can be used as an aid in training new people.
- It will show you where you can take measurements that will help you to run the process better.
- It will help you understand where problems occur and what some of the causes may be.
- It leverages other analytical tools by providing a source of data and inputs into these tools.
- It identifies and leads you to many important characteristics you will need as you strive to make improvements.

Individual maps developed by process members form the basis of process *management*. The individual processes are linked together to see the total effort and flow for meeting business and customer needs. To improve or to correctly manage a process, you must be able to describe it in a way that can be easily understood. The first activity of the Measure Phase is to adequately describe the process under investigation. Process Mapping is the most important and powerful tool you will use to improve the effectiveness and efficiency of a process.

During the project scope, project Team Members further specify project issues, develop a defined problem statement and brainstorm suspected sources of variation.

Similar to the process used in project selection, Team Members must strive to reduce the scope of their project to a level that ensures the problem is within the team's area of control, data can be collected to show both the current and improved states and improvements can be made within the project's four-month time frame.

A refined problem statement is a highly defined description of the problem. Beginning with the general problem statement, and applying what has been learned through further scoping, project teams write a refined problem statement that describes the problem in narrow terms, indicates a level where the team will begin its work and identifies the extent of the problem and how it is measured. Effective tools to scope projects include:

- Y/X Diagram
- Cause-and-Effect Diagram (Ishikawa)
- Cause-and-Effect Matrix
- FMEA (Failure Mode and Effective Analysis)
- Project Charter

5.11 Cascading Y = *f*(x)

A fundamental formula used in 6-Sigma training is that “Y” is a function of “X”. Y = *f*(x). In mathematical terminology, “Y” is the dependent variable while “X” is the independent variable. Expressed in another way, “Y” is an output resulting from a number of inputs or “Xs”. Building on this concept, it can be said that every “X” is correlated to a “Y” at some deeper level in the process. The diagram (Fig. 5.10) for this cascading relationship is as follows:

This method of “drilling down” to the specific issues is the fundamental technique for both project selection and project scoping. Those trained in 6-Sigma techniques are often heard describing issues in terms of the “Xs” and “Ys”.

☞Example: Delivery Timing, Y/X Diagram

Scope project

The project Team extends the Y/X chart used during project selection to further define their 6-Sigma project.

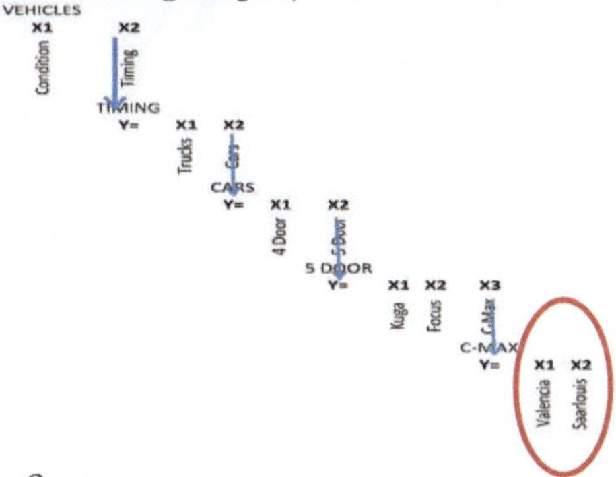

Refined Problem Statement

Delivery times for a car assembled at a US plant and shipped to Louisville Region dealerships are “on average” in excess of 35 days.

Fig. 5.10 Y/X diagram

5.12 Cause-and-Effect Diagram (Ishikawa)

A cause-and-effect diagram (Fig. 5.11) is a composition of lines and words representing a meaningful relationship between an effect, or condition, and its causes. To focus the effort and facilitate thought, the legs of the diagram are given categorical headings. Two common templates for the headings are for product-related and transactional-related efforts. Transactional is meant for processes where there is no traditional or physical product, i.e., it is more like an administrative process.

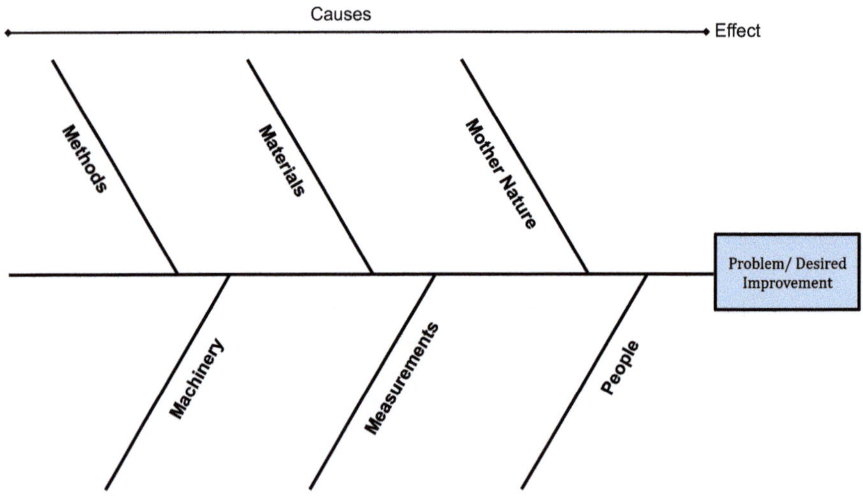

Fig. 5.11 Ishikawa diagram

Transactional processes are characterized as processes dealing with forms, ideas, people, decisions, and services. You would most likely use the product template for determining the cause of burnt pizza and use the transactional template if you were trying to reduce order defects from the order-taking process. A third approach is to identify all categories, as you best perceive them.

When performing a cause-and-effect diagram, keep drilling down, always asking why, until you find the root causes of the problem. Start with one category and stay with it until you have exhausted all possible inputs and then move to the next category. The next step is to rank each potential cause by its likelihood of being the root cause. Rank it by the most likely as a 1, second most likely as a 2, and so on. This may take some time. You may even have to create sub-sections, e.g., 2a, 2b, 2c, and then come back to reorder the sub-section into the larger ranking. This is your first attempt at really finding the Y = f (X). The top X's have the potential to be the critical X's, those X's which exert the most influence on the output Y.

Finally, we need to determine if each cause is a control or a noise factor. This is a requirement for the characterization of the process. Next, we will explain the meaning and methods of using some of the common categories. There may be several interpretations of some of the process mapping symbols; however, just about everyone uses these primary symbols to document processes.

The *Measurement* category groups Root Causes related to the measurement and measuring of a process activity or output.

The *People* category groups Root Causes related to people, staffing, and organizations.

The *Method* category groups Root Causes related to how the work is done, the way the process is actually conducted.

The *Materials* category groups Root Causes related to parts, supplies, forms, or information needed to execute a process.

The *Equipment* or *Machine* category groups Root Causes related to tools used in the process.

The *Environment* (a.k.a. Mother Nature) category groups Root Causes related to our work environment, market conditions, and regulatory issues.

📖 Definition: Cause-and-Effect diagrams are a visual tool to identify, explore, and graphically display all of the possible causes related to a problem or condition, in increasing levels of detail and to discover its potential causes. These diagrams:

- Force the team to focus on the actual content or nature of a problem.
- Generate a snapshot of the collective knowledge and awareness of the team.
- Help build consensus on problem causes and support for the solutions that result.
- Focus the project Team on causes instead of symptoms (X, not Y).

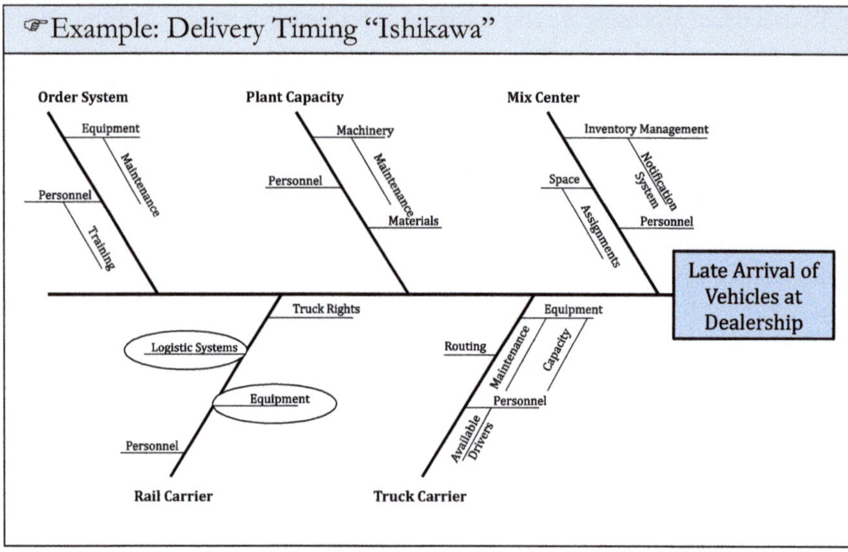

Fig. 5.12 Ishikawa diagram example

The resulting cause-and-effect diagram (Fig. 5.12) offers a visual representation of potential sources and causes of exterior vehicle damage. Information contained in this chart is very useful in developing a data collection plan and can often be helpful in writing the problem statement.

Table 5.4, based on information gathered during the Define Phase, the project team can now refine the problem statement. The refined problem statement is then "Exception claims submitted by the five, previously identified large-volume dealerships from the Southwest Region relating to exterior damage sustained during the delivery process either at the plant, en route to the Holding Yard, at the Holding Yard or en route to the dealership".

5.13 The Cause-and-Effect Matrix (X-Y Matrix)

The X-Y matrix (Table 5.4) Project Management Compilation Book.docx is a great tool to help us focus, as it is based on team experience and "tribal" (Tribal knowledge is any unwritten information that is not commonly known by others within a company.) knowledge. At this point in the project, it should be recognized that this is NOT hard data. As you progress through the methodology, don't be surprised if you find out through data analysis that what the team thought might be critical turns out to be insignificant. The great thing about the X-Y Matrix is that it is an unbiased way to approach definition around the process and WILL give you focus. The X-Y Matrix is an important tool for the many reasons we have already stated. Use it to your benefit, leverage the team, and it will help you progress through the methodology to accomplish your ultimate project goal.

Table 5.4 Cause-and-effect matrix

☞Example: Delivery Timing Cause and Effect Matrix

Rating of Importance to Customer	3	1	9	3											
	1	2	3	4	5	6	7	8	9	10	11	12	13	14	
Process Inputs	Verification of order acceptance	Online vehicle tracking	Delivery within 45 days	24-hour notification of delivery											Total
1 Order system	9	3	1	1											42
2 Plant	3	9	9	1											102
3 Rail carrier	1	9	9	9											120
4 Mix center	1	3	3	9											60
5 Truck carrier	1	3	3	9											60
6															
7															

5

Use your Fishbone Diagram as the source and type in the Inputs in this section, use common sense some of the info from the Fishbone may not justify going into the X-Y Matrix inputs. Enter your primary metric and any other secondary metrics across into this area. Weight these output variables (Y's) on a scale of 1–10; you may find that some have the same weight, which is just fine. If, at this time, additional metrics come to the surface, which is common, you may realize that you need to add secondary metrics to your project or even refine your primary metric.

For each X listed along the left, rank its effect on each corresponding metric based on a scale of 0, 1, 3, or 9. You can use any scale you choose however we recommend this on.

5.14 Failure Mode and Effects Analysis (FMEA)

Failure Mode and Effects Analysis or FMEA [*usually pronounced as F-M-E-A (individual letters) or "FEE-MA" (as a word) is a structured approach. At this point, a FMEA is developed with tribal knowledge in a cross-functional team. Later using process data, the FMEA can be updated and better estimates of detection and occurrence can be obtained. The FMEA is not a tool to eliminate X's but rather control the X's. It is also a tool to identify potential X's and prioritize the order in which the X's should be evaluated.

There are different types of FMEAs:

- *System FMEA*: Performed on a product or service product at the early concept/design level when various modules all tie together. The FMEA's entire module level tie together to form a system. As you go lower into a system more failure modes are considered.
  - Example: Electrical system of a car consists of the following modules: battery, wiring harness, lighting control module, and alternator/regulator.
  - System FMEA focuses on potential failure modes associated with the modules of a system caused by design.
- *Design DFMEA*: Performed early in the design phase to analyse product failure modes before they are released to production. The purpose is to analyse how failure modes affect the system and minimize them. The severity rating of a failure mode MUST be carried into the process PFMEA.
- *Process PFMEA*: Performed in the early quality-planning phase of manufacturing to analyse failure modes in manufacturing and transactional processes that may escape to the customer. The failure modes and the potential sources of defects are rated and corrective action taken based on a Pareto analysis ranking.
- *Equipment FMEA*: Used to analyse failure modes in the equipment used in a process to detect or make the part.
  - Example: Test Equipment failure modes to detect open and short circuits.

FMEAs (Fig. 5.13) are team tools like most in this phase of the methodology. They are applicable in most every project, manufacturing or service base. For all

☞Example: FMEA

___ System
___ Subsystem
___ Component
Model Year(s)/Program(s): ____________
Team: ____________

Process Responsibility: ____________
Key Date: ____________

FMEA Name/Number: ____________
Prepared By: ____________
FMEA Date (Orig.): ____________ (Rev.): ____________

Item/Function	Potential Failure Mode	Potential Effect(s) of Failure	Sev	Class	Potential Cause/ Mechanism of Failure	Occ	Current Process Controls (Prevent/Detect)	Det	RPN	Recommended Action(s)	Responsibility and Target Completion Date	Action Results: Actions Taken	Sev	Occ	Det	RPN
What is the process step?	In what ways does the Key Input go wrong?	What is the impact on the Key Output Variables (Customer Requirements) or internal requirements?	How severe is the effect to the customer?		What causes the Key Input to go wrong?	How often does cause of FM occur?	What are the existing controls and procedures that prevent either the cause or the Failure Mode?	How well can you detect cause or FM?		What are the actions for recuing the occurrence of the Cause, or improving detection?	Who's responsible for the recommended action?	What are the completed actions to take with the recalculated RPM? Be sure to include completion month/year				

Fig. 5.13 Failure mode and effects analysis (FMEA)

intents purposes, they are used in conjunction with your problem-solving project to characterize and measure process variables. In some cases, the FMEA will manifest itself as a management tool when the project concludes and, in some cases, it will not be appropriate to be used in that nature.

5.15 The Project Charter

The project charter (Fig. 5.14) expands on the business case; it clarifies the projects focus and measures of project performance and is completed by the Six Sigma Black Belt. The project charter is an important document—it is the initial communication of the project. The first phases of the Six Sigma methodology are defined and measured. These are known as "characterization" phases that focus primarily on understanding and measuring the problem at hand. Therefore, some of the information in the project charter, such as primary and secondary metrics, can change

☞Example: Project Charter

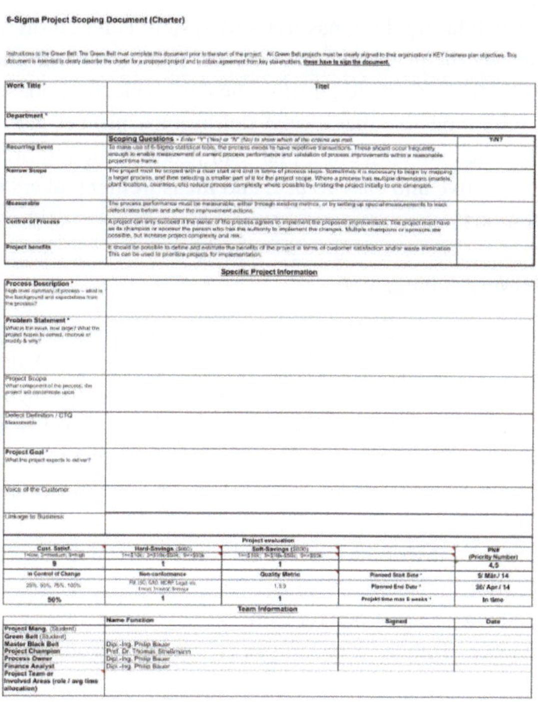

6-Sigma Project Scoping Document (Charter)

Work Title *	Titel
Department *	

	Scoping Questions - Enter "Y" (Yes) or "N" (No) to show which of the criteria are met	Y/N?
Recurring Event	[illegible]	
Narrow Scope	[illegible]	
Measurable	[illegible]	
Control of Process	[illegible]	
Project benefits	[illegible]	

Specific Project Information

Process Description *	
Problem Statement *	
Project Scope	
Defect Definition / CTQ	
Project Goal *	
Voice of the Customer	
Linkage to Business	

Project evaluation

Cust. Satisf.	Hard-Savings	Soft-Savings		PNr (Priority Number)
9	1	1		4,5
in Control of Change	Non-conformance	Quality Metric	Planned Start Date *	5/ Mär./ 14
25%, 50%, 75%, 100%			Planned End Date *	30/ Apr./ 14
50%	1	1	Projekt time max 8 weeks *	In time

Team Information

	Name Function	Signed	Date
Project Mang. (Student)			
Green Belt (Student)			
Master Black Belt	Dipl.-Ing. Philip Bauer		
Project Champion	Prof. Dr. Thomas Strelkmann		
Process Owner	Dipl.-Ing. Philip Bauer		
Finance Analyst	Dipl.-Ing. Philip Bauer		
Project Team or Involved Areas (role / avg time allocation)			

Fig. 5.14 Project charter

several times. By the time the measure phase is wrapping up the project charter should be in its final form meaning defects and the metrics for measuring them are clear and agreed upon.

Project charter definitions are *Problem Statement*—Articulates the pain of the defect or error in the process (this may be the Business Case restated). *Objective Statement*—States how much of an improvement is desired from the project. *Scope*—Articulates the boundaries of the project. *Primary Metric*—The actual measure of the defect or error in the process. *Secondary Metric(s)*—Measures of potential consequences (+/−) as a result of changes in the process.

5.16 Measurement System Analysis

The purpose of performing a measurement system analysis is to ensure the information collected is a true representation of what is occurring in the process. It is important to remember that total variation is the sum of process variation and measurement system variation. Therefore, minimizing measurement variation ensures that only process variation is reflected by the data. Upon concluding a measurement system analysis, the project team should have a high level of confidence that collected data will correctly depict variation in the process. Key Concepts are the operational definitions and the gage R&R.

One method of validating the measurement system is based on operational definitions constructed by the project team to ensure that all measurement takers completely understand what is expected during the data collection phase.

Following development of operational definitions, project team members will have validated that the data collection plan can produce the required data, the data collection tool is effective and easy to use, and measurement takers understand data collection expectations.

☞Example: Delivery Timing; MSA

Project team members use a "Walking the process" methodology to construct Operational Definitions and perform the Measurement System Analysis.

Prior to beginning the process, project team members will educate measurement takers on use of the Data Collection Tool and the format to use when logging time and date information. Measurement takers will also receive instruction on how to annotate process exceptions. Measurement takers receiving instruction include:

- Assembly Plant final inspection personnel (data collection initiators).
- Drivers who load vehicles on railcars.
- Drivers who unload vehicles at Mix Centre.
- Haul away carrier drivers who transport vehicles from Mix Centre to the Dealerships.

- Dealership inventory management personnel who receive the vehicles.

NOTE: The starting date for the order will be established using data from the vehicle ordering system.

Project team members will follow the delivery process beginning with the Assembly, Plant inspector, continuing through transfer to railhead, the Mix Centre and finishing with vehicle receipt at the dealership. "Walking the process" is repeated until project team members are confident that data compiled during the collection period accurately reflects the existing process.

5.17 The Histogram

The Histogram (Fig. 5.15) is a basic graphing tool that displays the relative frequency or the number of times a measured items falls within a certain cell size. The values for the measurements are shown on the horizontal axis (in cells) and the frequency of each size is shown on the vertical axis as a bar graph. The graph

☞Example: Delivery Timing: Histogram

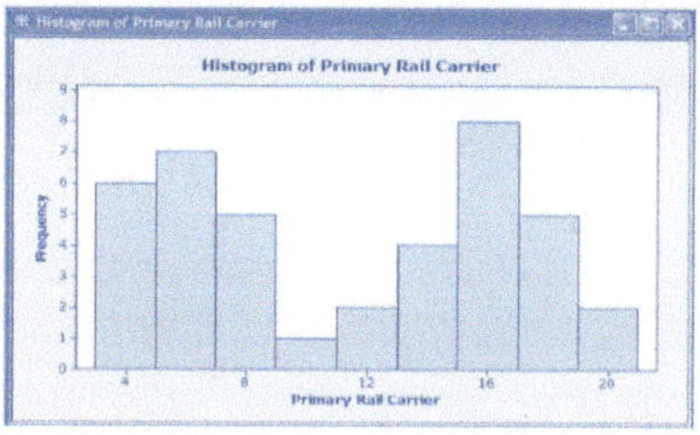

Histogram Analysis

The project team begins by calculating the total of each "LEG" of the delivery process. The resulting Histogram shows vehicle delivery data has a bi-modal (non-normal) distribution. Because this Histogram indicates non-normal data, the project team will likely continue their analysis by investigating how each process LEG impacts the overall results.

Fig. 5.15 Histogram

illustrates the distribution of the data by showing, which values occur most and least frequently. A Histogram illustrates the shape, cantering, and spread of the data you have.

It is very easy to construct, easy to use, and you will find it useful in many situations. This graph represents the data for the 20 days of arrival times at work from the previous lesson page. In many situations the data will form specific shaped distributions. One very common distribution you will encounter is called the Normal Distribution, also called the bell-shaped curve for its appearance.

Project Teams perform a graphical analysis on data collected during the previous step to gain direction regarding areas of potential improvement opportunities.

5.18 The Pareto Analysis

The Pareto analysis (Fig. 5.16) assists you in determining what inputs are having the greatest impact on your process is the Pareto Analysis approach. A bar graph used to arrange information in such a way that priorities for process improvement can be established.

☞Example: Delivery Timing

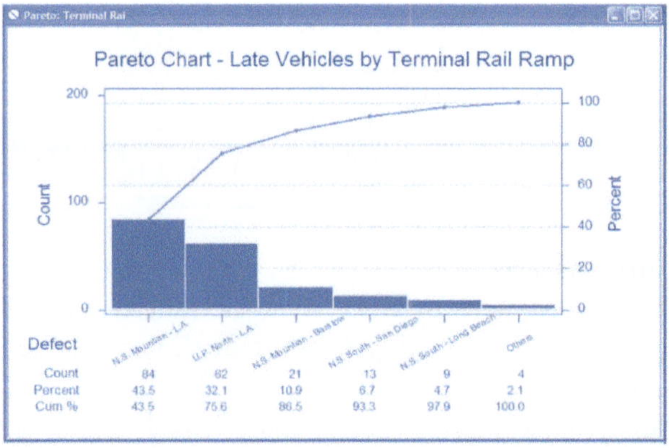

Pareto chart

The project Team wants to see if the rail carrier terminal ramp is affecting delivery time. The Pareto chart showing vehicles delivered after the 45-day target grouped by Terminal Rail Ramp. This Pareto chart identifies both Los Angeles rail ramps as potential significant factors.

Fig. 5.16 Pareto diagram

The 80–20 theory was first developed in 1906, by Italian economist, Vilfredo Pareto, who observed an unequal distribution of wealth and power in a relatively small proportion of the total population. Joseph M. Juran is credited with adapting Pareto's economic observations to business applications.

5.19 The Box Plot

A Box Plot (sometimes called a Whisker Plot) (Fig. 5.17) is made up of a box representing the central mass of the variation and thin lines, called whiskers, extending out on either side representing the thinning tails of the distribution. Box Plots summarize information about the shape, dispersion, and centre of your data. Because of their concise nature, it is easy to compare multiple distributions side by side.

These may be "before" and "after" views of a process or a variable. Or there may be several alternative ways of conducting an operation. Essentially, when you want to quickly find out if two or more distributions are different (or the same), then you create a Box Plot. They can also help you spot outliers quickly which show up as asterisks on the chart.

☞Example: Delivery Timing; Box Plot

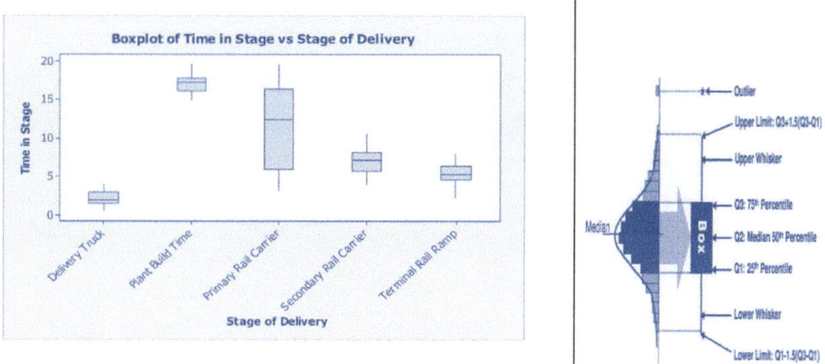

Boxplot

Boxplot showing the legs of the delivery process. Primary Rail Carrier has the greatest amount of variation and is the second-longest leg in terms of overall days. The Boxplot also shows that the Plant (building the vehicle) is the longest stage in terms of days, while dealer delivery truck is the shortest.

Fig. 5.17 Box plot diagram

A Box Plot is based on quartiles and represents a distribution as shown on the left of the graphic. The lines extending from the box are called whiskers. The whiskers extend outward to indicate the lowest and highest values in the data set (excluding outliers). The lower whisker represents the first 25% of the data in the Histogram (the light grey area). The second and third quartiles form the box, which represents fifty per cent of the data and finally the whisker on the right represents the fourth quartile. The line drawn through the box represents the median of the data. Asterisks represent extreme values or outliers. A value is considered an outlier if it is outside of the box (greater than Q3 or less than Q1) by more than 1.5 times (Q3-Q1).

You can use the Box Plot to assess the symmetry of the data: If the data are fairly symmetric, the Median line will be roughly in the middle of the box and the whiskers will be similar in length. If the data are skewed, the Median may not fall in the middle of the box and one whisker will likely be noticeably longer than the other.

5.20 The Run Chart

Use a Trend/Run chart (Fig. 5.18) to display trends within observation points over a specified time period. This chart is a simple time-ordered plot of data that can be used to test for the presence of special causes. The patterns of data points indicate

☞Example: Delivery Timing: Run Chart

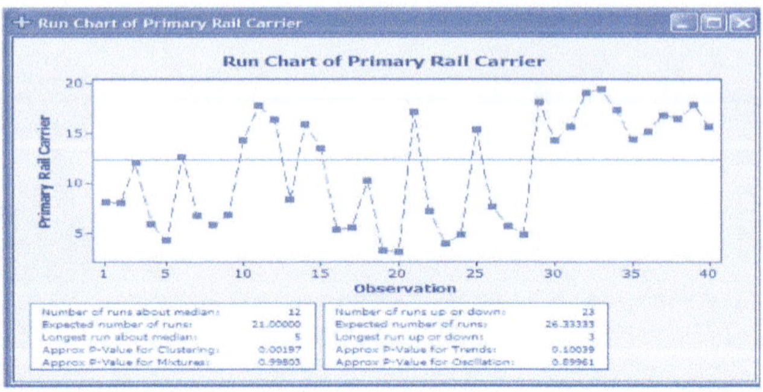

Run Chart

Based on the results of the Histogram and Scatter Plot, the project Team wants to learn more about variation existing in Primary Rail Carrier Stage, particularly those vehicles represented by data on the right-hand side of the histogram. The resulting chart shows a large amount of variation in the amount of time spent in the Primary Rail Carrier Stage.

Fig. 5.18 Run chart

trends or shifts occurring inside the process. Looking at the Time Series Plot, the response appears to be very dynamic. The benefit of this approach to charting is that you can see every data point as it is gathered over time. Some interesting occurrences can be revealed.

The project Team works with the assembly plant to determine why Sport Track models appear to be experiencing longer than average delays prior to loading on railcars for transfer to the Mixing Centre. Following interviews and direct observation, the project Team determines the following:

- Delayed Sport Track units are often orders that include the Cargo Cage option.
- Cargo Cage part availability issues mean that some Sport Track units leave the plant without the specified Cargo Cage installed.
- Production demands take priority with regard to Cargo Cage part shipments.
- Rework for Cargo Cage installation happens on Friday afternoons for units awaiting railcar loading.

5.21 Six Sigma as a Symbol, Level, and Measure

Variation is our enemy! Customers, both internal and external, have expectations relative to the deliverables from processes. Variation from those expectations likely dissatisfies them. Six Sigma is devoted to identifying, analysing, and eliminating defects and variation. The less variation within a process, the more predictable the process is, assuming the Mean is stable.

> 🕮 Definition: Sigma is a measure of deviation. The mathematical calculation for the Standard Deviation of a population is as shown in Fig. 5.19. *Sigma* can be used interchangeably with the statistical term Standard Deviation. *Standard Deviation* is the average distance of data points away from the Mean in a distribution. To measure the sigma value of a process, obtain the distance from the Mean to the closest specification limit to determine how many Standard Deviations it is away from the Mean. This is the *Sigma Level*!

Figure 5.19 depicts the percentage of data that falls between Standard Deviations within a Normal Distribution. Those data points at the outer edge of the bell curve represent the greatest variation in the process and can cause customer dissatisfaction.

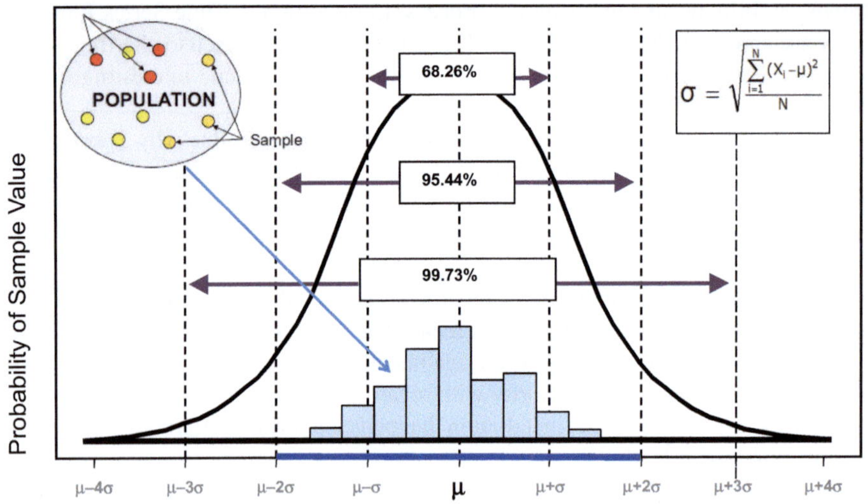

Fig. 5.19 Gauss Bell curve and related Six Sigma

5.22 Quality Management as Part of the Project Planning

In work breakdown structures—when quality is addressed—the work package… "Quality Assurance" is usually isolated. But as we know something can only be secured that was previously planned. For Quality management the tasks shown in Fig. 5.20 and the corresponding work packages should be taken into account for.

5.23 Quality Planning

The quality planning should be made on the basis of the company's quality policy and quality objectives. The quality planning must also take into account the results of the cost–benefit analysis. During the process the quality requirements, characteristics and metrics need to be agreed for all three areas (Product, project management process, and the Product Development process). Quality metrics is the operational definition of measures and methods for determining the value of what is being measured. (For example, adherence to delivery dates of the work packages can be measured after the project end, after the punctual beginning or the timely submission of the work package results in planned quality). Some well-known quality metrics in Software Development are the error density (number of failures per program length), error rate (the relative number of defective elements in relation compared to the total), or test coverage (the ratio of actual statements made a test compared with the theoretically possible statements; at a low test

Fig. 5.20 Quality management work-tasks-breakdown

coverage only small samples with a high test coverage over all features are completely tested). Often industry-oriented checklists can be used for quality planning. The result of its quality planning and the Quality management Plan should describe how Quality management is performed by the project Team. The Quality Plan should be accepted by all relevant stakeholders and known the project team.

5.24 Quality Control

In the Quality Control process the created product characteristics based on the quality plan are reviewed and checked to see whether they comply with the requirements and specifications. A further task of the quality control is also to identify and eliminate possible root causes. Quality Control is often performed by a special organizational functional project team. For this there are numerous tools, which were described in Sect. 5.9.

5.25 Quality Assurance

Quality assurance starts already during the planning process: the measures, processes, and those responsible must be defined, with whom you can use to secure the desired quality characteristics. Then, measures are carried out according to plan and continually checked.

5.26 Quality Improvement/Experience Backup

An important task of quality management is to ensure that the lessons learned in future phases of the project and new projects can be used for continuous improvement of quality. In many organizations, experience assurance is closely associated with knowledge management.

References

Akao, Y. (1972). "New Product Deployment and Quality Assurance—Quality Deployment System" (in Japanese), Standardization and Quality Control, 25, 14, 7–14.

Cohen, L. (1988). Quality Function Deployment and Application Perspective from Digital Equipment Corporation," National Productivity Review, 7, 3, 197–208.

A. Griffin, J. R. (1993). The Voice of the Customer Marketing Science pp. 1 - 27

Lobenwein, H. H. (1994). Unternehmenswert und Lean Management. Vienna.

McKay, A.. (2001). Requirements management: a representation scheme for product, Computer Aided Design Vol 33 No 7 pp 511e520

6 Project Organization

📖Definition: Project organization consists of a group of people and the associated infrastructure for agreements regarding leadership. Roles and Responsibilities, alignment with the business and functional processes.

This group of people can be either integrated directly into the project or indirectly involved, in which they try to influence the project. This group of people is also known as stakeholders. Typical examples of direct members are the project managers, who are responsible for the project, or the project staff, who operate as the executing instance. The project influencers count as indirectly involved. These are, for example, people from the departments where the project output will be used, and other department managers, who may be needed to provide resources for the project. The project resources need to be described independently regardless of people involved and therefore always you should speak about roles. A role is an abstract construct, which can be taken on by one or more persons (Role Responsible).

Whenever several people (or roles) work together on a task it is called teamwork. In projects, teamwork is an important element, since everyone must work together to achieve the project goal and results. Within this chapter the special teamwork needs are considered only marginally. An in-depth look into teamwork is the subject of Chap. 7. Everywhere where teamwork is essential, there is also the need to lead a team. The project manager in a project leads and must therefore also have appropriate leadership skills. Different leadership styles and qualities are part of the personal competencies. These include in particular leadership, commitment and motivation, assertiveness, relaxation and stress management and creativity, efficiency, advice, and value add. In addition to the management, personnel selection

P. Bauer, *A Comprehensive Project Management Guide*, Management for Professionals, https://doi.org/10.1007/978-3-031-68252-0_6

and training, related to the team building must be considered. The setup of the project team is not just approved by the project manager, but is also influenced by the functional managers who provide the project staff; usually even the Human Resources supports the team selection.

The synonymous *project management* and *project organization* are often used and seen as equivalent concepts, nevertheless to be able to confine between project organization and project management, the project organization has to be integrated into the management organization of the company, for example the integration into a matrix or functional project organizational structure. Related to the meaning of the overall definition of organization, *project quality planning* however relates to all controls and the management of projects. This includes the actual process of organizational change (process organization) in addition to establishing the organizational functions involved in a project with its tasks and competencies, and the relations between them (management organization).

Literature proposes a number of ways to formally integrate projects into a company's management organization. These recommendations can lead to the impression that projects can only be successful if organizational structures such as functional, matrix, or a pure project organizational structure are applied. The "Real life" often looks different: many, smaller projects are implemented successfully, hierarchy-free, and without a formal integration of the project team in the management organization. This is rather defined as a problem-solving group that deals ad hoc with project tasks. However, the concept of project management should also be applied here too; but only the management and leadership components are incorporated but not the organization element.

6.1 Participating in a Project

Project work is usually a cooperative problem-solving process in which all relevant knowledgeable, key competences, and responsible resources work together jointly. The project participants can be divided into two roles that are directly and indirectly involved in the project. Table 6.1 shows an overview of some roles in both groups.

Table 6.1 Roles as project participants

Direct Project Members	Indirect Project Members
• Contracting authority • Contractor • Steering committee • Project management (project leader) • Project manager or part of • Work package managers • Project member • Sub-contractor • Owner of the company • Team members	• Project controller • Project merchant • Project office manager • Project business office member • Program manager • Multimedia project manager • Head of department • Special field employee • Department coordinators • Applicant • Approval committee • Sponsor • Management (board of directors) • Director of quality planning units • QM officer • User representative • External consultants • Representatives of the company • Public authorities • Citizen's initiatives

Regardless of the type of project and the chosen organizational structure, three functional levels can be split into:

- Formal decision functions, which are the responsibility of the *projects principle*;
- Management functions, which is *project management* responsibility;
- Executional functions. This is conducted by the project group, supported by the *resources affected* directly by the project.

This circle of people actively involved in the problem-solving process reflects the totality of needs and the existing know-how in the respective problem area. The group is institutionalized for the duration of the project management phase structured as a special working group (Fig. 6.1); These working groups are formed for the coordination and implementation of the project task only and dissolve again at the end of the project. The work task content that is associated with the various working groups depends very strongly on the problem to solve. Usually another working group will be responsible for decisions affecting the overall project, as for those affecting only one particular subsystem or a particular aspect of the system.

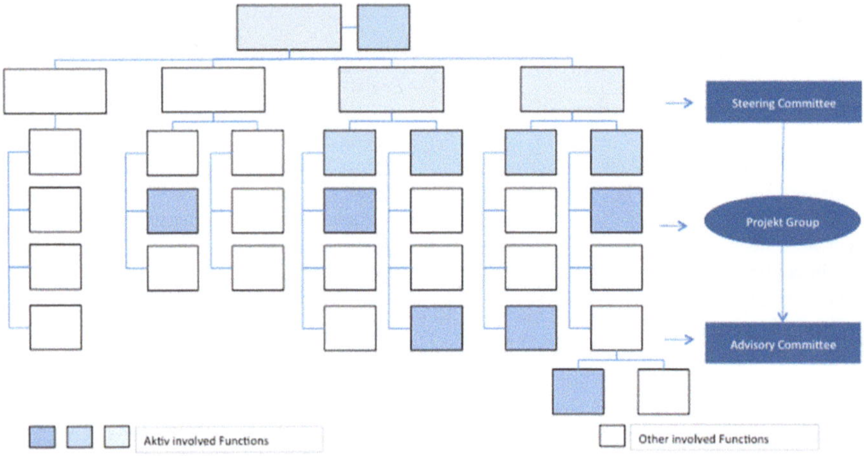

Fig. 6.1 Project resources

One of the main objectives of the structure is to reduce uncertainty and confusion that typically occurs at the project initiation phase. The structure defines the relationships among members of the project management and the relationships with the external environment. The structure defines the authority by means of a graphical illustration called an organization chart.

A properly designed project organization chart is essential to project success. An organization chart shows where each person is placed in the project structure. An organization chart is drawn in pyramid form where individuals located closer to the top of the pyramid have more authority and responsibility than members located towards the bottom. It is the relative locations of the individuals on the organization chart that specifies the working relationships, and the lines connecting the boxes designate formal supervision and lines of communication between the individuals.

The project manager must create a project structure that will meet the various project needs at different phases of the project. The structure cannot be designed too rigid or too loose, since the project organization's purpose is to facilitate the interaction of people to achieve the project ultimate goals within the specified constraints of scope, schedule, budget, and quality. The objective in designing a project structure is to provide a formal environment that the project manager can use to influence team members to do their best in completing their assignment and duties. The structure needs to be designed to help develop collaboration among individual team members, all in a cost-effective way with a minimum of duplication of effort and overlap.

The organization chart has a limited functionality; it only shows the hierarchical relationship among the team members but does not show how the project organization will work, it is for that reason that the design should consider factors that will facilitate the operation of the structure; these include communications, information flows, coordination, and collaboration among its members.

A constant interaction between the project work, on the one hand, and the overall organization objectives, on the other hand, is achieved through the connection of the project group with the Steering and Advisory Committee. Problem solutions obtained specifically by organizational projects are accepted due to the participation and involvement of competencies.

The alignment and the tasks of these three working groups are described in detail in the following chapter.

6.2 The Steering Committee

A project embodies often a kind of remote "thing" for most areas of a company that disturbs the routine processes. Taking this into account, the integration of a project into the organization is not always unproblematic—this applies in particular when a project is matrix organized. Projects can only handle successfully if the managers of the line organization involve themselves in the project management process, perceive their future tasks, and assume responsibility. For this purpose, a Steering Committee is set up provisionally where decision makers are grouped together for a project. This acts then as the *principle* of the project and then makes project decisions. The *Steering Committee* (Table 6.2) has to carry out the following tasks:

- The *Steering Committee* verbalizes the project contract with the broad objectives and the necessary or even desired boundaries for the implementation of the project. The rough objective setting gives the project manager a starting point for more detailed verbalization and operationalization of the project objectives.
- It defined the project group; it appoints the head of the project and formally determines the other members of the project group.
- It selects the members of the *Advisory Committee* from the functional supervisor groups of whose departments are affected by the project.
- The Steering Committee sets the project organization by ordering the project into the company's organization and sets the decision-making powers of the project leader in line with the entity. The Steering Committee must also make sure that these rules are made known to the involved line entity of the organization and to respect them.
- It determines the required project steps starting with the feasibility study up to introduction. The type and the number of project steps are to be adapted to the project tasks and the *project risk*. Generally, you can use the steps described in the chapter *risks & opportunities* of project management.
- Each step of the project will be formally released by interim decision-making of the Steering Committee. These decisions are intended to transition from one process step of the project to the next process step and that the project manager can review results regularly and receives the opportunity to intervene if there are significant deviations in timing from the original timing plan. He also gets the opportunity to make resulting corrections with regard to the project objectives if the overall organization objectives also change. Through formal decisions, the

project manager can maintain control over the project without investing too much time to meet his overall responsibility. At the same time, the regular releasing of intermediate results confirms the project group work and increases the project managers planning predictability. The decisions at the end or at the beginning of each project step should be communicated by a project status report to the Steering Committee on a regular basis by the project manager to present interim results, especially the results of the various project steps in the planning phases.

- The Steering Committee sets priorities, if multiple autonomous work tasks exist in the project and if these cannot be executed at the same time due to personal or financial bottlenecks. That is why particularly in organizational projects designed for multiple business units, it is essential to define the chronological order of work tasks in the individual departments. In this case the overall company's interests must be prioritized. A priority setting may also be necessary between activities in the project and in the line if individual project team members are only working part-time for the project.
- The Steering Committee enforces overall company's interests against the project manager and the line instances. This can be done by a decision of the hierarchical key representatives in the Steering Committee.

The *members* of the Steering Committee are recruited from the ranks of key decision-making and those who have responsibility of those areas that are affected directly by the project. Based on the tasks shown and due to the fact that if working on complex problems usually cross-functional decisions are made, the need to include the hierarchical top people in the Steering Committee. The supportive, dedicated leadership position in organizational projects often is top management or CEO level and is mandatory for a smooth scheduled project completion.

The meetings of the Steering Committee should be aligned depending on the scheduling of the various stages of the project. In addition, the Steering Committee should meet on a regular basis to consider and approve the status reports of the project leader. On the one hand, the Steering Committee does not want to be bothered daily by problems from the project, on the other hand it needs to assert its influence early enough to control the project and should meet at least every two months.

> 🕮 Definition: The temporary *Steering Committee* for special projects or programs is also referred to as Steering Committee, whereas the continuous and strategic board, which governs the project landscape in a company is *Control Panel* (or *Portfolio-Board*). The essential task of the Steering Committee is that the projects and programs are done properly, whereas the central task of the Control Panel is to make the right projects and programs in the company: the Steering Committee takes decisions within the framework of the project or program, and the Control Panel decides the framework of projects or programs on an overall company level.

Table 6.2 Roles and authorities of the steering committee and control panel

Index	Steering committee	Control panel
Tasks:	• Appoint project leader. • Project planning authorization. • Support the project manager. • Monitoring project progress. • Reporting to management. • Approve reports. • Relieve project manager.	• Identify necessary projects and programs. • Select projects and programs and approve. • Support of steering committees. • Monitor the progress of all projects and programs in the company. • Allocate and distribute project and program budgets. • Cancel, approve, or end projects/programs.
Competence:	• Decision about corrective actions. • Decision on changes of project content, dates, costs. • Decision on project tasks priorities.	• Decision on status of projects and programs (prioritization) and control the project landscape based on this decision (regulation).

6.3 The Advisory Committee

The Advisory Committee (often referred to as also *Technical Committee*) supports the project group—especially in larger project tasks and advises them on content issues; the committee consists of the functional department's owners affected by the project. The idea behind it is that planned changes can only be realized without serious problems if the intentions are already taken into account for in the planning phase. The Advisory Committee has the following technical tasks:

- Forward project-relevant expertise and technical information to the project group.
- The Advisory Committee has to check the feasibility of solutions developed by the project group and to assess their impact, risks, and effects.
- It forwards the results of the project group in the affected departments, so the acceptance of solutions increases.
- It informs the project group on any project-related changes in the problem area.
- It supported the project group in the preparation of documents for the meetings of the Steering Committee.

The Advisory Committee is an intermediary between the project group, on the one hand, and the units of the overall quality planning, on the other. It has merely an advisory and supportive function, with a veto privilege but no decision competency. In addition to the professional tasks the Committee also has a political function:

- The management affected is involved in the process of project implementation and therefore takes a direct responsibility in the design process and the results.

- The Advisory Committee represents the interests of the functional departments and aligns the project with them with the overall objectives of the company.
- The management acceptance of changes rises and intellectual resistance is reduced.

The members of the Advisory Committee are from the lower and middle management level and are appointed by the Steering Committee. Size and composition of the Advisory Board are not considered to be unchangeable, but are dependent on the project needs and adapted if necessary. For example, the affected departments may vary in the course of the project, when a restriction or extension of the issues is made. Corresponding changes in the line-up of the Advisory Committee will then be taken into account for.

The Advisory Committee or parts of them come together if necessary; they are invited to work meetings by the project teams. The Advisory Committee should be involved heavily in the process of project implementation and therefore meet every three to six weeks and the Steering Committee needs to be informed about the results of these working sessions at the same frequency.

6.4 Project Team Members

Project tasks can be solved by only one employee as a "stand alone" or by a working group. If you do not consider the labour-intense resources necessary based on capacity reasons, then the benefits of a working group are particular in the cumulative strength of individual members that can be used very efficiently (*Synergy Effect*). The correct long-term composition of the project team proves to be the *Critical Success* factor in project management.

The employee composition of the *project team* mainly depends on the character of the project task. Their superiors usually name the members according to their expertise. They then often work dedicated (full-time) in the project team and after completion of the project, they return to their old position. Due to the dedicated (full-time) character a *project group* becomes a *project team*. However, project staff can also be placed in smaller work task force to support a project only part-time.

The project group must not necessarily persist in the same configuration even during project execution; depending on the issue additional experts or sub-work groups can be created temporarily. These additional consulting experts usually work on a part-time basis in the project team, because the group members represent different departments, different hierarchical levels and have different knowledge.

Project teams underlie an internal structuring, which relates the tasks to special roles and responsibilities in the team. The communication structures within the project team and the external organizational units are of particular importance. The members of a project team can report internally in the team to a project manager. The project manager must be equipped with certain powers and responsibilities with regard to the implementation of the project, which can be set very differently. It may be set so that it is in line with the internal hierarchy and a related function of a team member. Instead, the project group can also be moderated and controlled by a *project coordinator*.

The project team has to have enough special and methodological expertise in the team to be able to solve a problem. In an organization project the following team members are needed:

- Internal specialists who have the necessary methodological knowledge of project management.
- Staff from the relevant departments that are specialists in their field of expertise.
- Depending on the problem and the chosen problem-solving strategy and the available know-how there may be a need for additional specialists as consultants who can be from other areas of the organization, as well as external consultants.

The individual members of the project group can either work full-time or only partially on the project. The project Steering Committee defines the respective timing and amount for temporary work tasks, specifying the period and time frame. For large and complex projects, members should work dedicated and full-time in the team, in order to ensure continuity. In this case, the project members need to be released from their routine tasks. Best practice shows that the project members should work on the highest prioritized tasks on a set number of weekdays and then on the other days of the week, they work undisturbed dedicated on their project tasks.

How many people should be in a core team—the nucleus of the group? No more than five to seven key members. Coordination and communication issues grow exponentially if more people are added to the core team. When additional resources are required, apply them on an as needed basis. If you have a requirement demanding more than five to seven people, reduce the individual team goals to a scope that can be covered by five to seven—or have more teams.

Roles (Table 6.3) that must be present include Champion/Sponsor, Leader, Facilitator, Technical expert, Coordinator, Chronicler, Communicator/Presenter, and someone to ensure the team keeps it collective eyes on the goal. One person may fulfil more than one role, or roles may be rotated or shared, but they must be done—if one of the teams is absent, then the team suffers from its performance.

Table 6.3 Roles and authorities of the project staff

Index	Project Staff
Tasks:	• Implementation of delegated task • Documentation of results • Support project manager • Control progress of the own tasks • Feedback of the results and the effort associated with result
Competence:	• Implementation of tasks • Preparation of decisions by the project manager

The establishment of specific, measurable, attainable, realistic, and time-framed goals for teams is absolutely essential to their success. If goals are not set for the team at the outset that meets those five criteria, then the first goal of the team is to develop goals and gain approval of their goals from their sponsor. Failure to do this is the single biggest reason that teams fail. Establishing the goals and making them known is the single best way to define and manage expectations and provide the basis for measuring progress and contribution.

This is where the saying "actions speak louder than words" really means something. The resources a team needs to meet its goals vary widely, based on any number of elements. The two resources that tell a team—any team—just how important their goals are to the organization are time and talent.

If team membership is simply layered on top of existing duties, if meetings are constantly delayed or cancelled because of other issues, if expertise cannot be made available by functional areas because the expertise is too busy working on other things, if briefing meetings with sponsors and leadership are difficult to schedule or keep getting changed, if team questions or concerns do not get quick review and response, then team goals aren't that important—regardless what is said.

The sponsor needs to be highly placed, actively engaged on a regular basis with the team, able to make things happen so the team can move forward to its goals, must have personal "skin" in the game, and has to have access to the very top leader on a routine basis. If those criteria are met, team performance is given a real chance to succeed—without it teams may be successful, but it will take longer and introduce a real chance for ineffectiveness and lack of enthusiasm.

Studies have shown that the top two things' people want in their work are being recognized as a contributing member of a worthy enterprise, and recognition and reward for their accomplishments. People want to identify themselves with their company. They want to know that what they do has value in the marketplace and has value to the success of their organization. The organization has to communicate that every position adds value—some may be more obvious than others, but the "we are all in this together" approach and philosophy of work leads to high performance.

Rewards and Recognition can come in many forms. Accomplishment on team projects needs to be publicized, and individual accomplishment within teams should lead to actions that make it clear that team participation and success lead to opportunities. One other thing about rewards and recognition—they can be lost in the helter-skelter of getting everything done. Schedule regular review times—at least monthly, to determine who should be recognized and rewarded, and make it a very public ceremony. If you find you cannot name quickly the people to reward, you really need to look at how the team is performing.

Review the essentials and compare them to your own organization, then change what you need to change to improve success—or to implement teams in your company. Doing so will ensure that you are accessing the collective genius of your organization—and that's like money in the bank—for everyone!

6.5 The Project Leader

With regard to the project management structure, two types can be distinguished:

- A *non-hierarchical* project group, where all team members have equal rights. The equality encourages a free and open cooperation. This type of cooperation strengthens the identification of individual group members with the project task and is suitable especially for projects where innovation and creativity is essential. Initial outside coordination and representation are transferred to individual members of the group, who then assume the function of a project speaker.
- In a *hierarchical* project group, a project member has special competencies and responsibilities with regard to problem solving and project implementation. The competencies of this people are very largely dependent on the selected type of organization. In an extreme competency structure group or people only have the right to be informed and the right for application. In some case the competencies go only as far as being a project coordinator.

The main tasks of the project manager (Table 6.4) include project planning and to take on the responsibility for the project management. Within the project-planning phase, he sets the project objectives and the resources required to achieve these goals, he does not have totally essentially responsibility for the target setting, but contributes to a large extent.

- They define the project objectives, checks their feasibility, documents then in a project charter, and makes sure that the objectives are commissioned to and approved by the Steering Committee.
- They are involved in the establishing of the project organization and propose the members of the project team.
- They are involved in the structuring of the project, in project steps and phases.

During the actual implementation of the project the project leader is fully personally responsible for the achievement of the timing- and cost- objectives primarily needing to do the following:

The project manager develops resource plans with a high granularity in line with the approved project plans and defines the timing and the funds together with the team members.

He reviews the planned project tasks with regard to the deadlines and costs. The project manager initiates appropriate corrective measures if the project deviates from plan. The project manager initiates appropriate corrective measures if serious deviations occur, he then also needs to inform the stakeholder authority.

He established measures and hardware resources for quality assurance and checks the quality of the project results. He also ensures the exchange of information within the project team and ensures complete project documentation. The project manager prepares the decisions of the Steering Committee, implements and releases them to the next stage of the project, continuously informs the head of the department concerned, and agrees with them regularly or on demand the project results.

Table 6.4 Roles and authorities of the project leader

Index	Project Leader
Tasks:	Project coordination and planning with steering committee Procurement of appropriate resources Coordination, management, and motivation of the project team Planning, control, and monitoring of schedules, cost, and quality objectives Representation of the project to the outside Implementation of the conclusion of the project
Competence:	Participation in definition of project goals Participation in the occupation of the project roles Technical authority Each according to the form of the project quality planning is also disciplinary authority empowered for all tasks in the project Require resource commitments

The tasks and competencies of the project manager in terms of leadership depend on the chosen integration structure of the project team into the management organization. In particular project managers should have the following competencies:

- He distributes project subtasks to the project team, also allowing him to plan the project member's vacation timings.
- He may propose measures for project members training, insofar as these are beneficial or necessary for the achievement of project goals.
- He has to resolve project team conflicts.

The management of complex projects experience is a full-time job as soon as more than seven people work full-time in the project team. In small project teams, project managers can perceive tasks in addition to his leadership that are related to the actual project implementation. Basically, there are three significantly related criteria for a project leader to success a project:

- To successfully complete all the project management tasks you need full support by top management. All stakeholders must be clear that the project promoter (the project Steering Committee or the top management) should not only be interested in the project, but also fully sponsors and supports the project manager.
- The project manager must be trained on the methodological skills of project management. This includes the knowledge and mastery of methods and techniques of project management. The methods should be consistently applied and understood by all stakeholders and accepted.
- Social skills involve above all the ability to the lead a team; These include the knowledge and mastery of methods and techniques of the personal management as well as the ability to convince, be sociable, have assertiveness and stamina.

6.6 Types of Project Organization

Of the several factors to consider when deciding on the design of project organizational structures, especially within an existing organization, the element that is significant is the extent of authority and responsibility top management is prepared to delegate to the project manager. An important function of the organization's top management is to design an organization that fully supports project management. This is done by redesigning the organization to emphasize the nature of the projects and adapting how roles and responsibilities are assigned.

The organization needs to define the project manager's job, degree of authority and autonomy, and relationship both to the organization, other projects and to other units in the organization. Upper management also should specify communication channels, methods of conflict resolution between the project and the rest of the organization. These areas are usually called program units and are centred on a specific development field. In this environment a project has three organization structures available for design and all are defined by the level of organizational authority given to the project manager:

- *Programmatic based*, in which project managers have authority only within the program focus or area
- *Matrix based*, in which the project manager shares responsibility with other program unit managers
- *Project based*, in which project managers have total authority.

6.7 Staff Unit Organization (Programmatic Based)

The programmatic focus refers to a traditional structure in which program sector managers have formal authority over most resources (Fig. 6.2). It is only suitable for projects within one program sector. However, it is not suitable for projects that require a diverse mix of people with different expertise from various programs. In a programmatic-based organization, a project team is staffed with people from the same area. All the resources needed for the project team come from the same unit. For instance, if the project is related to the quality area, the project resources come from the quality functional departments.

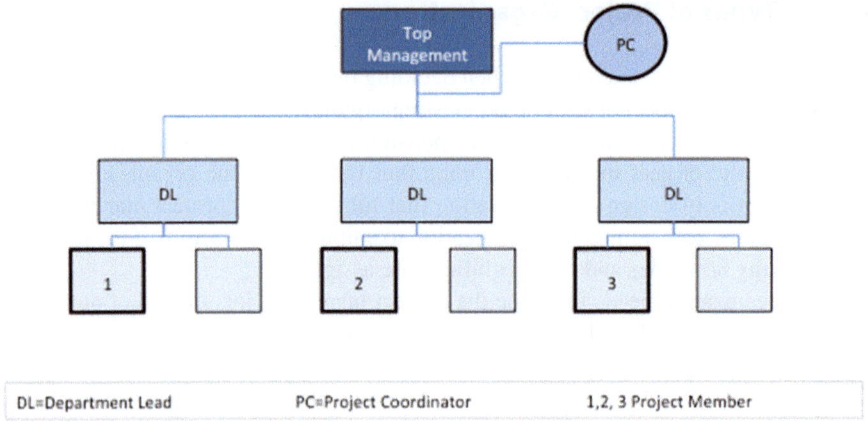

Fig. 6.2 Staff unit organization

The most obvious advantage (Table 6.5) of programmatic based projects is that there are clear lines of authority; in large projects, the project managers tend to also be the program unit manager. There is no need to negotiate with other program units for resources, since all of the staff needed will come from the same program area. Another advantage of this type of organization is that the team members are usually familiar with each other, since they all work in the same area. The team members also tend to bring applicable knowledge of the project.

A major disadvantage (Table 6.5) of the staff unit-based organization is that the program area may not have all of the specialists needed to work on a project. A quality project with environmental elements, for instance, may have difficulty-acquiring specialty resources such as civil engineers, since the only people available will work in their own program unit. Another disadvantage is that project team members may have other responsibilities in the program unit since they may not be needed full-time on a project. They may be assigned to other projects, but it is more typical that they would have support responsibilities that could impact their ability to meet project deadlines.

Table 6.5 Influence staff unit organization

	Staff Unit Organization
Features:	Employees remain in the line Project manager has no professional and disciplinary responsibility Project manager has only an advisory function Project execution occurs by the line
Application:	Small and non-critical projects Strategic cross-departmental projects High concern of many organizational units (for example, departments) In larger projects only if management clearly supports the project and the project management has enough personal authority (influence)
Advantages:	Eliminates need for organizational change High degree of flexibility in resource deployment Optimized utilization of resources possible Non-bureaucratic knowledge transfer (at least theoretically) possible
Disadvantages:	Complex processes of coordination and consultation Project manager has little capacity to enforce measures Risk or opportunity: identification with the project Line is loaded heavily

6.8 The Matrix Organization

Matrix-based project organizations (Fig. 6.3) allow program units to focus on their specific technical competencies and allow projects to be staffed with specialists from throughout the organization. For instance, Automotive Body specialists may report to one program unit, but would be allocated out to work on various projects. An engine specialist might report to the Powertrain unit, but be temporarily assigned to a project in another project that needs engine expertise. It is common for people to report to one person in the programmatic unit, while working for one or two project managers from other projects in different programmatic units.

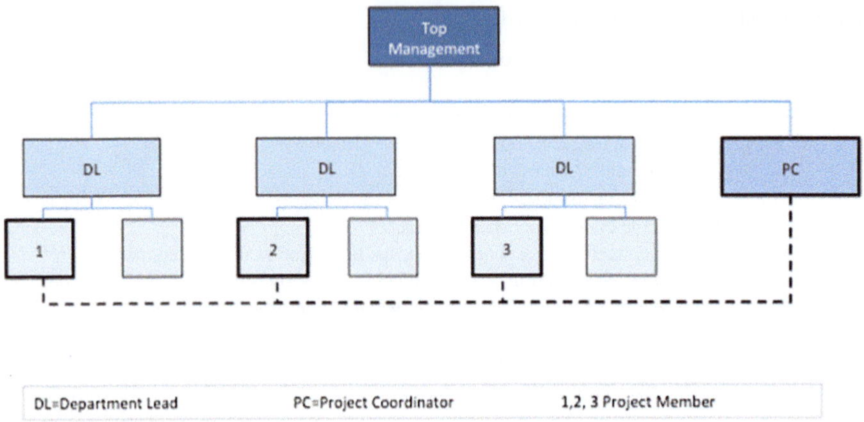

Fig. 6.3 Matrix organization

The main advantage of the matrix-based organization is the efficient allocation of all resources, especially scarce specialty skills that cannot be fully utilized by only one project. For instance, monitoring and evaluation specialists may not be utilized full-time on a project, but can be fully leveraged by working on multiple projects.

The matrix-based organization is also the most flexible when dealing with changing programmatic needs and priorities. Additional advantages to matrix management are: it allows team members to share information more readily across the unit boundaries, allows for specialization that can increase depth of knowledge, and allows professional development and career progression to be managed. It is easier for a program unit manager to loan an employee to another manager without making the change permanent. It is therefore easier to accomplish work objectives in an environment when task loads are shifting rapidly between programmatic units.

The main disadvantage is that the reporting relationships are complex. Some people might report to programmatic unit managers for whom little work is done, while actually working for one or more project managers. It becomes more important for staff members to develop strong time management skills to ensure that they fulfil the work expectations of multiple managers. This organization also requires communication and cooperation between multiple programmatic unit managers and project managers since that all be competing for time from the same resources.

Matrix management can put some difficulty on project managers because they must work closely with other managers and workers in order to complete the project. The programmatic managers may have different goals, objectives, and priorities than the project managers, and these would have to be addressed in order to get the job done. An approach to help solve this situation is a variation of the matrix organization, which includes a coordinating role that either supervises or provides support to the project managers. In some organizations this is known as the *Project Management Office* (PMO) (Fig. 6.4) dedicated to provide expertise, best practices, training, methodologies, and guidance to project managers.

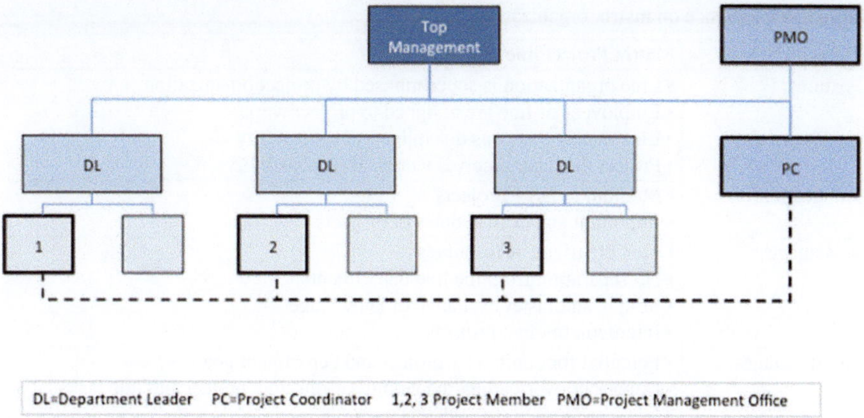

Fig. 6.4 Matrix organization with PMO

The PMO (Table 6.6) unit also defines and maintains the standards of project management processes within the organization. The PMO strives to standardize and introduce economies of scale in the implementation of projects. The PMO is the source of documentation, guidance, and metrics on the practice of project management and implementation. The PMO can also help in the prioritization of human resources assigned to projects.

Table 6.6 Influence on matrix organization

	Matrix Project line Organization
Features:	• Line organization is superimposed by project organization • Employees of line are assigned to project work • Line manager retains disciplinary responsibility • Project manager receives technical responsibility
Application:	• Medium to large projects • Important and critical dates of projects
Advantages:	• Flexible usage or resources • No separation from the line departments • Simple and faster exchange of knowledge • Interdepartmental projects
Disadvantages:	• Potential for conflict by project and department goals • Danger of overloading the employees through project and line tasks • Increased organizational expenses • Unattended project work due to day-to-day business

6.9 The Autonomous Project Organization

In this type of organization (Fig. 6.5) project managers have a high level of authority to manage and control the project resources. The project manager in this structure has total authority over the project and can acquire resources needed to accomplish project objectives from within or outside the parent organization, subject only to the scope, quality, and budget constraints identified in the project.

In the project-based structure, personnel are specifically assigned to the project and report directly to the project manager. The project manager is responsible for the performance appraisal and career progression of all project team members while on the project. This leads to increased project loyalty. Complete line authority over project efforts affords the project manager strong project controls and centralized lines of communication. This leads to rapid reaction time and improved responsiveness. Moreover, project personnel are retained on an exclusive rather than shared or part-time basis. Project teams develop a strong sense of project identification and ownership, with deep loyalty efforts to the project and a good understanding of the nature of project's activities, mission, or goals.

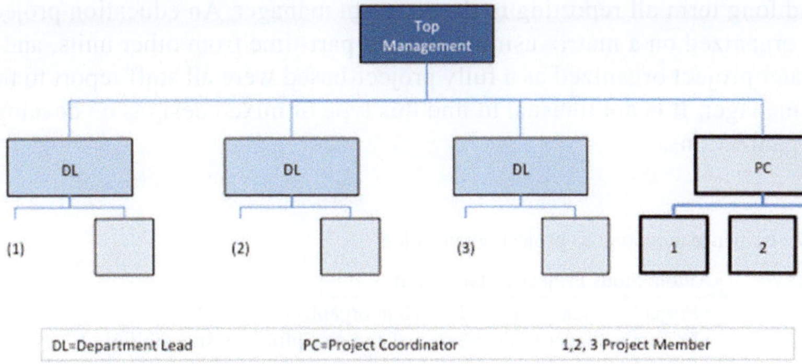

Fig. 6.5 Autonomous project organization

Pure project-based organizations are more common among large and complicated projects. These large projects can absorb the cost of maintaining an organization whose structure has some duplication of effort and the less than cost-efficient use of resources. In fact, one major disadvantage of the project-based organization is the costly and inefficient use of personnel. Project team members are generally dedicated to one project at a time, even though they may rarely be needed on a full-time basis over the life cycle of the project. Project managers may tend to retain their key personnel long after the work is completed, preventing their contribution to other projects and their professional development.

In this type of organization, limited opportunities exist for knowledge sharing between projects, and that is a frequent complaint among team members concerning the lack of career continuity and opportunities for professional growth. In some cases, project personnel may experience a great deal of uncertainty, as organization or donor's priorities shift or the close of the project seems imminent.

One disadvantage (Table 6.7) is duplication of resources, since scarce resources must be duplicated on different projects. There can also be concerns about how to reallocate people and resources when projects are completed. In a programmatic focus organization, the people still have jobs within the program unit. In a project-based organization it is not always clear where everyone is reassigned when the project is completed. Another disadvantage is that resources may not be needed as a full-time for the entire length of the project, increasing the need to manage short-term contracts with consultants and other subject matter experts.

A variety of this pure project approach is temporarily project-based organizations. This organization consists of a project team pulled together temporarily from their program unit and led by a project manager who does not report to a programmatic unit. The project manager has the full authority and supervision of the project team.

Another design is based on a mixed structure that includes a matrix, programmatic focus, and project based; this mix reflects the need for more flexibility in a development organization to accommodate different requirements. For example, a Six Sigma deployment program may have a couple of projects short term and long term all reporting to the program manager. An education project may be organized on a matrix using resources part-time from other units, and a large water project organized as a fully project-based were all staff report to the project manager. It is not unusual to find this type of mixed designs on development organizations.

Table 6.7 Influence autonomous project organization

	Autonomous Project Organization
Features:	• Project is a temporary independent organizational unit • Project manager has professional and disciplinary responsibility • Employees report to the project manager • Employees are removed from the lines after the end of the project • Resolution of organizational unit after project end
Application:	• Large and critical dates of projects • Minor organizational interfaces to other functions
Advantages:	• Unique powers and responsibilities • Hardly any potential for conflict through different task allocations • Identification with the project • Simple ways of communication
Disadvantages:	• Capacity problems through issues by allocating resources to only one project • Conflict potential during reintegration of the old area after project end • Increased if reintegration costs for training • Expertise drain

6.10 Choosing a Suitable Type of Organization

Choosing a suitable type of a quality planning for project management depends directly on the type and level of skills, which give the project manager a successful project execution. These are primarily related to the specific characteristics of the project. Table 6.8 contains a number of criteria and their importance for the different types of organizations.

- The type of *Staff project quality planning* is applied often for smaller projects as well as applied on projects, which involve several companies. Here the project manager also serves as interface for the non-corporate stakeholders.
- The pure *Project Organization* is suitable for long-term, large-scale projects, especially if they have relatively little contact points for the operational day-to-day business.
- The concept of *Matrix Project Organization* is due to its multipurpose and comprehensive design suitable for nearly any project, but especially if a company has to coordinate many projects at the same time. When working only on a few smaller projects, this form of organization requires a relatively high organizational effort. The matrix organization still requires a great openness of the line instances to group-oriented forms of cooperation.

Table 6.8 Criteria to select the type of project organization (PO)

Type of Project Organization (PO)				
Project criteria	Without PO	Staff-PO	Matrix-PO	Pure PO
Meaning	Low	Medium	Big	Very large
Scope	Low	Medium	Big	Very large
Uncertainty	Low	Medium	Big	Very large
Time pressure	Low	Medium	Big	Very large
Duration of the project	Short	Short	Medium	Long
Complexity	Very low	Low	Medium	High
Central control	Very low	Medium	Big	Very large
Employee	Additional	Additional	Part-time	Full-time
Personality	Not relevant	Minor relevance	Qualified PM	Very competent PM

The described areas may not be considered absolute rigid; Best practice shows that numerous combinations of these three basic forms are found in the industry. This is why it sometimes happens that pure project organization is only referred to the core group of full-time employees of the project, while the remaining staff stay in their old organization. In organizational projects often only the employees of the organization department are grouped into a project with professional and disciplinary leadership of a project manager; however, the employees of the departments affected by the organizational problem stay in their own organization. This is a pure *project quality planning* within the organization area. The project leader is then either the head of the organization area himself or a representative employee.

A chosen organization type must not necessarily be valid the whole duration of a project. Looking for innovative solutions requires different organizational frameworks as the implementation and enforcement of these ideas. Because the people involved sometimes change based on their qualifications and scope, a flexible adaptation of the project organization could then be appropriate.

7 Teamwork

7.1 Introduction

A team is a group of people who work together on one or more targets and they all vouch for. They do so by taking over different roles, in which they communicate with each other, with the aim to successfully coordinate their efforts.

This ability to work together was key factor in human communication and has proven itself until today. Beginning with the inventions in the aerospace industry right up to sequencing the human genome, this was only possible via a global network of specialists. Thus, teams initially allow quicker processes in development and production.

The work within the team and the gained experience also contribute to the development of individual personalities. People learn to set aside their own interests and to help each other in and team. This conflicts with the current patriarchal mindset, as we prefer individual performance that is also individual rewarded. We continue to learn to communicate effectively and often we need to find ways to resolve conflicts. Consequently, we adapt the suggestions and ideas of others, learn from our mistakes ("learning"), and mutually protect us from errors.

By working together, we learn more as if we would work alone. We benefit from mutual practical, but also emotional support. This successful working experience forges the team members together, leading to the experience of "affiliation" and "bonding". In successful teams we can contribute with our individual skills, develop and maintain a more collective and social identity at the same time.

Since the boom started in the 1990s, teamwork takes place in all areas and is a part of our everyday work life. However, there are doubts whether this trend towards teamwork is driven by the rational. The assumption is that teamwork is currently fashion thing, as managers believe they satisfy the wishes of employees and customers far more. But also, the structural changes in retail markets and buyer markets play a large role; for example, the ever faster new model development in the automotive industry.

P. Bauer, *A Comprehensive Project Management Guide*, Management for Professionals, https://doi.org/10.1007/978-3-031-68252-0_7

7.2 Basics and Definition

First, some terms are clarified. A well-established team definition is "A team is a group of individuals, which are mutually interdependent and jointly responsible for the achievement of specific objectives for the organization". There are additional characteristics for teams in a work context that are:

- Team members have more or less clearly defined roles.
- Teams have a clear identity and structure within the organization.
- Teams are not too small, nor too big (3–20 members).

To be able to talk about teamwork at all is perceived as effective, the following guidelines have been developed:

- The activity must be suitable for teamwork.
- The team members see themselves as a team and perceived from others within the organization as a team.
- The team has decision-making powers on the tasks.
- The team structure including the task, the members, and the standards must promote teamwork.
- The organization must support the needs of the team by procedures and guidelines.
- Feedback and coaching by experts is available, if needed from the team.

A team is a group of individuals

- That together produce a product or offer a particular service and
- That is accountable for the quality and its performance.

Members of a team

- Have shared objectives.
- They are jointly responsible for their achievement.
- You are dependent on the performance of the other team members.
- They influence the results through interaction with each other.

Because the team as a whole responsible for the final result of its work, one of the central tasks for each team member is to establish and maintain a network with the other members of the team.

> Conclusion; A project manager should be able to take on projects and to support then if there is sufficient evidence that a project is value added to the business. This is the only way to inspire the project members. If a project manager defines objectives for a project, but fails to convince them whether all these objectives will also actively be support by the team, they cannot expect full support and therefore full team effort. It is their task to ensure the team accepts all objectives.

7.3 Ability to Work in a Team

In many organizations team ability represents a commonly used criterion for new employees that need to comply to with full extent. This is also seen in the media where companies seeking potential candidates request teamwork ability. In many rankings for the most important skills for managers, teamwork is at the top, ranked before willingness to learn, self-motivation, and the ability to communicate. Then what is team ability?

> 🕮 Definition: Team ability as "the individual willingness and capability for the effective and solidary cooperation in small learning groups of a size between 3 and 6 participants".

Team ultimately means ability to cooperate with others in the context and to achieve results with regard to an objective that is clearly described and coordinated effectively. At the same time, this interaction of the individuals should be experienced positively. It is based on task-related criteria (performance, efficiency) and relationship-related criteria (satisfaction, relationship quality).

Consequently, it becomes clear that the ability to work on a team is basically the ability of being able to work together. This overall requirement can be substantiated with several aspects of the topic, such as:

- Ability to Communicate
- Interaction/Contact ability, ability to Cooperate
- Conflict resolution skills
- Integration ability
- Consensus

The communication skill alone is not sufficient, however a mandatory prerequisite. A good performance in the team does not automatically conclude that the team members communicate well with each other, but because they cooperate well.

If a person has these competencies, it can be assumed the he has the team ability. This bundling of these skills allows a person to be able to integrate in every team. It also must be ensured by the leaders that the same people are also willing to use these competencies.

7.4 Optimize Team Meetings

High-functioning teams are what make high-performing companies very effective. Whether the task is to create an innovative service or implement a new system, groups rather than individuals are shouldering more of the burden than ever before.

The ideal team merges individual talents and skills into one super-performing whole with capabilities that surpass those of even its most talented member.

Yet, in reality, many teams fail to get dose to that ultimate ideal. Members do not work together as seamlessly as they could. People disengage, information goes unshared, wires get crossed, and time and money are wasted.

7.5 Make Time for Team Members

Interpersonal understanding is critical to trust, which, in turn, is critical for the flow of ideas and information. What distinguishes top teams from the rest? High-performing teams aren't the result of happy accident, research shows. They achieve superior levels of participation, cooperation, and collaboration because their members trust one another, share a strong sense of group identity, and have confidence in their effectiveness as a team. In other words, such teams possess high levels of group emotional intelligence (EQ).

Building an emotionally intelligent team requires developing emotional competence for the group as a whole. A team, like any social group, is governed by shared attitudinal and behavioural norms, which, though sometimes unspoken, are understood within the group. Teams that enjoy high levels of groups have established norms that strengthen trust, group identity, and group efficacy. As a result, their members cooperate more fully with one another and collaborate more creatively in furthering the team's work.

Implementing the following three practices will get your efforts to build your teams EQ off to a solid start:

Interpersonal understanding is critical to trust, which, in turn, is critical for the flow of ideas and information. The group must be aware of each member's skills and personality. When a group is first formed, it's smart to hold a launch meeting that has time built in for introductions and socializing. Members can get acquainted with one another as they start hammering out team goals and creating a shared vision of success.

Once a team is established, taking 5 min at the beginning of regular meetings for members to share work progress and personal reflections helps fortify the groups understanding of each individual and how they all contribute to a common goal. "People on teams where people knew one another better were more efficient and got more work done".

7.6 Surface and Manage Emotional Issues

It's important to establish comfortable, group-sanctioned ways to express the anger, tension, and frustration that arise in a team endeavour and to positively redirect that energy. "Inevitably, a team member will indulge in behaviour that crosses the line, and the team must feel comfortable calling the foul".

1. *First,* humour and playfulness can be helpful tools in defusing conflict and relieving tension. One team at the worldwide innovation consultancy IDEO (Palo Alto, Calif.) tossed soft toys over cubed walls when feelings ran high. Besides lightening the mood, this action served as a reminder that the group had established norms for expressing difficult emotions, thereby making them feel less threatening to individuals and to the group as a whole. In another approach, the Xerox team members wrote down their gripes, dipped them to play money in denominations from €1 to €100 depending on how serious they felt the issue to be, and dropped them into an "opportunities" jar, their gripes were discussed at meetings, starting with problems attached to larger denominations.

   The process enhanced the group's emotional competence in several ways. First, it increased trust by fostering openness and decreasing the temptation for members to express their frustration in destructive ways.
2. *Second*, those with complaints saw them dealt with fairly and positively. In response to a complaint that an overly gregarious (and unnamed) team member was a distraction, the group developed a good—natured solution: small placards for the backs of their chairs reading "The doctor is in" or "The doctor is out": Holmes explains that when the doctor was "in", visiting was OK; when the doctor was "out", it wasn't.

   Establish comfortable, group-sanctioned ways for the team to express anger and tension and to positively redirect that energy. "Inevitably, a team member will indulge in behaviour that crosses the line, and the team must feel comfortable calling the foul".
3. *Third*, the jar truly did offer opportunities by enabling members to expand skills while helping forward the team's work. For example, the "opportunities" jar revealed that members were unable to get past the Xerox firewall when working offsite. The individual who volunteered to troubleshoot was not an IT specialist but had enough computer knowledge, curiosity, and persistence to find and eliminate the glitch.

7.7 Celebrate Success

Building the EQ of a team also requires the expression of positive emotions, such as gratitude for going the extra mile or pride in a job well done. Recognizing individual and group achievements not only strengthens a team's identity, but it also spotlights its effectiveness and fuels its collective passion for excellence. For instance, Xerox Canada created a "Wall of Fame" to honour members of the Sarbanes-Oxley team.

> ☞ Giving each other high fives, toasting one another at dinners, or simply dapping for someone in a meeting-it's amazing, what such simple acts can do for building a sense of solidarity, efficacy, and identity.

7.8 Principles of Team Leadership and Facilitation

Human beings are social by nature. People tend to seek out the company of other people. This is a great strength of our species, one that enabled us to rise above and dominate beasts much larger and stronger than ourselves. It is this ability that allowed humans to control herds of livestock to hunt swift antelope and to protect themselves against predators. However, as natural as it is to belong to a group, there are certain behaviours that can make the group function more (or less) effectively than their members acting as individuals.

We will define a group as a collection of individuals who share one or more common characteristics. The characteristic shared may be simple geography, i.e., the individuals are gathered together in the same place at the same time. Perhaps the group shares a common ancestry, like a family. Modern society consists of many different types of groups. The first group we join is, of course, our family. We also belong to groups of friends, sporting teams, churches, and so on. The groups differ in many ways. They have different purposes, different time frames, and involve varying numbers of people. However, all effective groups share certain common features. In their work, joining together the following characteristics of an effective group is:

- Group goals must be clearly understood, be relevant to the needs of group members, and evoke from every member a high level of commitment to their accomplishment.
- Group members must communicate their ideas and feelings accurately and clearly. Effective, two-way communication is the basis of all group functioning and interaction among group members.
- Participation and leadership must be distributed among members. All should participate, and all should be listened to. As leadership needs arise, members should all feel responsibility for meeting them. The equalization of participation and leadership makes certain that all members will be involved in the group's work, committed to implementing the group's decisions, and satisfied with their membership. It also assures that the resources of every member will be fully utilized and increases the cohesiveness of the group.
- Appropriate decision-making procedures must be used flexibly if they are to be matched with the needs of the situation. There must be a balance between the availability of time and resources (such as member's skills) and the method of decision-making used for making the decision. The most effective way of making a decision is usually by consensus (see below). Consensus promotes distributed participation, the equalization of power, productive controversy, cohesion, involvement, and commitment.
- Power and influence need to be approximately equal throughout the group. They should be based on expertise, ability, and access to information, not on authority. Coalitions that help fulfil personal goals should be formed among group members on the basis of mutual influence and interdependence.

- Conflicts arising from opposing ideas and opinions (controversy) are to be encouraged. Controversies promote involvement in the group's work, quality, creativity in decision-making, and commitment to implementing the group's decisions. Minority opinions should be accepted and used. Conflicts prompted by incompatible needs or goals, by the scarcity of a resource (money, power), and by competitiveness must be negotiated in a manner that is mutually satisfying and does not weaken the cooperative interdependence of group members.
- Group cohesion needs to be high. Cohesion is based on members liking each other, each member's desire to continue as part of the group, the satisfaction of members with their group membership, and the level of acceptance, support, and trust among the members. Group norms supporting psychological safety, individuality, creativeness, conflicts of ideas, growth, and change need to be encouraged.
- Problem-solving adequacy should be high. Problems must be resolved with minimal energy and in a way that eliminates them permanently. Procedures should exist for sensing the existence of problems, inventing and implementing solutions, and evaluating the effectiveness of the solutions. When problems are dealt with adequately, the problem-solving ability of the group is increased, innovation is encouraged, and group effectiveness is improved.
- The interpersonal effectiveness of members needs to be high. Interpersonal effectiveness is a measure of how well the consequences of your behaviour match intentions.

These attributes of effective groups apply regardless of the activity in which the group is engaged. It really doesn't matter if the group is involved in a study of air defence, or planning a prom dance. The common element is that there is a group of human beings engaged in pursuit of group goals.

7.9 Selecting a Facilitator

Facilitators should possess four basic capabilities:

He or she should be able to anticipate the complete problem-solving and decision-making processes.
He or she should use procedures that support both the group's social and cognitive process.
He or she should remain neutral regarding content issues and values.
He or she should respect the group's need to understand and learn from the problem-solving process.

Facilitation works best when the facilitator takes a strategic and comprehensive view of the problem solving and decision-making processes and selects, from a broad array, the specific methods that match the group's needs and the tasks at hand.

He also supports the group's social and cognitive processes, freeing the group members to focus their attention on substantive issues. All group members trust the facilitator as a neutral party who has no biases or vested interest in the outcome and helps the group understand the techniques being used and helps the group improve its own problem-solving processes.

7.10 Facilitating the Group Task Process

Team activities can be divided into two subjects: *task-related* and *maintenance-related*. Task activities involve the reason the team was formed, its charter, and its explicit goals.

The facilitator should be selected before the team is formed, they should assist in identifying potential team members and leaders and in developing the team's charter.

The facilitator also plays an important role in helping the team develop specific goals based on their charter. Goal setting is an art and it is not unusual to find that team goals bear little relationship to what management actually had in mind when the team was formed. Common problems are goals that are too ambitious, goals that are too limited and goals that assume a cause-and-effect relationship without proof. An example of the latter would be a team chartered to reduce scrap assuming that Part X had the highest scrap loss (perhaps based on a week's worth of data) and setting as its goal the reduction of scrap for that part. The facilitator can provide a channel of communication between the team and management. Facilitators can assist the team leader in creating a realistic schedule for the team to accomplish its goals.

Facilitators should assure that adequate records are kept on the team's projects. Records should provide information on the current status of the project. Records should be designed to make it easy to prepare periodic status reports for management. The facilitator should arrange for clerical support with such tasks as designing forms, scheduling meetings, obtaining meeting rooms, securing audio visual equipment and office supplies, etc.

Other activities where the facilitator's assistance is needed include:

Meeting Management Schedule the meeting well ahead of time. Be sure that key people are invited and those they plan to attend. Prepare an agenda and stick to it! Start on time. State the purpose of the meeting clearly at the outset. Take minutes. Summarize from time-to-time. Actively solicit input from those less talkative. Curtail the overly talkative members. Manage conflicts. Make assignments and responsibilities explicit and specific. End on time.

Communication The idea that "the quality department" can "assure" or "control" quality is now recognized as an impossibility. To achieve quality the facilitator must enlist the support and cooperation of a large number of people outside of the team.

The facilitator can relay written and verbal communication between the team and others in the organization. Verbal communication is valuable even in the era of instantaneous electronic communication. A five-minute phone call can provide an opportunity to ask questions and receive answers that would take a week exchanging email and faxes. Also, the team meeting is just one communication forum; the facilitator can assist team members in communicating with one another between meetings by arranging one-on-one meetings, acting as a go-between, etc.

7.11 Facilitating the Group Maintenance Process

Study the group process. The facilitator is in a unique position to stand back and observe the group at work. Are some members dominating the group? Do facial expressions and body language suggest unspoken disagreement with the team's direction? Are quiet members being excluded from the discussion?

When these problems are observed, the facilitator should provide feedback and guidance to the team. Ask the quiet members for their ideas and input. Ask if anyone has a problem with the team's direction. Play devil's advocate to draw out those with unspoken concerns.

7.12 Stages in Group Development

Groups of many different types tend to evolve in similar ways. It often helps to know that the process of building an effective group is proceeding normally. The *Forming—Storming—Norming—Performing* model of group development and performance developed was first proposed by American Psychologist Professor Bruce Tuckman in 1965, who maintained that these phases are all necessary and inevitable in order for the team to grow, to face up to challenges, to tackle problems, to find solutions, to plan work, and to deliver results. This model (Fig. 7.1) has become the basis for subsequent models.

7.13 Phase Model by Tuckman

The *Forming—Storming—Norming—Performing* model of group development & performance developed was first proposed by American psychologist Professor Bruce Tuckman in 1965, who maintained that these phases are all necessary and inevitable in order for the team to grow, to face up to challenges, to tackle problems, to find solutions, to plan work, and to deliver results. This model (Fig. 7.2) has become the basis for subsequent models.

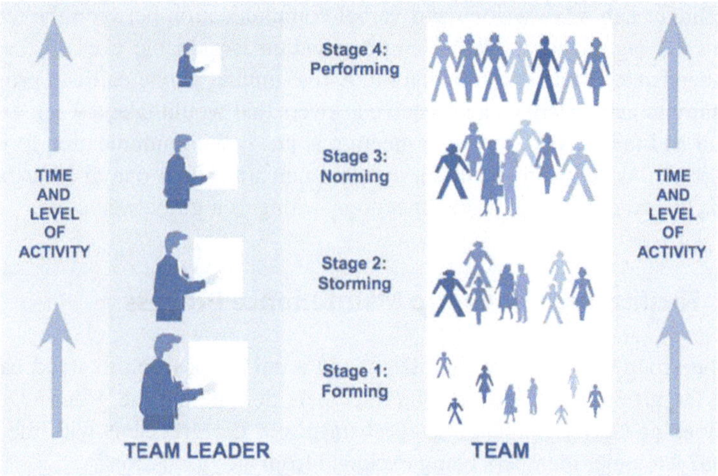

Fig. 7.1 Tuckman's model: Team development and performance development

During the *forming* stage a group tends to emphasize procedural matters. Group interaction is very tentative and polite. The leader dominates the team dynamics management, including conflict resolution, decision-making process and plays a very important role in moving the group forward.

The *storming* stage follows forming. Conflict between members, and between members and the leader, is characteristic of this stage. Members question authority as it relates to the group objectives, structure, or procedures. It is common for the group to resist the attempts of its leader to move them towards independence. Members are trying to define their role in the group. It is important that the leader deal with the conflict constructively. There are several ways in which this may be done:

- Do not tighten control or try to force members to conform to the procedures or rules established during the forming stage. If disputes over procedures arise, guide the group towards new procedures based on a group consensus.
- Probe for the true reasons behind the conflict and negotiate a more acceptable solution.
- Serve as a mediator between group members.
- Directly confront counterproductive behaviour.
- Continue moving the group towards independence from its leader.

During the *norming* stage the group begins taking responsibility, or ownership, of its goals, procedures, and behaviour. The focus is on working together efficiently. Group norms are enforced on the group by the group itself.

The final stage is *performing*. Members have developed a sense of pride in the group, its accomplishments, and their role in the group. Members are confident in their ability to contribute to the group and feel free to ask for or give assistance.

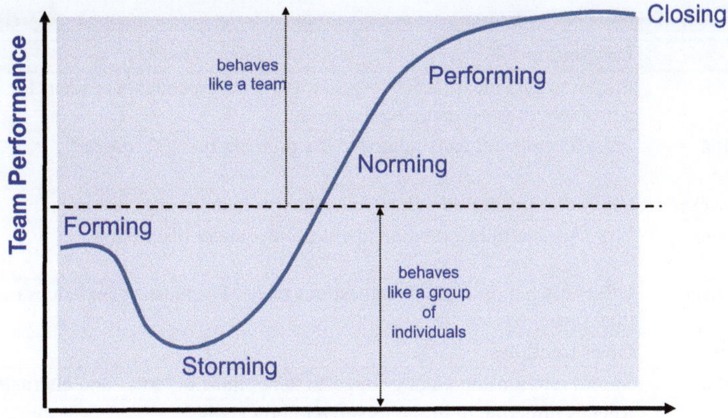

Fig. 7.2 Tuckman's model: Team performance cycle

7.14 Member Roles and Responsibilities

There are two basic types of roles assumed by members of a group: *task roles* and *group maintenance* roles. Group task roles are those functions concerned with facilitating and coordinating the group's efforts to select, define, and solve a particular problem. The group task roles shown in Table 7.1 are generally recognized.

Table 7.1 Group task roles

Role I.D.	Description
Initiator	Proposes new ideas, tasks, or goals; suggests procedures or ideas for solving a problem or for organizing the group.
Information seeker	Asks for relevant facts related to the problem being discussed.
Opinion seeker	Seeks clarification of values related to problem or suggestion.
Information giver	Provides useful information about subject under discussion.
Opinion giver	Offers his/her opinion of suggestions made. Emphasis is on values rather than facts.
Elaborator	Gives examples.
Coordinator	Shows relationship among suggestions; points out issues and alternatives.
Orientor	Relates direction of group to agreed-upon goals.
Evaluator	Questions logic behind ideas, usefulness of ideas, or suggestions.
Energizer	Attempts to keep the group moving towards an action.
Procedure technician	Keeps group from becoming distracted by performing such tasks as distributing materials, checking seating, etc.
Recorder	Serves as the group memory.

The development of task roles is a vital part of the team building process. Team building is defined as the process by which a group learns to function as a unit, rather than as a collection of individuals.

7.15 Counterproductive Group Roles

In addition to developing productive group-oriented behaviour, it is also important to recognize and deal with individual roles (Table 7.2), which may block the building of a cohesive and effective team. The leader's role includes that of process observer. In this capacity, the leader monitors the atmosphere during group meetings and the behaviour of individuals. The purpose is to identify counterproductive behaviour. Of course, once identified, the leader must tactfully and diplomatically provide feedback to the group and its members. The success of project is, to a great extent, dependent on the performance of groups.

Table 7.2 Counterproductive group roles

Role i.d.	Description
Aggressor	Expresses disapproval by attacking the values, ideas, or feelings of other. Shows jealousy or envy.
Blocker	Prevents progress by persisting on issues that have been resolved; resists attempt at consensus; opposes without reason.
Recognition seeker	Calls attention to himself/herself by boasting, relating personal achievements, etc.
Confessor	Uses group setting as a forum to air personal ideologies that have little to do with group values or goals.
Playboy	Displays lack of commitment to group's work by cynicism, horseplay, etc.
Dominator	Asserts authority by interrupting others, to manipulate and claim superior status.
Help-seeker	Attempts to evoke sympathy and/or assistance from other members through "poor me" attitude.
Special-interest pleader	Assert the interests of a particular group. This group's interest matches his/her self-interest.

7.16 Conflict Resolution

Conflict management is a duty shared by the facilitator and the team leader. The facilitator can assist the leader by assuring that creative conflict is not re-pressed, but encouraged. Explore the underlying reasons for the conflict. If "personality disputes" are involved that threaten to disrupt the team meeting, arrange one-on-one meetings between the parties and attend the meetings to help mediate.

The first step in establishing an effective group is to create a consensus decision rule for the group, namely:

No judgement may be incorporated into the group decision until it meets at least tacit approval of every member of the group.

Adopting the following behaviours can facilitate this minimum condition for group movement:

- Avoid arguing for your own position. Present it as lucidly and logically as possible, but be sensitive to and consider seriously the reactions of the group in any subsequent presentations of the same point.
- Avoid "win–lose" stalemates in the discussion of opinions. Discard the notion that someone must win and someone must lose in the discussion; when impasses occur, look for the next most acceptable alternative for all the parties involved.
- Avoid changing your mind only to avoid conflict and to reach agreement and harmony. Withstand pressures to yield, which have no objective or logically sound foundation. Strive for enlightened flexibility; but avoid outright capitulation.
- Avoid conflict-reducing techniques such as the majority vote, averaging, bargaining, coin flipping, trading out, and the like. Treat differences of opinion as

indicative of an incomplete sharing of relevant information on someone's part, either about task issues, emotional data, or gut level intuitions.

- View differences of opinion as both natural and helpful rather than as a hindrance in decision-making. Generally, the more ideas expressed, the greater the likelihood of conflict will be; but the richer the array of resources will be as well.
- View initial agreement as suspect. Explore the reasons underlying apparent agreements; make sure people have arrived at the same conclusions either for the same basic reasons or for complementary reasons before incorporating such opinions into the group decision.
- Avoid subtle forms of influence and decision modification. E.g., when a dissenting member finally agrees, don't feel that having his own way on some subsequent point must reward him.
- Be willing to entertain the possibility that your group can achieve all the foregoing and actually excel at its task. Avoid doom saying and negative predictions for group potential.

Collectively, the above steps are sometimes known as the "consensus technique". In tests it was found that 75% of the groups who were instructed in this approach significantly outperformed their best individual resources.

7.17 Management Role

Perhaps the most important thing management can do for a group is to give it time to become effective. This requires, among other things, that management work to maintain consistent group membership. Group members must not be moved out of the group without very good reason. Nor should there be a constant stream of new people temporarily assigned to the group. If a group is to progress through the four stages described earlier in this chapter, to the crucial performing stage, it will require a great deal of discipline from both the group and management. Another area where management must help is creating an atmosphere within the company where groups can be effective.

References

Michael Gessler. (2011). Kompetenzbasiertes Projektmanagement (PM3) Handbuch für die Projektarbeit, Qualifizierung und Zertifizierung auf Basis der IPMA Competence Baseline Version 3.0 / unter Mitwirkung der spm swiss project management association (4. Auflage ed., Vol. 1). Nürnberg: GPM Deutsche Gesellschaft für Projektmanagement.

http://www.projectsmart.co.uk/5-essentials-to-project-team-success.php. (2015). 5 Essentials to Project Team Success. Web: Web.

8 Problem Resolution

Project work is normally accompanied by problems. There is no project manager who does not use most of his time for solving problems. Is this normal? Is this really necessary? Working on problems means recognizing and solving problems and is actually not the exception—but it has become some sort of a routine. Project leaders experience daily situations such as:

☞Example **Case Problem**: A pillar of a newly built bridge is anchored well on stone. After some time, it is recognized that the stone is embedded in clay and is moving. The structure of the bridge is at risk. This is classical problem as it is not always possible to know and detect all possible failure modes and conditions, especially with innovative and complex projects.

☞Example **Method Problem**: A project manager must write a five-page report weekly about his project. That annoys him particularly because this report is not read and there is no feedback on it. This is a methodological problem; an inherently meaningful method is handled incorrectly, by demanding something that is not necessary and appears meaningless.

☞Example **Organizational Problem**: The project manager must urgently initiate an order, if this is done too late, the project finish date will shift in the wrong direction. But the project manager is dependent on the signature of two supervisors and one is on vacation. This is a typical case in which the roles and responsibilities are not sufficiently clearly settled, leading to problems.

P. Bauer, *A Comprehensive Project Management Guide*, Management for Professionals, https://doi.org/10.1007/978-3-031-68252-0_8

☞Example **Action Problem**: A team member delivers his work package qualitatively inadequate and far too late despite a clear timing agreement. Other project team members can therefore not continue with the next project steps. The team member has no convincing arguments.

☞Example **Decision Problem**: Two project managers need a particular employee to work full-time on two projects at the same time, to be able to keep the project end dates. The Steering Committee must decide which project to be given to the employees. But the Steering Committee does not decide as it fears the consequences of not working on one of the projects and for not delivering the projects on time.

☞Example **Behaviour Problem:** The project team consists of a group of specialists with individual opinions that follow only the objectives of their individual departments. As a result, no consensus is found, solutions are blocked, and the whole project execution fails and a whole bunch of problems develop.

☞Example **Political Problem:** A big client of a company is the customer of a project. The client will not commit himself on the objectives and specifications of the project, but calls for rapid progress. The management of the company doesn't dare to force the client to finally sign off the specification, because he is key business customer and must not be upset.

8.1 Key Takeaways

All projects have problems of various kinds and with a wide variety of effects. These problems result from the increasing complexity of the projects. The effect of these problems can severely limit the success of the project and even stop it. A problem is described as a difference between a nominal and a value and how the gap can be closed; this difference can occur particularly for plan values and also for the behaviour of the people in the project.

The most important phase in the event of problem-solving is the clarification phase, where the issue is clearly described and where all information is collected about the problem. Problems all have a root cause, but the problem is mostly identified by its symptoms.

The solutions to the problem are developed using the creativity techniques and by using systematic structuring. As there are several alternative solutions all must be found because the first alternatives are not often the best. The method of cost–benefit analysis provides a very good approach to be able to select from the variety of solutions and pick the most significant and most suitable solution.

The implementation of the proposed solution completes the problem-solving process. The effect of problem-solving must be reviewed periodically, especially at the end of the process. Out of each problem solved there is potential for improvement for the company in the sense of a Continuous Improvement, Lessons Learnt, and Failure Mode Avoidance.

References

Michael Gessler. (2011). Kompetenzbasiertes Projektmanagement (PM3) Handbuch für die Projektarbeit, Qualifizierung und Zertifizierung auf Basis der IPMA Competence Baseline Version 3.0 / unter Mitwirkung der spm swiss project management association (4. Auflage ed., Vol. 1). Nürnberg: GPM Deutsche Gesellschaft für Projektmanagement.

Prof Dr. Shulte Zurhausen, M. (2010). Project-/Change Management/Organisation Lerneinheit 1. Hagen: Institut für Verbundstudien der Fachhochschule NRW.

Pm4dev, Project Management For Development Organizations. (2007). Web: Web.

Project Structures 9

Projects are unique missions with complex character and initially hard to overlook. The process of **project structuring** breaks down the units according to different aspects/issues into small manageable tasks (work breakdown structure). It must be insured that no tasks resulting from the interfaces, which are necessary for the completion of the project, are forgotten. The consequence is the need for a complete illustration of all elements of the project and their relationships to each other—the **project structure**.

The structuring of the project is a project management process, which begins in the definition phase (DIN 69901-2) with a top-level structure and is continued in the planning phase with a project structure plan and the definition and description of work packages.

The project structure should be developed by the project team to ensure that all project participants have the same understanding of the tasks, e.g. type and content, range of activities, assignment of responsibilities, and time required.

The work breakdown structure is often referred to as "mother of all plans"—the central instrument of order in the project, which has implications in all other areas of the project.

The frequently encountered rationale is that there is no need for a work breakdown structure and no work package, you could put everything in a process and schedule plan, is a dangerous mistake. That appears latest if important deliverables have been forgotten in the associating process or the performance allocation is wrong.

Disturbances in the project process quality issues; contract disputes are just a few of the possible consequences.

Some important objectives of the project structure are shown in Table 9.1.

P. Bauer, *A Comprehensive Project Management Guide*, Management for Professionals, https://doi.org/10.1007/978-3-031-68252-0_9

Table 9.1 Purpose of the work breakdown structure

1. Representation of the project object in its entity
2. Detection of lack of clarity in the definition of objectives
3. Provision of all operational and therefore controllable units of work (work packages, tasks)
4. Map logically all work packages
5. Creating transparency in the project
6. Promoting a common vision of the project subject
7. Promote a consistent order principle
8. Communication in change management
9. Allocating work packages to subcontractors

9.1 Fundamental Principles and Structures

In the framework of project processing, structures are designed, used, and maintained for different tasks. Each structure uses one or more aspects of the project mass that needs to be organized as classification criteria. Aspects may represent concepts, methods, properties, documents, and so on. From a conceptual perspective, aspects become attributes of project elements.

Main Dimensions of Projects

- Aspects of the project structures can be classified from the main dimensions of projects: project objects are parts of the affected project activity system that is changed by project management and has enough information: project objects are also called process objects, products, and results.
- Project activities change objects and produce information: project activities are parts of project processes. This creates the project results.
- Project information (knowledge), usually in documents, describes the project objects and the project activities ("will", "plan", and "is").

Project objects, project activities, and project information build up a triangle or a cube. The three dimensions (Fig. 9.1) are described in short with the words "Objects", "Activities", and "Information" for the next illustration.

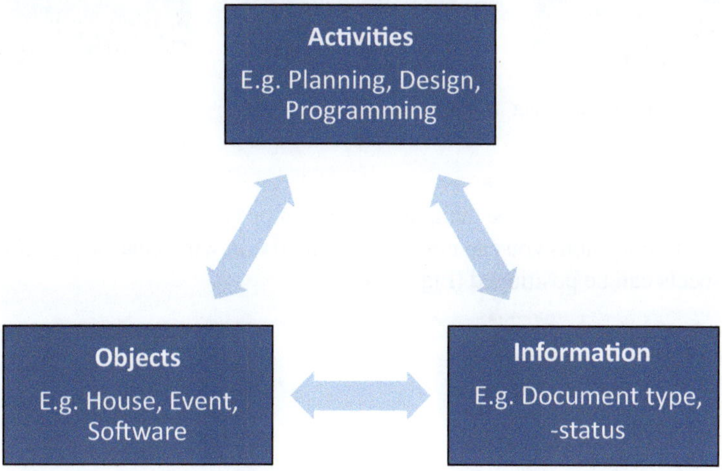

Fig. 9.1 Main dimensions of projects as a triangle

Aspects for project structures (Fig. 9.2) can be classified on the other hand from the point of view of primary leadership dimensions in the project (connection to the company)

- **Project content** ("Thing"): Which project objects are affected by which project activities or affect the project and what project information (knowledge) issued or created? For example, a work package, a subtask.
- **Project agreements** govern the tasks in the project or how is someone affected in the project environment, e.g. basic agreement for work packages, contracts, work orders.
- **Project organizations with their roles and involvement:** Who and how does an affected team member contribute to the project result? Or is his area somehow affected?

"Content", "Agreements", and "Organizations" create a chain of relationships: Contents relationships are linked to the organizations by agreements/contracts.

Fig. 9.2 Aspects of structuring

> Definition: From the main dimensions of projects and the primary management dimensions you can now create a matrix, in which the various classes of aspects can be positioned (Fig. 9.3).

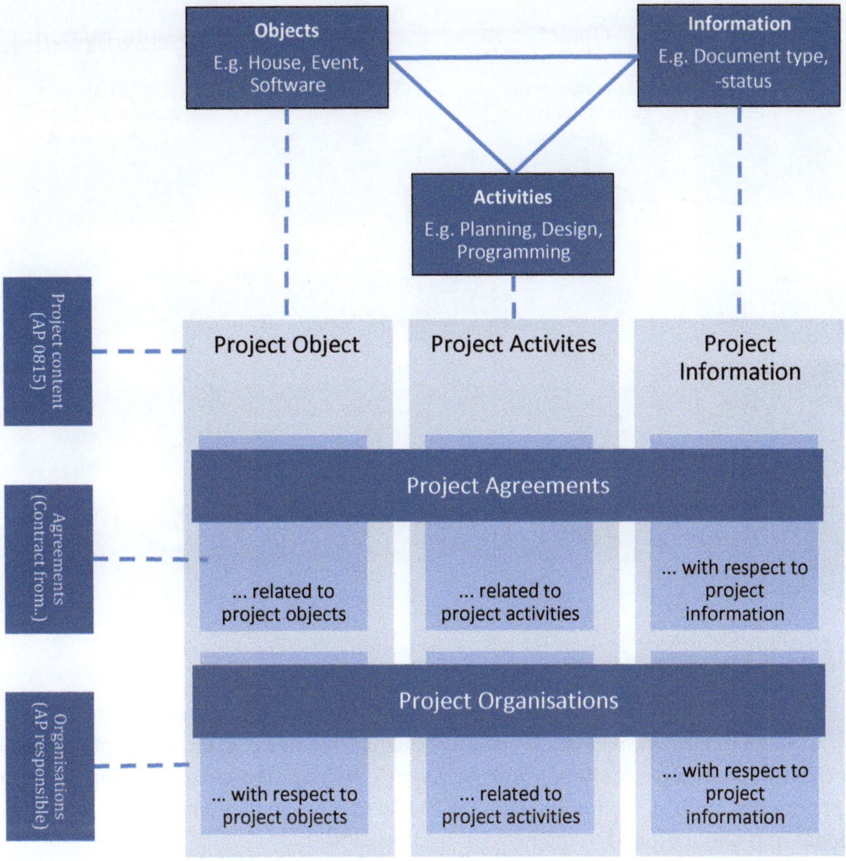

Fig. 9.3 Matrix with various classes of aspects

A core element of the project structuring is the work package (WP). Work packages combine values from one or more aspects of the project content (Fig. 9.4).

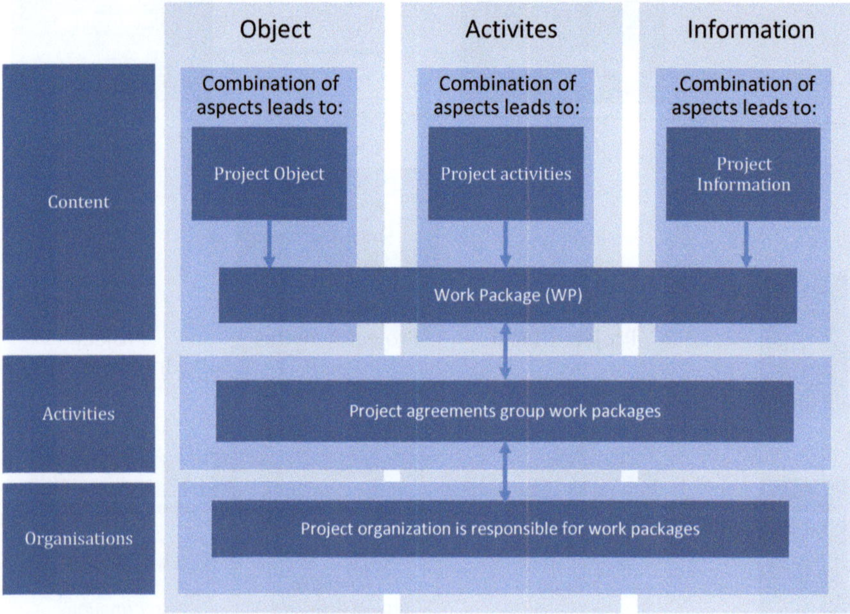

Fig. 9.4 Classification of the work packages

Conclusion: Work packages (usually) change the system, i.e. the content of the project or even the structure. Work packages (WP) are the content of fundamental agreements, such as contracts. Each (WP) has to have an agreement of an organizational unit and assigned to the project organization.

Complex projects are generally separated based on various views or aspects in which the simplest form is a work breakdown structure (WBS) that can no longer meet these complex hierarchical structured requirements.

To capture the complexity of the project, different aspects and views are necessary that inevitably lead to several different work breakdown structures, e.g.:

- **Object-oriented**
- **Phase-oriented**
- **Activity-oriented**
- **Organization-oriented**
- **Cost-oriented**

In this case, we talk about multidimensional project structuring (Fig. 9.4). For simple, non-complex projects, a simple hierarchical project breakdown structure (WBS) is generally sufficient. The essential common aspects are: **Object Orientation**, **Activity Orientation,** and **Phase Orientation.** If more aspects need to be represented, such as a cost structure or an area structure, then these can be illustrated using an encoding system.

9.2 Work Breakdown Structure Set-Up

A hierarchical tree structure—i.e. by layers—is used for the construction of the work breakdown structure.

Elements of the WBS (work breakdown structure) are:

- The so-called root elements—projects, programs
- Sub-projects or tasks, which can be further resolved
- Work packages in the smallest resolved elements

The illustration of a work breakdown structure with its elements is shown in Fig. 9.5.

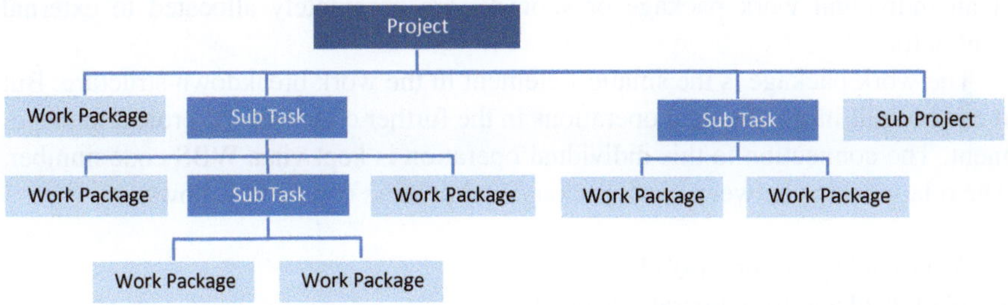

Fig. 9.5 Work breakdown structure according to DIN

We recommend dividing the overall task and the project, beginning with the root element sub-projects, tasks, and work packages into various individual levels (top-down). This process is called **breakdown method** related to DIN. The breakdown method begins with the first level, which represents the name of the project. Then the project is broken down according to a specific classification criterion into different elements. These then shape the second level. The work breakdown structure is finished if all parts of the project are separated into single work packages (DIN 69901-3: 2009).

It has to be ensured that the down-streamed elements in the lower level are fully mapped in the upper parent level. The project Breakdown Structure needs to contain all project tasks that also reflect the total cost structure. The interfaces are significantly dangerous elements as they confine the performance. Work packages can be forgotten or incorrectly split and assigned wrongly. This is in particular significant if an individual work package or subtasks are completely allocated to external contractors.

The work package is the smallest element in the work breakdown structure. But it can be split into individual operations in the further course of the project management. The connection to this individual operation is kept via a WBS code number. The relationships between work package and process can be as follows:

- Work package to process (1:1)
- Work package for n operations (1:n)
- M-Work packages to 1 summary task (m:1)

With these we can be create work breakdown structures with varying degrees of detail:

- Rough schedules for the management
- Workflow for the control level
- Detail workflows the working level

This aspect is important in the transition from the WBS to the **Network Plan**/workflow of importance.

Figure 9.6 shows the basic structure of the **Project Breakdown Plan** and the essential definitions. The root element is in the top level of the WBS. Sub-projects, tasks, and work packages are hierarchically in the lower levels.

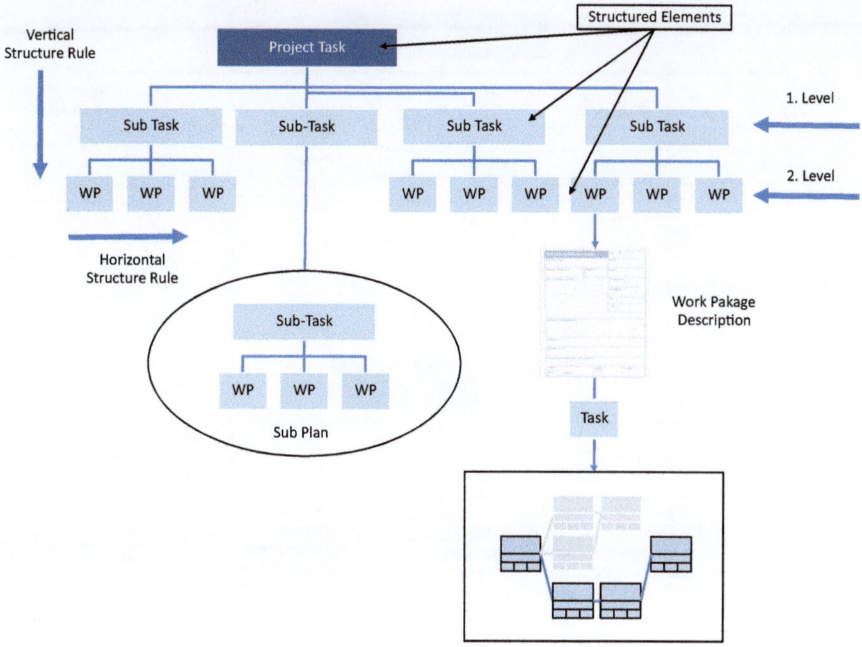

Fig. 9.6 Build of a work breakdown structure

9.3 Principles of Project Structuring

Whilst structuring the project you should consider that projects sometimes completely differ in their characteristics such as:

- Type of project (investment, quality planning projects)
- Complexity (number of the participating departments, sub-projects, etc.)
- Scope of the project (budget)
- Duration of the project (short term up to 6 months, long term up to 10 years)

It requires some experience to define the best possible structure for a project. Following outline principles are often applied as a structuring guide:

- Structure on the object—object-oriented
- Structure on required functions in the project—function- or activity-oriented
- Structure on project phases—phase-oriented
- Structure on responsible organizational units—organization-oriented

Using the "pure" structure for best practice in principle is rare; the mixed-oriented structures are used more often.

Object-Oriented Classification

The project is split into its **Parts, Components**, and **Assemblies.**

The example in Fig. 9.7 shows an object-oriented structure. The work packages are still too big and can be split even further to the next level.

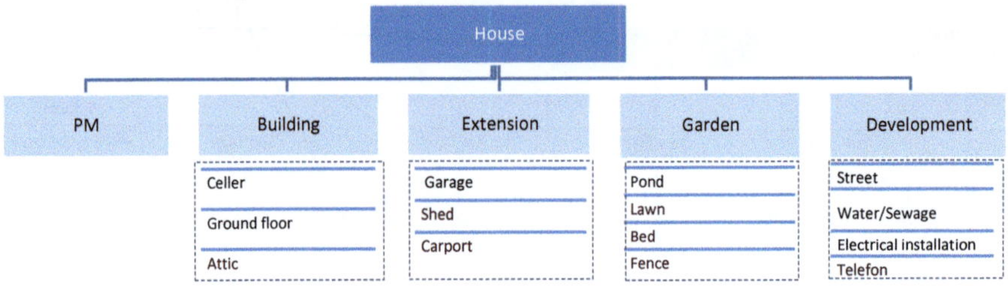

Fig. 9.7 Object-oriented classification

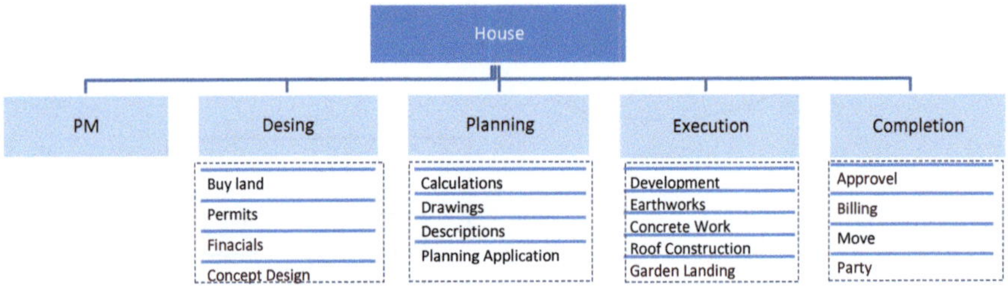

Fig. 9.8 Functional-oriented classification

The activity-oriented (functional-oriented) classification (Fig. 9.8) has subtasks in the first level (functions); actions that are necessary for the completion of the project are cascaded into the other lower levels as processes.

9.4 Work Package Construction

If the classification principle of structuring is set, then the process can continue into 2 directions:

- **Horizontally** within a level to the various objects, phases, and activities (functions): The clean content definition of the elements is important to determine completed, clearly defined elements. This may also result in defining work tasks per element that helps the control functions later on in the project.
- **Vertically** in various levels of increasing detail according to the principle: As accurate as needed, not as accurate as possible. In addition, detailing is possible at any time by inserting another level, if required.

Work packages are the smallest element in the WBP. They include a defined performance with appropriate needs on resources and costs. Performance must be clearly based on the specification book and be capable to control.

In early project phases, the scope/content of a work package can be described roughly; in later stages, e.g. in the process of procurement of services with the controlling process it is necessary to define handlebar work packages. Attempts to define the magnitude of work packages by metrics are not goal targeted. Then the experience of the respective project manager is needed.

Characteristics of Work Packages

- The work includes an enclosed activity that clearly segregates against other work packages.
- Necessarily, the work package completes with a defined result.
- The work package can be—with the exception of the top ones—at all structure levels.
- The work package size should be controllable and manageable—from the point of view of the respective user.
- The work package should be assigned clearly to an organizational unit or internal or external contractors. This aspect plays a major role in the procurement of services and contract design as well as controlling.
- Work package responsibilities need to be assigned.
- A code number can uniquely identify the work package.

Description of Work Packages (Fig. 9.9)
In addition to the WBS the individual work packages must be clearly described and specified:

- Information on the identification
  - Project number and project name
  - Work package description including WBS code number
  - Responsible organization unit, responsible employee
- Information on content/performance (delivery object)
  - Scope of work
  - Results
  - Tasks
  - Dates, resources
  - Cost/Performance
  - Interfaces

<table>
<tr><th colspan="2">Description of Activity</th><th colspan="2">Sourcing of required equipment</th></tr>
<tr><td>Work package</td><td>Pre-Study</td><td>Activity No.</td><td>2.1</td></tr>
<tr><td>Objective</td><td colspan="3">Availability of all equipment to start the manufacturing of the heli- copter and to prepare the measurement construction</td></tr>
<tr><td>result</td><td colspan="3">Availability of the following components:
- Scissors
- Stop watch
- Paper template
- Folding ruler</td></tr>
<tr><td>execution</td><td colspan="3">- Supply equipment from personal inventory
- Purchasing of paper template</td></tr>
<tr><td>Requirements and particularities</td><td colspan="3"></td></tr>
<tr><td>Work load</td><td colspan="3">- 30 min working time</td></tr>
<tr><td rowspan="2">Budget</td><td rowspan="2">- 30 min working time
- Paper template (5.000 €)</td><td>Start time</td><td>End time</td></tr>
<tr><td>12:00</td><td>12:10</td></tr>
<tr><td>Responsible</td><td colspan="3">- Team leader</td></tr>
<tr><td>Personnel</td><td colspan="3">- Quality engineer
- Recycling engineer</td></tr>
</table>

Fig. 9.9 Work package template/example

9.5 Key Takeaways

Through the process of project structuring the project is split and cascaded into different small, manageable units regarding different viewpoints and aspects that are easier to handle for more planning and control phase in the process. The work breakdown structure developed in a project team is the central regulatory instrument that affects all other project management processes.

Based on the objectives, the content of the project, and the project phase plan, the split can be accomplished down to the smallest elements—the work packages. This is done based on different viewpoints, aspects such as object, activities, information, project content, agreements, and organization.

The work breakdown structure has to contain all activities completely and faultlessly, which are required for the project. Depending on the intended use and the respective characteristic aspects we distinguish between object-oriented and activity-oriented (function-oriented, phase-oriented, and mixed structures).

Work packages include activity, resource, and cost requirements and—most important—the establishing of a responsible owner for the work package. For the unique identification the work packages have to have an encoding classification system for secure identification.

The use of standard structure plans may be useful for the structuring of recurring projects or sub-projects.

References

Michael Gessler. (2011). Kompetenzbasiertes Projektmanagement (PM3) Handbuch für die Projektarbeit, Qualifizierung und Zertifizierung auf Basis der IPMA Competence Baseline Version 3.0 / unter Mitwirkung der spm swiss project management association (4. Auflage ed., Vol. 1). Nürnberg: GPM Deutsche Gesellschaft für Projektmanagement.

Deutscher Normenausschuß (Hrsg.): D1N 69901: Projektmanagement. (2009a). Berlin.

Deutscher Normenausschuss (Hrsg.): DIN 69902 Projektwirtschaft, Einsatzmittel, Begriffe. (2009b). Berlin.

Scope and Deliverables 10

This chapter focuses on the definition of a project, including the designation of who is responsible for what progress by when. By definition, those applying project management methods must answer some or all of these questions in the first phase of their system improvement or new system design projects. Also, according to what may be regarded as a defining principle of project management, projects must be cost-justified or they should not be completed. Often in practice the needed cost justification must be established by the end of the **define** phase.

The most relevant strategies associated with answering these questions relate to identifying so-called subsystems and their associated key input variables (KPIVs) including the Voice of the Customer (VOC) and key output variables (KOVs).

Therefore, the chapter begins with an explanation of VOC and the concept of systems and subsystems. Then, strategies are briefly defined to help in the identification of subsystems and associated goals for KOVs. Next, specific methods are described to facilitate the development of a project charter.

As a preliminary, consider that the first step in important projects involves searching the available literature. Search engines such as Google can be relevant and, also, technical indexes such as the science citation index. Finally, consider using governmental resources such as the National Institute of Standards (NIST), the Patent Office web sites, and the Federal Statistical Office.

10.1 The Customer (VOC)

What is a customer? Every process/system has a deliverable. The person or entity who receives this deliverable is a customer. There are two different types of customers, **External and Internal**. People generally forget about the Internal customer and they are just as important as the customers who are buying your product. There are different types of customers, which dictate how we interact with them in the

P. Bauer, *A Comprehensive Project Management Guide*, Management for Professionals, https://doi.org/10.1007/978-3-031-68252-0_10

process. In order to identify customer and supplier requirements we must first define who the customers are:

- **External**
  - Direct: those who receive the output of your services; they generally are the source of your revenue.
  - Indirect: those who do not receive or pay for the output of your services but have a vested interest in what you do (government agencies).
- **Internal**
  - Those within your organization who receive the output of your work.

Knowing your customer is more than just a handshake. It is necessary to clearly understand their needs. Using Six Sigma understanding the customer needs are called “CTQs” or Critical to Customer characteristics.

Doing this allows you to find all of the necessary information that is relevant between your product/process and customer, better known as CTQs (Critical to Quality). The CTQs are the customer requirements for satisfaction with your product or service.

There are four steps that can help to understand the customer. These steps focus on the customer’s perspective of features, the company’s integrity, delivery mechanisms, and perceived value versus cost. Voice of the Customer or VOC seems obvious; after all, we all know what the customer wants. Or do we? The customer’s perspective has to be foremost in the mind project leader throughout the whole project cycle.

1. **Features**
   (a) Does the process provide what the customers expect and need?
   (b) How do you know?
2. **Integrity**
   (a) Is the relationship with the customer centred on trust?
   (b) How do you know?
3. **Delivery**
   (a) Does the process meet the customer’s time frame?
   (b) How do you know?
4. **Expense**
   (a) Does the customer perceive value for cost?—How do you know?

10.2 Systems and Subsystems

A system comprises inputs and outputs, whilst a “subsystem” is a self-contained system within a larger one, sharing some inputs and outputs with its parent system. Figure 10.1 illustrates three subsystems nested within a system (see Example of Subsystems Inside a System on page 202).

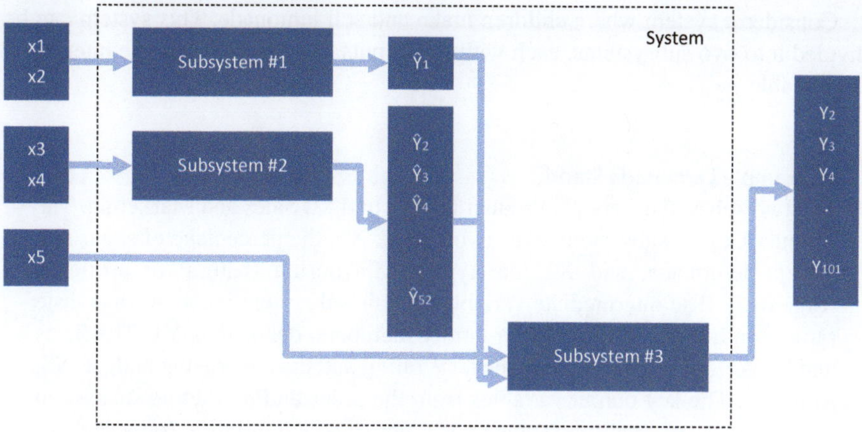

Fig. 10.1 Example of subsystems inside a system

The primary objective of the "define phase" is to pinpoint specific subsystems and concentrate on them. Typically, the key deliverable from this phase is a charter, which outlines goals for subsystem outputs.

☞ Example: In relation to a chess game system, one strategy to increase one's chance of success is to memorize recommended lists of responses to the first set of "opening" moves. The first opening set of moves constitutes only a fraction of the inputs needed for playing an entire game and rarely by itself guarantees victory. Yet, for a novice, focusing attention on the chess opening subsystem is often a useful strategy.

Figure 10.1 illustrates output variables $\hat{Y}1$, …, $\hat{Y}52$ from subsystems that are specific to those subsystems and are not direct outputs of the entire system. We designate these as "intermediate variables", which are key outputs (KOVs) from subsystems serving as inputs to other subsystems. Thus, individuals in one subsystem may not directly control intermediate variables but might influence them within a different subsystem context.

For instance, in chess, scoring is an intermediate variable that assigns points to captured pieces. A high score in one phase of the game does not guarantee victory, but scores often help predict outcomes. Experts analysing endgame strategies may attribute specific point values to different moves. Generally, winning or losing constitutes the primary output variable for the entire system.

Consider a system where children make and sell lemonade. This system can be divided into two subsystems, each with two inputs and outputs, and one intermediate variable.

☞ Example Lemonade Stand

The two subsystems are (1) Product Design and (2) Sales and Marketing. The Product Design subsystem takes two inputs: X1, the percentage of sugar in a cup of lemonade, and X2, the type of flavouring (natural or artificial) (Fig. 10.2). The intermediate variable for this subsystem is the average taste rating (on a scale of 1–10) from family members, denoted as $\hat{Y}1$. The Sales and Marketing subsystem uses the taste rating and the advertising budget, X3, as inputs. The key output variables from the Sales and Marketing subsystem are the profit, y1, and the average customer satisfaction rating (on a scale of 1–10), Y2.

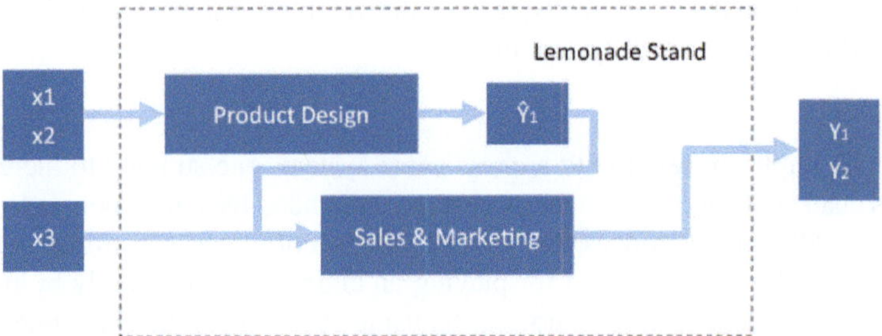

Fig. 10.2 Lemonade stand system with two subsystems

10.3 The Project Charter

A written "Charter" often marks the conclusion of the project's initial phase. This charter outlines the project's objectives, the responsible parties, and the timeline (Fig. 10.3) for a summary of key issues typically covered in charters. The primary focus when developing a charter is to clarify what can be achieved within the project's time frame and with the available resources. The term "Scope" is used to formally describe the project's tasks, whilst "Deliverables" refer to the outcomes associated with the project scope. Although traditionally deliverables are tangible objects, they can also be intangible, like equations or key ideas.

Creating a charter can be a complex, political process. Assigning the selected team for a specified duration represents a significant and risky investment by management, who are essentially betting that the project's deliverables will be valuable upon completion. The main reason for a formal design phase is to separate the complex, management-level decisions from the more technical, detailed decisions necessary for completing the project and its deliverables.

Developing a charter involves creating a semi-formal contract between management and the project team, delineating what is "in scope" and what is "out of scope" or unnecessary for project success. This agreement helps protect team members from new, unanticipated demands, known as "scope creep", which might arise during the project's subsequent phases. Protection against scope creep fosters a supportive environment, increasing the likelihood of delivering the project on time and within budget.

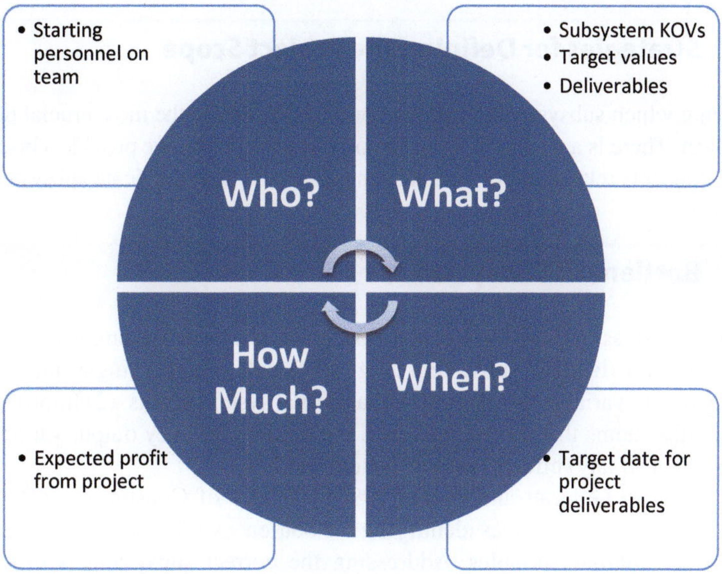

Fig. 10.3 Possible issues addressed by a project charter

Project **goals** in the charter are typically articulated as targets for system key output variables (KOVs). Often, the project's scope requires that measurable KOVs be intermediate variables associated with subsystems. According to the principle of cost justification, at least one KOV for these subsystems must likely impact the bottom-line profits of the major system. Frequently, projects concentrate on a small subsystem that isn't fully autonomous within a company, making it challenging to assess the project's financial impact on the company's bottom line. Nonetheless, making an effort to establish this linkage is generally deemed essential.

10.4 Strategies for Defining the Project Scope

Identifying which subsystem to improve or design is likely the most crucial decision in a project. There is a wealth of literature on this topic. Here, we provide a brief overview of concepts related to bottleneck subsystems and near-duplicate subsystems.

10.5 Bottleneck Subsystems

The relevant ideas to consider are as follows: (1) In a large system, there is almost always one **"bottleneck"** subsystem (Fig. 10.4), which has a single intermediate, truly key output variable that directly impacts total system profits. (2) Improvements to other subsystems that do not influence the bottleneck's key output variable will have minimal (if any) effects on total system profits.

According to Goldratt and Cox's (1992) "Theory of Constraints" (TOC), the improvement process involves identifying the bottleneck subsystems and enhancing the truly key output variables. Addressing the correct subsystem is crucial for impacting total system profits effectively.

Many individuals may not have the opportunity to work on bottleneck subsystems. Consequently, TOC suggests that their efforts are unlikely to significantly impact the bottom line. Additionally, any bottom-line savings predicted by those not working on these subsystems should be viewed with scepticism. However, TOC provides some reassurance: if the bottleneck system is improved or alleviated by others, the previously considered subsystem may become the new bottleneck, presenting an opportunity for future impact.

10.6 Go-No-Go Decisions

The term **"Categorical Factor"** refers to inputs that have only qualitatively distinct settings. **"Design Concept"** is used to describe one specific setting of a categorical factor. For example, in the context of a car, a rear engine is a design concept that represents one setting of the categorical factor "engine type". When developing systems and subsystems, the number of design concepts considered at any one time is limited due to resource constraints. The phrase "**Go-No-Go** Decisions" pertains to the possible exclusion of certain design concepts or projects from further consideration. For instance, a costly method for arc welding aluminium might be discarded in favour of a more economical alternative following a go-no-go decision.

A key objective in improvement or design projects is to make these go-no-go decisions decisively. For example, when addressing an automotive joining design problem, the design concept of snap tabs might compete with screws. The team would assess the strength of snap tabs to determine which concept to adopt.

Another related consideration is the presence of nearly identical subsystems. For example, multiple product lines could potentially benefit from changing their joining method to snap tabs. This scenario allows one subsystem to be tested, leading to multiple go-no-go decisions across similar systems. "Worst-case analysis" refers to the practice where engineers experiment with the most challenging subsystem and then make go-no-go decisions for all other nearly identical systems based on the results.

☞ Example: Lemonade Stand Improvement Strategy

Children are selling pink and yellow lemonade on a busy street bustling with potential customers. Both types of lemonade contain the same fraction of sugar. However, word-of-mouth feedback indicates that both lemonades, especially the pink one, are perceived as too sweet, resulting in lost sales. The cost of materials is negligible. Using the Theory of Constraints (TOC) and worst-case analysis, identify a subsystem for improvement with one key input variable (KIV) and one key output variable (KOV).

The answer is: TOC suggests targeting the apparent bottleneck, which in this case is the product design subsystem, as shown in Fig. 10.4. This focus is recommended because manufacturing costs are minimal, and potential customers are already aware of the products. A worst-case analysis strategy further narrows down the focus to the pink lemonade design subsystem. The rationale is that determining the optimal fraction of sugar input factor (X1) for the pink lemonade is likely to enhance sales for both pink and yellow lemonade. A reasonable intermediate variable to concentrate on would be the average taste rating ($\hat{Y}1$).

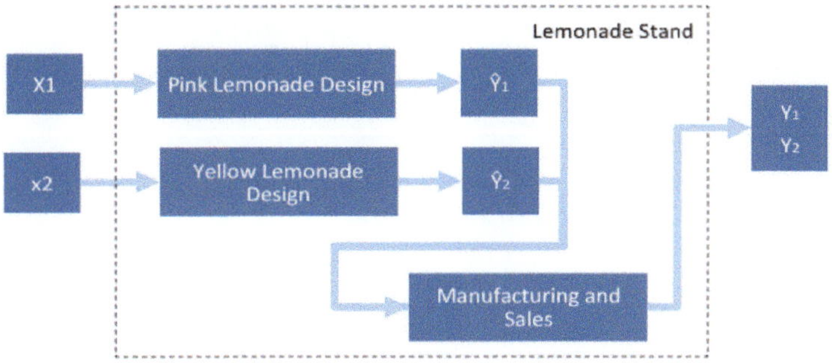

Fig. 10.4 Lemonade stand subsystems and strategy

10.7 Methods for Scoping

Several methods are valuable during the define phase, including **Pareto Charting** (Sect. 5.18) and **Benchmarking**, which sets a standard for system outputs useful for evaluating design choices. Meeting rules are also important, as meetings are a common feature in virtually all organizations and project phases. They are particularly relevant in the define phase because developing an effective charter often requires input from many people. Additionally, methods such as process mapping and value stream mapping can also contribute to the development of project charters.

Reference

Michael Gessler. (2011). Kompetenzbasiertes Projektmanagement (PM3) Handbuch für die Projektarbeit, Qualifizierung und Zertifizierung auf Basis der IPMA Competence Baseline Version 3.0 / unter Mitwirkung der spm swiss project management association (4. Auflage ed., Vol. 1). Nürnberg: GPM Deutsche Gesellschaft für Projektmanagement.

11 Project Phases

Subsequently, the abstract delves into the typical phases of the project life cycle, including initiation, planning, execution, monitoring and controlling, and closure. It discusses the primary objectives and activities associated with each phase, emphasizing the iterative and interdependent nature of project work and the need for continuous alignment with project goals and stakeholder expectations. Basics:

Phases (Fig. 11.1) of a project are divided into time and/or objective sections. Phases create a first basic rough structure, provide orientation, and reduce the complexity of a project. Each phase meets specific goals in the overall project, resulting in the question how does a phase perform and what is the output. It results in the questions: In which sections can the project be divided (**Phases**)? And what output is generated out of these phases (**Milestones**)?

Milestones are defined events of particular importance. These include in particular (1) **Deliverables** or even intermediate results, (2) **Tests** such as inspections, intermediate inspections, or also reviews, and (3) **Decisions** (e.g. may the next phase start or not: go/no go)? Milestones are also usually placed at the beginning (phase release) or at the end of a phase (phase end) and therefore also mark the (4) **Phase Transitions**.

The structuring of a project into phases and milestones offers several advantages:

- Structuring the project into sections allows a first fundamental orientation at an early stage and reduces complexity. A phase plan allows an early high-level overview of a project.
- Project phases are a possible structuring principle to create a work breakdown structure and thus create a "link" between gross and fine planning. It also offers a grid for fine structuring.
- Project phases allow the phase-related mapping and phase-based controlling of milestone targets, resources, costs, and financial resources. For this reason, they are useful for project planning and project management.

P. Bauer, *A Comprehensive Project Management Guide*, Management for Professionals, https://doi.org/10.1007/978-3-031-68252-0_11

- Project phases allow phase-related planning and the adapting of the project Organization. The phase transitions provide a systematic occasion to clarify competences, responsibilities, and authorities for the next phase.
- Milestones allow the orderly completion of a project section (closeout) as well as the orderly transition to the next section of the project (startup). They are very helpful for quality assurance (e.g. quality gate) and finally for the project closure.
- Milestones allow a continuous integration of the project contracting authority or Steering Committee through the decisions at the end of each phase and the individual phase release.
- Milestones allow a continuous goal orientation for employees, the experience of phase achievements, and a synchronization of the teamwork. These are also tools for leadership and motivation!

However, there are drawbacks by structuring a project by phases and milestones:

On the one hand, a phase plan reduces the complexity of a project; on the other hand, the early planning phases and milestones can restrict the flexibility required. Project planning seen as anticipating future actions has limits, if the stakeholders do not have the necessary experience, to realistically anticipate activities and events. Planning also then reaches limits when the individual experience level is high, but the substantive requirements are unstable and change in the course of the project. Especially innovative projects, which have often indistinct and unstable requirements, cannot be planned in a technocratic and strictly sequential manner very well.

A way of flexibility could then be to subdivide the project into phases, without however creating a detailed plan for the entire project. The detailed planning is done then only at the end of a phase and for the succeeding phase. This principle is used for example in PRINCE 2:

Planning the next phase always happens at the end of the previous phase. However, for the transition phase the "transfer principle" applies: Basically, the transition to the next phase is "locked". Only if the project has shown the results required are still to plan and the business case is still on track ("viable") and the next phase is planned, the Steering Committee then decides to enter into the next phase. The principle of locks restricts the flexibility in the transition phase.

The solution to the problem "Planning ahead is not possible" is not to avoid planning altogether, but to shorten the interval between detailed planning and execution. A similar method that includes the agile project management represents yet another way. These methods are similar, because they also work with the shortening of the time intervals. They are different, since they use daily team meetings to adjust. The detailed planning is not by releasing detailed planning documents (e.g. PRINCE 2), but by communicating locally. Similar is also the use of so-called **time boxes** that is part of the APM agile project management, a method that incorporates various elements of SCRUM, plays a central role, and remembers one of the combination of phase and milestone: "A time box defines a unchangeable set time frame; at its end there should be an amount of results in specific detail and quality including available formal documentation. As the results are not achieved as planned, these are then moved into the succeeding time box. To do this, the results actually achieved are determined at the scheduled finish date. A time box is a tool for planning and monitoring a development process. On the other hand, it does not dispense the use of planning but shapes a flexible transition phase between the time boxes.

> 🕮Conclusion: Phases, milestones, and the design of transitions in any form whatsoever represent a necessary PM—Instrument; however, this predictive modelling never captures the 1:1 reality to 100% but is still necessary.

11.1 Project Management and Project Phases

DIN 69901–2: 2009 differentiates on the one hand project management phases and on the other project phases. Project **management phases** are equally present in all projects as they are regardless of the specific problem or the specific context fundamental requirements of project work. Project management phases according to DIN 69901–2:2009 are:

- **Initiating phase**: All the activities and processes of the formal initialization of a project (e.g. clarify responsibilities, outline project objectives)
- **Definition phase**: All activities and processes for the definition of a project (including the definition of objectives, estimation, and feasibility assessment)
- **Planning phase**: All the activities and processes of the formal planning of a project (including event and work packages planning, create costs and funding plan, analyse risks, create resource plan)
- **Steering phase**: All of the activities and processes of the formal control of a project (including the control of dates, resources, costs and funding, risks, quality, goals)
- **Closing phase**: All activities and processes to the formal termination of a project including preparation of the project completion report, cost calculation, preserve experience (prevent recurrence), termination of the contract).

The sum of the above-mentioned project management phases forms the project life cycle. The phases are each named after those PM activities that mostly characterize a PM phase.

Project phases, unlike the project management phases, are product-specific and contextual. They differ from project type to project type (e.g. investment projects or quality planning projects) from branch to branch (such as building trade or information/communication) and from quality planning to quality planning.

11.2 Milestones and Gateways

As mentioned at the beginning, each phase closes or starts with at least one milestone; however, milestones can also lie within a phase. As a valid rule of thumb: we can determine that the time intervals between the milestones of the total duration of a project are dependent on length of the project. Milestones can also be determined by other factors such as risk, quality, and/or the project quality planning form. Nevertheless, milestones are derived particularly from the objectives of the project. Event goals can also be part of the project's objectives (see Chap. 3).

It is also essential for milestones to follow the same objective setting logic as the project goals and to operationalize them, to make them measurable. For this indicators or criterion is required. Each review is unpredictable without predefined criteria. In process model's milestone results are often stored in specifications, checklists, or forms. This applies especially to product-centric process models that define the timing, dependencies between processes, and responsibilities about products (results) and activities. The V-Modell XT and PRINCE 2 follow this philosophy. It also distinguishes who is involved as a milestone: The ordering party or Steering Committee is involved in external milestones. The responsibility for the decision (such as go/no go) is at the principal or at the Steering Committee level. Internal metrics can themselves be internal milestones for the project and even be control elements for the project manager.

Stages and gates: NASA developed the stage-gate principle in the 1960s. Characteristic of a gate is that all activities of a phase must be completed before the next phase can be started. Gates are located at the end of a phase and contain measurement and decision points throughout the course of the project. They correspond to the milestones at the end of a phase. The key focus is particular on whether there are any results. Not only the project is taken into consideration but also especially the environment (including market relevance, competition, technological development). The gate itself remained a lock; this approach however often leads to delays. In the concepts of the third generation (from the middle of the 1990s), overlaps are finally allowed by phases: sequence phases can begin as soon as a defined minimum standard is achieved; adjustments are possible within a defined period in the succession phase (see figure 60).

In addition to securing the product quality, the quality of supplier integration and the overall quality of synchronizing processes play a central role from the very beginning, which is why the gates are often also called **quality gate.** To additionally secure quality, the interaction between processes and structures and the operational and organizational structures on the one hand and the project and root organization on the other hand count heavily.

At a quality gate the progress of a project is assessed, evaluated, and decided whether to move to the next quality gate; in addition, the objectives can be adjusted and the release of the next project phase can be delayed or even cancelled. An auditor (so-called **Gatekeeper**) is selected normally by the Steering Committee to recommend the next steps based on their analysis and results.

Quality gates can help to control the project landscape in an organization using a comprehensive process. The testing of quality gates is often called reviews. Some people have the opinion that good project management should include no more than six gates, because otherwise too much attention will flow into the gate reviews. In any case, the number of quality gates is to be kept as low as possible, whilst the number of milestones is dependent on the number of phases, as well as the objectives.

Milestones secure the process of being able to work in a goal- and results-oriented manner in the project and are also an important control instrument for the project manager. Milestones motivate and fulfil the goal functions **Control, Orientation, Connections, Coordination,** and **Selection**. Quality gates have broad requirements (project and environment, checking and synchronization, project team and customer/Steering Committee) and are an important control instrument in particular in project environments. The following illustration shows a vehicle development phase model (Fig. 11.1).

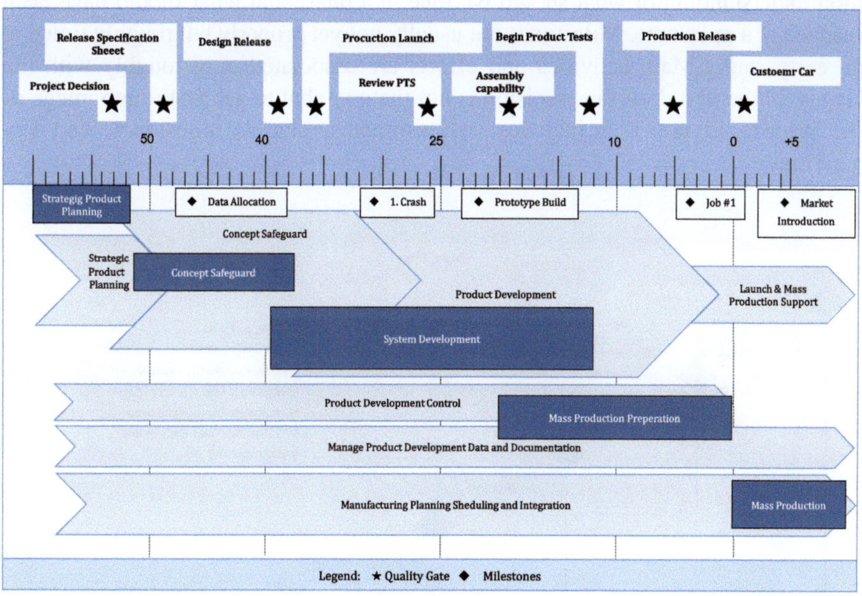

Fig. 11.1 Phase model automotive product development

11.3 Phase Plan

Phase plans can be created already at an early stage, to get a quick overview of the upcoming project. Already with the first target draft it is possible to create a rough phase plan. It is helpful to use a basic schema and to divide the task into five phases related to DIN (69901–2). This is then substantiated based on context and product specifics (targeting system) and further concretized within the progressive planning process. To at least roughly specify the phases, it is helpful to even name and define the main activities at the beginning. Frequently only a top-down complexity estimation is possible. This first estimate is usually very inaccurate (possibly deviations up to 300%). Therefore, it is very useful to use **Analogy Conclusions**: Do industry-specific guidelines exist? Are there references based on project types or company-specific process models? Is there any useful experience from other projects?

The naming of phases and milestones is usually company-specific and it is also irrelevant how they are named. However, it is far more important that there is a common understanding of what should be done in a phase and what should have been reached at a milestone. Milestones are usually not yet properly but roughly timed at an early stage. Main activities and efforts are associated only roughly with the stages. In the first draft the precision is not the goal, but to get first rough image of the project. Figure 11.2 includes cost estimates, phases, milestones, and key activities.

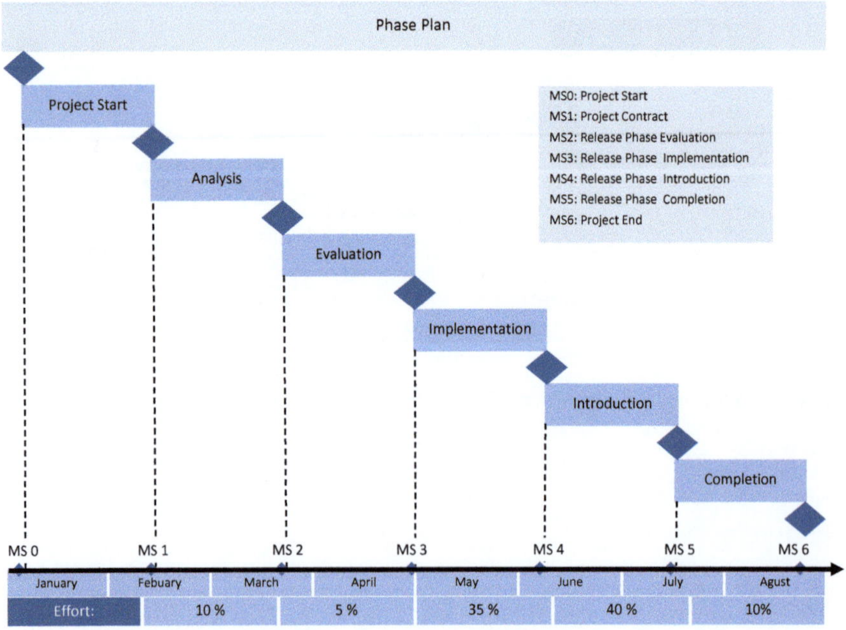

Fig. 11.2 Phase plan example

11.4 Process Models

The task of a project is to develop one or more solutions for a specific problem. This process is also known as the problem-solving process. A method contains the rules for the targeted and efficient solution of problems. A number of so-called process models were specially developed for the execution of projects.

> Definition: A process model is a standardized model to support a consistent approach in project execution.

The following features characterize process models:

- There are several steps that must be run through whilst developing a project solution.
- These steps are arranged in chronological and/or logical order.
- The steps must be repeated in exceptional or non-exceptional cases.

The use of process models can even be mandatory, for example the HOAI process—"Ordinance on the fees of architects and engineers" (see Table 11.1 Six Sigma (DMAIC, DFFS), KAIZEN, LEAN, KANBAN. A process model selected for a project must always be adapted to the current tasks of the project and the necessary activities must be aligned to the scope and goals.

This customization and detailing process is called **tailoring**.

Table 11.1 Work phases referred to the § HOAI

1. Establishing the basis of the project
2. Preliminary design
3. Final design (system and integration planning)
4. Building permission application
5. Execution drawings
6. Preparation of contracted assignment
7. Assisting assignment process
8. Project supervision
9.Project control and documentation

> Definition: Tailoring involves the adaptation and detailed planning of a process model in a specific project task.

The tailoring of selected process model leads to a catalogue of the procedures which shapes the basis for the further planning of the project.

11.5 The Process Model of System Engineering

The concept of system engineering consists of a set of methods and procedures that facilitate the intellectual discussion of complex issues. The concept of system engineering finds its original application in the design of technical systems, where the design is mainly based on cause–effect and processes interactions. The concept corresponds to the idea of creative engineering activity, which is reflected in the term "engineering". In the industry the system thinking method is increasingly being used, in particular for solving technical information interface problems, and has demonstrated extraordinary capability; the application of the system approach is not only limited to technical issues, but can be applied readily for managerial and organizational problems.

The system engineering process model describes the process of problem-solving from the first kick-off through system planning, realization, and control: it is based on the following four fundamental ideas.

1. **The process principle "From the Rough to the Detail"**

   The process principle "From the Rough to the Detail" specifies to view and include initially a wide observation area and then to gradually narrow it down step by step. According to the hierarchical system thinking the problem is then structured and described regarding its major subsystems and interfaces. Only global goals are defined and a general solution framework is established. In the further process the problem is increasingly detailed and defined.

   The principle "From the Rough to the Detail" (also named "**Top-Down**" Principle) is to prevent problem analysis and problem-solving from being started; in fact, a total concept needs to be developed for complex problems. However, it does not exclude that similar known problem solutions that have occurred in the past are used for introducing direct specific detailed solutions. This results in the "bottom-up approach" which is basically the summation of the individual actions.
2. **Structure of the System Design in Stages**

   The process of system design is a breakdown of logical and chronologically detached steps. The process is divided into several manageable and controllable sections, each associated with characteristic results. By doing this, generally the steps of system planning, system execution, and system implementation and introduction are differentiated. The level of the system planning according to the two first principles is further differentiated and divided in the planning stages of the feasibility study, the main study, and pre-studies.

3. **The Principle of the Progressive Alternative Solutions/Rejection** (Fig. 11.3)
   There are usually several ways of solving a problem. It corresponds with the procedure principle of system engineering to provide a broad overview of the solutions that are possible on a certain detailed level. This involves less solution variants, which differ only in details, but rather the search for fundamental alternatives.
   With respect to the principle of the process "From the Rough to Detail" the principle of alternative development applies to all levels of detail; however, this would increase the number of possible solution options with each further step. The further scoping of all alternatives would then need immense time and efforts to handle.

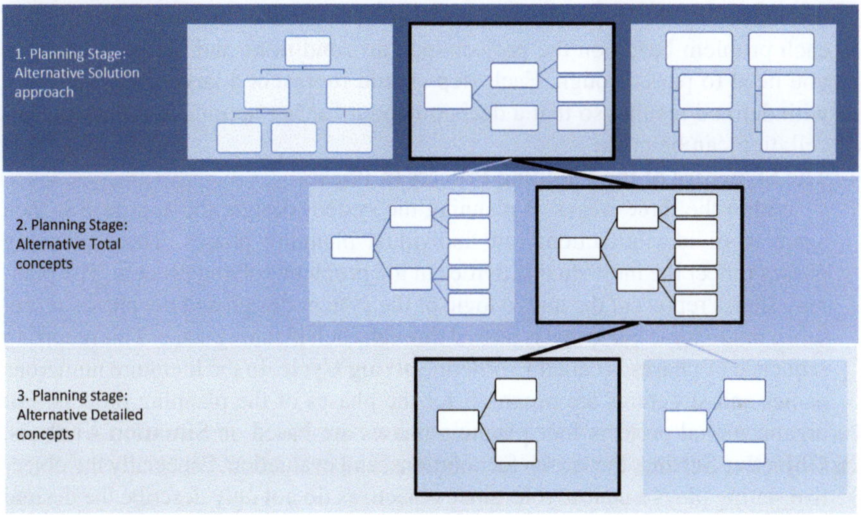

Fig. 11.3 Progressive alternative composition and rejection

The step-by-step breakdown sometimes does not seem feasible due to not having a complete overview of all detailed questions. In this case you must step back and return to a higher level and find a new problem-solving structure to follow. If the risk associated with the selected problem-solving structure is too high and the risk of following more than one alternative solution is manageable, it can make sense also to simultaneous follow alternative solutions and break them down into more detailed levels. Even if the alternative solutions are not feasible there is still high confidence that the **one** problem solution will be feasible. There is a big risk if the principle of progressive alternative solution is not considered because all possible solutions are then put forward in an advanced phase of the system planning. This is normally too late as this would mean to either jump back to the system planning or to do without an optimal solution. The number of levels for a project depends on the scope and the importance of a problem; consequently, you need to adapt each problem based on the project-specific conditions and define what steps you need to pass through. Each step should represent a largely shielded unit with defined results, so that a decision about further actions or a project cancellation can be made.

4. **The Structure of the Planning Process in Phases**

   Within the three stages of planning the system design, the approach is then again to divide the actions into individual planning phases. These planning phases reflect the individual activities in the problem-solving process. The planning stages represent the macro logic of the system design and the phases represent a micro logic cycle that is passed through each planning stage. This recurring sequence of phases is called **Problem-Solving Cycle**. In the literature numerous names and structures are proposed for the phases of the planning process. For organizational projects four planning phases are based on **Situation Analysis**, **Objective Setting**, the search for solutions, and evaluation. Especially the objective setting plays a central role, since objectives do not only describe the desired target state but also serves as guidance in finding solutions as well as being used as a performance metric.

11.6 Process Model for Handling Organizational Projects

Organizational structures are considered as a tool to achieve the objectives of the institution "Organization" well and efficiently. The organizational structures can be designed in a conscious and rational analytical manner and if needed it can adjust. The organizational design is seen as an essential management function; here the term **Functional Quality Planning** comprises all of the incoming activities. The organizational change or redesign aims primarily at the rationally planned changes of existing or introduction of new management, information, and process structures and intervenes by changing the entire or parts of the organizational structure of a company. The limit setting for the responsible assigned organizational change leader largely influences the success of the organizational measures.

Reorganization (also restructuring) is probably the most common type of organizational change. The systems and resources or the technical infrastructure are very often subject to reorganization. The improvement of processes, the reduction of jobs, and the introduction of new management structures are also typical reorganization measures. Usually, companies do not have unstructured organizations resulting in not having the need to create a total new organizational structure. Even if there is no formal organizational structure usually informal structures exist which must be defined.

A process model has a great value for the work of the organization: it offers safety and guidance in solving complex design problems and supports a consistent, systematic, and goal-oriented approach together with the ideas of project management. The project progress is controlled by clearly defined intermediate verifiable results that offer valuable assistance in monitoring the project progress. The model shown in Fig. 11.4, has proved itself to be practical for the work of the organization:

- The problem-solving process is divided in principle into the stages of **Planning, Implementing, Establishing,** and **Controlling**. The process model used here is based on the principle "From the Rough to the Detail" using a detailed structure and cascading further step by step with the pre-study, the main study, and partial studies. These develop into **six-stage** project execution.
- In the three planning stages of the project, the creative problem-solving activities are executed; this is divided into **four planning phases.** This could also be a five-stage Six Sigma DMAIC process.

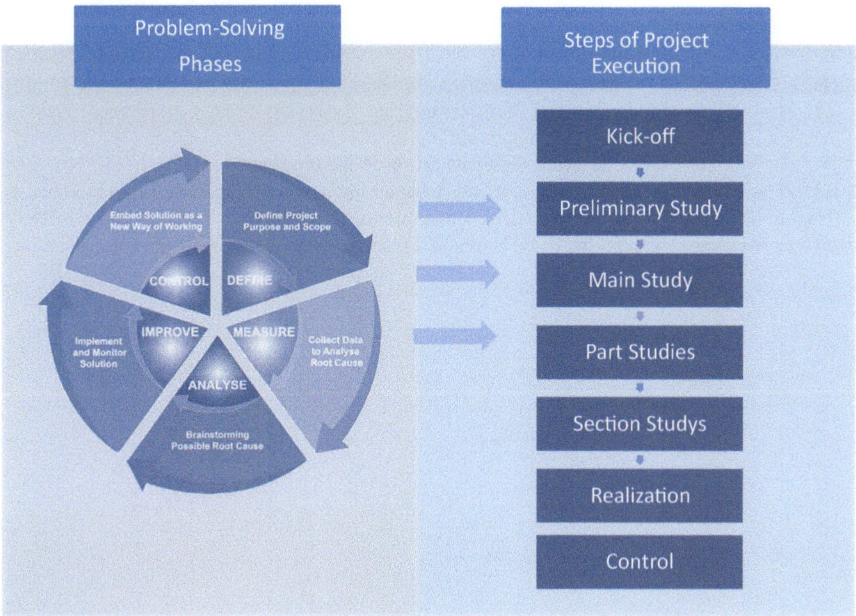

Fig. 11.4 Stages and phases of an organizational project

To use a model in the organizational design is critical, because by using a rational analytical procedure you think you are following a secure path; unluckily this does not work. Many organizational projects fail, because common phenomena such as rejection, resistance, and the struggles for power are not adequately accounted for.

It is therefore appropriate to combine the approach of the organization design with elements of organizational development and to add more levels of intervention. Methods, which consider the voice of participants and the people concerned, have the highest probability and the best chances to be implemented and successful.

Individual activities of the problem solution process can be effectively supported by appropriate techniques. The techniques represent the toolbox of project work. These tools have their specific fields of application; like all tools the success depends on the proper usage. For that matter the following recommendations should be followed:

- By using alternative techniques, the balance between resource expenses, timing impact, and the correctness and accuracy of the obtained statement is optimal.
- The degree of perfection used with these technologies should also be dependent on the correctness and accuracy of the results. In addition, all involved should understand the techniques used to be able to understand the results and statements.

As a reference chapter (Sect. 5.9) describe the usage and some technologies of process models:

References

Michael Gessler. (2011). Kompetenzbasiertes Projektmanagement (PM3) Handbuch für die Projektarbeit, Qualifizierung und Zertifizierung auf Basis der IPMA Competence Baseline Version 3.0 / unter Mitwirkung der spm swiss project management association (4. Auflage ed., Vol. 1). Nürnberg: GPM Deutsche Gesellschaft für Projektmanagement.

Prof Dr. Shulte Zurhausen, M. (2010). Project-/Change Management/Organisation Lerneinheit 1. Hagen: Institut für Verbundstudien der Fachhochschule NRW.

Deutscher Normenausschuß (Hrsg.): D1N 69901: Projektmanagement. (2009). Berlin.

Agile Project Management 12

At the beginning of the new millennium, the book *Extreme Programming Explained* by Kent Beck propagated a paradigm shift away from the traditional plan-driven ways of acting in software projects. The term "agile development" chosen a short time later by Beck and similarly qualified colleagues strives for higher effectiveness of project work through flexible, "lightweight" processes.

It was initially limited to the software world and was only marginally noticed by established project management. However, agile working methods in development also require tailored "agile" management. The protagonists of agile software development have therefore always taken care of project management in agile projects. These agile management approaches are always interesting for all types of projects, even outside the software area, when you are dealing with unpredictable projects. Agile software development has now become agile project management.

Since its inception in the 1960s, project management has been characterized by engineering and systems engineering approaches that originally emerged in the aerospace industry. Projects then begin with the elaboration of as complete a set of requirements as possible for the result to be developed, which are documented in extensive specifications for development projects. This is followed by an initially rough and then increasingly refined system design; the development, design, and programming work; and finally the testing and system introduction.

This approach, also known as the waterfall model, sounds good in principle, but has always had its weaknesses: The requirements determined at the beginning of the project with great effort often proved to be incomplete and unstable in the further course of the project. In addition, global competition, growing market dynamics, and more complex technologies since the 1990s required ever shorter project durations and more frequent technical changes during the project. Many customers were also overwhelmed to formulate their requirements for a new system precisely at the beginning of the project.

Most of the methods they found were not completely new but were based on the iterative and incremental process models already presented in the 1970s in which a

P. Bauer, *A Comprehensive Project Management Guide*, Management for Professionals, https://doi.org/10.1007/978-3-031-68252-0_12

software system is broken down into subsystems and functionality is added and improved.

12.1 Agile Project Management Using the Example of Serum

At this point, the process of agile projects is first illustrated by the example of the **serum method**. Compared to other agile approaches, serum is more focused on the **management of projects** than on software engineering issues. The serum method is therefore also a **representative example of agile project management**. Serum assumes that development processes are so complex and dynamic that they **cannot be reliably planned either in whole or in parts.** Traditional **work package** and scheduling techniques are not suitable for such uncertain planning situations. Instead, serum works with an experience-driven, empirical project management method that dispenses with binding plan specifications. Serum projects are divided into **individual iterations (sprints),** which usually always last **30 days.**

The term **"serum"** (= crowd) comes from **rugby**. There, a serum takes place when the players of a team stand close to the ball to discuss how they want to win the ball as quickly as possible after the throw-in. This team coordination method is transferred to the project process. The next figure shows the process. Central elements are the **product backlog,** the **sprint backlog**, the **serum meeting,** and the **sprint review** (Fig. 12.1).

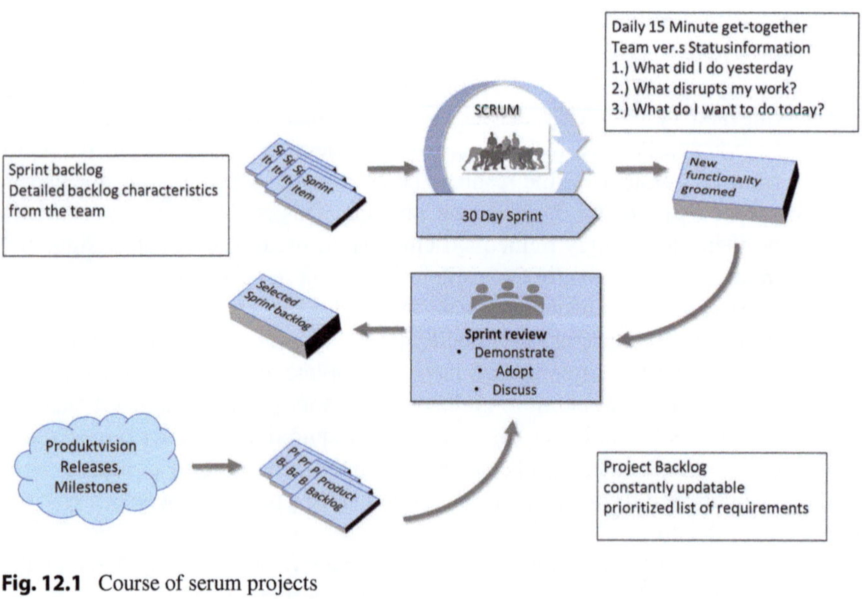

Fig. 12.1 Course of serum projects

1. **Product backlog**. Based on a rough product vision, the requirements for a new system are recorded in an open, changeable, and expandable feature list at any time, the so-called product backlog (= "order backlog"). The functional and performance characteristics contained in the list are determined by the customer (in the form of a customer representative or product manager) and prioritized.
2. **Sprint backlog**: The features and functions to be implemented in the next sprint are selected from the product backlog at the beginning of the sprint in a joint meeting of the project team and customer representatives. In addition, an overarching sprint goal is defined in a concise sentence, which is the guideline for sprint acceptance 4 weeks later. The selected characteristics are transferred by the team from the product backlog to a sprint backlog and detailed. During the sprint, this list can no longer be changed by the customer representative. The team members (not the Scrum Masters) agree among themselves by whom and in what order the requirements from the sprint backlog are processed. In order to be able to assess how many features can be realized, they also estimate the time required.
3. **Serum meeting:** During the sprint, a short meeting takes place every morning for ongoing coordination, in which the work progress is compared and problems that have arisen are discussed. The remaining tasks to be realized by the end of the sprint are recorded in a feature burndown chart which is updated in each serum meeting. If it turns out that not all features can be implemented within the sprint, the serum master can remove less prioritized features from the sprint backlog. If more time is available than expected, the serum master adds additional features from the product backlog.
4. **Sprint review**: After completion of the sprint, the newly developed functionality is demonstrated to the customer and the results are subjected to an informal review by the team and customer representatives. From the product backlog, the features for the next sprint are selected and the feature burndown chart (Fig. 12.2) for the overall project is updated.

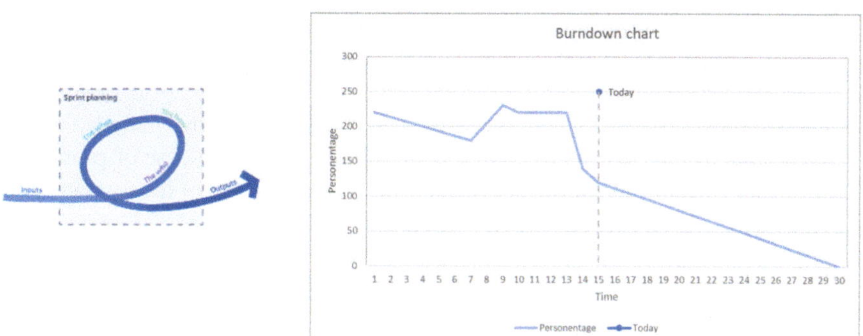

Fig. 12.2 Feature burndown chart

After the sprint review, the feature burndown metric is populated with the used resources versus the standard sprint duration of 30 days showing then the work task progress.

12.2 Agile Manifesto

Most agile approaches are based on the fact that they try to reduce the pure design phase to a minimum and to get to executable software as early as possible in the development process, which can then be submitted to the customer for joint coordination at regular, short intervals (iterations). In this way, it should be possible at any time to respond flexibly to customer requirements and thus increase overall customer satisfaction.

In four guiding principles it is formulated that in case of doubt:

- People and their cooperation are more important than processes and tools.
- Functioning software/items are more important than extensive documentation.
- Cooperation between stakeholders is more important than contracts.
- Flexible response to change requests is more important than sticking to a rigid plan.

Agile methods are lightweight processes that actively involve users in the project to determine, prioritize, and verify the requirements for the project outcome. They rely more on the implicit knowledge of the project team than on extensive documentation.

12.3 Core Features

Core features of agile methods are:

- **Iterative incremental approach**: Agile methods provide the customer with a functional system as quickly as possible, which is improved in short iteration loops and extended with additional functions.
- **Timeboxing:** The individual iterations are run in fixed time periods, which means that everyone involved can rely on the fixed dates. In case of problems, there will be no postponement but an adaptation to the scope of the version to be created.
- **Self-organizing teams**: The members of the team are basically equal. The team has the autonomy to organize itself in such a way that it can best meet the work requirements.
- **Change-friendly project culture**: In contrast to the classic waterfall model, requirements and technologies are not placed under change control in the "design freeze" but can be easily changed during the product development cycle. Changes are seen as a friend, not an opponent of the project. Agile methods try to use the so-called rule of ten of error costs (costs of a change increase from phase to

phase by a factor of 10) and to keep the cost curve for changes as flat as possible. This enables higher creativity and faster benefit for the customer in the project.

12.4 Agile Development

The methods of agile development are divided differently, distinguishing between:

- **Technical working practices,** such as simple design, refactoring (repeated code cleansing during programming), and test-driven development.
- **Communication methods**, for example metaphors as a project vision, programming in pairs.
- **Management methods**, for example continuous version delivery in short cycles, planning games.
- Agile project management can be understood as a management method and the communication method of agile development in a broader sense. The agile methods are often divided into the areas of **agile system analysis, agile architecture, agile programming, agile documentation, agile project management,** and **agile organization.** The agile project management is understood as a pragmatic and situation-appropriate management of projects focused on its essentials, in which **customer satisfaction**, **motivated teams**, and effective **risk management** are the focus. This definition reflects today's prevailing idea of agile project management very well. The agile organization can also be counted as project management in a broader sense.

12.5 Agile Project Management

An independent methodological framework for agile project management outside of software projects was published in 2004. This distinguishes between three customer- and product-oriented and three leadership style-oriented agile management principles:

Customer benefits through innovative products:

- **Deliver customer value.**
  - Work with **iterative**, requirement-based process models.
- **Collaborative leadership style:**
  - Be adventurous
  - Be adaptable (**self-organizing, disciplined**) teams
  - Simplify, whenever possible

Many of these principles are derived from the methods of lean production and lean development in the automotive industry. One of the most important principles there is the **systematic** reduction of **waste** that does not provide any benefit to the customer. Project management must also free its projects from waste and focus on delivering the results expected by the customer.

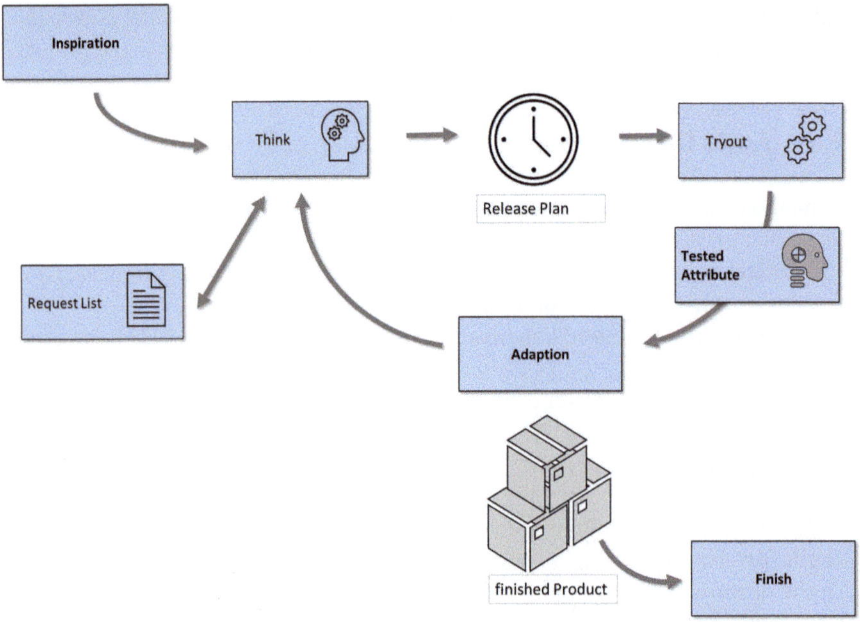

Fig. 12.3 Agile project management process

Agile Projekt Management Process

1. **Inspiration (instead of initiation)**—Determining the product vision and scope of delivery, identifying stakeholders, and team building: Instruments for the product vision are the visionary product packaging, the elevator test statement, and a rough product structure plan. A **one-page project profile** is used to define the scope of the project. Other practices of this phase are the composition of personnel, the stakeholder analysis, the definition of the customer–supplier–team interface, and the definition of rules of the game for teamwork.
2. **Thinking (instead of planning)**—Development of a requirement-oriented release, milestone, and iteration plan: The product breakdown structure is broken down into a feature breakdown structure like the BOM in production. Performance requirements and functional features of the feature structure plan are displayed in **index cards (user stories**, feature maps; often handwritten; see figure on pin boards on which they can be easily plugged back and forth. In the case of larger, distributed teams, the **cards are managed electronically** with software programs designed for this purpose. An iteration plan can be developed by simply arranging the feature **cards on boards** in the appropriate iterations. Estimation exams and risk analyses are integrated into the course of the planning meetings.
3. **Trial and error (instead of execution)**—Delivering tested features in **short iteration cycles** and continuous risk management: The main management tasks

of this phase are the provision of a collaborative working environment and team management. Instruments are coaching, daily team meetings, cooperative decision-making, and daily customer contacts. The team members themselves are responsible for resource utilization management and the most cost-effective implementation of technical changes.

4. **Adapt (instead of control)**—review of the delivered products, the project situation, and team performance; adaptation measures, if necessary: Instruments of this phase are customer focus groups, technical reviews, self-assessment of team performance, and metric-based project status reports (e.g. the **feature burn-down charts** already mentioned or the tracking of the number and value of the delivered features and the expected project end date).
5. **Completion**—complete project, pass on experience, and celebrate: Instruments are the same as in the fourth phase as well as special project completion checklists and the project retrospective.

Reference

Philip Bauer, Agile Training course, Ford Motor Company

Scheduling 13

The first part of the chapter describes the process steps of sequencing and scheduling. This is based on phase planning (Chap. 3) and the project structure (Chap. 9) and shows how at first glance a complex project can be broken down into manageable units (work packages, operations). The result of sequencing and scheduling is a first timing schedule. Taking resources and costs into account you have created a binding plan/target specification for all stakeholders.

In the second part, the network technology is described as central planning and control tool. The name used for this method is usually "PERT" but we normally use it in the context of the precedence diagram **method** (PDM) (network diagram technology tool) showing the concepts and the procedure for calculating dates, as well as important elements (such as buffers and critical paths). The project manager will certainly never calculate a timing schedule manually as there is corresponding software support available. But he should know the basics correctly to be able to interpret a schedule and check for plausibility.

At the end of the chapter, valuable tips and examples for establishing networks and choosing detail levels, as well as proposals for simple work techniques and different types of illustrations, are presented.

13.1 Project Planning Transfer from Schedule Planning into Phase Planning

Simultaneously during the phase planning a rough scheduling section with milestones at the end of each phase is processed. The activities (usually wide detailed) are found as a "Node" (Action) in the schedule plan, as well as the milestones shown as "Events". The first step of project complexity reduction has been done with the help of the phase planning process.

The phase structure selected at the planning phase must but not necessarily be applied into the project structure (Chap. 9). The project structuring can also be done

P. Bauer, *A Comprehensive Project Management Guide*, Management for Professionals, https://doi.org/10.1007/978-3-031-68252-0_13

based on functional, object-oriented, or organizational aspects. Usually a mixed-oriented outline approach at different levels depending on the project or project type is selected.

> 🕮 Definition: project structuring is the next step after the planning phase to the further breakdown of a complex project into phases and therefore detailing into tasks and work packages and thus establishing the requirements for the sequence and scheduling planning.

The project structure plan shows all tasks in a project (as an amount of work packages) that is required to deliver the performance expected (Chap. 10) and provides transparency:

- What to do?
- Who is doing what?
- Who is responsible for what?

The project structure plan gives no information about:

- The order of work package processing
- The interfaces between projects/tasks and work packages
- The exact timing and implementation timing

The final step in project planning on its way from "Rough to the Fine" is the transfer of the work breakdown structure into the schedule plan. Figure 13.1 illustrates this.

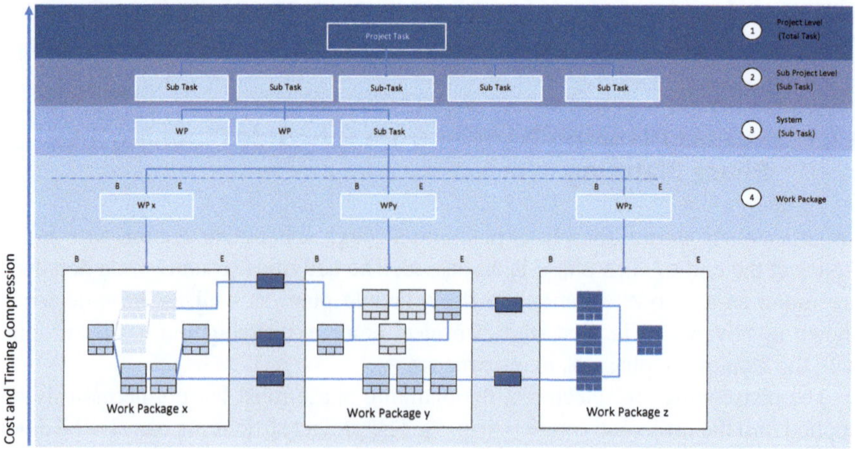

Fig. 13.1 From the project structure plan into the schedule plan

Definition: Work package is the smallest unit in the project structure plan; in the schedule plan all the elements regardless of the detail are referred to as "Node" (Action).

1. The first step in creating a schedule plan is the definition of the content and level of detail related to the work actions that need to be processed. Depending on the complexity of the work package this can be solved differently:

   Usually, a work package includes a series of interdependent steps ("1: n relationship"); these are actions that need to be planned and controlled individual. In this case, a "Sub-Network" develops from a work package (see illustration in Fig. 13.1).

   Single manageable work packages do not need to be broken down to more detail and can be entered as a "Node"(Action) into the schedule plan ("1:1 relationship").

   For specific purposes, such as for the compression of time schedule information (Rough Network Planning, Frame Schedule Planning), several work packages can be summarized to one "Node" ("m: 1-relationship").

13.2 Define Technological Node Sequence

2. In the second step, the actions are to be linked together logically so that a process workflow (network) is developed.

- Which clearly defines each node interactions
- How actions can be structured, after the other, parallel, overlap, or run independently of each other.
- What time interval is required between the nodes?
- Stakeholders are already forced in an early phase of the project to clarify and identify interfaces. Based on practical experience there are high risks in individual work packages, because up front there is no exact knowledge on the technical feasibility or other important information that could be missing.

13.3 Transfer Work Breakdown Structure into the Schedule Plan

3. In the third step, the stakeholders estimate realistically the time frame for the nodes—first without explicit consideration resources.

It is essential that the project manager makes sure that individual appraiser does not incorporate (hidden) buffers for their own security. Only he (project manager) alone is permitted to incorporate a buffer and only if the predetermined fixed finish date allows it.

After defining the node timings and the intervals between the nodes you can calculate the **Earliest** and **Latest** dates for each node and in addition the time-critical processes ("critical path") as well as the time-based range ("buffer"). The total calculation then results in a first **Preliminary Plan**.

13.4 Determination of Resource Needs and Resource Balancing

The first-time scheduling of the project plan is normally done without taking the resources needed into account.

4. In the fourth step, the allocation of resources occurs.

- Employees with certain qualifications
- Equipment, like machinery, facilities
- Materials or production facilities
- Node costs/work packages

If single actions cannot be executed because of restricted resources between the originally scheduled times or during the relevant period, then the schedule structure must be changed, e.g., by using sequential processing instead of parallel execution of actions or by stretching the time of a work package. After the adjustment timing is recalculation. The next step is then the optimization of the process and schedule plan.

13.5 Process and Schedule Plan Optimization

5. The next step follows the optimization of the process and schedule plan.

The schedule calculation taking into account all resources can often lead to an undesired result where the required project finish date may not be met. In this case, an iterative process begins to optimize the process and schedules in cooperation with all responsible stakeholders. To reduce the schedule timing, you can also change the process structure by, e.g., overlap Nodes and reduce the action execution timings by, e.g., increased resources.

At this stage of the process and scheduling planning, alternative processes can be used to simulate the impact on the project end date or on other target factors, such as cost or resource/equipment requirements.

🕮 Important: In any case, it is important at this stage of scheduling to strictly ensure that no unrealistic assumptions are incorporated in the planning and the previous planning is destroyed completely.

13.6 Release of Execution Plan

6. The optimization project schedules and process plan need to be reviewed and released from the responsible functions (such as principal, management, project management, suppliers).

The dates in this execution plan then change to binding plan/target dates for all involved. This schedule is often an important part of the contract with the project contractor. Under circumstances subsequent non-compliance with contractually fixed project end dates can lead to penalties.

With the release, the project plan is subject to change management; i.e. changes must be documented and must be approved by the authorized functions. The stage of project planning is now finished; however, the sequence and schedule management is still ongoing. In the subsequent implementation phase, there is hardly a project without planning changes. Reasons are:

- Alterations by the client
- Delays, such as loss of resources or by delayed delivery by sub-contractors
- Technical difficulties in the realization of individual work packages
- The need for test replication because of failed tests

The sequence and schedule management in the implementation phase is inextricably linked to the **monitoring and control phase** (Chap. 21 Project Controlling: Control and Reports).

13.7 Basics of Gantt and Network Diagram Technology

Relationships between activities are easier to recognize if they are presented using graphics such as bar charts or a network of connected boxes. The type of bar chart used to illustrate activity relationships in a project is the **Gantt chart**. The Gantt chart was developed by Henry Gantt and used on major projects, including building the Hoover Dam and the US interstate highway system. The Gantt chart is a time-scaled graphic that represents each activity with a bar that reflects the duration, start, and finish time, as shown in Fig. 13.2.

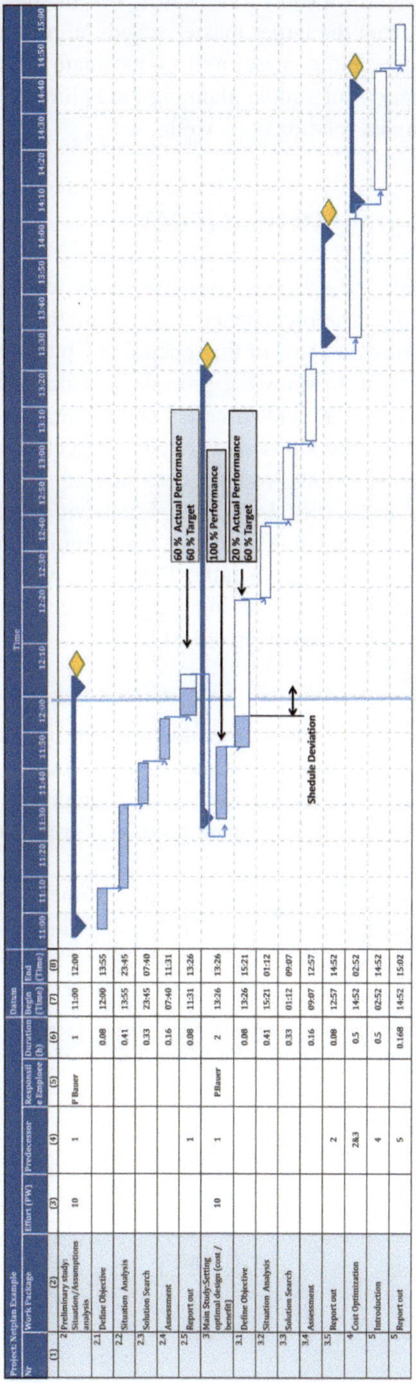

Fig. 13.2 Example Gantt chart

A Gantt chart is easy to read and provides sufficient information for project team members to plan activities within a short time frame. For many larger projects, a 2-week bar chart, extracted from the larger master schedule, provides the information needed for team members and contractors to coordinate activity details. The Gantt chart provides information for simple planning but is limited because a Gantt chart does not illustrate complex relationships well.

13.8 Precedence Diagram Method (PDM)

People recognize relationships and patterns more effectively when they look at diagrams like the one in Fig. 13.3. The precedence diagram method (PDM) is a technique for graphically displaying the logic of the schedule by placing the activities in boxes with arrows between them to show the precedence–successor relationships. The boxes in this type of diagram are called nodes and the arrows indicate finish–start relationships. This type of diagram is also called a project network diagram.

Before creating a project schedule, you need to identify and understand the dependencies between project activities. Incorrectly identifying these dependencies typically causes projects to come in late. One of the benefits of PDM is that it helps in understanding project dependencies visually. PDM is a visual representation technique that depicts the activities involved in a project. Precedence diagrams are also known as project network diagrams (Fig. 13.3).

PDM helps you to:

- **Communicate:** The visual representation makes it easier for you to communicate the flow of project execution or the project activity flow.
- **Identify missing activities**: When an activity is not identified, it will never be done. By visually representing the activities, there is a greater chance for your team to identify missing activities.
- **Identify dependencies**: Each activity is dependent on some other activity. When a dependency is not identified, the project will be delayed until such a time that

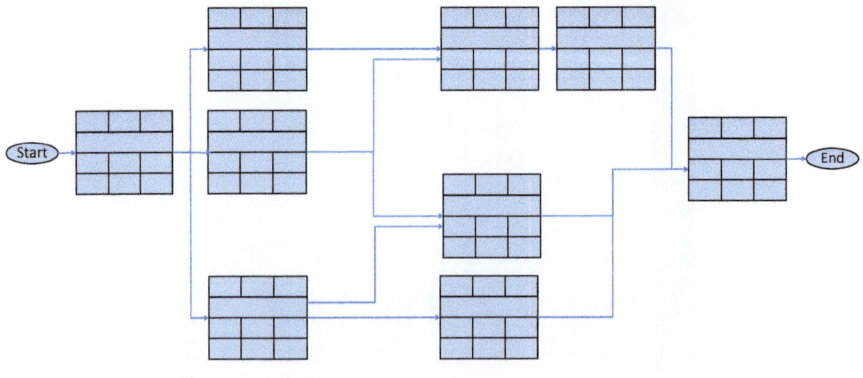

Fig. 13.3 Project network diagram

identification occurs. For example, if there is a critical component that is being produced by a third-party vendor, the final product is dependent on the vendor. So, even if you complete all other activities, the project will not be complete until the vendor supplies the critical component.

- **Identify critical activities:** Certain activities have a greater impact on project schedule than others. By using PDMs, you can determine the activities critical to the project schedule. This is known as the critical path method (CPM).
- **Create a project schedule:** The final goal of PDM is to create a practical and robust project schedule.

13.9 Types of Dependencies

The individual relationships determine the logical order processing of the individual actions (Nodes): (1) which action is necessary before the next task ("followers") can start? (2) Which event must occur before the next phase of the project can begin? (3) What mandatory time interval must exist between two nodes? (4) Is it possible to process two nodes in parallel (partially)?

There are **four** types of dependencies that you need to be aware of before creating a precedence diagram.

1. **Finish–start** (Fig. 13.4): In this dependency an activity cannot start before a previous activity has ended. For example, you cannot cook a meal before gathering all the ingredients. Therefore, the activity "Gather Ingredients" needs to finish before the activity "Cook Meal" can begin. This is the most commonly used dependency.

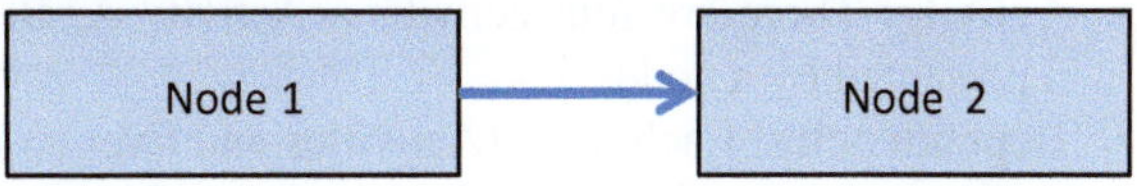

Fig. 13.4 Node dependencies: finish–start

2. **Start–start** (Fig. 13.5): In this dependency there is a defined relationship between the start of activities.

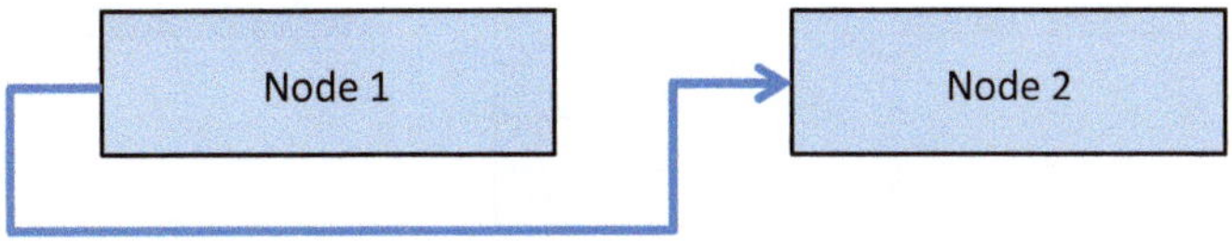

Fig. 13.5 Node dependencies: start–start

3. **Finish–finish** (Fig. 13.6)**:** In this dependency there is a defined relationship between the end dates of activities.

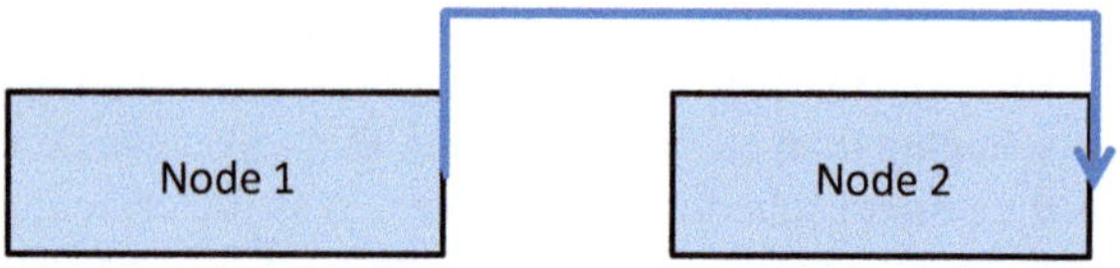

Fig. 13.6 Node dependencies: finish–finish

4. **Start–finish** (Fig. 13.7)**:** In this dependency there is a defined relationship between the start of one activity and the end date of a successor activity. This dependency is rarely used.

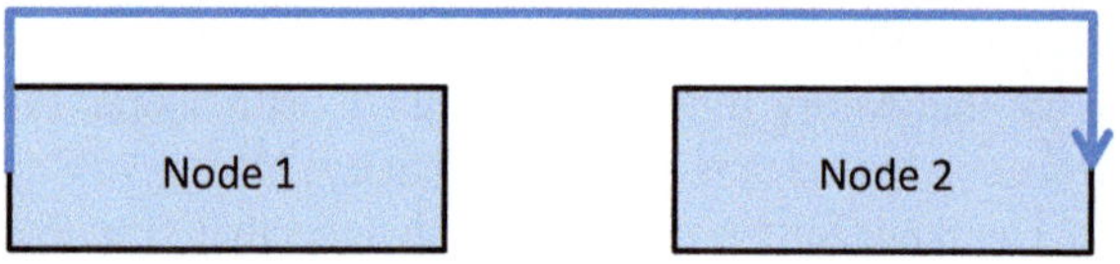

Fig. 13.7 Node dependencies: start–finish

Precedence Diagram Notation

The image (Fig. 13.8) displays a simple precedence diagram.

You'll notice that the precedence diagram has the following features:

- **Events:** The start and end oval shapes signify events. An event is a point in time having no duration, which is also known as a milestone. A precedence diagram will always have a start and an end event.
- **Activity:** There are four activities (Activity A, B, C, and D); each activity is represented by a node.
- **Dependencies:** Each node (Activities and Events) is connected by using unidirectional arrows. This signifies the relationship between activities. The relationship between activities can either be predecessor or successor. For example, in

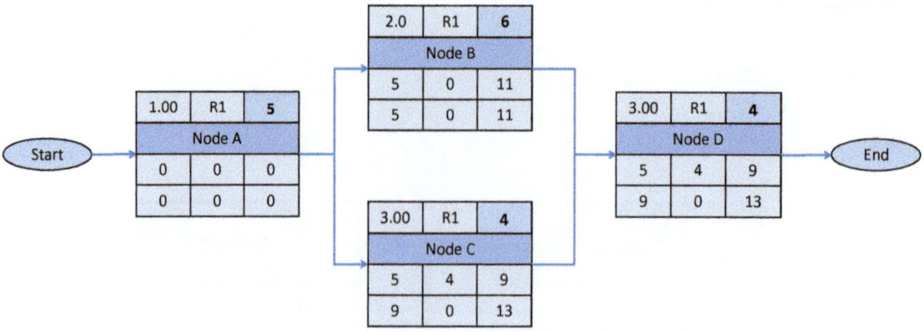

Fig. 13.8 Simple project network diagram

the image, Node A has no dependency; Nodes B and C are dependent on Node A, whilst Node D is dependent on Nodes B and C.

Since the node represents the activities, precedence diagrams are also called "**Activity-on-the-Node**" diagrams.

A network diagram will always have the start and end events. They may also have other events called milestones. For example, kill-points are milestones. In a network diagram, the start of an activity must be linked to the end of another activity.

13.10 Specify Predecessors and Successors Given a List of Project Activities

This is the first step to creating a precedence diagram (project network diagram). In this step, the project activity dependencies are identified. The precedence diagram (project network diagram) needs to clearly illustrate these dependencies.

Whilst creating a list of project activities, you need to ask yourself the following questions:

- What project activities happen before the activity being examined?
- What project activities can happen at the same time with this activity?
- What project activities happen after this activity?
- For example, suppose you are constructing a shed and the following activity list has been defined: Purchase Wood; Hire Workers; Dig Foundation; Lay Foundation; Harden Foundation Cement; Purchase Plot; Select Design; Assemble Shed; Purchase Paint; Paint Shed, Dry Paint; Furnish Shed.
- Suppose you are examining the purchase wood activity, ask yourself the three questions listed above.
- **What project activities happen before the activities being examined?** Some activities that may occur before the "Purchase Wood" activity include Purchase Plot and Select Design.
- **What project activities can happen at the same time with this activity?** Some activities that may occur at the same time as "Purchase Wood" activity include Hire Workers and Purchase Paint.
- **What project activities happen after this activity?** Some activities that may occur after the "Purchase Wood" activity include Assemble Shed.

From the answers, we have determined the predecessors and successors of the Purchase Wood activity (Table 13.1). Similarly, you can examine each project activity and develop relationships between each one (see the image below—click for a larger view). You will then have a table of project activities, which also contains information about predecessors and successors.

The activity list would contain the entire scope. Generally, the scope of work that needs to be completed is broken into more manageable phases (releases and

Table 13.1 Node list (Build Shed)

Index	Node description	Predecessor	Duration
A	Purchase plot	-	5
B	Hire workers	Purchase plot	6
C	Select design	Purchase plot	4
D	Purchase paint	Purchase plot	3
E	Dig foundation	Hire workers	4
F	Purchase wood	Select design	2
G	Paint shed	Purchase paint	4
H	Lay foundation	Dig foundation, purchase wood	5
I	Assemble shed	Purchase wood, paint shed	8
K	Dry paint	Paint shed	7
L	Harden foundation cement	Lay foundation	3
M	Furnish shed	Assemble shed, dry paint, harden foundation cement	4

iterations). Each phase will have its own precedence diagram (project network diagram). Prioritizing scope that provides maximum value is important.

13.11 Arrange Project Activities in Order of Execution to Create a Precedence Diagram

After creating the table, you can then proceed to constructing the precedence diagram (project network diagram). An example precedence diagram is shown in the image. Refer to the table whilst creating the project network diagram. The visual representation helps you to identify missing activities. In this example, "Cut Wood" may be a missing activity, that'll depend on "Hire Workers". Can you spot any other missing activities?

Usually, there are multiple paths of completion for any project; hence the precedence diagram may vary. For example, in Fig. 13.9, we could make Purchase Paint dependent on Purchasing Wood. This would alter the precedence diagram and consequently the project schedule.

> 🕮 Important: You also need to be aware of leads and lags between activities.

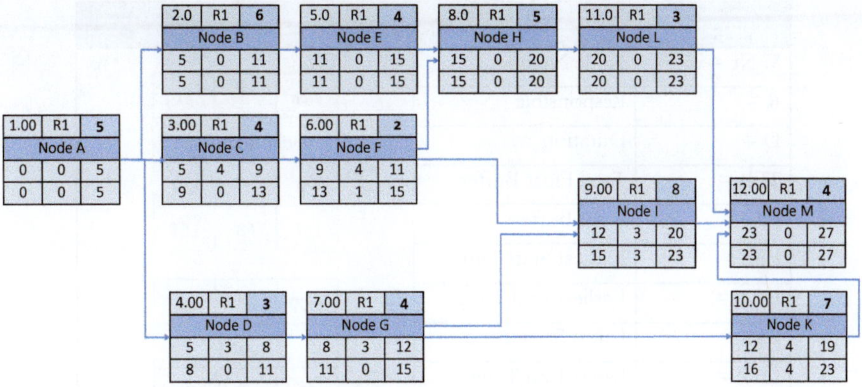

Fig. 13.9 Project network diagram (Build Shed)

13.12 Node Standard Related to DIN 69900

The duration of each activity is determined mostly by comparing and predicting. The calculation of each activity duration and the resulting slack is a key element to focus on whilst developing network diagrams.

> 🕮 Float, sometimes called slack, is the amount of time an activity, network path, or project can be delayed from the early start without changing the completion date of the project.

Each event and each activity has an earliest (possible) and a latest (allowed) position in the allowed time sequence. In the precedence diagram method, the activities are shown as nodes and drawn as rectangles. These rectangles contain—as listed in Fig. 13.10—the earliest and latest start and end time of the operation and additional key scheduling information.

Each node "Point in Time" calculation is basically done in two steps:

1. Initially a f**orward** calculation starting from the planned earliest start date stepping through each node one at a time until to the latest end dates. The result is consequently the **earliest** start and finish dates of all activities.
2. In step two you **reverse** the calculation; proceed starting from the project end date towards the earliest starting date. The result is then the **latest** start and finish dates of each single activities.

By performing both calculations you obtained the **earliest** start and end time, on the one hand, and the **latest** start and end date, on the other hand, for each node. If there is a difference between the result of the forward and the reverse calculation a slack exists; the node therefore has a time buffer. A node with slack can be moved

Abbreviation	Description
V. Nr =	Node Number
R =	Responsible
D =	Duration
TFB =	Total Float Buffer
FB =	Float Buffer
EST =	Earliest Start Time
EET =	Earliest End Time
LST =	Latest Start Time
LET =	Latest End Time
FBB =	Free Float Buffer
IB =	Independent Buffer

Notation

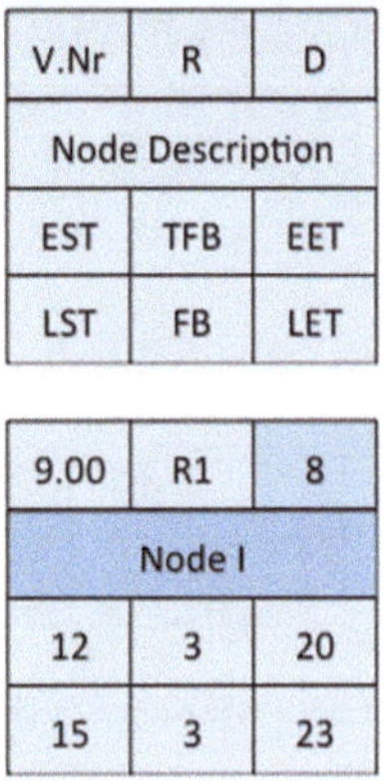

Fig. 13.10 Node standard related to DIN 69900

between the earliest start date and its latest end date without affecting the project. Buffer times therefore expand the scope in the project planning and control. However, if the earliest and latest dates are the same, the node is on the **critical path**.

📖 Definition: The critical path is a connection of all activities, whose earliest and latest timings are equal.

Each project must logically have one and can have two or more critical paths and the critical path is time determining. The total duration of the project is the sum of the durations of critical activities that are on this path. The naming for the critical path results in the impact of a temporal node delay on the corresponding project total end date. The critical paths are especially highlighted in network diagrams.

13.13 Forward and Backward Time Calculation

The standardized precedence diagram calculations are based on DIN 69900 and are shown in Table 13.2. These calculations are normally supported by software applications, but to learn the algorithm, the manual forward (Fig. 13.11) and backward (Fig. 13.12) calculation sequence is shown step by step.

Table 13.2 Standardized precedence diagram calculations (DIN 69900)

Forward calculation:	Float (Slack) calculation:
EST J = maxi (EET i, j)	TFB = LST j – EST j
EST E = 0 (Index E = End Node)	FB = min k (EST j, k) – EET j
EET j = EST j + D j	FFB j = LST j – max i (LET i,j) (Additional Metrics)
Backward Calculation:	IB j = (0; min k (EST j, k) – max I (LET i, j) – D j) (Additional Metrics)
LET j = min k (LST j, k)	
LST E = 0 (Index E = End Node)	
LST j = LET j - D j	

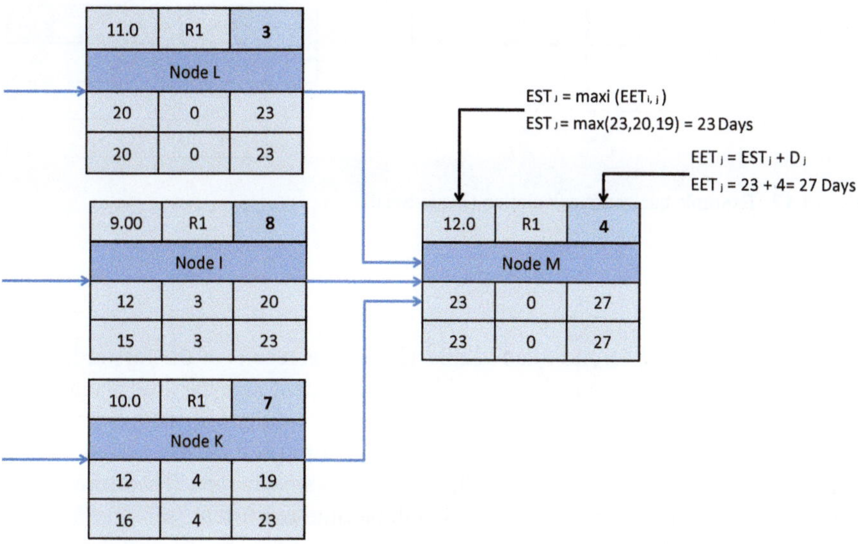

Fig. 13.11 Example forward calculation (Build Shed)

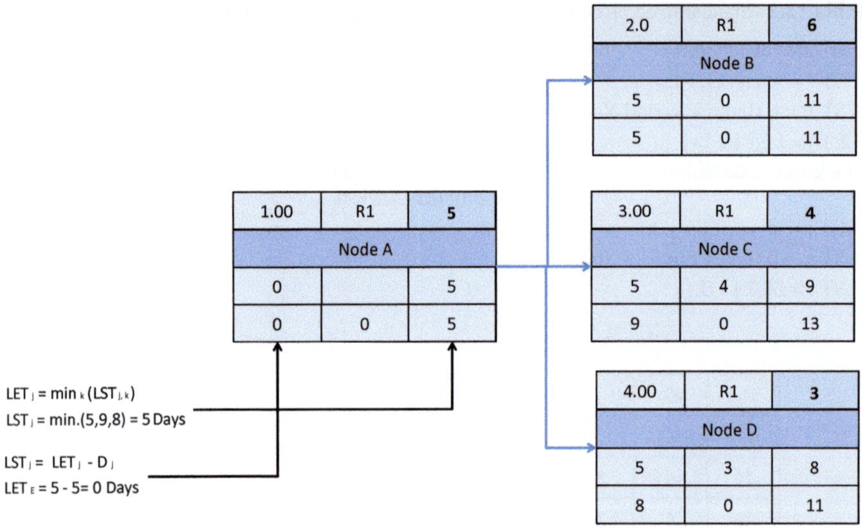

Fig. 13.12 Example backward calculation (Build Shed)

Using the example "Build Shed" Table 13.3 shows results of the forward, backward, and buffer calculations. Beware of being consistent with the time planning, as there can be no **negative buffer**. If the consistency conditions for time are not met, the network nodes must be checked, by looking for specified fixed dates. These fixed dates are the main factors that influence the negative buffers. Therefore, if you are not using fixed deadlines the network will be time-consistent.

The backward (reverse) calculation runs through each node by taking all successors into account and selecting the smallest node LST for the current node selected.

In precedence diagram (project network diagram), the buffer for the events can only be calculated after the forward and backward calculation for the single nodes (Fig. 13.13).

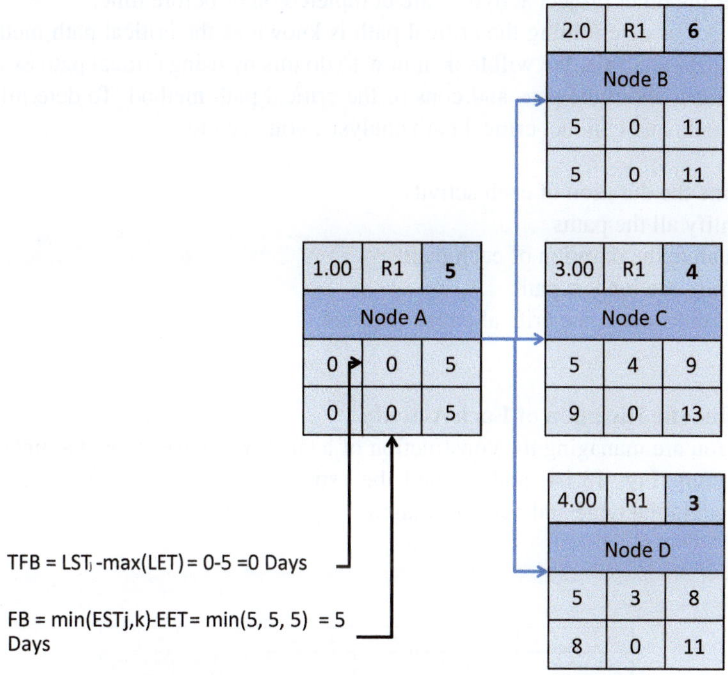

Fig. 13.13 Example buffer calculation (Build Shed)

13.14 Critical Path Method: Examples Using the Precedence Diagram

Not all project activities have the same impact on delaying the project. Use the critical path method and critical path analysis to identify the most important activities which can impact the project schedule.

After creating the precedence diagram, you can identify the activities that would, if delayed, cause your project to come in late. This is the critical path definition. A delay in any of the critical path activities will delay the entire project, regardless of whether the other project activities are completed on or before time.

The act of determining the critical path is known as the critical path method or critical path analysis. We will look at how to do this by using critical path examples and to learn about the pros and cons of the critical path method. To determine the critical path and conduct critical path analysis, you need to:

- Define the duration of each activity
- Identify all the paths
- Calculate the duration of each path
- Identify the longest path
- Let's consider some critical path examples

1. **Define the Duration of Each Activity**

   You are managing the construction of a shed. You have created a precedence diagram (Fig. 13.14) and defined the estimated duration of each activity, as shown in the table and network diagram (Table 13.3).

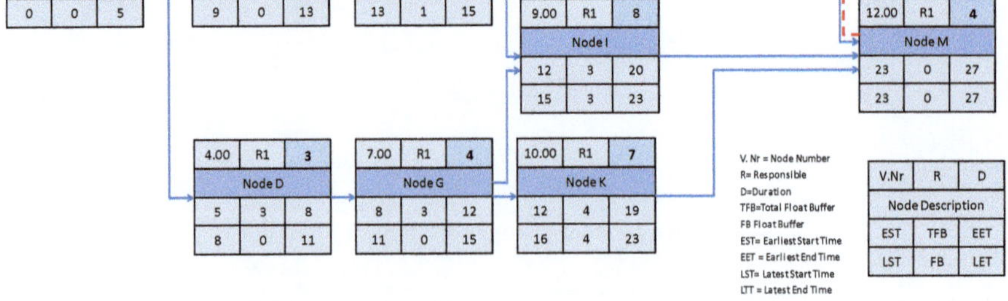

Fig. 13.14 Project network diagram (Build Shed) with critical path

Table 13.3 Project network table (Build Shed)

Index	Node description	Predecessor	Duration	EST	EET	LST	LTT	TFB	FB
A	Purchase plot	–	5	0	0	5	5	0	0
B	Hire workers	Purchase plot	6	5	5	11	11	0	0
C	Select design	Purchase plot	4	5	9	9	13	4	0
D	Purchase paint	Purchase plot	3	5	8	8	11	3	0
E	Dig foundation	Hire workers	4	11	11	15	15	0	0
F	Purchase wood	Select design	2	9	13	11	15	4	1
G	Paint shed	Purchase paint	4	8	11	12	15	3	0
H	Lay foundation	Dig foundation, purchase wood	5	15	15	20	20	0	0
I	Assemble shed	Purchase wood, paint shed	8	12	15	20	23	3	3
K	Dry paint	Paint shed	7	12	16	19	23	4	4
L	Harden foundation cement	Lay foundation	3	20	20	23	23	0	0
M	Furnish shed	Assemble shed, dry paint, harden foundation cement	4	23	23	27	27	0	0

2. **Identify All the Paths**

   The precedence diagram shown in the image has one critical path one path, as shown above:

3. **Calculate the Duration of Each Path**

   To do this, you can simply add the duration of each activity in each path; you get Table 13.4:

Table 13.4 Critical path calculation (Build Shed)

Path	Nodes	Duration	Total
Path 1 Critical*	A + B + E + H + L + M	5 + 6 + 4 + 5 + 3 + 4 =	27 days
Path 2	A + C + F + H + L + M	5 + 4 + 2 + 5 + 3 + 4 =	23 days
Path 3	A + C + F + I + M	5 + 4 + 2 + 8 + 4 =	23 days
Path 4	A + D + G + I + M	5 + 3 + 4 + 8 + 4 =	24 days
Path 5	A + D + G + K + M	5 + 3 + 4 + 7 + 4 =	23 days

The durations calculated assume that there is no scope creep. In real projects, scope creep can be expected. However, it is up to the project manager to control the degree of scope creep. Read the Managing Scope Creep article for more about controlling and monitoring scope creep.

Each path has a different duration (Table 1.1). That means the critical path method or the critical path analysis is required to determine the most important path. As a project manager, you will need to keep an eye on the critical path.

4. **Identify the Longest Path**

   The longest path is the critical path. From the above calculations, we can see that Path 1 is the longest. Therefore, if activity on this path is delayed, then the project will be delayed. After identifying the critical path, you can deduce the activities that when delayed will not impact the project.

   For example, do you think the project will be delayed if the "Purchase Paint" activity is delayed by 3 days? If the answer is no, the project will not be delayed. What if the "Purchase Paint" activity came in 8 days late? To answer the question recalculate to determine the amount of time; path 4 or 5 may be late but without delaying the project.

   As you can see, the critical path method or critical path analysis is very useful for determining activities that can lead to project delay. In theory the critical path method and critical path definition is always the same and follows the steps mentioned in this article.

   Last, you might want to also use Chap. 4 practices that can help you protect your project from time and cost over-runs.

13.15 Tools Used to Create a Precedence Diagram

In a complex project, you will probably not create the precedence diagram (project network diagram) manually as we have done in this example. You will most likely use software, such as PS8, to create the precedence diagram. However, even in the software, you will need to manually enter the project activities list and the dependencies between them. The software you use, such as PS8 or Microsoft project, will consist of a variety of other useful features, like automatically creating the critical path and a Gantt chart.

References

Prof Dr. Shulte Zurhausen, M. (2010). Project-/Change Management/Organisation Lerneinheit 1. Hagen: Institut für Verbundstudien der Fachhochschule NRW.

Deutscher Normenausschuss (Hrsg.): DIN 69900: Projektmanagement - Netzplantechnik. (2009). Berlin.

Resources 14

14.1 Resource Management

The resources of an organization consist of people, materials, equipment, knowledge, and time. Organizations typically have limited resources; therefore, trade-offs on what project resources are expended and when are made every day within organizations. A resource allocation plan is an important tool in effective management of scarce resources.

The timing of the need of those resources can be and should be determined within the project schedules. A resource plan, which describes the type of resource needed and the timing of that need, is critical to effective resource management. As the project schedule changes, the resource plan must also be flexible enough to adjust as these changes occur.

In developing resource plans, there is little chance that the project manager will have all of the necessary resources assigned to the project at its start. The fact is when starting a project, the details of that project are typically unknown. Therefore, knowing the types and duration of resources necessary is not always possible.

Known knowns are events that can be planned for. In building the schedule, some deliverables can be decomposed in sufficient detail creating tasks, whilst other deliverables will only be known at the highest level. When details of a deliverable are not sufficiently known, a planning package should be used.

The details of the deliverables defined within planning packages can be considered known unknowns, or risks. In these instances, the work has not been fully decomposed.

Known planning events, as well as planning packages, can be assigned individual resources and durations that have been established by the people who will be doing the work. The only difference is in planning packages; the duration and resource estimates are typically less accurate. The use of historical information or industry standards can provide a higher degree of confidence in estimates, when available.

P. Bauer, *A Comprehensive Project Management Guide*, Management for Professionals, https://doi.org/10.1007/978-3-031-68252-0_14

It is not necessary to have all deliverables decomposed and assigned to individuals prior to beginning work on a project. In fact, it is very common to set a baseline schedule and resource plan based on planning package estimates.

As the project progresses, these known unknowns become clearer to the project team warranting changes within the project schedule and resource plan.

Events that cannot be planned for are called unknown unknowns. These events are not known in the realm of possibilities, yet could occur. An example is a warehouse fire that destroys inventory and delays the project completion. This would not normally be factored in as a known event during the project planning, so it is an unknown.

Since projects are unique and temporary endeavours, project managers will always work in a world of unknowns. Therefore, resource management and planning should continue throughout the project life cycle.

14.2 Between Offer and Demand

Resource management consists of planning, monitoring, and control of resources in projects, with the goal to recognize and plan the needed resources for projects, but also for all other activities within an organization at an early stage, and to align the available resources accordingly. The use of these resources is then to be agreed with the responsible management and the resource allocated to the project is controlled and also that the business objectives are met. In addition, a further part of the resources management is to plan and control the necessary long-term capacities and competences as well as to align a medium-term staff development.

Essentially, resource planning can be seen as a comparison between offers and demand shown in Fig. 14.1.

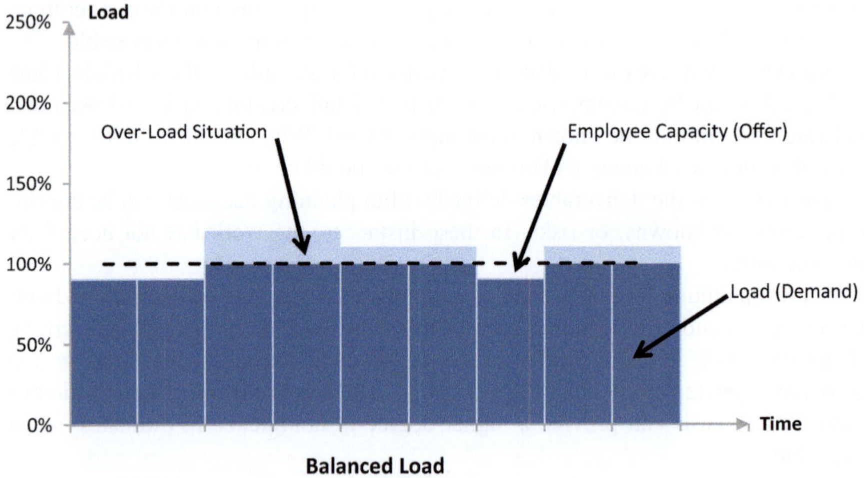

Fig. 14.1 Resource planning—offer and demand

Resource planning aims to apply and control different types of resources in projects: people, machines and equipment, technical aids, etc. The main focus in the following chapter is on the human resources, as these dominate among the different resources in most projects. Science has mainly focused on creating precise mathematical models, which are not suitable and do not meet the requirements for human resource planning. The optimization potential here is much larger compared to the "hard" resources.

Projects are rarely performed "on the desk". They tend to run mostly within one or more companies (or organizations). A functioning resource management requires therefore the consideration of all projects to be run in these organizations, as well as to consider all other activities. This has far-reaching consequences on the design of resource management.

Resources are those assets of the firm, including the time of employees, that are used to accomplish the objectives of the project. The project manager should define, negotiate, and secure resource commitments for the personnel, equipment, facilities, and services needed for the project. Resource commitments should be as specific as possible. Generally, resource utilization is specified in the project budget.

14.3 The Three Main Dimensions What, Who, When

The following items should be defined and negotiated related to the "Build a Shed" example:

- What will be built?
- By whom?
- When?
- How will it be delivered?
- How much will it cost?
- Who will pay?
- When will payment be made?

Of course, there are always other opportunities for utilizing resources. On large projects, conflicts over resource allocation are inevitable. It is best if resource conflicts can be resolved between those managers directly involved. However, in some cases, higher levels of management must address resource conflicts. Senior managers should view resource conflicts as potential indications that the management system for allocating resources must be modified or redesigned. Often, such conflicts create ill will among managers and lead to lack of support or even active resistance to the project. Too many such conflicts can lead to resentment towards quality improvement efforts in general.

14.4 Resource Loading and Resource Levelling

A project manager has several choices on how to meet demands of his/her many projects. Two simple choices are resource loading and resource levelling.

1. **Resource loading**

   Resource loading mainly involves your manpower or employees. In resource loading, each employee is assigned a task or a percentage of a project (X % of the whole). Usually, it's 25% of the whole. Then the employee is assigned other tasks until he or she reaches 100% booked. This would then mean that the employees couldn't take on any additional work.

   With resource loading, a project manager can predict an employee's hours for the year and see how tasks can be assigned. This also allows the project manager to decide whether or not additional employees or contractors are needed to complete the scheduled projects.

   The downside to resource loading is that employees cannot be 100% booked. Other things may arise to take away their time, such as unexpected problems that need to be fixed. An employee should always be under 100% booked. Resource loading increases the chance that a project will not be completed on time because employees are overloaded with projects.
2. **Resource levelling**

   Whilst resource loading mainly deals with manpower, resource levelling deals with both time (project starting and ending date) and resources, including manpower and budget. Resource levelling tries to balance the conflicting interests of projects with the available resources.

   Resource levelling generally breaks things down into two categories: time and available resources. Some projects need to be finished within a certain time frame. These projects will use all the available resources (money and manpower) to complete the project by a certain date.

14.5 Juggling Your Resources with Resource Levelling

Project management is all about juggling your resources and your projects. Resource levelling allows project managers to balance resources over the course of a project and try to resolve conflicts between resources. Levelling is a key component of project management. To read about other key factors related to project resources, read Ronda Bowen's article, "Key elements of resource management".

Resource levelling tries to take the available resources and compare them to the demands of ongoing projects. Often, many projects or tasks will overlap, creating strain on resources, especially manpower. Resource levelling tries to take these competing demands and allocate resources effectively.

Many times, this either means that a project will have to be delayed whilst other projects are completed. But sometimes this is not feasible. Often tasks need to be done for the project to be finished on time. A delay in one task could deeply affect the rest of the project.

Another way to implement resource levelling is to lengthen the time it takes to finish a specific task. As opposed to a particular task taking 1 week, a project manager could extend this to 2 weeks to make sure that there are enough resources to complete this particular task. Yet again, this could affect the overall project. When levelling, the ultimate goal is always to fix over-allocation. Read Ronda Bowen's article about resource allocation for some ideas on ways you can achieve this goal.

Whilst resource levelling can assure that money and manpower are available for all competing projects and tasks, it could affect your critical path. This can be a problem since you cannot tell in the beginning which tasks will be essential to the critical path. If a task that is delayed does affect your critical path, your project could become overdue and make for very unhappy clients.

To make resource levelling more effective, a project manager should measure time in days and hours. This is easier to measure than any other dimension.

14.6 Two Main Types of Resource Levelling

Resource levelling generally breaks things down between finishing a project within a certain length of time and finishing a project with only the resources available. Projects that are going to be completed within a time limit use all the needed resources. These projects are usually those on the **critical path**.

Projects that only use the resources that are available can be stretched out until the necessary resources become obtainable. If the number of projects scheduled exceeds the needed resources, then those projects will have to be put off until a later date.

Overall, resource levelling helps a project manager decide whether or not he or she should quickly finish a project by using the maximum number of resources needed for that project. The alternative is to stretch out how long a project will take to ensure that enough resources are available to finish that project.

14.7 Estimate Processing Effort

A meaningful, accurate resource planning relies on a realistic and exact estimation of processing expenses and efforts. Predicting the errors resulti directly in he load situation and the end dates.

The estimate of the costs processing is not an exclusive resource-planning domain. The knowledge of expenses and efforts is also the key requirement for cost planning. The cost estimate is therefore primarily addressed in the context of cost management. The following chapter gives an overview of the most important cost and effort estimation methods.

Compare with similar predecessor projects As you standardize more projects the database and thus the project experience get larger. For an innovative IT project, this will be problematic due to the absence of sufficiently similar predecessor projects. In the construction of a power plant, however the estimation of engineering costs and efforts data from past power plant construction projects can be used.

Use a larger database of comparable projects This approach is a continuation of the first method. For heavily standardized project types such a database can be built and maintained within a company. Additionally, there are also external databases with defined process models. Especially in the building sector and for IT projects there are corresponding attempts. We are speaking about attempts, because even with this method the truth is approximated, in some cases resulting in serious mistakes. These supposedly exact methods give a feeling of pseudo safety and the feeling that even simpler methods are often inferior.

Prediction and expert surveys Having access to the expertise of the staff who are familiar with the relevant type of projects or work packages obviously leads to good results, since this kind of "state of the art" can be purchased. Those experts finally rely on the usual methods. From this point of view, this approach is not really an alternative method. It is rather a particular type of estimating procedure. The outcome is significantly dependent on choosing the right experts. It is very important to have a well-moderated approach with the goal to obtain different genuine opinions and experiences.

Parametric methods This method uses simple or complex mathematical formulas to calculate the cost and efforts of an entire project or any part of it. Example: An architect needs to estimate the cost for the renewal of a public place; he will simply use the ground area and multiply it with the price per square metre. For the calculation of engineering services costs there are extremely sophisticated formulas and mechanisms that are even mandatory and standardized in certain countries. Other parameters in addition to areas are (1) enclosed space, (2) dimensions, (3) weights, and (4) performance metrics (e.g. used in the power plant generator construction), but also the (5) levels of quality and the (6) number of functions and interfaces in software projects. The risk of errors mentioned above also applies in this method.

Function Point Method and COCOMO (constructive cost model) represent the parametric methods for computer science projects. The base for the estimation is the scope of functions or the target system. The additional parameters (1) product development process complexity, (2) deployed development tools, and the (3) project team qualifications are used.

Detailed structuring of the project The project is broken down into its component parts: work packages are defined. These can then be split into single work actions (nodes). This approach must be applied anyway for the continuing project planning. At this point in time the refinement is deliberately pulled ahead for the purpose of the cost and effort estimation to increase their accuracy. In almost all cases, this approach leads to higher and usually more realistic cost and effort values than the lump-sum estimate. With this you can successfully encounter the widespread optimism of project planners for cost and effort estimation.

Usually, different methods are used in combination for a single project, depending on the phase of the project (degree of accuracy requirements), the type of the elements concerned, the volume of the element, as well as the extent of risks and uncertainties.

The matter is that it would be important to reliably estimate cost and efforts in the early stages of projects, because decisions are made about projects being executed or not. But right at this moment, the uncertainty of planning is still very great. Smart project managers take care to communicate this context most emphatically with their project clients: project leaders are strongly advised, to specify a bandwidth or uncertainty for the estimation and to document the assumptions and methods used.

The serious estimate of costs and efforts is relatively common in practice. The following process steps for resource planning—determining the available capacity and the systematic distribution of expenses on resources and the timeline—are however still the exception.

> 🕮 Tip: The cost estimate provided is not just a planning task at the beginning of the project. It must accompany the project over its whole lifespan. This is because on the one hand the accuracy of estimates increases with the project progressing and on the other hand for projects that are already underway need periodically residual cost estimates. This is a mandatory requirement to keep the resource planning up to date.

14.8 Capacity Planning

The guiding principle of all planning is "Bottleneck Planning":

If the dates of an activity are fixed—then the capacity needs to be planned so that the fixed dates are achieved or the human resource capacity is established—or based on that capacity the end dates need to be set. In organizational projects the staff is usually the bottleneck, so that the timing of the project activities is based on the available staff. There are mainly two reasons for projects being under **timing pressure**:

- In the course of projects, often-urgent functional tasks are taken on as priorities using the current available capacities resulting in the non-availability of the scheduled project capacity.
- Individual employees are simultaneously involved in several activities, without taking this into account carefully enough.

Therefore, an additional capacity planning should be performed generally directly after the time scheduling. Because:

- During project planning potential bottlenecks are identified in advance and therefore early preventive actions can be taken up front.
- If there are no capacity bottlenecks, a better utilization of the project staff can be aspired by distributing the under and over capacities evenly.

The personnel requirements needed are planned during the capacity-planning phase. The degree of capacity needed for each project team member is determined within a specific time period; the load is usually illustrated by using a load profile chart (Figs. 14.2 and 14.3). The charts show both EST and EET timing on whether the staff capacity available for an employee is below the total project capacity threshold having then free capacity to be used for other activities, or the employee is exceeding the threshold and therefore a burden sharing or new resources are required.

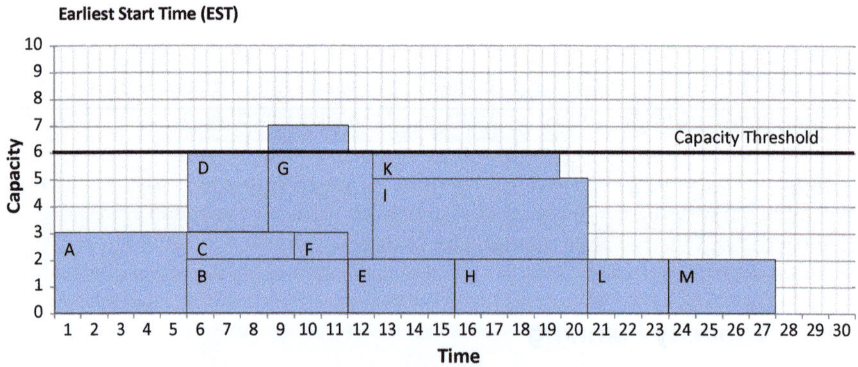

Fig. 14.2 Uneven balanced capacity load (EST) (build shed)

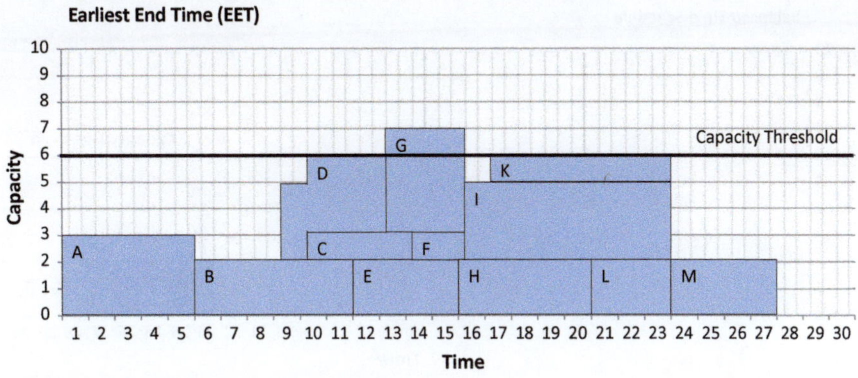

Fig. 14.3 Uneven balanced capacity load (EET) (build shed)

The capacity load balance can be done as follows:

- The dates of the non-critical activities are modified (restricted by the nodes time buffer) logically resulting in overall balanced capacities and schedules.
- The project staff activities are distributed differently. Only employees with wide knowledge, expertise, and an acceptable load can support the strained employees.
- Increase the entire available staff capacity; this is done either by reinforcing temporal integration of the staff who contribute only part-time on the project or by adding additional internal or external project team members.
- The milestone dates can be moved so that the basic dates of the scheduling change.

In practical project planning the scheduling and capacity planning cannot be separated because schedules and resources commonly interact. The capacity and scheduling are therefore a continuous, iterative process to be performed until the existing bottlenecks are removed and a more or less uniform distribution load of all project staff achieved. In Fig. 14.4 you see the result of the iterative resource optimizing.

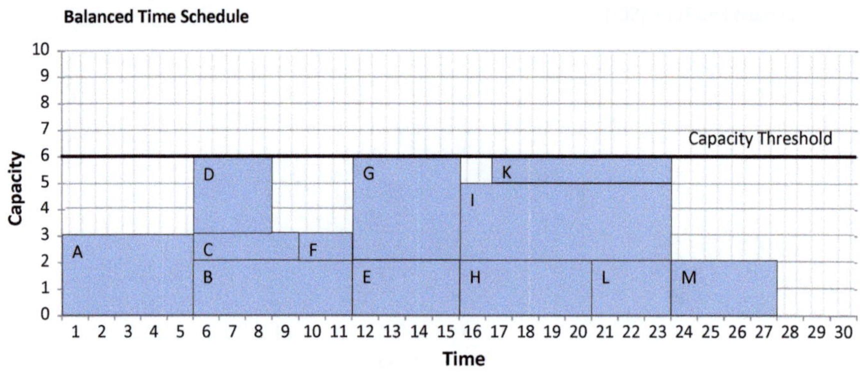

Fig. 14.4 Balanced capacity load (build dhed)

References

Michael Gessler. (2011). Kompetenzbasiertes Projektmanagement (PM3) Handbuch für die Projektarbeit, Qualifizierung und Zertifizierung auf Basis der IPMA Competence Baseline Version 3.0 / unter Mitwirkung der spm swiss project management association (4. Auflage ed., Vol. 1). Nürnberg: GPM Deutsche Gesellschaft für Projektmanagement.

Prof Dr. Shulte Zurhausen, M. (2010). Project-/Change Management/Organisation Lerneinheit 1. Hagen: Institut für Verbundstudien der Fachhochschule NRW.

15 Cost and Finance

An important part of a project manager's job is managing money. All types of organizations must manage their money well in order to fulfil their mission, including not-for-profit and government organizations. The tools and methods used to manage money on a project vary depending on the phase and complexity of the project. This chapter first describes the methods used to estimate the cost of a project, create a budget, and manage the cost of activities whilst the project is being executed. It then covers a major component of cost management—the procurement process.

To achieve the objectives of the project, the management team often needs to look outside the internal organization for additional help. The process of obtaining goods and services from providers who are outside of the organization is called procurement. We will discuss ways of selecting the work that will be procured and the different methods and processes for procuring the equipment, materials, and services for the project.

The procurement effort on projects varies widely and depends on the type of project. Often the client organization will provide procurement services on less complex projects. In this case, the project team identifies the materials, equipment, and supplies needed by the project and provides product specifications and a detailed delivery schedule. When the procurement department of the parent organization provides procurement services, a liaison from the project can help the procurement team better understand the unique requirements of the project and the time-sensitive or critical items of the project schedule.

On larger, more complex projects, personnel are dedicated to procuring and managing the equipment, supplies, and materials needed by the project. Because of the temporary nature of projects, equipment, supplies, and materials are procured as part of the product of the project or for the execution of the project. For example, workbook materials might be procured for the product of the project, and the computers and software might be equipment procured for the execution of the project work. At the end of the project, equipment bought or rented for the execution of the

P. Bauer, *A Comprehensive Project Management Guide*, Management for Professionals, https://doi.org/10.1007/978-3-031-68252-0_15

work of the project are sold, returned to rental organizations, or disposed of some other way.

More complex projects will typically procure through different procurement and management methods. Commodities are common products that are purchased based on the lowest bid. Commodities include items like concrete for building projects, office supplies, or even lab equipment for a research project. The second type of procurement includes products that are specified for the project. Vendors who can produce these products bid for a contract. The awarding of a contract can include price, ability to meet the project schedule, the fit for purpose of the product, and other considerations important to the project. Equipment specially designed and built for a research project is an example of what might be provided by a project vendor. These vendors' performances become important parts of the project, and the project manager assigns resources to coordinate the work and schedule of the vendor.

The third procurement approach is the development of one or more partners. A public relations firm that is awarded the advertising contract for a major project and a research firm that is conducting critical subparts of the research are examples of potential project partners. A partner contributes to and is integrated into the execution plan. Partners perform best when they share the project vision of success and are emotionally invested in the project. The project management team builds and implements a project procurement plan that recognizes the most efficient and effective procurement approach to support the project.

15.1 Estimating Costs

During the conceptual phase when project selection occurs, economic factors are an important consideration when choosing between competing projects. To compare the simple paybacks or internal rates of return between projects, an estimate of the cost of each project is made. The estimates must be accurate enough so that the comparisons are meaningful, but the amount of time and resources used to make the estimates should be appropriate to the size and complexity of the project. The methods used to estimate the cost of the project during the selection phase are generally faster and consume fewer resources than those used to create detailed estimates in later phases. They rely more on the expert judgement of experienced managers who can make accurate estimates with less detailed information. Estimates in the earliest stages of project selection are usually based from previous projects that can be adjusted and scaled to match the size and complexity of the current project or by applying standardized formulas.

15.2 Analogous Estimate

An estimate that is based on other project estimates is an analogous estimate. If a similar project cost a certain amount, then it is reasonable to assume that the current project will cost about the same. Few projects are exactly the same size and complexity, so the estimate must be adjusted upwards or downwards to account for the difference. The selection of projects that are similar and the amount of adjustment needed is up to the judgement of the person who makes the estimate. Normally, this judgement is based on many years of experience estimating projects, including incorrect estimates that were learning experiences for the expert.

☞ **Example:** Peter asked a friend for advice about the cost of his building a shed. His friend replied, "I built a shed a little smaller than yours last year and the quality was about the same. I did it with a company named Karibu construction and a few friends. It cost about 999 € for the Workers, Paint, Foundation, Wood, Shed Assembly and Furnishing." Because of the similarity of the projects, John's initial estimate of the cost of the move was less than 1200 € and he decided that the cost would be affordable and the project could go forward.

Less experienced managers who are required to make analogous estimates can look through the documentation that is available from previous projects. If those projects were evaluated using the Darnall-Preston Complexity Index (DPCI), the manager can quickly identify projects that have similar profiles to the project under consideration even if other people managed those projects. Comparing the original estimates with the final project costs on several previous projects with the same DPCI ratings gives a less-experienced manager the perspective that it would take many years to acquire by trial and error. It also provides references, which the manager can use to justify the estimate.

15.3 Parametric Estimate

If the project consists of activities that are common to many other projects, average costs are available per unit. For example, if you ask a construction company how much it would cost to build a standard office building, they will ask for the size of the building in square metre and the city in which the building will be built. From these two factors—size and location—the company's estimator can predict the cost of the building. Factors like size and location are parameters—measurable factors that can be used in an equation to calculate a result. The estimator knows the average cost per square foot of a typical office building and adjustments for local labour costs. Other parameters such as quality of finishes are used to further refine the estimate. Estimates that are calculated by multiplying measured parameters by cost-per-unit values are parametric estimates.

☞ Example: To estimate the time for the foundation digging needed for Peter's shed, the parameter used by a building company in the Internet is the area and dimensions and the weight of the shed. The company assumes that the weight and dimensions are important parameters to determine how big the foundation should be and how much concrete is needed. Once the size is determined, other parameters, such as concrete quality, are used to estimate the cost.

15.4 Estimating Costs to Initiate Projects

Once the project is selected, more accurate estimates are often needed to raise funds and agree on contracts with vendors in the initiation phase.

☞ Example: Peter recalled that his friend also told him how tiring it was to do all the work and help assemble the shed himself, and some shed parts were damaged when the load shifted inside the truck. Peter decides to call in a few favours from two friends, to help him and to unpack and control the parts before the truck leaves again and to hire some of the skilled labour like that needed to assemble the shed properly.

15.5 Vendor Bid Analysis

If vendors will provide services or products, the cost of those services can be determined by issuing a request for proposal (RFP). The RFP describes the work, service, or product to be provided by the vendor and the quality level required. The RFP is sent to a list of vendors who are qualified—meet standards of reliability and capability—to perform this type of work. They respond with a proposal for completing the work described in the RFP, including an estimate of the cost. Some government organizations are required to use the qualified vendor with the lowest bid. Other organizations are not bound to take the lowest bid but are usually required to justify their reasons for not doing so.

☞ Example: Using RFPs to make estimates on Peter's shed: Peter wants to find out how much it would cost to hire a skilled crew to build the shed and the concrete foundation from the same company. He is not sure if any companies offer this option, so he decides to ask three different companies for bids. He also decides to ask for bids on a standard shed assembly that includes all phases of shed building as a comparison to see if his cost-saving plan is worth the extra effort.

The project management team can review the responses by several vendors to the RFP to determine if their estimate of the cost of that aspect of the project is close to the estimate made during the project selection stage. If the estimates by the vendors are much higher than expected, and if the project cannot be completed for the cost that was used to select the project, the selection decision might have to be reconsidered. Reconsidering the selection of the project should take into consideration the economic ratings of the competing projects that were not chosen and who the project champions are for the projects that would be affected.

Some vendors may suggest an alternative way to meet the objective of the RFP in a more cost-effective manner that does not match the specifics of the RFP. Such alternatives can reduce costs if they are acceptable.

15.6 Bottom-Up Estimating

The most accurate and time-consuming estimating method is to identify the cost of each item in each activity of the schedule, including labour and materials. If you view the project schedule as a hierarchy where the general descriptions of tasks are at the top and the lower levels become more detailed, finding the price of each item at the lowest level and then summing them to determine the cost of higher levels is called **bottom-up** estimating.

Example: Bottom-up estimate for Peter's move. After evaluating the bids by the moving companies, Peter decides the savings are worth his time if he can get the assembly done with the help of his friends. He decides to prepare a detailed estimate of costs for tools and materials. He looks up the prices for tools and materials on company websites and prepares a detailed list of items, quantities, and costs, as shown in Table 15.1.

Table 15.1 Detailed cost estimate

Index	Category	Node Description	Activite	Duration	EST	EET	Node Cost	Total Cost
A	Pre-planning	Purchase plot	1.0	5	0	0	€30.00	€150.00
B	Human resources	Hire workers	2.0	6	5	5	€20.00	€120.00
C	Pre-planning	Select design	1.0	4	5	9	€10.00	€40.00
D	Materials	Purchase paint	1.0	3	5	8	€25.00	€75.00
E	Houerly work	Dig foundation	3.0	4	11	11	€40.00	€160.00
F	Materials	Purchase wood	1.0	2	9	13	€15.00	€30.00
G	Houerly work	Paint shed	2.0	4	8	11	€20.00	€80.00
H	Houerly work	Lay foundation	3.0	5	15	15	€30.00	€150.00
I	Houerly work	Assemble Shed	2.0	8	12	15	€20.00	€160.00
K	Delay	Dry paint	-	7	12	16	€10.00	€70.00
L	Delay	Harden foundation	3.0	3	20	20	€60.00	€180.00
M	Houerly work	Furnish shed	1.0	4	23	23	€30.00	€120.00
							Sum	€1,335.00

This type of estimate is typically more accurate than an analogous or parametric estimate. In this example, the sum of the shed building is estimated to be 1335.00 €.

The detail can be rolled up—subtotalled—to display less detail. This process is made easier using computer software. On projects with low complexity, the cost estimates can be done on spreadsheet software. On larger projects, software that manages schedules can also manage costs and display costs by activity and by category. For example, the subtotal feature could be used in Excel and collapsed to show the subtotals for the two categories of costs, as shown in Table 15.2.

Table 15.2 Sum of detailed cost estimate by category

Category	Count - Node	Sum - Total Cost
Delay	2	€250.00
Houerly Work	5	€670.00
Labour	1	€120.00
Materials	2	€105.00
Pre-Planning	2	€190.00
Totel	**12**	**€1.335.00**

An activity can have costs from multiple vendors in addition to internal costs for labour and materials. Detailed estimates from all sources can be reorganized so those costs that are associated with a particular activity can be grouped by adding the activity code to the detailed estimate.

Table 15.3 Detailed cost associated with activities

Index	Category	Node Description	Activite	Duration	EST	EET	Node Cost	Total Cost
A	Pre-planning	Purchase plot	1.0	5	0	0	€30.00	€150.00
B	Human resources	Hire workers	2.0	6	5	5	€20.00	€120.00
C	Pre-planning	Select design	1.0	4	5	9	€10.00	€40.00
D	Materials	Purchase paint	1.0	3	5	8	€25.00	€75.00
E	Houerly work	Dig foundation	3.0	4	11	11	€40.00	€160.00
F	Materials	Purchase wood	1.0	2	9	13	€15.00	€30.00
G	Houerly work	Paint shed	2.0	4	8	11	€20.00	€80.00
H	Houerly work	Lay foundation	3.0	5	15	15	€30.00	€150.00
I	Houerly work	Assemble Shed	2.0	8	12	15	€20.00	€160.00
K	Delay	Dry paint	-	7	12	16	€10.00	€70.00
L	Delay	Harden foundation	3.0	3	20	20	€60.00	€180.00
M	Houerly work	Furnish shed	1.0	4	23	23	€30.00	€120.00
							Sum	€1,335.00

Category	Count - Node	Sum - Total Cost
Delay	2	€250.00
Houerly Work	5	€670.00
Labour	1	€120.00
Materials	2	€105.00
Pre-Planning	2	€190.00
Totel	12	€1.335.00

The detailed cost estimates can be sorted by activity and then subtotalled by activity to determine the cost for each activity (Table 15.3).

15.7 Establishing a Budget

Once you have broken your project down into activities, you will be able to calculate your overall project costs by estimating and totalling the individual activity costs. This process of subtotalling costs by category or activity is called **cost aggregation**.

15.8 Budget Timeline

Costs are associated with activities and since each activity has a start date and a duration period, it is possible to calculate how much money will be spent by any particular date during the project. The money needed to pay for a project is usually transferred to the project account shortly before it is needed. These transfers must be timed so that the money is there to pay for each activity without causing a delay in the start of the activity. If the money is transferred too far in advance, the organization will lose the opportunity to use the money somewhere else, or they will have to pay unnecessary interest charges if the money is borrowed. A schedule of money transfers is created that should match the need to pay for the activities. The process of matching the schedule of transfers with the schedule of activity payments is called reconciliation.

Index	Activity	1	2	3	4	5	6	7	8	9	10
1	Cost	50,00 €	200,00 €	50,00 €	300,00 €	500,00 €	200,00 €	100,00 €	400,00 €	300,00 €	500,00 €
2	Total Spend	50,00 €	250,00 €	300,00 €	600,00 €	1.100,00 €	1.300,00 €	1.400,00 €	1.800,00 €	2.100,00 €	2.600,00 €
3	Transfers	400,00 €	900,00 €	700,00 €	600,00 €						
4	Total funding	400,00 €	400,00 €	400,00 €	1.300,00 €	1.300,00 €	1.300,00 €	2.000,00 €	2.000,00 €	2.600,00 €	2.600,00 €
5	Cash in Account	350,00 €	150,00 €	100,00 €	700,00 €	200,00 €		600,00 €	200,00 €	500,00 €	

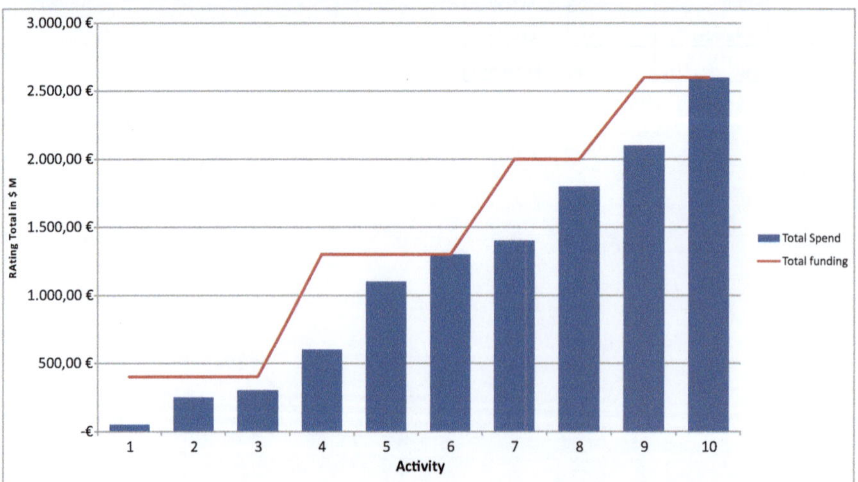

Fig. 15.1 Fund transfers and expenditures

Refer to Fig. 15.1 which shows the costs of ten major activities in a project. Funds are transferred into the project account four times. Notice that during most of the project, there were more funds available than were spent except at activity 6 when all the available funds were spent.

In the project budget profile shown in Fig. 15.1 there is no margin for error if the total of the first six activities exceeds the amount of funding at that point in the project.

Contractual agreements with vendors often require partial payment of their costs during the project. Those contracts can be managed more conveniently if the unit of measure for partial completion is the same as that used for cost budgeting. For example, if a builder is building a house, the contract may call for partial payment after 25% of the structural works have finished.

15.9 Managing Cash Flow

If the total amount spent on a project is equal to or less than the amount budgeted, the project can still be in trouble if the funding for the project is not available when it is needed. There is a natural tension between the financial people in an organization, who do not want to pay for the use of money that is just sitting in a checking account, and the project manager, who wants to be sure that there is enough money available to pay for project expenses. The financial people prefer to keep the company's money working in other investments until the last moment before transferring it to the project account. The contractors and vendors have similar concerns, and they want to get paid as soon as possible so they can put the money to work in their own organizations. The project manager would like to have as much cash available as possible to use if activities exceed budget expectations.

15.10 Contingency Reserves

In most projects, unforeseen events often arise, leading to costs exceeding the initial estimates. If estimates consistently remain under the actual costs, the estimating method should be reevaluated, as the estimates might be inflated. Whilst predicting which specific activities will incur higher costs is challenging, it is prudent to anticipate that some will. Estimating the probability of these occurrences falls under risk analysis, which will be explored in a later chapter.

Rather than inflating each cost estimate, a budget is set aside specifically for handling unforeseen but statistically predictable cost increases. These funds are known as contingency reserves.

Since it is likely that these funds will be utilized, they are included in the overall project budget. If the **contingency reserve** is sufficient to cover unexpected expenses, the project can be completed within the budget.

15.11 Management Reserves

If an event occurs during the project that necessitates a change in scope, funds may be required to address the situation before negotiating the scope change with the project sponsor or client. This situation could present either a challenge or an opportunity. For instance, if a new technology emerges that significantly improves the project, there would be additional costs and a scope change, but the enhancement would be worthwhile. Funds can be allocated at the manager's discretion to accommodate needs that alter the project's scope. These funds are known as management reserves. Unlike contingency reserves, they are not typically expected to be spent and are not part of the project's budget baseline, although they can be included in the total project budget.

15.12 Evaluating the Budget During the Project

A project manager must consistently compare actual expenditures with the budgeted amounts and report this information to managers and stakeholders. It's essential to establish a clear method for measuring and reporting progress.

☞ Example of reporting budget progress for Peter's shed: Peter estimated the shed move would cost around 1200 € and take about 16 days. Eight days into the project, Peter has spent 300 €. He tells his friends that the project is on track because he's halfway through the timeline but has only spent a fifth of the budget. However, Peter's friend Alice points out that his report is insufficient because he didn't compare the actual expenditure to the budgeted amount for the tasks that should have been completed by the eighth day. As Alice highlights, a budget report must compare the actual spending to the expected spending for the project's current phase. Basic measures such as the percentage of activities completed, percentage of measurement units completed, and percentage of budget spent are sufficient for simpler projects, but more sophisticated techniques are necessary for complex projects.

15.13 Earned Value Analysis

For medium- and high-complexity projects, a widely used method is **earned value management (EVM).** EVM involves periodically comparing budgeted costs with actual costs throughout the project. This method integrates the scheduled activities with detailed cost estimates for each task, allowing for the assessment of partial completions when only some of the associated costs have been incurred.

The budgeted cost of work scheduled (BCWS) includes the detailed cost estimates for each activity in the project. The planned value (PV) represents the amount of work that should have been completed by a specific date. Whilst some sources use these terms interchangeably, planned value is specifically used in formulas to denote the sum of the budgeted costs up to a particular point in the project. For clarity, this text will maintain this distinction in the definitions.

☞ Example: Planned value on day six of Peter's shed project: By day six of the project, Peter should have taken his friends to lunch and bought the paint materials. The segment of the BCWS that corresponds to these tasks is the planned value (PV) for that day. The details of the planned value for day six are shown in Table 15.4.

Table 15.4 Planned value for lunch and materials

Description	Quantity	Cost
Lunch	3	45,00 €
Hire workers for foundation work	10	42,57 €
Hire workers for woodwork	15	60,82 €
Hire workers for assambly	7	46,57 €
Do survey with friends to selectd design (Coffe shop)	7	26,25 €
Buy paint	3	23,85 €
Buy brushes	3	38,00 €
Buy foil	2	7,70 €
Buy tape	2	3,00 €
Buy turpentine	2	5,90 €
	PV=BCWS	**299,65 €**

The **budgeted cost of work performed** (BCWP) is the cost that was budgeted for the work that has actually been completed. Summing the BCWP values up to a specific point in the project gives the earned value. The actual cost, on the other hand, is the total of the amounts actually spent, which may differ from the estimated budget.

☞ Example: Comparing plane value, estimated value, and actual cost in Peter's shed building project on Day Six: The two friends of Peter's were both trying to lose weight and just wanted a nice salad. Consequently, the lunch cost less than expected. Peter makes a stop at a store that sells moving supplies at discount rates. They do not have all the items he needs, but the prices are lower than those quoted by the building company. They have a very good price on brushes so he decides to buy an extra one. He returns with some of the items on his list, but this phase of the job is not complete by the end of day six. Peter bought half of the paint, all of five other items, twice as many brushes, and none of four other items. Peter is only 6 days into his project, and his costs and performance are starting to vary from the plan. Earned value analysis gives us a method for reporting that progress (Table 15.5).

Table 15.5 Planned value, earned value, and actual cost

	Budget Cost of Work Shedule (BEWS)		Budget Cost of Work Perfomance (BEWP)		Actual Cost	
Description	Quantity	Cost	Quantity	Cost	Quantity	Cost
Lunch	3	45,00 €	3,00 €	45,00 €	3,00 €	35,00 €
Hire workers for foundation work	10	42,57 €	5,00 €	24,78 €	5,00 €	27,80 €
Hire workers for woodwork	15	60,82 €	15,00 €	60,82 €	15,00 €	48,94 €
Hire workers for assambly	7	46,57 €				
Do survey with friends to selectd design (Coffe shop)	7	26,25 €	7,00 €	26,25 €	7,00 €	18,25 €
Buy paint	3	23,85 €				
Buy brushes	3	38,00 €	3,00 €	38,00 €	6,00 €	52,00 €
Buy foil	2	7,70 €				
Buy tape	2	3,00 €	2,00 €	3,00 €	2,00 €	1,50 €
Buy turpentine	2	5,90 €				
	PV=BCWS	299,65 €	EV=BCWP	197,85 €	AC=ACWP	183,49 €

The initial schedule projected a planned value of 299.65 € by day six. However, the work completed was valued at 197.85 € (earned value) according to the estimates, whilst the actual expenditure was only 183.49 €.

15.14 Schedule Variance

The project manager needs to determine if the project is on schedule and within budget. The variance between planned and actual progress provides this information. Schedule variance (SV) is calculated as the difference between the earned value (EV) and the planned value (PV). The formula is **SV = EV − PV.** If the earned value is less than planned, the schedule variance is negative, indicating the project is behind schedule.

☞ Example: Schedule variance on Peter's shed: Peter's moving plan required spending 299.65 € by day six, which is the planned value (PV). The difference between the planned value and the earned value (EV) is the schedule variance (SV). Using the formula **SV = EV − PV**, we find SV = 197.85 € − 299.65 € = (101.80) €. A negative SV shows the project is behind schedule.

Cost variance (CV) is the difference between the earned value (EV) and the actual cost (AC). The formula is **CV = EV − AC**. A positive CV indicates the project is under budget.

☞ Example: **Cost variance on Peter's shed:** The difference between the earned value of 197.85 € and the actual cost of 183.49 € is the cost variance (CV). Using the formula **CV = EV − AC**, we find CV = 197.85 € − 183.49 € = 14.36 €.

15.15 Variance Indexes for Schedule and Cost

The schedule variance and cost variance indicate whether spending is behind or ahead of schedule and whether the project is over or under budget. However, they do not show how these variances compare to the total budget. The ratio of earned value (EV) to planned value (PV) indicates project completion. This ratio is known as the **schedule performance index** (**SPI**), calculated as **SPI = EV/PV**.

☞ Example: For Peter's shed project, the SPI is 0.66 (SPI = 197.85 €/ 299.65 €= 0.66). An SPI value less than one means the project is behind schedule.

The ratio of earned value (EV) to actual cost (AC) is the cost **performance index** (CPI), calculated as **CPI = EV/AC.**

☞ Example: Cost performance index for Peter's shed: In this case, CPI = 197.85 €/183.49 €= 1.07. A value greater than one indicates the project is under budget. A cost variance of positive 14.36 € and a CPI value of 1.07 suggest that Peter is getting more value for his money than planned by day six. Conversely, a schedule variance (SV) of negative (101.80) € and an SPI of 0.66 indicate that he is behind schedule in adding value to the project (Fig. 15.2).

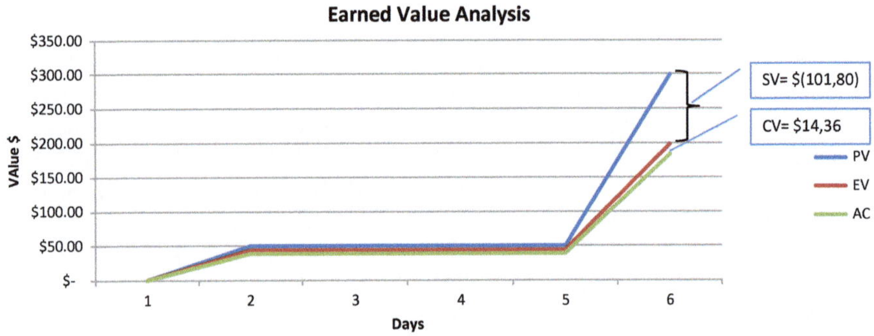

Fig. 15.2 Schedule variance and cost variance on day six of the shed build

Throughout the project, the manager assesses the schedule using metrics like schedule variance (SV) and schedule performance index (SPI) and monitors the budget using metrics such as cost variance (CV) and cost performance index (CPI). These tools provide insights into how well the project is adhering to its planned schedule and budgetary allocations.

15.16 Estimated Cost To Complete The Project

Midway through the project, the manager assesses the accuracy of cost estimates for completed activities to forecast the remaining costs needed to finish the project, known as the estimate to **complete (ETC).**

To calculate ETC, the manager evaluates whether the observed cost variances up to this point will continue into the future. For instance, if unexpected weather conditions caused higher costs initially, it's unlikely to impact future expenses similarly. If the manager determines these variances are atypical, ETC is calculated as the difference between the original **budget at completion** (BAC) and the **earned value** (EV) accrued so far. This is expressed as **ETC = BAC – EV**.

☞ Example: Estimate to complete Peter's shed: In Peter's shed construction, Peter managed to purchase most items at a discount store with limited inventory and decided to buy extra lifting straps. Costs for packing materials were based on prices from the moving company where he still needs to buy remaining items. Peter concludes these factors causing variances won't affect future costs like truck rentals or hotel fees. Thus, he calculates ETC as BAC (1633.00 €) minus EV (197.85 €), resulting in 1371.90 €. Formulaically, ETC = 1633.00 € – 197.85 €= 1371.90 €.

If the manager believes the observed cost variances will persist, influenced by factors like increased labour or material costs, ETC is adjusted by dividing it by the cost performance index (CPI). For instance, if labour costs were estimated at 80,000 € (EV) but actually cost 85,000 € (AC), yielding a CPI of 0.94 (CPI = EV/AC).

To calculate ETC assuming typical future costs, the formula is ETC = (BAC – EV)/CPI. If the project's BAC is 800,000 €, then ETC = (800,000 € – 80,000 €)/0.94 = 766,000 €.

15.17 Estimate Final Project Cost

The costs incurred up to the present differ from the original estimates; the overall project cost estimate will be impacted. This revised estimate is known as the estimate at completion (EAC) (Table 15.6). The EAC is calculated by adding the estimate to complete (ETC) to the actual cost (AC) of the activities already performed. The formula is expressed as **EAC = AC + ETC.**

☞ Example Estimate at completion for Peter's shed: The updated estimate at completion (EAC) for Peter's shed project is now calculated as **EAC** = 183.49 €+ 1455.15 € = **1638.64 €**.

Table 15.6 Summary of terms and formulas for earned value analysis

Term	Acronym	Description	Fromula	Peter's Shed
Actual Cost	AC	The money actually spent on projects up to the present		183,49 €
Budget at Completion	BAC	Original budget for the project (same as BCWS)		1.633,00 €
Cost Performance Index	CPI	Ratio of earned value to actual cost	CPI = EV / AC	1,08 €
Cost Variance	CV	Difference between earned value and actual cost	CV= EV-AC	14,36 €
Earned Value	EV	Sum of estimates for work actually done up to the presen		197,85 €
Estimate at Completion	EAC	Revised estimate of total project cost	EAC= AC + ETC	1.618,64 €
Estimate to Complete	ETC	Money to complete the project if early cost variance is atypical	ETC = BAC- EV	1.435,15 €
Estimate to Complete	ETC	Money to complete the project if early cost variance is typical	ETC = (BAC - EV) / CPI	1.331,01 €
Planned Value	PV	Sum of the estimates for work done up to the present		299,65 €
Schedule Performance Index	SPI	Ratio of earned value to planned value	SPI = EV /PV	0,66 €
Schedule Variance	SV	Difference between earned value and planned value	SV= EV- PV	101,80 €

15.18 Key Takeaways

1. Additional funds are set aside in a contingency reserve to handle activities where costs surpass estimates. Additionally, a management reserve is allocated to address significant opportunities or challenges that necessitate a scope change, ensuring funds are available immediately before the scope change can be formally negotiated.
2. Schedule variance is the difference between the earned value (EV) of work completed and the planned value (PV) of work that should have been completed by now. Similarly, cost variance (CV) is the difference between the earned value (EV) and the actual cost (AC).
3. The schedule performance index (SPI) is calculated as the ratio of earned value (EV) to planned value (PV). The cost performance index (CPI) is the ratio of earned value (EV) to actual cost (AC).
4. The formula to calculate the **estimate to complete (ETC)** depends on whether the cost variance to date is expected to persist. If the cost variance is atypical, the ETC is the original total budget (BAC) minus the earned value (EV). If the cost variances are typical and expected to continue, the ETC is adjusted by dividing the difference between BAC and EV by the CPI. The **estimate at completion (EAC)** is determined by adding the actual cost (AC) incurred so far to the estimate to complete (ETC).

References

Michael Gessler. (2011). Kompetenzbasiertes Projektmanagement (PM3) Handbuch für die Projektarbeit, Qualifizierung und Zertifizierung auf Basis der IPMA Competence Baseline Version 3.0/unter Mitwirkung der spm swiss project management association (4. Auflage ed., Vol. 1). Nürnberg: GPM Deutsche Gesellschaft für Projektmanagement.

Prof Dr. Shulte Zurhausen, M. (2010). Project-/Change Management/Organisation Lerneinheit 1. Hagen: Institut für Verbundstudien der Fachhochschule NRW.

Accettura, A., Bergsma, K., Boszak, T., Callaway, J.L., Cote, N. Doepker, C. Harbidge, M., Her, S., Hlushko, T., Holmes, J., Knight, M., MacDowell, P., Marshall, C., McDougall, L., Prima, A., & Story, T. (2021). Project Management for Instructional Designers, First Canadian Edition. Retrieved from http://pm4id.ca. Licensed under a Creative Commons Attribution NonCommercial ShareAlike (BY-NC-SA) license.

16 Procurement

16.1 Project Procurement

The approach to acquiring supplies and equipment for a project is influenced by its complexity profile. For a small, low-complexity project, the procurement services of the parent organization may suffice. In an organization where project resources are dispersed across various departments, these departments may provide the necessary supplies and equipment. The project procurement cycle encompasses activities from the decision to purchase through to payment and contract closure.

16.2 Procurement Plan

Once the decision to purchase goods or outsource services is made, a procurement plan is developed. This plan includes:

- Selecting appropriate relationships and contract types for each purchased good or service
- Preparing and evaluating RFQs (Requests for Quotes) and RFPs (Requests for Proposals)
- Awarding and managing contracts
- Ensuring quality and timely performance
- Managing contract changes and closing contracts

The time required for each step varies with the project's complexity and is incorporated into the project master schedule. Delays in procurement activities can impact the project's critical path, necessitating special attention.

P. Bauer, *A Comprehensive Project Management Guide*, Management for Professionals, https://doi.org/10.1007/978-3-031-68252-0_16

16.3 Selecting the Contract Approach

The technical teams typically outline the work to be outsourced. The project management team then considers:

- Is the work or material a commodity, a customized product/service, or a unique skill/relationship?
- What type of relationship is needed: supplier, vendor, or partnership?
- How should the supplier/vendor be approached: RFQ, RFP, or personal contact?
- How well defined is the scope of work?
- What are the risks and who should assume them?

These considerations help determine the procurement approach and the most appropriate contract type, factoring in risk management. The procurement team utilizes the answers to the initial three questions to decide on the approach for acquiring goods or services. The remaining questions help in determining the most suitable contract type.

A crucial aspect in selecting the contract approach is assessing which party will assume the most risk. The team identifies the risks that the project will manage and those that will be transferred to the contractor. Generally, the project management team prefers to handle the project risk. However, in certain situations, contractors possess greater expertise or control, allowing them to more effectively manage the risks related to their contracted work.

16.4 Soliciting Bids

Solicitation involves requesting prices and supporting information from bidders, usually through RFQs or RFPs. Senior management handles partnership establishment on a case-by-case basis.

16.5 Qualifying Bidders

Potential bidders are individuals or organizations capable of supplying the materials or executing the work needed for the project. For smaller, less complex projects, the parent company often maintains a list of suppliers and vendors with a proven track record of providing goods and services, along with their performance records. For unique projects without such a list, the project team compiles a list of potential suppliers and qualifies them to bid on the project work. Qualified bidders are then added to the bidders list and informed about the project bidding schedule.

A supplier's eligibility is assessed based on their ability to meet project requirements and demonstrate financial stability. This includes the capability to meet quality specifications and adhere to the project schedule. During periods of high economic activity, suppliers may be overwhelmed, so the project team ensures that potential suppliers have the capacity and a history of meeting deadlines before adding them to the bidders list.

Financial stability is another crucial criterion for inclusion on the bidders list. A credit check or financial report from a reputable financial information provider will give insights into the potential bidder's financial health. These services typically include:

- Proprietary rankings and predictive creditworthiness scores
- Public filings such as suits, liens, judgements, and standardized financial disclosure documents conforming to the uniform commercial code.
- Comprehensive payment history, including financial statements and history.

16.6 Request for Quote

An RFQ (Request for Quote) emphasizes price. It is used when the type of materials or services is clearly defined and available from multiple sources. The contract typically goes to the bidder who can meet the project's quality and schedule requirements at the lowest price.

16.7 Request for Proposal

An RFP (Request for Proposal) considers price but prioritizes meeting the project's quality or schedule requirements. Developing a proposal in response to an RFP can be costly for the bidder, so the project team should only issue an RFP to companies that are genuinely eligible to win the bid.

16.8 Evaluating Bids

The evaluation of bids in response to RFQs (Request for Quotations) for commodity items and services primarily focuses on price. Typically, the contract is awarded to the bidder with the lowest total price, which includes the costs of goods or services, shipping or delivery expenses, warranties, and any additional services that add value to the project.

In contrast, the evaluation of bids based on RFPs (Request for Proposals) is more intricate. It involves assessing both the price and the technical approach proposed by the bidder. The project team must include experts capable of understanding the technical aspects and the value each proposal brings to the project. For more complex projects, the administrative part of the proposal is evaluated and scored by one team, while another team assesses the technical aspect. The combined scores from these evaluations determine the best proposal for the project.

16.9 Awarding the Contract

Once the project team has chosen the bidder that offers the best value, a project representative verifies all conditions of the bid and the contract with the prospective contractor. For simpler contracts, such as those for printed materials, this involves reading and signing the contract to ensure the supplier comprehends the terms and project schedule requirements. However, for more complex projects, a thorough discussion is necessary. This includes outlining the goals, identifying potential obstacles, reviewing the project schedule and critical dates, and establishing processes for resolving conflicts and enhancing work performance.

16.10 Planning Session Follows Contract Award

For a design project aimed at developing major training for a global company, the project manager organized a three-day planning session with two key partners after the contracts were awarded.

The session began with the project manager emphasizing the goal of creating an environment where each partner could exceed their profit expectations. He explained that achieving this would require a mutually supportive team, where everyone contributed to improving project performance and reaped the benefits of enhanced outcomes. The focus then shifted to identifying solutions to potential problems and strategies for boosting performance. Although this might seem straightforward, it involved several days of in-depth discussions and conflict resolution. The substantial effort invested in aligning the project team and contractors can greatly enhance overall project performance.

16.11 Managing the Contracts

Different contract types require varying levels of effort and specific skills to effectively manage them. The manager overseeing supplier contracts focuses on developing meticulous specifications and ensuring strict adherence to these guidelines. Meanwhile, the manager handling vendor contracts verifies that the contractors bidding for the work possess the requisite skills and capacity to meet project schedules. They continuously monitor vendor performance against project requirements, offering guidance and support as necessary.

In contrast, the manager of partnering arrangements works towards aligning all parties around common objectives and operational processes. Each role demands distinct competencies and effort levels.

Certain project items, known as long lead items, receive early attention from project leadership. These could include equipment custom-designed for the project, curriculum tailored for training purposes, or specialized bioreactors for biotech projects. Such items often require weeks, months, or even years to procure and finalize. Identifying these long lead items early allows the project team to initiate procurement activities promptly, as relying on standard procurement cycles could potentially delay the project.

Following the award of contracts, the project team meticulously monitors the contractor's performance against predefined criteria within the contract. Typically, contractors deliver products or services that meet quality standards and support project timelines. Occasionally, there may be instances where contractors fail to meet project expectations. In such cases, some project managers opt to enforce contractual penalties or incentives to improve performance. Alternatively, other managers collaborate with contractors to devise innovative solutions that enhance performance and meet project requirements. This flexible approach in contract management accommodates various strategies to address underperforming contractors, ensuring project success.

Managing contractor performance is crucial to achieving overall project objectives, complementing the efforts of the project team itself.

16.12 Logistics and Expediting

Equipment and materials essential for the project must undergo transportation, inventory management, warehousing, and often require secure storage. This specialized field is known as logistics. Project logistics can be managed internally by the project team or included as part of the Request for Proposal (RFP) or Request for Quote (RFQ) process.

In international projects, where materials may need to be imported, the procurement team handles customs procedures. Smaller projects often rely on logistical support from their parent company, whereas larger projects typically outsource these responsibilities to specialized logistics firms. For more extensive and intricate projects, the procurement team includes dedicated logistical expertise.

The project's progress heavily relies on the timely procurement of materials. The delivery schedule of these materials directly impacts project timelines, often necessitating earlier acquisition than conventional procurement practices dictate. Long lead items are integrated into contracting plans early on, requiring contractors to detail how they will support the project schedule.

In complex projects, critical items may be scheduled for delivery after their required date. In such cases, the procurement team collaborates with contractors to expedite manufacturing or transportation processes. Contracts often prioritize the fabrication and delivery of equipment to align with project schedules. The project logistics team explores strategies to reduce transportation times, such as expediting critical equipment directly from manufacturers, as exemplified by a project in Argentina that flew crucial equipment from Sweden instead of shipping it, thereby saving significant transit time despite higher logistics costs. Ultimately, these efforts enhance project value and ensure efficient project delivery.

16.13 Key Takeaways

1. The procurement plan encompasses several crucial steps: defining the scope of materials or services needed, selecting the appropriate contractual approach, inviting bids, choosing suitable bidders, overseeing project execution, and finalizing contracts.
2. Decisions regarding contract types hinge on several factors: the availability of suppliers, vendors, or partners for the required materials or services, the clarity of work specifications, risk allocation strategies, the task's criticality to project timelines, and the necessity for cost certainty.
3. Companies vying for contracts undergo rigorous evaluation based on their track record and current financial health. Requests for Quotation (RFQs) prioritize price competitiveness, while Requests for Proposals (RFPs) scrutinize both price and proposed methodologies.
4. Long lead-time items, essential for project timelines, are closely monitored and managed. Items crucial to schedules or experiencing delays are managed by designated expeditors. Logistics planning includes coordinating delivery, storage, and transportation logistics, alongside rigorous quality inspections of work and materials. These measures ensure that project needs are met efficiently and effectively.

References

Accettura, A., Bergsma, K., Boszak, T., Callaway, J.L., Cote, N. Doepker, C. Harbidge, M., Her, S., Hlushko, T., Holmes, J., Knight, M., MacDowell, P., Marshall, C., McDougall, L., Prima, A., & Story, T. (2021). Project Management for Instructional Designers, First Canadian Edition. Retrieved from http://pm4id.ca. Licensed under a Creative Commons Attribution NonCommercial ShareAlike (BY-NC-SA) license.

Michael Gessler. (2011). Kompetenzbasiertes Projektmanagement (PM3) Handbuch für die Projektarbeit, Qualifizierung und Zertifizierung auf Basis der IPMA Competence Baseline Version 3.0 / unter Mitwirkung der spm swiss project management association (4. Auflage ed., Vol. 1). Nürnberg: GPM Deutsche Gesellschaft für Projektmanagement.

Prof Dr. Shulte Zurhausen, M. (2010). Project-/Change Management/Organisation Lerneinheit 1. Hagen: Institut für Verbundstudien der Fachhochschule NRW.

17 Contracts

Due to the potential risks associated with legal agreements, procurement activities are typically governed by the policies and procedures of the parent organization. Once the project management team identifies which aspects of the project will be outsourced and determines the necessary relationships to support the project execution plan, the procurement team initiates the development of a contracting strategy.

On smaller and less complex projects, contract development and execution are often overseen by the parent company or by a part-time project assignee. Conversely, larger and more intricate projects may require dedicated procurement teams with specialized contracting expertise. The contracting plan establishes the framework for interactions between the project and subcontractors (suppliers, vendors, or partners), outlining procedures for accommodating changes that may arise during project execution. This change management process is used for client agreements in project management.

The contracting strategy is tailored to support the project's procurement approach, taking into account factors such as:

- The degree of uncertainty in the scope of required work
- Allocation of risk for unexpected cost escalations
- Criticality of meeting scheduled milestones
- Requirement for predictable project costs

Various types of contracting approaches are available, each suited to different project environments and methodologies. Legal contracts underpinning the procurement plan typically fall into two main categories: fixed-price contracts and cost-reimbursable contracts, each offering variations tailored to specific project needs.

For more comprehensive insights into contracting practices, please refer to (Michael Gessler, 2011) chapter 1.14.

P. Bauer, *A Comprehensive Project Management Guide*, Management for Professionals, https://doi.org/10.1007/978-3-031-68252-0_17

References

Accettura, A., Bergsma, K., Boszak, T., Callaway, J.L., Cote, N. Doepker, C. Harbidge, M., Her, S., Hlushko, T., Holmes, J., Knight, M., MacDowell, P., Marshall, C., McDougall, L., Prima, A., & Story, T. (2021). Project Management for Instructional Designers, First Canadian Edition. Retrieved from http://pm4id.ca. Licensed under a Creative Commons Attribution NonCommercial ShareAlike (BY-NC-SA) license.

Michael Gessler. (2011). Kompetenzbasiertes Projektmanagement (PM3) Handbuch für die Projektarbeit, Qualifizierung und Zertifizierung auf Basis der IPMA Competence Baseline Version 3.0 / unter Mitwirkung der spm swiss project management association (4. Auflage ed., Vol. 1). Nürnberg: GPM Deutsche Gesellschaft für Projektmanagement.

Prof Dr. Shulte Zurhausen, M. (2010). Project-/Change Management/Organisation Lerneinheit 1. Hagen: Institut für Verbundstudien der Fachhochschule NRW.

Contractual Law in Projects 18

Contract law is integral to nearly all technical aspects of project management competencies and indirectly impacts all other elements as well. Understanding the basic concepts of contract law is essential for effective project management. Project managers and team members consistently deal with contracts, and compliance with these contracts is synonymous with successful project completion.

Project managers must grasp the essential legal aspects of contracts. They need to know when contracts become effective, the importance of legal terms, the consequences of mistakes, and how to document contract fulfilment. Contract and claim management processes are available to support optimal contract fulfilment and revenue generation.

Contract law is crucial for project managers. They must read and comprehend the contract before commencing work on a project. Understanding the contractual objectives aligns with understanding the project objectives. Familiarity with all contractual obligations and their corresponding sanctions for failures is necessary for compliance. This understanding enables the identification of risks associated with the overall contract and the various phases of the contract, allowing for proactive risk management. In particular, recognizing the risks of non-compliance is vital.

This book does not delve into Contract Law in detail. For more comprehensive knowledge, please refer to (Michael Gessler, 2011) Chapter 1.14c.

References

Michael Gessler. (2011). Kompetenzbasiertes Projektmanagement (PM3) Handbuch für die Projektarbeit, Qualifizierung und Zertifizierung auf Basis der IPMA Competence Baseline Version 3.0 / unter Mitwirkung der spm swiss project management association (4. Auflage ed., Vol. 1). Nürnberg: GPM Deutsche Gesellschaft für Projektmanagement.

Prof Dr. Shulte Zurhausen, M. (2010). Project-/Change Management/Organisation Lerneinheit 1. Hagen: Institut für Verbundstudien der Fachhochschule NRW.

P. Bauer, *A Comprehensive Project Management Guide*, Management for Professionals, https://doi.org/10.1007/978-3-031-68252-0_18

19 Organization and Change Management

The expectation of a company's organization is much higher than just to solve the structural questions. There are two points of view:

- The company has an organization. If they want to achieve their goals, they need to set general standards.
- The company is an organization. The company is a target-oriented social system where people have their own ideas and do not necessarily correspond to the operational objectives.

The importance and focus of change management in the company increases as change management takes a high priority ranking of important problem areas in the company. The reasons for changes are change processes which are time-consuming and expensive and are not just executed for the sake of change.

Then "Why change?" Why do companies take on change processes, knowing very well which difficult territory to walk on? Especially changes process "shaping the future of the company" and thus are inevitably risky.

"You must be aware that there is no more difficult venture, no dubious success and no more dangerous attempt to introduce a new order of things. Because every change has enemies that had advantages in the old order and the defenders of the change, who hope for benefits of the new order. This Equanimity comes in part from the fear of the opponents, partly by the distrust of the people who have real confidence to the new situations, if they have been convinced by its durability. It is, therefore, that the enemies attack the new order at every possible opportunity and the others defend the new order weakly" (Niccolò Machiavelli, 1469–1527).

"Progress is a nice word. But its engine is 'change' and has many enemies."

(KENNEDY, n.d.)

Today, almost every company faces challenges with project characters. This has developed ultimately based on the big trends of our time: globalization, increasing dynamics, scarcity of resources, time, and money, and new developments and rapid

P. Bauer, *A Comprehensive Project Management Guide*, Management for Professionals, https://doi.org/10.1007/978-3-031-68252-0_19

progress; e.g. in the IT information technology area where the organizations were originally designed for decidedly linear (public administrations) tasks they are increasingly rethinking their internal structures and working processes to handle the pending projects more successfully.

19.1 What Is Change Management?

Change management is a structured approach that helps project management teams to manage the *"human"* **aspects** of change in order to:

- Anticipate and manage issues effectively
- Use change management techniques and tools to:
  - Analyse present state
  - Define future state
  - Develop an effective transition plan

The main reasons and drivers for changes in the companies are always questions or problems associated with the growth and cost. If you would reduce the root cause to a single business transformation objective, what would this be for your company? (Fig. 19.1)

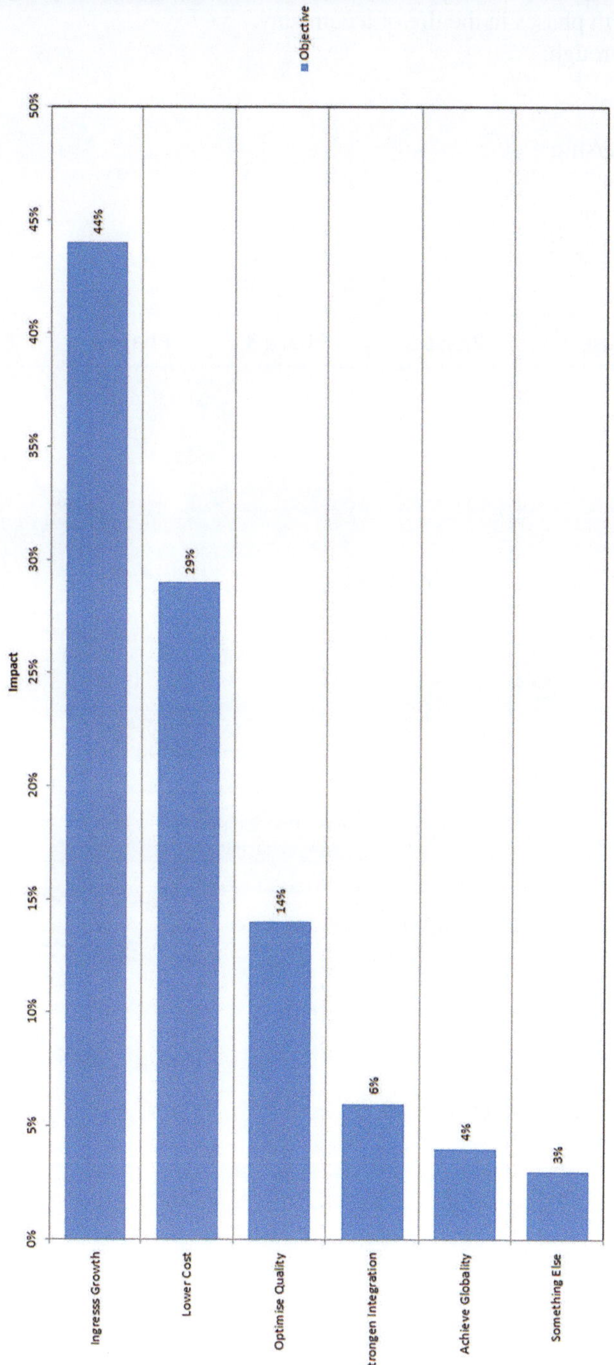

Fig. 19.1 Drivers for changes in the companies

In the growth model of the economic theorists Larry E. Greiner (Fig. 19.2) there are five growth phases in the life of a company.

Growth through:

- Creativity
- Firm leadership
- Delegation
- Coordination
- More team spirit

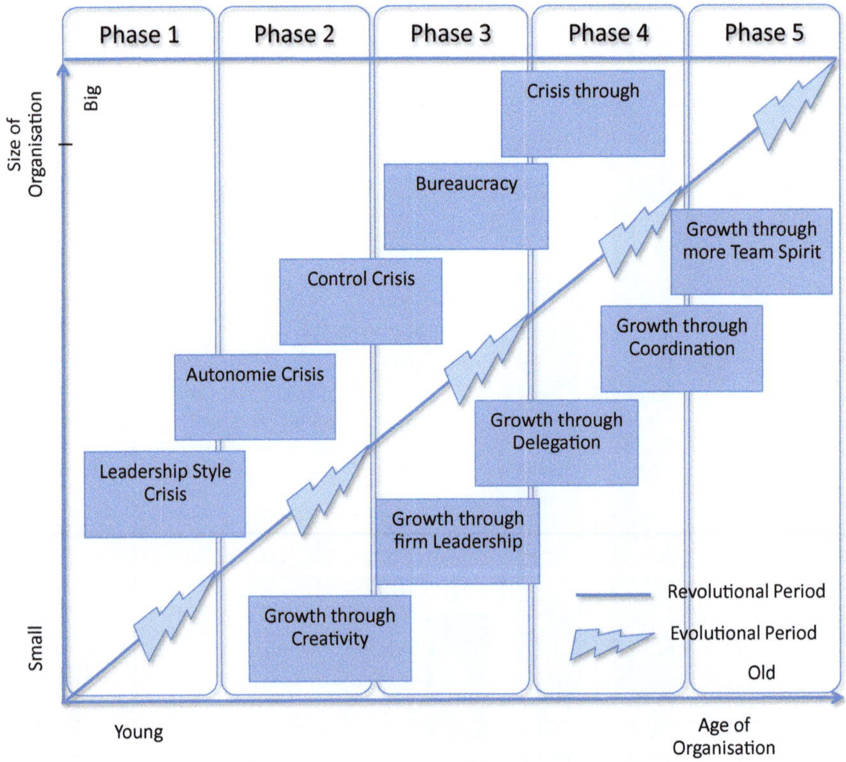

Fig. 19.2 Larry E. Greiner's five growth phases

By looking at a company as a complex system, it is clear that in the frame of a change strategy, every single intervention has also an effect on the overall system (joined-up thinking). To see these interactions at any time is a prerequisite for the change management processes. The company is represented in simplified form, divided into four fields of action, and shows the dependencies of the areas and the task of change management, which is intended to ensure the coordination and alignment of the causal relationships (Fig. 19.3).

Fig. 19.3 Areas of change management

19.2 Application of Strategies

The strategy is often called the King's discipline in the context of corporate governance. The strategy gives indications to the company and to the employees in which direction the company wants to move.

19.3 Application of Culture

The corporate culture is the entity of the values created in the course of time in an organization, to understand **moral concepts**, **standards,** and **codes of conduct**, e.g., Ford's **"One Ford"** or the Toyota production system. In addition to the classical approaches (JIT, Kaizen, lean, group work), the so-called hard facts also ("soft facts") play an important role in the company's success.

What is Culture?

- Culture is a result of behaviours and beliefs that have been learned and shared by members of a social group like a department or function.
- Culture is the written and unwritten rules about what is valued and how things are done.

Sometimes it is even necessary to adapt a controlling culture to pave the way for a new future (Table 19.1).

Table 19.1 Unwritten rules

Dimensions	Examples of "Unwritten rules"
Power/Hierarchy Status within functions (line, staff), authority, empowerment, risk-taking	The highest-ranking person has the last word
Relationships Social support, competition, induction of newcomers, attitude towards mistakes	Make your friends inside your own functional unit
Commitment Decision process, meeting committed deadlines, accountability, consequences, if rules are not followed	People who work long hours are promoted (work-life balance)
Communication Honesty, candour, e-mails, phone calls, meetings, presentations, access to your management	I can talk to my boss openly about problems

19.4 Culture: Identifying Unwritten Rules

19.5 Vision and Mission Statement

A requirement in management is that successful companies should have a vision. The vision is a credible and at the same time attractive picture to understand future corporate developments. Therefore, a vision statement (Fig. 19.4) should be able to answer the following three questions.

Fig. 19.4 Vision statement

- Strategies: Where are we today?
- Vision: Where are we going?
- Mission statement: How do we get there?

• If you do not have a goal, any path is right! • Define present state • Identify stakeholders • Find out about people and their attitudes • Identify their culture • Research the history • Define future state	• Help them define future state and get commitment • Find out which people will win/lose • Think about future culture • Design transition phase • Develop and apply actions • Overcome resistance • Communicate effectively • Influence and motivate

19.6 Application Area Organization

Functional organized companies with clear hierarchy levels are increasingly being developed into a process-oriented business structured direction, thus trying to close the organizational gap (Fig. 19.5). The main focus of the process-oriented organizations is the unique alignment of all activities based on the customer needs. (Customer focus also called VOC “Voice of the Customer”.)

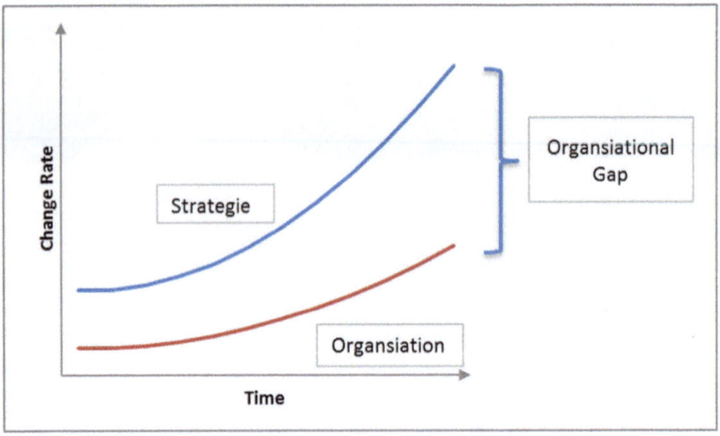

Fig. 19.5 Organizational gap

19.7 Application Area Technologies

Technology can be seen as applied knowledge, which is closely associated with procedures, methods, and machines. In the industry it is primarily related to manufacturing processes whilst in the trade and the service industry, it is related mainly to information and communication technology.

> ☞ As an example, a bank sells a portion of its products/services on the Internet (direct banking). This is primarily a technical change, but at the same time this has a serious impact on the strategy, the organization, and the culture. If you would reduce the problem only to the technology change, it will always boomerang!

Summary

All four fields of actions (Fig. 19.3) should be considered in the overall context. Any change, whether externally initiated or triggered from the inside, has an effect on the organization. This permanent "unplanned change" should be managed by implementing a planned change management or better yet a proactive change management process. The optimal fit between the four areas of application fields of action with the goal of achieving an approximate state of equilibrium (balanced condition) or stability and change should be the objective: change and resistance.

Changes

In many cases change is accompanied by the feeling of insecurity, fear, and helplessness. Every person reacts differently to this threat. From the organizational perspective, in this context one speaks of **resistance.** "The word resistance relates to the mental barriers, showing in an active and passive denial of changes". Of course, not every person behaves the same in changing conditions. Therefore, the classification, which is seen in (Fig. 19.6), seems useful.

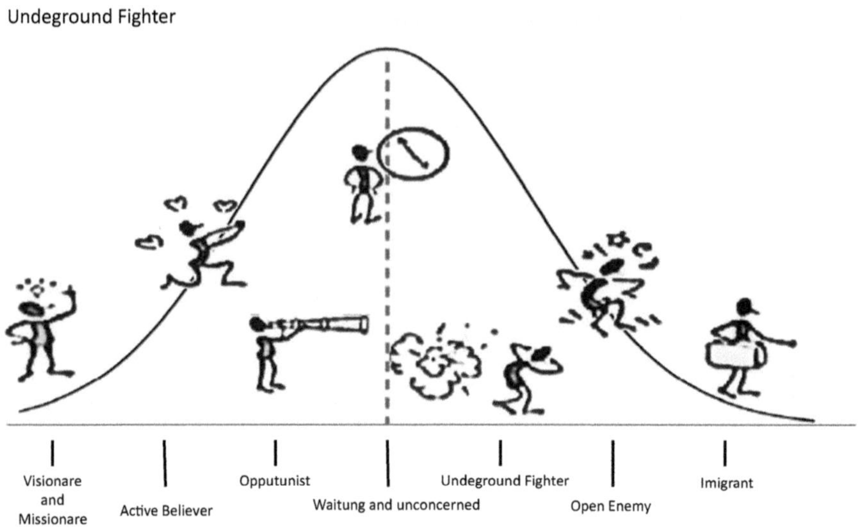

Fig. 19.6 Resistance classification

- Faced with change, people …
- Tend to be **annoyed**
- Tend to think of what they have to give up
- Tend to **feel alone**
- Can handle only so **much change**
- Are at different levels of **readiness**
- Doubt they have the **resources**, time, energy, money, or skills to handle change
- Revert to old behaviour when the **pressure is off**

19.8 Types of Resistance

Resistance to change can be different. **Rational resistance** is based on logical reasons and can probably be broken with appropriate communications.

The **political resistance** is about aspects of power. The process of change may impact the loss of a hierarchical position or loss of a social status. A separation of these persons may be inevitable.

The **emotional resistance** results in the fear from the new and the unknown. This resistance is often the hardest to tackle, because logical arguments are opposite to subjective feelings.

The model (Fig. 19.7) illustrates a general process for transitions. It was developed to describe the bereavement (death of a loved one) process, which is one of the most difficult transitions we have to go through.

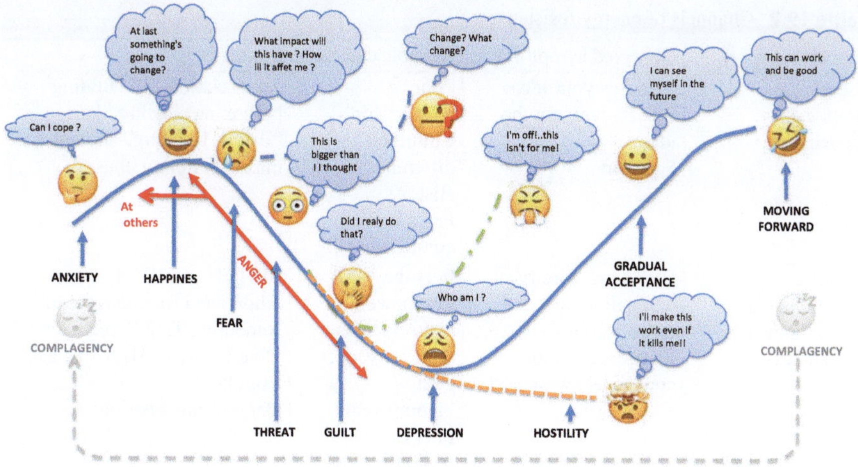

Fig. 19.7 The fisher transition curve

19.9 Methods to the Overcoming of the Resistance

The following key methods to overcome resistance have developed over time:

- Timely and open communication
- Building trust
- Qualification and competence building
- Coaching
- Reward the promoters of change
- Creation of early and rapid success experiences
- Allow errors
- Rapid stabilization of achieved communication
- Make participants from person concerned

There Is No Change Without Resistance

Resistance is normal, if it deals with the new. If there's no resistance, you should listen more in depth as those affected accept the change with resignation; this then will develop into much bigger problems. Resistance is always an encrypted message (emotional resistance). Non-observance of resistance leads to blockages. (Action = Reaction). Go with the resistance, not against it. (Channel the energy of resistance) (Table 19.2).

Table 19.2 Channels of energy resistance

Levels	Observed symptoms	Possible causes	Strategies
Level 3 Personal resistance	Opposes your ideas Resists you, not the ideas Sarcasm	Poor relationship Cultural differences History Personality conflicts	Start relationship building before introducing ideas "Bridge building" strategies during planning phases
Level 2 Emotional or physiological resistance	Blood pressure rises, adrenaline flows, pulse increases Triggered without conscious awareness	Fear they will lose power/ control status, face, or respect Feel incompetent Feel isolated Exceeds personal tolerance levels	LISTEN to THEM Align need for change with something THEY value and identify what THEY can gain from it. One-on-one meeting
Level 1 Technical resistance	Vocal disagreement Rational argument Doesn't understand	Lack of information Disagree with the idea Confusion	Presentations Q & A sessions INVOLVE THEM

A noted consultant suggests that one of the biggest mistakes people make is that they think they have to "fight" or "overcome" resistance. Resistance is an emotional response people have to the change you are introducing. Behind the resistance are "feelings" and you can't talk people out of their feelings. Feelings are neither good nor bad. They are just feelings. The best way to deal with feelings is to encourage full expression. Listen, understand, and be empathetic. Once expressed, an interesting phenomenon occurs—they lose their strength and pass like a storm. Because people feel they have been heard. If you fight the resistance or don't allow it to be expressed, the opposite occurs—Feelings grow in strength, along with their resistance.

One of the principles in Covey (1989) supports this premise. *Habit 5: "Seek first to understand, then to be understood."* To learn more about resistance, read Chap. 8 (Understanding Resistance) and Chap. 9 (Dealing with Resistance) of (Block, 2011) *Flawless Consulting,* and *Habit 5* from (Covey, 1989), *Seven Habits of Highly Effective People.* One of the most powerful strategies to keep in mind is:

The **N**eed or **M**otivation to change must be GREATER than the **R**esistance to maintaining the status quo **(N or M > R).** Motivation is not making people do things. It is getting them to want to do things. People get excited about change when they feel they are a part of it. They respond with enthusiasm when they have a role in helping define solutions or how to make things happen.

Research indicates that 51% of the time individual decisions are less accurate than group methods. Involving people in the process of making change happen helps you accomplish three things: (1) reduce resistance, (2) develop better ideas and decisions, and (3) helps you move people through the curve quicker.

Facing Resistance

- Resistance is nature's way of telling you something important is going on!
- Do not take the resistance personally.
- Allow your stakeholders to express their underlying concerns directly.
- Conflicts are a symptom of resistance.

DO NOT IGNORE RESISTORS!

19.10 Building Relationships

Listen! be conscious of your behaviour towards others. **Learn about others** by asking them about their interests and experience. Ask if you can **come to customers' team meetings.** Take this chance to introduce yourself and your project. Keep a **calendar of birthdays,** hire dates of team members, etc., and remember people on significant dates, either verbally or by sending a note. Leave your office and get out into the areas of your project work whenever possible **(get into THEIR reality)** (Fig. 19.8).

Fig. 19.8 Motivate and influence—your motivation

Different strategies:

- The first impression you make when you meet people is a lasting impression. Maintain eye contact with people, greet them, and treat them with respect regardless of their position. You'll have a great pay-off with little invested energy. Most important, however, is to be sincere. If they think you are putting on a show, you'll create mistrust and Level 3 Resistance.
- Building relationships is not a one-way communication. So, listen and find out your colleague's interests and experience. Maybe you'll discover common hobbies or similar assignments in the past.
- When you are meeting a new colleague, bring with you tables, visualized charts, and real examples of "out of specification limit" like parts or the customer complaint letter.

19.11 Concept of Organizational Changes

The requirement of all change management is to be able to plan—and to control the unpredictable in any way. This should be the minimum requirement for management. The planning is done with the help of two established concepts.

Organization design: (technical approach) this considers the efficiency and functionality of the company's structures. People play a rather secondary role. The concept is based on "hard facts"; starting points are **negotiation failure, strategic organization,** and **technology.**

Organization development: This approach brings the people into the main focus, by improving the organizational framework conditions and then expecting more motivated employees and hence an increase in effectiveness. The concept of organization development opts for many more "soft facts", i.e. more in the range of the company **culture.**

19.12 Organization Design

This concept is based on system engineering, so the engineering approach to problem-solving; it is based on the following four fundamental ideas:

- **Basic idea:** Principle "From the Rough to the Detail". Here the focus on the problem is deliberately wide at the beginning, to not get in too much detailed problem-solving. (Rough process engineering.)
- **Basic idea:** Principle of gradual formation of alternatives and selection. Initially different alternatives are looked for, not only by just following one solution path.
- **Basic idea:** Stepwise breakdown of a system design. Now the whole issue is being disassembled into sub-processes and selective decisions are prepared.
- **Basic idea**: Outline the planning process in stages. Stages within the overall problem (macro logic) are divided into steps (micro logic) (Fig. 19.9).

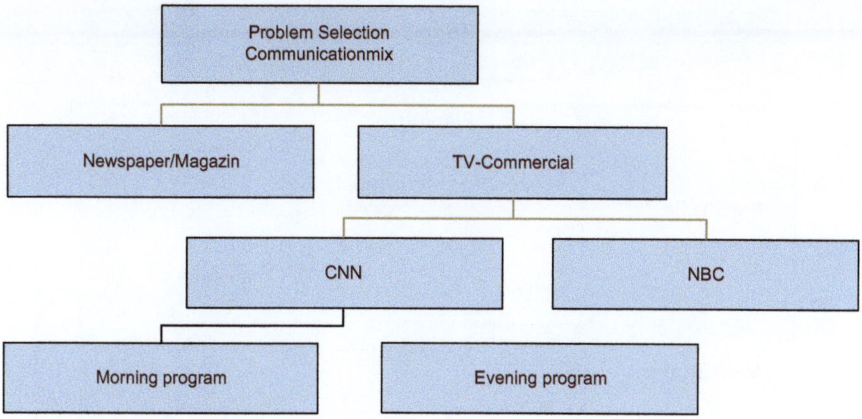

Fig. 19.9 Organizational design

19.13 How to Change Management Through Organizational Design

The proposed course of action or way of thinking makes it clear that this approach can be quite suitable to use for many organizational problems. But be warned to reduce organizational problems solely to a logical level. Also, on sheer simple structured problems people are involved and the change process gets to another dimension, where they can no longer be solved quickly without behavioural concepts (Fig. 19.10).

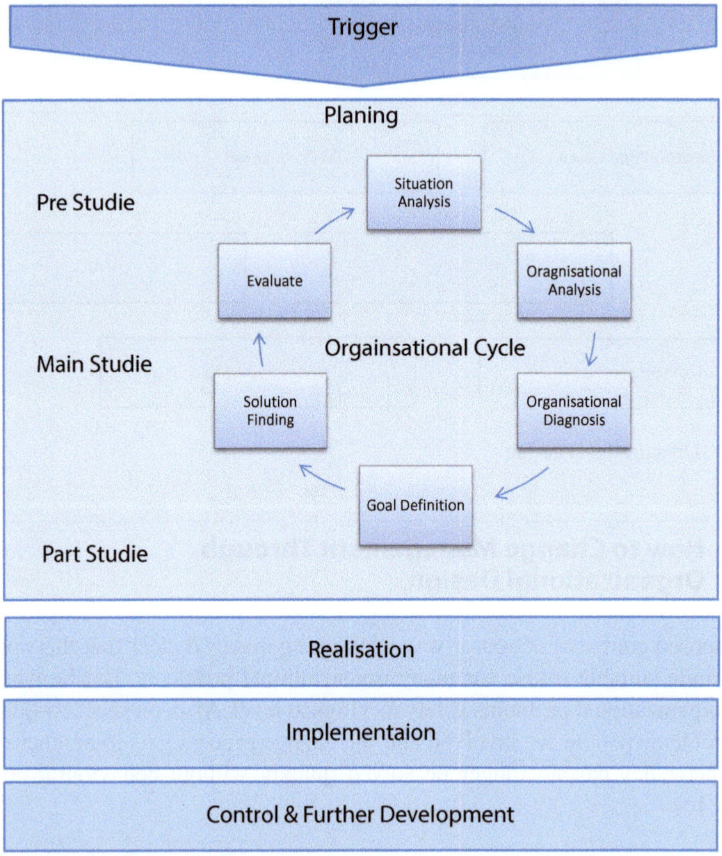

Fig. 19.10 Organizational change management

19.14 Force Field Analysis

Force field analysis is a change management technique, which was originally conceived by the psychologist Kurt Lewin for use in social situations. It displays and analyses the forces driving movement towards a goal (helping forces) or restraining movement towards the goal (hindering forces).

A big block represents the change we want to implement. Then we list all the driving forces for the change. These can be arguments in favour of the change, benefits of the change, and also groups or individuals who will support or benefit from the change. We rank these by giving each force a number from 1 to 10; the stronger the force, the higher the number.

We then list all the drawbacks, risks, costs, and reasons not to make the change. We also list those groups, departments, or individuals who might oppose the change or suffer some negative consequence of the change. We then draw all the forces as arrows bearing onto the block in the middle as shown in Fig. 19.11.

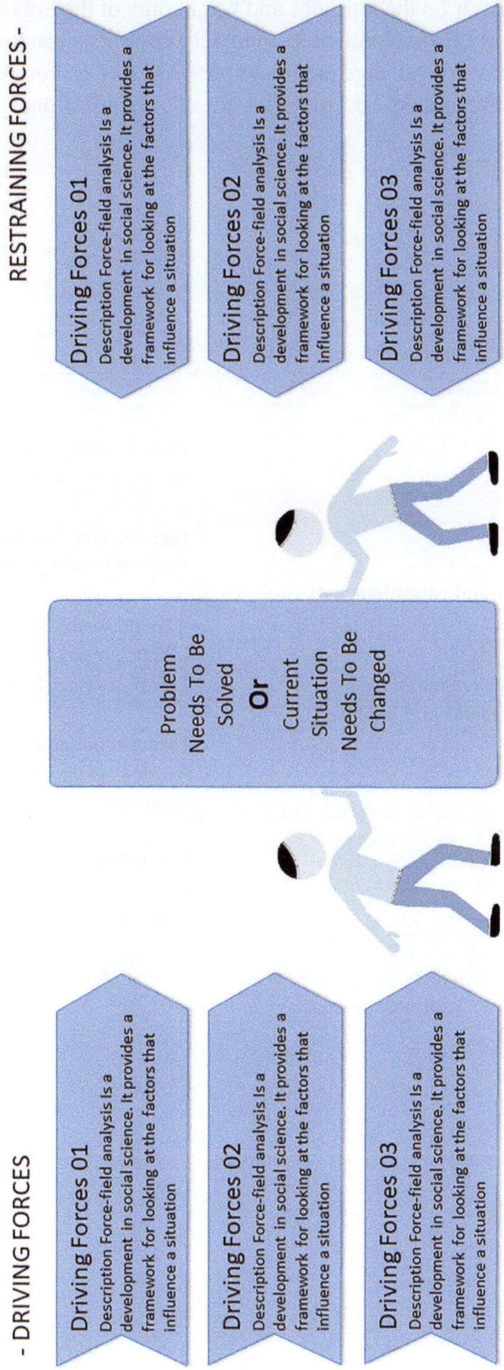

Fig. 19.11 Force field analysis

The human being is at the heart of this approach. Organizational development attempts therefore to enter on the attitudes and behaviours of the organization members. The model of Kurt Lewin (force field approach) controls consciously individuals and groups in a process of change; see example (Fig. 19.12). Forces are effective in every situation; the model is the classic of organizational development (Table 19.3).

Table 19.3 Example force field analysis by LEWIN

Force Field Analysis by LEWIN	
1. Problems describe:	
Us upsets, that ...	There is little communication to the higher management
2. Define target:	
How can we make that ...	There is more direct communication to senior management
3. Forces of influence of and conditions list:	
What inhibits ...	What promotes.
1. Old power structures	1. Young leaders with vision
2. Afraid to name the problem unfiltered.	2. Transparency, Communication
4. Powers of influence weight and analyse:	
The most limiting factor is ...	The most promotional factor is
Managing Director	Positions in the market and resources
5. Proposals for change:	
The inhibitory factors to eliminate or mitigate	To reinforce the promotional factors and support
The must CEO leave	Low sales
6. Action plan:	
Agree on specific measures:Who is doing what, when, and with whom, to achieve the desired changes	Opt out Managing Director

19.15 Organizational Development: Lewin Model

For every organizational process it is key to change the **force fields**. The process (Fig. 19.12) can be explained by three terms and procedures. **Unfreeze:** *generate feelings of guilt and security despite of change*, **Change:** *coaching*, **refreeze:** *stabilize*.

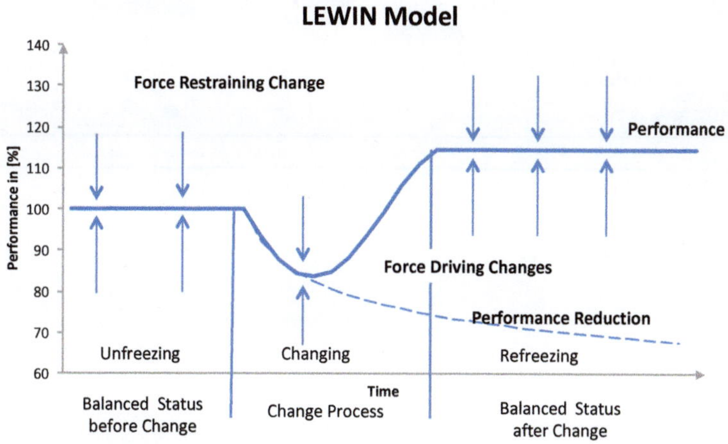

Fig. 19.12 Lewin model graph

Specifically, each change management process must begin at a point in time. Meaning: where the organization should first be intervened? Possible approaches are top-down approach, bottom-up approach, centre-out approach (wedge approach), multiple—nucleus approach (spot strategies) (Fig. 19.13, p .317).

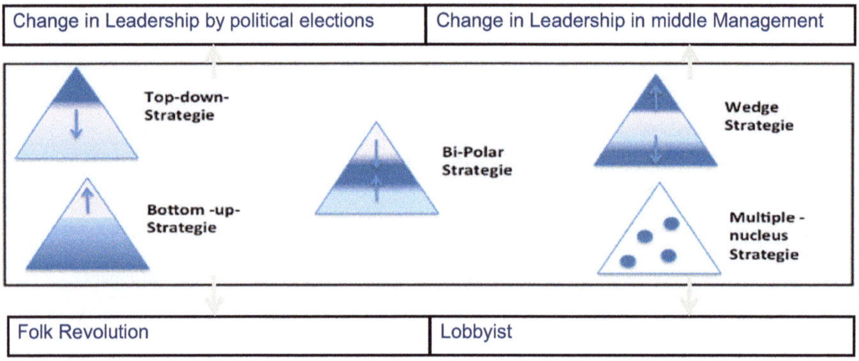

Fig. 19.13 Spot strategies

19.16 Change Management and Company Culture

No matter what in the context of a change management process measures: it always has impact on the whole. It can be stated that successful change management aims to change the culture of an organization. The iceberg expresses that a large part of the company's culture is located under water; only the factual level is visible (Fig. 19.14).

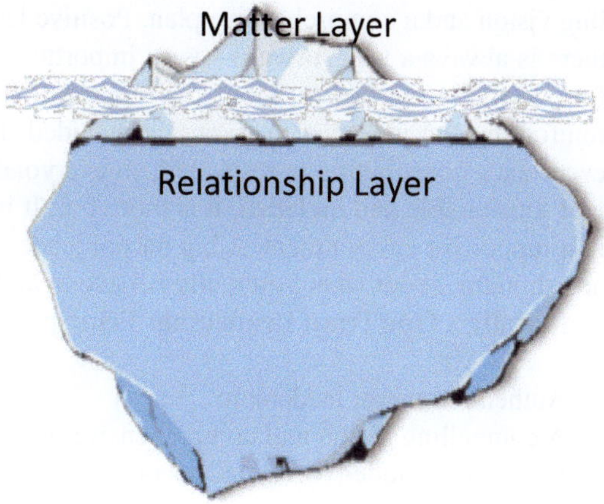

Fig. 19.14 Iceberg layer

Organizational change is cultural change.

For the Ford Motor Company, the cultural change was symbolic "One Ford". Alan Mulally became CEO of Ford in September 2006. At that time the company was just months away from running out of money. Congress had offered all three US automakers a bailout and GM and Chrysler put their hand out. But Ford had a plan to reform operations, build great cars, and overcome its non-functional culture. The plan was called One Ford.

Today Mulally's One Ford strategy is one of the greatest turnaround stories in history: taking Ford from near death to the most profitable automaker in the world.

At the most fundamental level, it is an honour to serve—at whatever type or size of organization you are privileged to lead, whether it is a for-profit or nonprofit. It is an honour to serve. Starting from that foundation, it is important to have a compelling vision and a comprehensive plan. Positive leadership—conveying the idea that there is always a way forward—is so important, because that is what you are here for—to figure out how to move the organization forward. Critical to doing that is reinforcing the idea that everyone is included. Everyone is part of the team and everyone's contribution is respected, so everyone should participate. When people feel accountable and included, it is more fun. It is just more rewarding to do things in a supportive environment. A big part of leadership is being authentic to who you are, thinking about what you really believe in and behaving accordingly.

Mulally's One Team Leadership Principles:

- Authentic servant leadership
- A compelling vision and comprehensive plan
- Everyone included, everyone accountable

19.17 The Learning Organization as a Model for the Future

Learning does not take place automatically in a company. The willingness and ability to learn cannot be seen as a natural prerequisite for all employees. Also, the company has to have a positive and impartial framework towards the new.

There are four basic forms of organizational learning:

- **Learn from experience (learning by doing):** Experiences from the past
- **Mediated learning:** Learn from the experience of others
- **Incorporation of new knowledge:** "Inclusion" foreign knowledge
- **Self-referential learning**: Linking/reactivation form existing knowledge

Intangible assets

If **knowledge becomes a decisive competition factor**, then companies must establish the appropriate conditions for it. For these organizational forms are needed, which can adapt to the changes of markets by **looking ahead** and having the skills to implement acquired knowledge and organizational measures into **new strategies** rapidly.

19.18 Value Component of the Knowledge Assets of a Learning Organization

There are four subcomponents (Fig. 19.15):

- **Human capital:** the human capital of a company includes the ability of his staff and managers to create added value for the customers and stakeholders.
- **Structure capital:** Structured capital is the company's ability to learn to be innovative and to adapt quickly to environmental changes.
- **Partner and customer capital:** The outsourcing of non-core competencies to "partners" as for example in the automotive industry and their suppliers. The cooperative partnership with the suppliers also applies to the cooperation with the customer in a similar way.

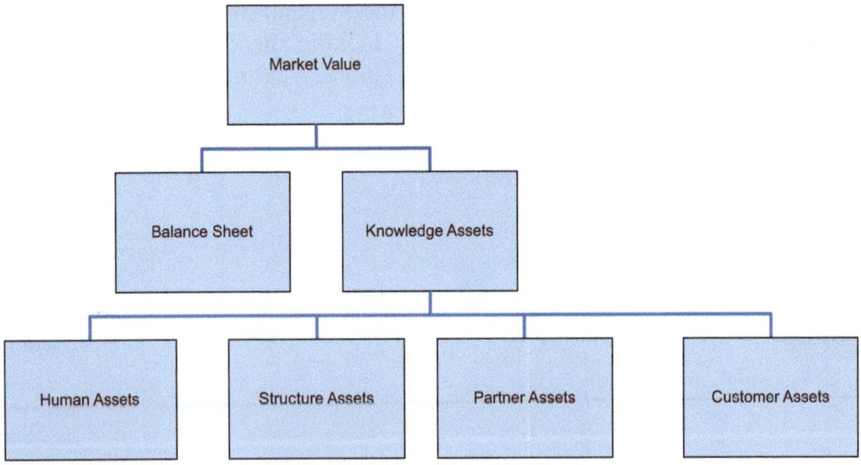

Fig. 19.15 Knowledge assets of a learning organization

A model approach for integrative knowledge management includes 4 phases: (Fig. 19.16).

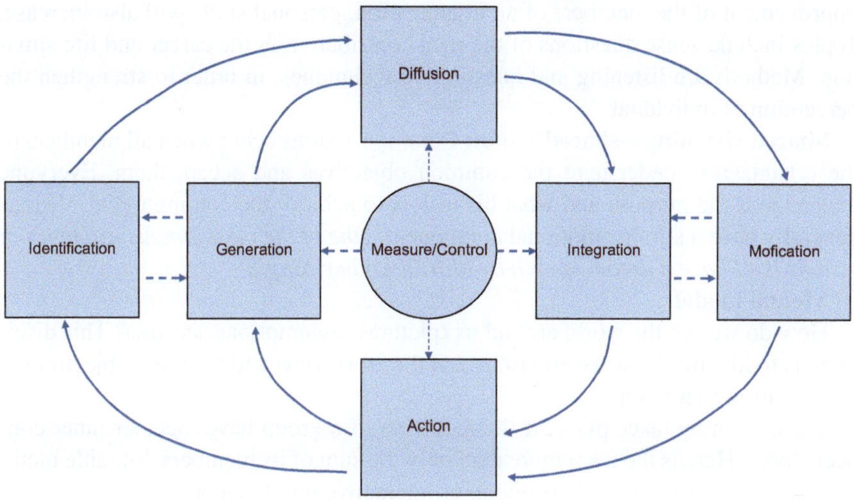

Fig. 19.16 Model of integrative knowledge management

Phases of integrative knowledge management

- **Phase 1: Identification**: Information collection and use, "what, which, like".
- **Phase 2: Diffusion:** Exchange of knowledge to achieve learning success. Means how and how well the knowledge is communicated: "Quality of communication".
- **Phase 3: Modification and integration:** What happens to the information? **Ignore, integrate, or modify**.
- **Phase 4: Action:** recording and conversion of the obtained knowledge.

19.19 The Learning Organization

Today it is more than important to encourage all levels of staff to learn. Today management skills are required at all levels. (The employee as an entrepreneur = An employee as a businessman in the company). To sustainably achieve the learning organization Peter Senge formulated "five disciplines": the disciplines support themselves mutually, and the capabilities of the organization increase gradually using a stepwise development process.

Thinking in systems: constitutes the conceptual framework of thought: this is to expose the departure from the linear thinking (cause effect). In system thinking, the context of operations and parts is seen, where the essence of the individual components of subordinate system determines the system as a whole, e.g. effects of too few "cup holders" in the car.

Personal mastery—individual self-improvement: By the continuous self-improvement of the members of an organization, personal skills will also increase. Topics include sense questions of the own contribution in the career and life situation. Methods are listening and questioning techniques, in order to strengthen the perception of individual.

Shared visioning—shared vision: Common visions occur when all members of the organization understand the common objectives and accept them. Everyone understands the purpose and what his task is to achieve the common goal. Visions generally have a strong emotional component. *One of the most famous examples of visions is "I have a dream speech by Martin Luther King".*

Mental model

How do we see the world around us (pictures, assumptions, stories)? This discipline is to identify these assumptions and the worldview and to assess objectivity.

Learning in a team

Team learning takes place, if the members of a group have together inner connectedness. Here is the team more than only the sum of its members. Suitable methods to use are methods such as dialog or interactive mind mappings.

An **exemplary example** from the sports arena is the "Klinsmann" project (Tables 19.4 and 19.5).

Table 19.4 Klinsmann's six steps to macro change

<table>
<tr><th colspan="2">Six steps to macro change</th></tr>
<tr><td colspan="2">Managers should consider the following points when changing their business at the organizational level:</td></tr>
<tr><td>Sense of urgency
• At the beginning of a fundamental change there must be a comprehensive analysis
• Don't be afraid to openly address problems and uncomfortable truths
• Keep showing the need for change</td><td>Dynamics and freedom of action
• Encourage your employees to come up with new ideas. Initiatives and risk-taking
• Make sure that your employees can do their work undisturbed and are spared from power struggles and unfounded resource bottlenecks. Consistently and promptly reform the structures that hinder the implementation of your vision
• Always focus on content, not people, in all your efforts</td></tr>
<tr><td>Strong leadership coalition
• Nominate a team for the change project that is technically beyond any doubt and also has the necessary human qualities
• As a compromise, only appoint team members who you are 100 percent convinced of.
• Introduce decentralized structures, delegate, and have trust in your team members</td><td>Visible successes
• Communicate important project milestones right from the start
• Try to generate success as early as possible. Make improved performance and success publicly visible and celebrate them</td></tr>
<tr><td>Vision and strategy
• Give the change a clear direction early on using a vision
• Make sure that the vision contains both a goal and a behavioural component
• Develop a suitable strategy to implement the vision
• Integrate your employees into the vision and strategy development process
• Use every possible channel and opportunity to communicate vision and strategy</td><td>Anchoring in everyday life
• Make sure that the change project is not tailored to one person alone
• Create structures that enable change on a broad basis
• Attract and promote employees in every phase of the project who can implement the change.</td></tr>
</table>

Table 19.5 Klinsmann's four "I's" of leadership in change projects

The four "I's" of leadership in change projects				
When a company changes, it's not just about organizational changes. Those responsible must also win over each individual employee for the change project at the micro level through an identifying, inspiring, intellectual, and individual leadership style				
Leadership style	**Identifying**	**Inspiring**	**Inspiring**	**Individually**
Proceed	Convey enthusiasm • Act as an identification person • Take action everyone with integrity and authenticity • Stand in front of your team to protect them, even in times of crisis	Convey enthusiasm • Act as an identifying person • Take action everyone with integrity and authenticity • Stand in front of your team to protect them, even in times of crisis. • Motivate employees with a captivating vision • Don't try to "sell" tasks, but rather show the contribution and importance of each individual to the success of the project	• Constantly stimulate your employees mentally. This will give you ideas and innovations • Break established thought patterns by following conventional paths	• Analyse strengths and weaknesses of your entire team in order to deploy and develop employees in a strength-oriented manner • Treat each of your employees individually, and give them confidence
Self-check	Would your employees follow you if your title and status were taken away?	Do your employees always know the overarching goal of their actions and their specific contribution to it?	Are you more of an authoritarian or a participative boss?	Are you able to do this on an ad hoc basis for each of your employees to name your three greatest strengths and your values?"

The success of the federal football is not a "motivation miracle" but the result of pure hard work. It is the result of a professionally planned and implemented change project. Can you infer project factors on the basis of a successfully professionally conducted change process? You can by yourself—such as Klinsmann—by following the 6 steps of change shown here at the macro level.

1. **Create a sense of urgency**
2. **Establish strong leadership coalitions**
3. **Develop visions and strategies and always communicating**

4. **Allow momentum and give freedom of action**
5. **Achieved and secure visible successes**
6. **Anchor new approaches in everyday life**

References

Prof Dr. Shulte Zurhausen, M. (2010). Project-/Change Management/Organisation Lerneinheit 1. Hagen: Institut für Verbundstudien der Fachhochschule NRW.

KENNEDY, R. F. (n.d.). Progress is a nice word. But its engine is 'change' and has many enemies.

Block, P. (2011). Flawless Consulting.

Covey, S. (1989). Seven Habits of Highly Effective People. USA.

20 Claim Management

The claim is a specific requirement of one contracting party for time extension for completion and/or additional payment that could be notified to the other contracting party on the basis of an event or circumstance that is foreseen in a contract clause or otherwise in connection with the contract.

Claim management (CM) is a system for monitoring and assessment of risks realization variations and their economic impact for the purpose of claim preparation and enforcement. It is a system for the early solution of problems, obstructions, and complications. Claim management starts to be crucial with the recent economic situation in construction.

In case of a public procurement project, applicable law often affects change and claim procedures and causes many difficulties to all the participants of construction projects. The fact that the contractor is able to claim in conformity with the contract is a question of survival. Nowadays, it is very important to be able to implement CM in a company quickly and efficiently.

After years of growth construction companies have to face a rapid change of external environments. Their strategies must be changed thanks to budget restrictions caused by the global economic crisis.

New very competitive global markets are being established. The contractors often bid without profit, risk, and overhead surcharges. Sometimes they bid even under the foreseen overall cost to win in a particular tender. It is quite common that large construction projects are not prepared well by the employer. In such circumstances claim management starts to be crucial.

In case of a public procurement project applicable law often affects change and claim procedures and causes many difficulties to all the participants of construction projects. The fact that a contractor is able to claim in conformity with the contract is a question of survival (Klee, 2013).

Claim management is a discipline which has its origins in the Anglo-American area and raises very diverse legal and economic questions. The focus is on the requirements, by national regulations. In particular the VOB to claim management

P. Bauer, *A Comprehensive Project Management Guide*, Management for Professionals, https://doi.org/10.1007/978-3-031-68252-0_20

provided is a way to avoid supplementary not discarded by the application of cooperation models and alternative contract types, as well as de-risking by the use of certain forms. In addition, the procedural ways to enforce and mitigate claims also can be disclosed.

20.1 Term Definition Claim

Errors, changes, and adjustments to the original contract inevitably occur in large and complex construction projects during the construction phase. The resulting additional costs and delays lead to compensation or damages of the contracting parties. Claims which arise after conclusion of the contract are named as claims or supplements or supplementary claims. If a claim is a disputed claim that results from changes that occurred after conclusion of the contract, this then leads to different requirements of the contractual partners.

20.2 Claim Management

Claim management is a holistic process that accompanies the project from the beginning to the end to minimize the risks of the job and the assurance of guaranteed job earnings. This needs an as exact as possible contract design and analysis covered in the planning phase of a building project to identify potential claims. The operational implementation and control of all measures for treating, documenting, ensuring enforcement, and defining claims is in the implementation phase. This in particular is an objective of the project quality, costs, and deadlines: Moreover, claim management as a basis for identifying, implementing, and mitigating claims requires organizational structures within the company. The claim will then decide on the strategy and the framework conditions of how claim manager needs to resolve the issue. In addition, he brings together standardized processes such as the use of forms, meeting minutes, or construction day report to unique and consistent documentation. The processes within the organization structure should be designed that all information about possible contractual variations in writing and promptly converge manager at the claim. The basis of the claim management relates to the four components of the law: **economics, technical and organizational planning,** and **control** of a **construction process.**

20.3 Claim Management Strategies

The influence factors of a claim management strategy can be very diverse. In many companies, claims against the contractors cause often disruption of the business relationship or a sign of the lack of flexibility. In addition, also external factors affect the claim management strategy of a company. These are in particular the increased competitive pressure and resulting lower margins, but also the rising raw material prices and the declining expenditure of public clients. Therefore, a company must determine what starting position exists for a project and on this basis choose an appropriate strategy, as the realization of the claim management is related to the strategy.

20.4 Difference Between Claim and Change

The difference between a claim and a change lies in their definitions and contexts of use: A claim is an assertion or statement that something is true or factual, often requiring proof or evidence from a contracting partner. It can refer to a demand for something considered one's due, such as an insurance claim or a legal claim. Change refers to the act or process of becoming different, altering something from one state to another. It involves transformation, modification, or substitution, whether in physical form, status, or project conditions (Fig. 20.1).

Claim

- Additional or not delivered supplies/(cooperate) services where the responsibility is debatable.
- Responsibilities are not disputed but the scope of services and their impact on cost, dates, etc., are.
- Only reimbursement of additional costs and/or shift of dates are negotiated largely between project and contract partners.

Change

- New/additional offer or altered/additional services.
- Appointments or other contractual terms and conditions.
- Profit margins can be recalculated and appointments can be made shifted.
- A process that runs in the project itself.

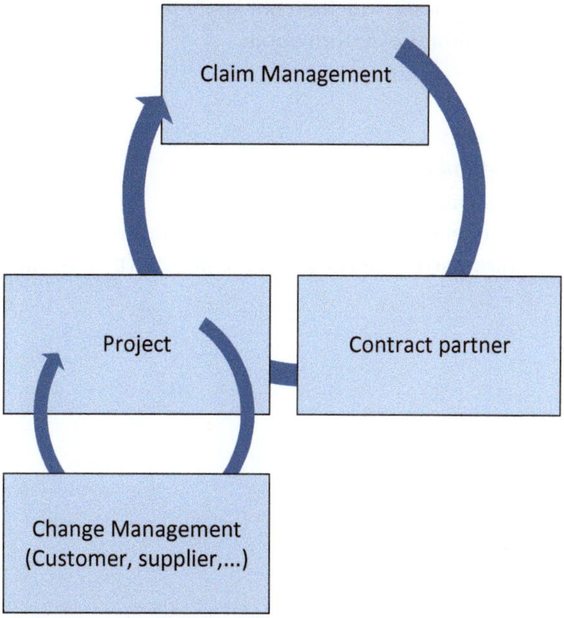

Fig. 20.1 Difference between claim and change

20.5 Objectives in Claim Management

Objectives

- Early detection of risks
- Additional revenue opportunities.
- Identification and development of one's own claims against a contracting party
- Prevent the formation of (foreign) claims
- Minimize additional costs in project management
- Enforcing (justifiable) claims against a contract (e.g. participation services)
- Defence of (not justifiable) claims by a contractor (e.g. additional services)
- Prevention of (expensive) litigation

20.6 Addressees and Triggers in Claim Management

In claim management, "Addressees" are the parties to whom the claims are directed, such as insurance companies or legal entities. "Triggers" are events or conditions that initiate the claim process, like accidents, natural disasters, or breaches of contract.

Triggers:

- Participation of the customer or trades or services by sub-contractors/free-lancers are:
- Be provided on time
- Not provided in the required quality
- Not provided in required quantity
- Change in project execution (by the contractor, the customer, or a third party).
- Change in scope (extensions, but have different interpretation of the scope by the contractor, the customer, or a third party)
- Assumptions, which do not apply to
- False promises/information

Addressee:

- **Customer**
- Sub-contractors/freelancers
- Account owner, owner of delivery, delivery units, project manager
- Third-party claims against the project (by customer, UAN/FL)

Triggers:

- **Contract**
- Contract clauses that are not unique (e.g. performance claims)
- Terms and conditions with advance availability
- Contradictions in the agreement
- Different interpretation of the contract (such as claims for damages)

20.7 Claim Contracts

A claim contract is an agreement between the organization and an outside provider of a service or materials via a contract. To limit misunderstandings and make them more legally binding, contracts are usually written documents that describe the obligations of both parties and are signed by those with authority to represent the interests of the parties.

There are several **types** of contracting approaches and each supports different project environments and project approaches. The legal contracts that support the procurement plan consist of two general types of contracts: the **fixed-price** and the **cost-reimbursable** contracts, with variations on each main type (Fig. 20.2).

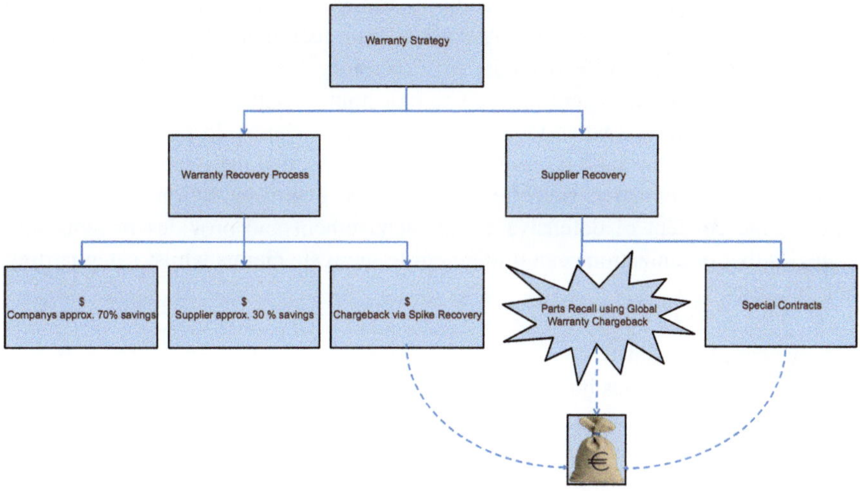

Fig. 20.2 Organizational chart example of different types of claim contracts

20.8 Offensive and Defensive Claim Management

Aggressive claim management is a proactive approach that organizations employ to assertively address and resolve contractual claims. In a business landscape where disputes can be costly and time-consuming, adopting strategies for effective claim management is crucial. This chapter explores the concept of aggressive claim management and provides insights into strategies that organizations can implement to navigate claims assertively.

- High claim potential
- At the slightest suspicion to open a claim
- Maximum or excessive claims
- Question all counter-claims and exploit all counter-arguments
- Accept only contracts that have an economical benefit for us
- Promotion of one's own claims by concealment of facts

Aggressive claim management is about taking a proactive stance to identify, address, and resolve contractual claims efficiently. By implementing early identification, transparent documentation, effective communication, and strategic negotiation tactics, organizations can navigate claims assertively and foster positive business relationships. Incorporating these strategies into a comprehensive claim management framework positions businesses to protect their interests and maintain a reputation for fair and effective contract execution.

Defensive claim management is a strategic approach that organizations employ to protect their interests when faced with contractual claims. In the complex landscape of business transactions, disputes are inevitable, making it essential for businesses to adopt defensive strategies for effective claim resolution. This chapter explores the concept of defensive claim management and provides insights into strategies that organizations can implement to navigate claims whilst safeguarding their interests.

- Low claim potential.
- Claim only for serious infringements.
- Actual amount is debited.
- Accept legitimate counter-claims.
- Contracts are customer-friendly.
- Exploit all the possibilities of claim prevention.

Defensive claim management is an integral aspect of effective risk mitigation and dispute resolution. By leveraging contractual analysis, strategic communication, legal expertise, and a proactive approach to risk management, organizations can navigate claims whilst safeguarding their interests. Implementing a comprehensive defensive claim management strategy positions businesses to respond assertively to claims and protect their reputation and financial well-being.

20.9 Four-Step Success Claim Process

A successful claim process involves a systematic and strategic approach to address contractual claims efficiently. Here is a four-step success claim process:

- **Claim identification and documentation:**
- *Early detection:* Promptly identify potential claims by establishing effective monitoring mechanisms and regularly assessing contract performance against agreed-upon terms.
- *Documentation:* Thoroughly document all relevant information related to the claim, including communications, changes in scope, delays, or any deviations from the original contract terms. Clear and comprehensive documentation is essential for building a strong case and understanding the nature of the claim.
- **Internal Evaluation and Decision-Making:**
- *Cross-functional collaboration:* Assemble a cross-functional team involving legal, project management, finance, and relevant subject matter experts. Collaborate to analyse the claim comprehensively, considering legal implications, contractual obligations, and potential financial impacts.
- *Risk assessment:* Conduct detailed risk assessment to understand the potential consequences of the claim. Evaluate the merits of the claim and assess the organization's exposure. This step involves weighing the costs and benefits of different resolution strategies.
- **Strategic resolution planning:**
- *Negotiation strategy:* Develop a strategic negotiation plan based on the evaluation of the claim. Consider alternative dispute resolution (ADR) mechanisms, such as mediation or arbitration, to expedite resolution.
- *Communication strategy:* Craft clear and strategic communications to present the organization's position. Articulate the facts, legal arguments, and contractual obligations in a way that enhances the organization's position and minimizes the risk of escalation.
- **Implementation and monitoring:**
- *Resolution implementation:* Execute the chosen resolution strategy, whether it involves negotiating a settlement, engaging in ADR, or pursuing legal action. Ensure that all parties involved understand and comply with the agreed-upon terms.
- *Continuous monitoring:* Monitor the resolution process to track compliance with the agreed-upon terms and ensure the effective closure of the claim. If necessary, implement corrective actions to prevent similar issues in the future.

By following this four-step success claim process, organizations can systematically address contractual claims, minimize financial and reputational risks, and maintain positive business relationships. The process emphasizes early detection, thorough evaluation, strategic planning, and effective implementation to navigate claims assertively and achieve successful resolutions. Achieve with **consensus → change management and with dissent → claim management.**

20.10 Claim Prevention

Claim prevention is a proactive approach aimed at minimizing the occurrence of contractual claims before they escalate into disputes. Effective claim prevention involves careful planning, clear communication, and proactive risk management. Here are key strategies for preventing claims:

- Dynamics of projects—100% claim avoidance is difficult.
- Understand and jointly accepted targets in relation to the
- Services, dates, and costs.
- Common understanding of project (content, appointment, quality).
- Clean project definition and planning.
- Clear and distinct contracts.
- Jointly accepted and unambiguous milestones.
- Fully documented contract deviations.

Prevention by project management:
Claim prevention in project management is a critical aspect of ensuring the successful execution of projects whilst minimizing the risk of disputes and claims. Proactive project management strategies can help identify, address, and prevent issues before they escalate into formal claims. Here are key project management practices for effective claim prevention:

- **Comprehensive project planning:**
- *Detailed project scope:* Clearly define and document the project scope, including deliverables, timelines, and performance expectations. A comprehensive understanding of the project scope helps in preventing scope creep and associated claims.
- *Risk identification:* Conduct thorough risk assessments during the planning phase to identify potential issues and challenges that could lead to claims. Develop risk mitigation plans to address and manage identified risks.
- **Clear communication and documentation:**
- *Stakeholder communication*: Establish open and transparent communication channels with all project stakeholders. Regularly communicate project progress, milestones, and any changes to expectations.
- *Document everything:* Maintain detailed and accurate project documentation, including meeting minutes, decisions, and changes. Clear documentation provides a historical record and supports effective communication.
- **Effective change management:**
- *Formal change control processes*: Implement formal change management processes to document and manage any changes to the project scope, schedule, or budget. This helps prevent claims arising from unapproved or undocumented changes.

- *Change approval protocols*: Define clear protocols for obtaining approvals for changes, ensuring that all modifications are agreed upon by relevant stakeholders.
- **Proactive risk management:**
- *Regular risk reviews:* Conduct regular reviews of project risks and update the risk register as needed. Proactively address identified risks to prevent them from evolving into issues that could lead to claims.
- *Contingency planning:* Develop contingency plans for high-impact risks, providing a structured approach for managing unforeseen events and reducing the likelihood of claims.
- **Performance monitoring and quality assurance:**
- *Key performance indicators (KPIs)*: Define and monitor KPIs to assess project performance against established benchmarks. Timely identification and correction of performance issues prevent disputes and claims.
- *Quality control measures:* Implement robust quality control measures to ensure that deliverables meet the specified standards. High-quality work reduces the risk of claims related to substandard performance.
- **Contractual clarity:**
- *Clear contract terms*: Ensure that the project contract contains clear and unambiguous terms. Clearly define roles, responsibilities, and deliverables to minimize the potential for misunderstandings and disputes.
- *Legal review:* Involve legal experts to review contract terms and conditions, ensuring that they are enforceable and provide adequate protection to both parties.
- **Stakeholder engagement:**
- *Proactive issue resolution:* Encourage stakeholders to report issues promptly. Establish a structured process for resolving issues at the project level before they escalate into formal claims.
- *Conflict resolution training:* Equip project managers with conflict resolution skills to address interpersonal conflicts within the project team, preventing disruptions that could lead to claims.
- **Continuous learning and improvement:**
- *Post-project reviews:* Conduct comprehensive post-project reviews to analyse successes and challenges. Use insights gained to update project management processes and improve claim prevention strategies for future projects.

By integrating these project management practices, organizations can foster a proactive approach to claim prevention. This not only safeguards project success but also contributes to positive stakeholder relationships and the overall reputation of the project management team and the organization as a whole.

Prevention by contract management:
Effective contract management plays a crucial role in preventing claims and disputes by establishing clear expectations, responsibilities, and mechanisms for dispute resolution. Here are key strategies for claim prevention through contract management:

- **Clear and precise contract language:**
- *Avoid ambiguities*: Draft contracts with clear and unambiguous language to minimize the potential for misinterpretation. Clearly define terms, obligations, deliverables, and performance metrics.
- *Define key concepts:* Clearly define key concepts and obligations, including milestones, payment terms, and any special conditions, to reduce the likelihood of disputes.
- **Thorough contract review and approval**:
- *Legal expertise:* Involve legal experts to review and approve contracts before execution. Legal professionals can identify potential pitfalls, ensure compliance with relevant laws, and enhance the enforceability of contract terms.
- *Cross-functional review:* Conduct a cross-functional review involving relevant stakeholders, including project managers, finance, and subject matter experts. This ensures that the contract aligns with the operational capabilities and expectations of all parties involved.
- **Effective change management procedures:**
- *Document changes*: Establish robust procedures for documenting and managing changes to the contract. Changes may include scope adjustments, timeline modifications, or cost variations. Ensure that all changes are agreed upon in writing by both parties.
- *Change approval process*: Implement a formal change approval process that involves obtaining approvals from authorized personnel, reducing the risk of unauthorized modifications leading to claims.
- **Performance metrics and key performance indicators (KPIs):**
- *Clearly defined metrics:* Define clear performance metrics and KPIs in the contract to objectively measure the performance of each party.
- *Regular performance assessments:* Conduct regular assessments against established metrics to identify and address performance issues promptly, preventing disputes from arising due to perceived breaches.
- **Dispute resolution mechanisms:**
- *Incorporate ADR clauses:* Include alternative dispute resolution (ADR) clauses in contracts. Specify mechanisms such as mediation or arbitration to resolve disputes outside of traditional litigation.
- *Clearly define escalation procedures:* Clearly outline procedures for escalating disputes, including timelines and steps for resolution. Having predefined processes streamlines the resolution of disagreements before they become formal claims.
- **Periodic contract audits:**
- *Regular audits*: Conduct periodic audits of existing contracts to ensure ongoing compliance with terms and conditions.
- *Identify and address issues*: Identify any potential issues or deviations from the contract terms during audits and address them proactively to prevent claims from arising.

- **Effective communication channels:**
- *Open lines of communication:* Foster open and transparent communication channels between contracting parties. Encourage regular updates on project progress, changes, and potential challenges.
- *Address issues promptly:* Promptly address any concerns or issues that may arise during the contract period to prevent them from escalating into formal claims.
- **Training and awareness:**
- *Contract management training:* Provide training to personnel involved in contract management to ensure a thorough understanding of contractual obligations and effective management practices.
- *Promote awareness:* Foster awareness among stakeholders about the importance of adhering to contract terms and the potential consequences of non-compliance.
- **Continuous improvement:**
- *Learn from past contracts:* Conduct post-contract reviews to analyse successes and challenges. Use insights gained to update contract management processes and improve claim prevention strategies for future contracts.
- *Feedback loops:* Establish feedback loops with stakeholders to gather insights on contract performance and areas for improvement.

By implementing these strategies, organizations can establish a robust contract management framework that not only prevents claims but also contributes to positive and collaborative relationships between parties involved in the contract.

20.11 Claim Management Tips

Knowing all of your claims from the very first day on is key and applies to all the project team. Create a basis for a claim by defining and naming measurables with the contractor, by documentation and protocols, and by clarifying the communication channels with the contractor. Counting, measuring, and weighing are elements many contracts are not clear enough of.

Plan all claims and request claims in a timely manner, document differences (delay) regularly, and communicate deviations. Check the implementation of the claims by quantitative and qualitative acceptance and documenting deviations (time, budget, quality) and communicate variances early enough to intervene so that deviations and actions can be agreed with the contractor.

Hold regular claim meetings with the customer and sub-contractors and introduce the tracking of the participation performance/performance delivery and track the claims by a claim list.

20.12 Claim Manager Role

The project manager and the project owner are responsible for claim management, and the registration, processing, and tracking of claims are supported by the claim manager. The function of the claim manager should be an independent role and typically represents a full-time activity. The function can also be integrated into the responsibilities of a process or project owner who is responsible during the operational phase and who has the greatest interest in the defence or positioning of claims. Also, the legal department (if present) must be involved for all claims with serious consequences.

The **claim manager** is responsible for the compilation and maintenance of the claim documentation and to review and document the basis of claims (e.g. checks/ searches in contracts) and document the potential impact (cost, time, quality). Furthermore, he is involved in the creation of his own claims and the registration of claims for counterparty compilation of counterstatements for external claims. Regular communication with the contractor about the status of the claims (at least monthly, better weekly) is key to ensuring the team has the same knowledge base. The clam manager should also compile and distribute the claim reports.

Necessary characteristics of a claim manager are knowledge of human nature and negotiating skills, broad technical and methodological knowledge, the ability to work under pressure and be durable, complex thinking skills, and a quick wit. Not only the character plays a role but also the necessary powers of a claim manager who is authorized in the project team for document collection and that the claim manager receives room for negotiation from management, which he can exploit in the negotiations; to finally complete the claim negotiations, the claim manager receives the authority to legally sign the negotiated protocol and last but not least responsibility of the claim **documentation**.

The **documentation** (Table 20.1) of claims is a key element to be able to defend claims, as you have facts to underline your analysis and work. Similar to the FMEA that is used in quality that can underline suspension order with facts.

Table 20.1 Example management documentation

ID	Claim description	Impact of deviation	specific causes and activities with impact on cost, time or quality	Detail description	Target State in accordance with contract	Contract / project - reference document
1	Customer has not provided the workspace on time	The Project work could not start as planned. Sheduled end date cannot be held.	Project staff have been deployed according to original planning and can not be used for other purposes.	see column E	Customer has to provided the workspace for developer.	Chapter 8, paragraph 3, individual contract

Impact on costs				Effect on time	Effect on quality
Resource	Effort in hours	Personnel cost	Expenses / travel fees /.	Description of the shift	Description of not feasible quality requirements
Jones Smith Brown	8 8 8	$ 1.680,00		Start default planned: xx.yy.zzzzneuer planned to start: aa.bb.cccc shift of the following milestones to x W eeks	none

In addition, he leads the **project team** that coordinates the support for claim documentation. He follows up and controls the claim detection and warning, transfer of contextual information, and development claim strategy proposals.

In general, **project controlling** (Fig. 20.3) is **both** the planning function and the function that tracks progress against the plan. Project control provides critical information to all the other functions of the project and works closely with the project manager to evaluate the cost and scheduling impact of various options during the life of a project. The following are typical activities included within the project control's function:

- Estimating
- Tracking costs
- Analysing trends and making projection planning and scheduling
- Managing change
- Tracking progress against schedule

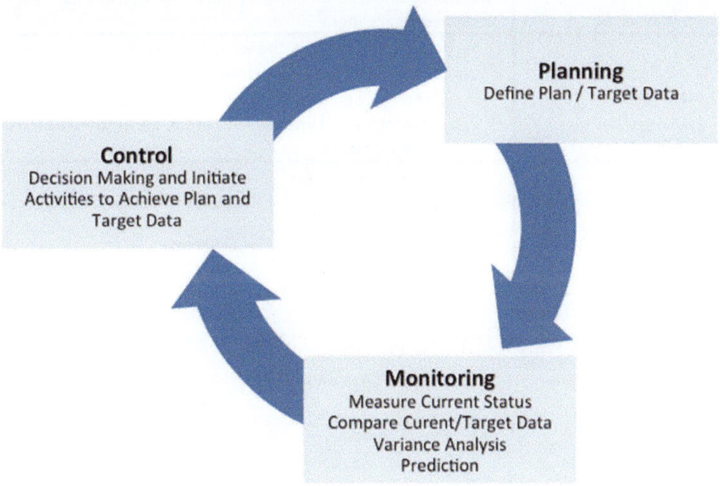

Fig. 20.3 Claim management project controlling circle

20.13 Establish Project Performance Data

Generally, the following data listed (Table 20.2) should be collected for a project status. The relationship between **performance** and **quality**, the **schedules,** and the **costs** requires a holistic approach. A one-sided schedule and cost control would quickly lead to a trade-off on system performance and quality especially for organization projects.

Table 20.2 Project status collection

Performance Data	Data Collection Needs
① Result/Performance (Content/Quantity/Quality)	• Current progress degree, i.e. current completion status (for all activites)
②Dates	• Actual status dates, i.e. actual start date (for all begun activites) and the actual finish date (only for completed activites) • Estimated end date or estimated remaining time for the currently required result/performance or the updated planed duration for all unfinished activites.
③Effort (Hours/Cost)	• Actual work effort i.e. the actually incurred hours and costs (for all completed and in-progress activies). • Estimated remaining efforts (in hours and costs) for the / result/performance currently required or the updated plan required for in-progress tasks
④Process Quality	• Customer satisfaction • Employee satisfaction • Satisfactionin the project environment • Riks development

20.14 Check Claim Schedules and Costs

Tracking the project parameters is primarily a question of information **processing** and **visualization**. Unfortunately, the network diagram (PDF) technology offers little opportunity to visualize the progress of the project. Schedules can be tracked using bar (Gantt) charts (Fig. 20.4) by proportionally **shading** the activity bar to the achieved percentage of completion.

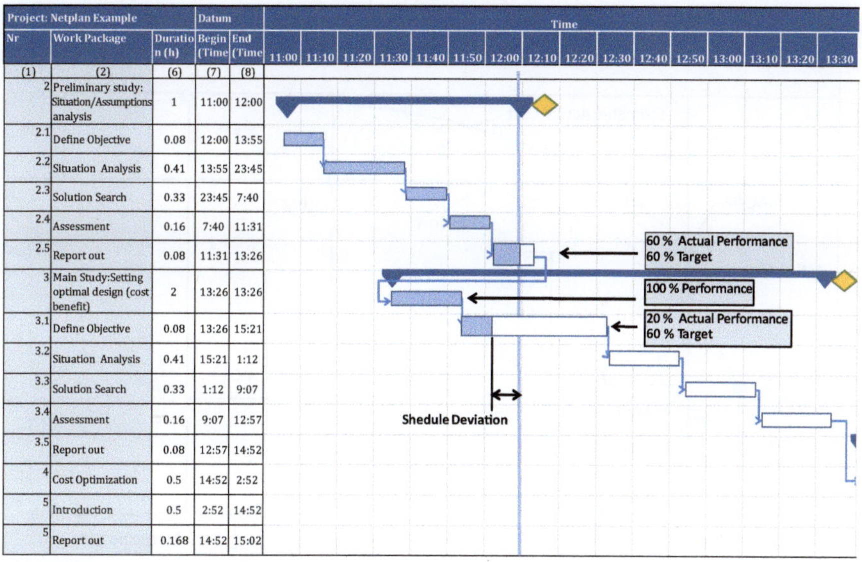

Fig. 20.4 Gantt chart

Check Costs

The instrument of the earned value analysis (EVA) (Fig. 20.5) aims to predict the future development of the project on the basis of the previous history of the project and to create a numbers-based early warning system as well as an assessment of the project situation. It tries to include all three elements of the magical triangle at the same time and incorporate them into the project evaluation. The earned value analysis is based on the thought of the costing and refers to the service provided in the form of planned and actual costs on the project duration.

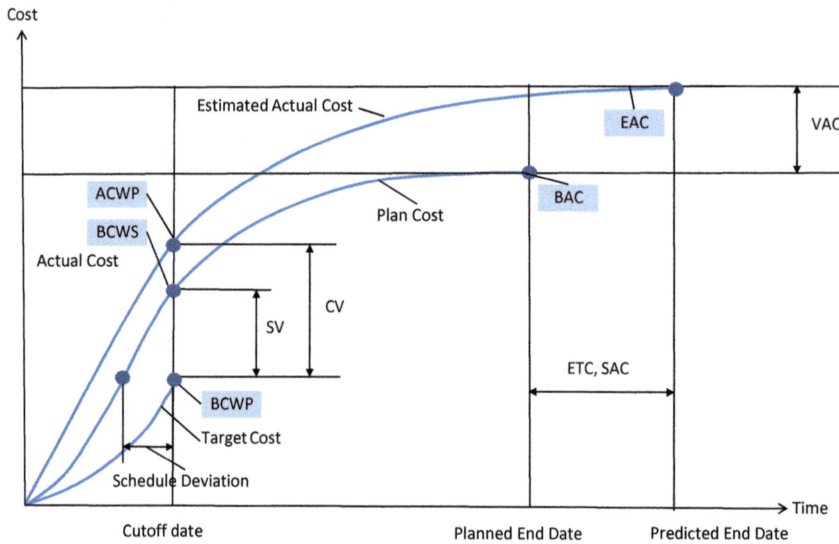

Fig. 20.5 Earned value analysis (EVA)

Control of the Quality Performance

The performance and quality control extend to the actual working results of a project. They should show whether the results correspond to the time and cost efforts. Even if the project requirements for time and cost are **met** then there is no guarantee that the project meets all contractual requirements **without significant** rework and cost that then calls for claim management.

The **milestone trend analysis** is a very simple and convenient instrument to display the status of the project. Prerequisite for their application is a realistic schedule and carefully defined milestones. The milestone trend analysis is a single chart that is updated during the entire project life cycle. The **horizontal** timeline marks in the respective reporting date and the **vertical** axis the time planned for the individual report dates or updated milestone dates (Fig. 20.6).

- If the curve is pointing up, a time delay exists.
- If the curve remains horizontal, the schedules are in track.
- If the curve is pointing downwards, an earlier completion than planned to be expected.

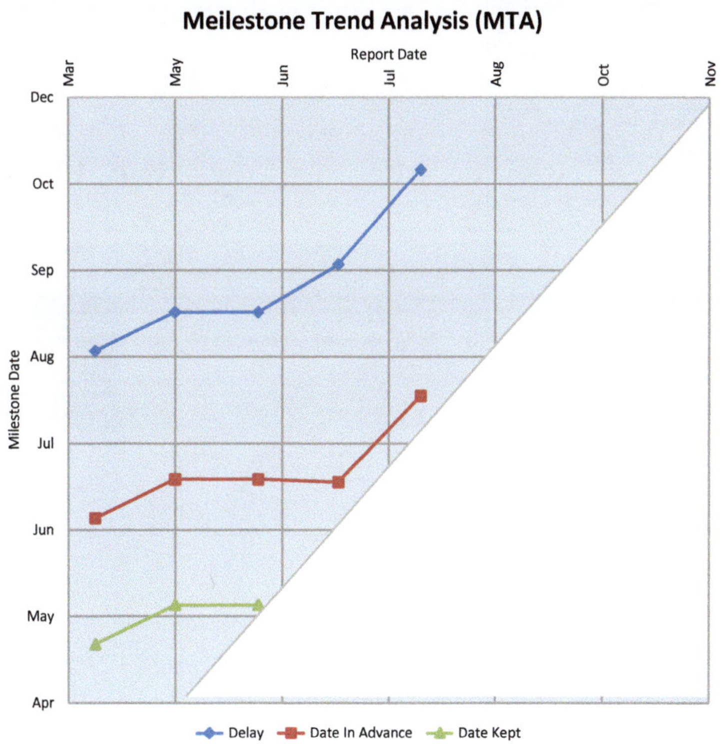

Fig. 20.6 Milestone trend analysis

20.15 Well, Prepared for the Claim Negotiations!

A legitimate claim that is well prepared and presented is not rude but professional. This needs a precisely researched and a well-documented claim with details on who, when, and what has been consolidated. The documentation must be understandable for everyone (even for outsiders) and has to be complete and as factual as possible (no challenge, no charges, no blame).

Caution! The other party is perfectly prepared for the claim negotiations as well; do not underestimate the other claim party and be prepared for all questions or push-backs (Fig. 20.7). Almost all claim's negotiations end up as a compromise (win/win); only in exceptional cases does it lead to a win/lose situation; you need to compromise in your own team and discuss and compromise variants up to your own "pain threshold". Examples of compromises in claim negotiations payment terms, payment schedules, and payment concessions make the occasion according to "live and let live".

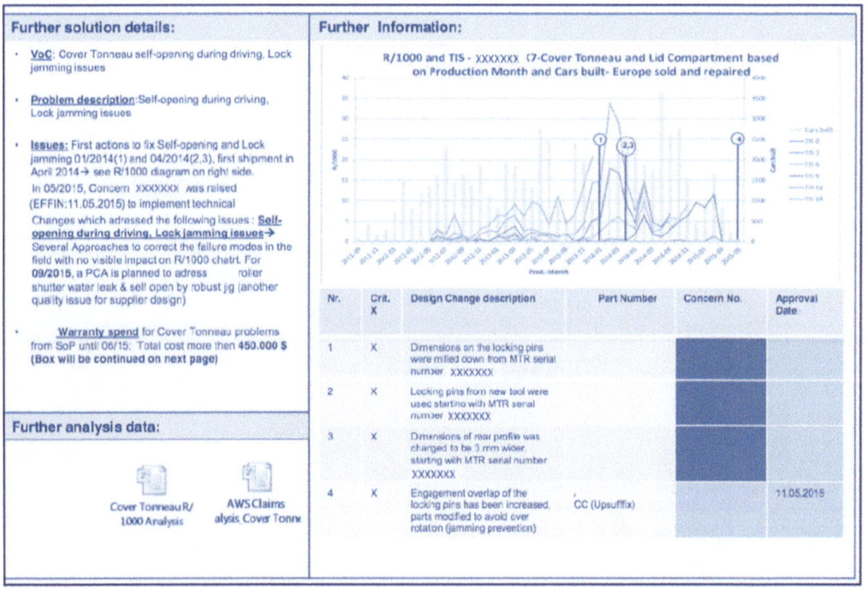

Further solution details:

- **VoC**: Cover Tonneau self-opening during driving, Lock jamming issues
- **Problem description**:Self-opening during driving, Lock jamming issues
- **Issues:** First actions to fix Self-opening and Lock jamming 01/2014(1) and 04/2014(2,3), first shipment in April 2014→ see R/1000 diagram on right side.
  In 05/2015, Concern XXXXXXX was raised (EFFIN:11.05.2015) to implement technical Changes which adressed the following issues : **Self-opening during driving, Lock jamming issues**→
  Several Approaches to correct the failure modes in the field with no visible impact on R/1000 chatrt. For **09/2015**, a PCA is planned to adress roller shutter water leak & self open by robust jig (another quality issue for supplier design)
- **Warranty spend** for Cover Tonneau problems from SoP until 06/15: Total cost more then **450.000 $** **(Box will be continued on next page)**

Further analysis data:

Cover Tonneau R/1000 Analysis
AWS Claims alysis Cover Tonn

Further Information:

Nr.	Crit. X	Design Change description	Part Number	Concern No.	Approval Date
1	X	Dimensions on the locking pins were milled down from MTR serial number XXXXXXX			
2	X	Locking pins from new tool were used starting with MTR serial number XXXXXXX			
3	X	Dimensions of rear profile was changed to be 3 mm wider, starting with MTR serial number XXXXXXX			
4	X	Engagement overlap of the locking pins has been increased, parts modified to avoid over rotaton (jamming prevention)	CC (Upsufffix)		11.05.2015

Fig. 20.7 Claim report example

20.16 Factors that Drive Contractual Claims

Contractual claims are a common aspect of business and legal transactions, arising when one party believes that the other has failed to meet its contractual obligations. These claims can lead to disputes, legal battles, and financial repercussions. Understanding the factors that drive contractual claims is crucial for businesses to navigate contracts effectively and mitigate the risk of disputes.

Understanding the factors (Fig. 20.8) that drive contractual claims is essential for businesses to proactively manage their contracts and mitigate the risk of disputes. Effective communication, clear contract terms, and proactive risk management strategies can contribute to successful contract execution and minimize the likelihood of claims, fostering positive and enduring business relationships.

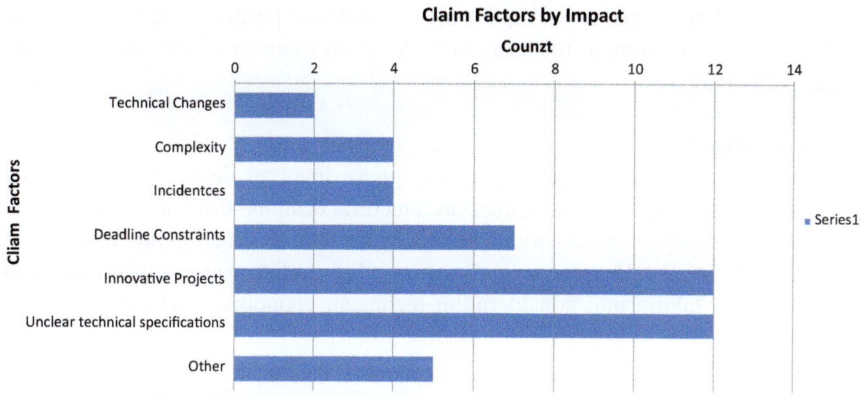

Fig. 20.8 Key factors that drive claims

20.17 EPC: Engineering Procurement Construction

EPC stands for engineering, procurement, and construction (Fig. 20.9) and is a prominent form of **contracting agreement** in the construction industry. It represents a comprehensive approach to project management, covering the entire project life cycle from initial design and engineering through procurement of materials and equipment to the actual construction phase.

The engineering and construction contractor will carry out the detailed engineering design of the project, procure all the equipment and materials necessary, and then construct to deliver a functioning facility or asset to their clients. Companies that deliver EPC projects are commonly referred to as **EPC contractors.**

The EPC phase of the project is also known as the **execution phase** which normally follows what is known as a FEED or front-end engineering design phase. The FEED is a basic engineering design used as the basis for the EPC phase. The FEED can be divided into separate packages covering different portions of the project. The FEED packages are used as the basis for bidding on when the client offers the EPC work to the market.

- **Engineering:**
- *Design and planning*: The engineering phase involves detailed planning and design of the project. This includes architectural designs, structural engineering, and other technical specifications necessary for the construction process.
- *Feasibility studies*: Engineers conduct feasibility studies to assess the viability of the project, taking into consideration technical, economic, and environmental factors.
- **Procurement:**
- *Sourcing materials and equipment:* Once the design is finalized, the procurement phase involves sourcing and purchasing all the necessary materials, equipment, and services required for construction.
- *Contracting:* The EPC contractor is responsible for negotiating and managing contracts with suppliers and sub-contractors. This includes ensuring that all materials and services meet the specified quality and standards.
- **Construction:**
- *On-site construction*: The construction phase is the physical realization of the project. It involves the actual building, assembly, and installation of components as outlined in the design and planning phase.

- *Project management*: EPC contractors manage the construction process, coordinating activities, ensuring safety compliance, and overseeing the work of subcontractors to ensure the project stays on schedule and within budget. The EPC approach offers several advantages:
- **Single point of responsibility**: One entity, the EPC contractor, is responsible for the entire project. This reduces the complexity of project management and streamlines decision-making processes.
- **Cost certainty:** EPC contracts often include a fixed-price agreement, providing the client with cost certainty and protecting them from unexpected budget overruns.
- **Efficiency:** The integrated nature of EPC projects promotes efficiency in communication and coordination. Engineering, procurement, and construction activities are closely aligned to optimize the project timeline.
- **Risk mitigation:** EPC contractors assume a significant portion of the project risks, including cost overruns and delays. This allows the client to transfer risk to the contractor and focus on other aspects of their business.

EPC contracts are commonly used in industries such as energy, oil and gas, infrastructure, and large-scale industrial projects. The success of an EPC project relies on effective collaboration between the client and the EPC contractor, emphasizing clear communication, detailed planning, and adherence to quality and safety standards.

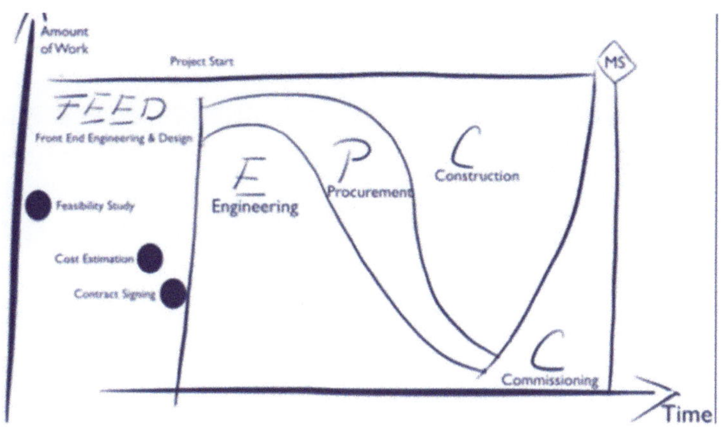

Fig. 20.9 EPRC scheme

References

Prof Dr. Shulte Zurhausen, M. (2010). Project-/Change Management/Organisation Lerneinheit 1. Hagen: Institut für Verbundstudien der Fachhochschule NRW.

Klee, L. (2013). Script Management of Contractor's Claims in Construction Projects. (C. U. Prague, Ed.) Retrieved 2015, from http://ssrn.com/abstract=2405813

http://www.brighthubpm.com/project-planning/. (n.d.). BRIGHT HUB PROJECT MANAGEMENT. New York.

Project Controlling: Control and Reports 21

In general, project controlling is both the planning function and the function that tracks progress against the plan. Project control provides critical information to all the other functions of the project and works closely with the project manager to evaluate the cost and scheduling impact of various options during the life of a project.

Sometimes accounting functions such as payroll, budgeting, and cash management are included within project controls. On larger projects, accounting functions are typically separate because the accounting culture tracks expenses to the nearest penny, and cost estimating and tracking by project controls can often be off by hundreds and sometimes thousands of dollars. The lack of definitive information necessitates the development of cost estimates within ranges that are often inconsistent with accounting practices. Separating these two functions allows each to operate within their own accuracy comfort zone. The following are typical activities included within the project control's function:

- Estimating
- Tracking costs
- Analysing trends and making projections planning and scheduling
- Managing change
- Tracking progress against schedule

The project control team gathers this information from all the functions on the project and develops reports that enable each functional manager to understand the project plan and progress against the plan at both the project level and the functional level. On large complex projects, some project managers will assign project control professionals to work within the major functions as well as the project management office. This approach allows each function to plan and track the function's work in more detail. The project control manager then coordinates activities across functions. The illustration (Fig. 21.1) shows the tasks on project controlling in projects based on the "magical triangle".

P. Bauer, *A Comprehensive Project Management Guide*, Management for Professionals, https://doi.org/10.1007/978-3-031-68252-0_21

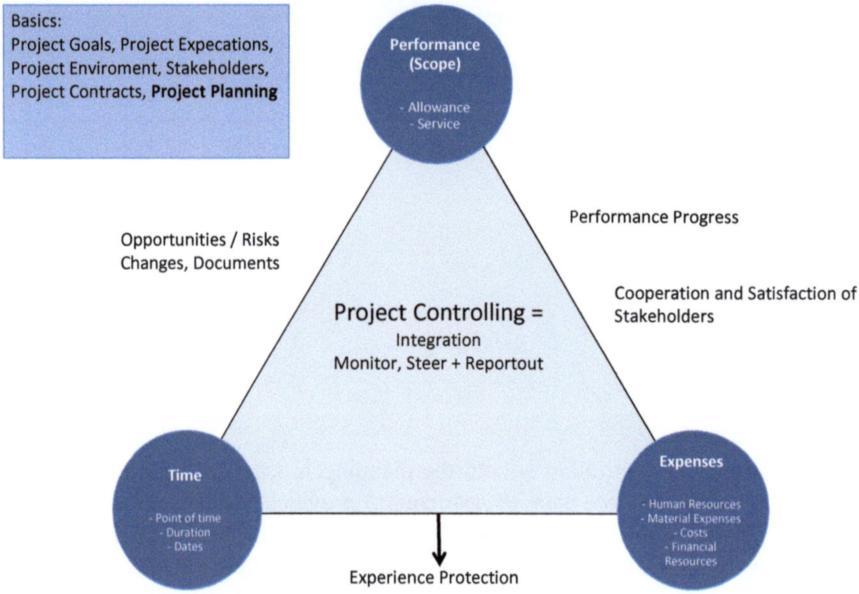

Fig. 21.1 Integrative tasks of project controlling—in individual projects

21.1 Fundamentals of Project Control

Integration in project management means summarizing, coordinating, monitoring, and controlling all activities, aspirations, and interests and focusing on results with regard to the achievement and the success of the project objectives. The ability to integrate is a key feature of the project manager. Effective integration requires an appropriate personality, adequate expertise, and knowledge of human nature, organizational skills, and certain leadership characteristics dealing with people.

This understanding of integration leads to the necessity of continually integrated consideration of the effect relationship of the following aspects in projects.

(1) The different areas of project management, i.e. Schedule, Resources, Cost and Funding, Contract, Risk, Documentation, Configuration, and Change Management etc.
(2) The three partial processes steps of project management: **Planning Monitoring** and **Control**
(3) The three project targets ("magic triangle"): Results/performance (or in other words: scope), expense, and time
(4) The different project members [also known as interested parties, multi-stakeholder] coming form from a wide range of functional technical areas of interest, project cultures, countries, etc.

The organizational and content integration in the different project management areas (1) and the different project members (4) are sometimes referred to as interface managers. The needs for this type of project integration get clear immediately and might also be called "outer" or "external" integration from the perspective of project management.

The other aspects of integration (2), (3) concern the "Internal" or the integration essence of project management. The integration aspect (3) states that the project status and project progress as a (non-integrated) individual observation and comparison of individual project outcomes such as planned and actually achieved schedules and actually incurred costs are meaningful and are very commonly used.

Conclusion: The isolated statements to individual targets in the chapter before can show an incomplete picture of the true project situation and could give the recipient a false impression about the real project status resulting in wrong decision-making. This is why the integrated approach has always a significant relevance.

21.2 Sub-processes Monitoring and Control

The complete cycle of the project management process (Fig. 21.2) starts with the (origin-) planning and the assignment of plan values. This has to be done for at least for those project areas that will be later in terms of project targets also monitored and controlled. As a general rule: The systematic monitoring and control of the project execution is not possible without having a pre-project planning in place. Therefore, project controlling should be actively involved already during the project planning phase.

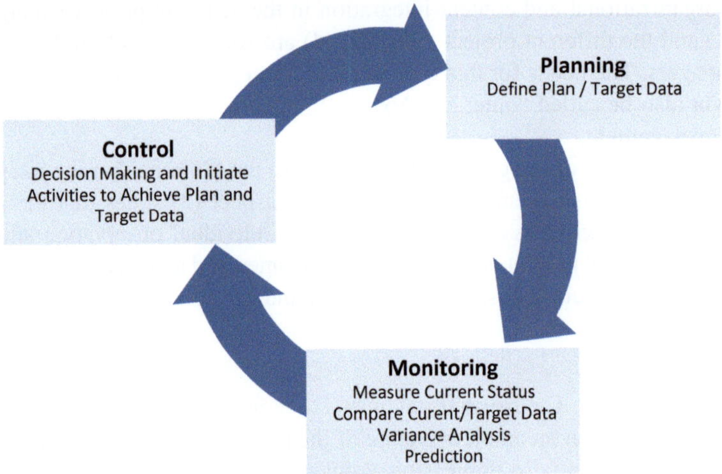

Fig. 21.2 Three sub-process of project management

21.3 Establish Project Performance Data

The delivered project results, i.e. the provided performance and achievements, are at first significant for a robust (verifiable) statement about the actual physical project progress. The project lead needs to focus on the data that is needed to evaluate the required performance and achievements. These are however often structured and detailed differently but usually specified in the following documents:

- In the **Project Assignment**, **Customer Contracts**, **Contracts**, etc.
- In the **Specification Letters** (performance specifications, functional specifications, etc.)
- In the **Work Breakdown Structure** or **Project Structure Plans** and the **Work Package Descriptions**
- In the **Process and Schedule Plan** and **Node** (activity) descriptions

Each of these performance and achievement descriptions need to be synchronized with each other to create manageable project tasks. The minimum is to describe the work packages as precise as possible not only including the required numbers but also the required qualities. Depending on the project details a project task can be positioned on any structural level of the project, tasks such as subtasks, work packages, or even single project activities. For all nodes (activities) plan data should usually be available, consequently then being able to compile the performance data (1)–(3) in this detail. This is not necessarily required most of the time but can be meaningful related to the cost consideration.

Generally, the following data listed (Table 21.1) data should be collected for a project status.

Table 21.1 Performance data acquisition table

Performance data	Data collection needs
1. Result/performance (content/quantity/quality)	• Current progress degree, i.e. current completion status (for all activities)
2. Dates	• Actual status dates, i.e. actual start date (for all begun activities) and the actual finish date (only for completed activities) • Estimated end date or estimated remaining time for the currently required result/performance or the updated planed duration for all unfinished activities
3. Effort (hours/cost)	• Actual work effort, i.e. the actually incurred hours and costs (for all completed and in-progress activities) • Estimated remaining efforts (in hours and costs) for the/result/ performance currently required or the updated plan required for in-progress tasks
4. Process quality	• Customer satisfaction • Employee satisfaction • Satisfaction in the project environment • Risks development

21.4 Content of the Control

The contents of the control and the control procedures are agreed with the responsible project planner. By having a detailed breakdown of project work packages and activities up front, it will be easier to control during project execution. All existing documents of the detailed planning are used as control documents such as schedule lists, network diagrams, or Gantt charts.

21.5 Control Metrics and Timings

Primarily the individual stages and phases of the problem solution process, the project progress, the resource impact, and the cost development are subject to be controlled. The relationship between **Performance** and **Quality**, the **Schedules,** and the **Costs** requires a holistic approach. A one-sided schedule and cost control would quickly lead to a trade-off on system performance and quality especially for organization projects.

21.6 Check Schedules and Costs

Project progress (also project status) and the development of costs are determined with schedule and cost control. This is done by a periodic comparison of the planned and actual schedule dates and costs. This is based on the network (PDM) plans, the detail plans, and the work packages with associated activities and costs. The individual project members usually do the data collection; appropriate forms can significantly simplify the collection and the analysis (Table 21.2).

Table 21.2 Example collection form

Project:							Work Package			
Logistics (Pre-Studie)							Situation Analysis			
							Production planning/Sales			
Employee Peter Smith							Calendar Week: 40		Page 1/1	
Activity	Expenditure of time (Hours)						Effort ACTUALS Week	Effort ACTALS Total	Effort PLAN Total	Effort PLAN Delta
	M	D	M	D	F	S				
Create the interview Guide	8	8	2				18	18	16	0
Perform the interviews with production			6	8	6		20	20	80	60

Tracking the project parameters is primarily a question of information processing and visualization. Unfortunately, the network diagram (PDM) technology offers little opportunity to visualize the progress of the project. Schedules can be tracked using bar (Gantt) charts by proportionally shading the activity bar to the achieved percentage of completion. A completely shaded bar corresponds to a closed, which means 100% finished activity. The length of the bar in the Gantt chart represents the planned proportional duration. The shaded length shows the actual project activity performance, which is proportional to result (Fig. 21.3).

To achieve a situation-oriented picture with regard to the schedules and the costs they need to be related to actual project performance. If the project is delayed then you need to relate target costs with the actual cost at the same point in time. The same situation applies to a project schedule delay. To be able intervene as soon as the project is delayed it is significantly important to have the cost data shortly at hand. This principle applies especially for large projects where the speed of supplying information is essential and has a higher priority than the accuracy. The use of project management software can considerably facilitate the calculation of project costs.

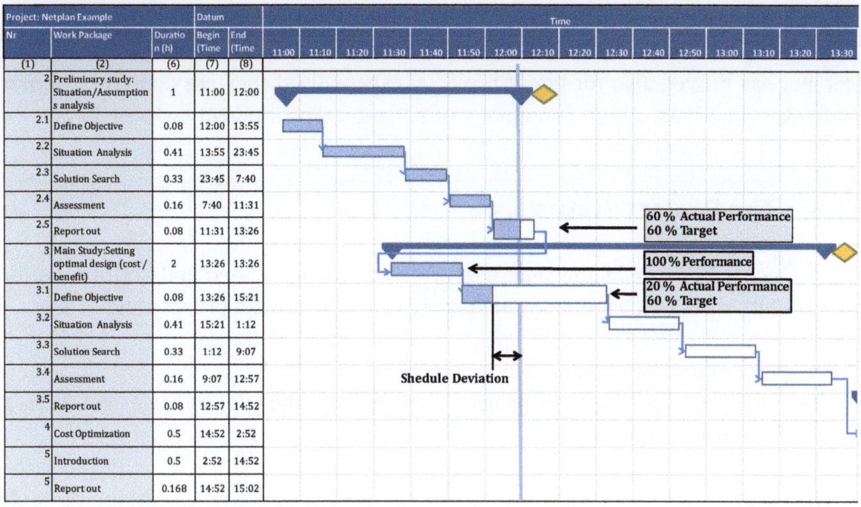

Fig. 21.3 Schedule deviation in Gantt chart

In the framework of project control, data capturing should not only focus on actual status, but also on forecasting on the expected future processing of the individual work packages. The controlling instrument, **earned value analysis**, aims to predict the future development of the project based on the historical project development; in addition the metrics can be used as an early warning system to gain an overall project status overview.

21.7 Control of the Quality Performance

The performance and quality control extend to the actual working results of a project. They should show whether the results correspond to the time and cost efforts. Even if the project requirements for time and cost are met, there is no guarantee that the project meets all contractual requirements without significant rework and costs. The system performance and the system quality can only be reviewed at the end of a work package where verifiable results are then available.

Especially in the early stages of a project, defects and errors have a significant impact on the total cost of the project. The later the correction measures are carried out, the higher is the additional effort on time and money. The project manager must therefore attempt to recognize quality defects as early as possible and to take countermeasures immediately. The aviation industry has developed effective review procedures for large projects to ensure the successful completion of the project. The development status of a project is subjected upon reaching certain review milestones. These review milestones coincide with the completion of each project stage. However, it is also possible given there is a suitable project structure, to review individual results of work within a project level. After successful verification the individual work packages are clearly and accurately completed to be prepared for the next project stage. The review concept is suitable not only for technologies projects, but has proved also for larger projects, especially if they are done by external contractors and have a high percentage of software development tasks in them.

21.8 The Project Status

The project status reflects the state of a project in a compressed and uniform build. It represents a periodic summary and reporting of the project process and serves:

- The preparation for management reporting
- The purpose, to provide the project manager and the project team members a picture of the overall project.

The project status is captured via the work package or activities passing through the project stages:

- At the beginning each work package and activities are **Planned**"; processing has not yet begun.
- The status of "in progress" expresses that work has been was started on a work package or an activity.
- Planned and unplanned interruptions will be marked "**Interrupted**".
- The processing is "**Completed**", when the output of a work package is available.
- A work package will receive the status "**Signed Off**", if the result of the quality assurance has been positive.

Project status reports should have a standard format. Table 21.3 shows detailed status reports on the level "Employees—Activity—Week" and is designed primarily for the internal information of the project manager. For the regular Steering Committee report out a compression level is sufficient on the "Work Package—Monthly" level.

21.9 Control of Projects

Project management includes all project-internal activities that are required to successfully carry out the project in accordance with the planned values. The project management is a continuous task throughout the whole project lifetime and is done by **Active Control**, by

- Formally releasing the work package at the beginning
- The project manager actively engages as soon as schedules or cost overruns are expected
- The project manager is constantly informed about the progress of the project and looks for and identifies roadblock together with the respective project staff and develops appropriate solutions

Table 21.3 Example project status report

Project:			Page 1/1		Date CW46	
Logistic (Pre-studies)						
Nr.	Work package	Effort	Effort	Start/End date	Start/End date	Status
		PLAN	ACTUALS	PLAN	ACTUALS	
(1)	(2)	(4)	(5)	(6)	(7)	(8)
1	Situation analysis	30	30	40/43	40/43	C
	Production planning/Sales					
2	Situation analysis	25	28	40/44	40/45	C
	Procurement /Warehouse management					
3	Objective setting	8	2	45/45	46/?	E
	Logistic concept					
4	Frame concept	50	0	46/49	?/?	P
	Logistics					
–	Total	113	60	40/49	40/?	E

Status: *P* planned, *E* executing, *I* interrupted, *C* completed

The effects of these active control measures are to eliminate and detect possible deviations as soon as possible. The reactive management process focuses on eradicating **Actuals versus Target** deviations. It is essential to investigate the causes of all deviations and in particular its impact on the projects next milestone. Actuals versus Target deviations are the result of planning errors or mistakes in project execution. Usually planning mistakes are related to different causes:

- The objectives and the project task or the conditions of the project were changed without having the project planning adjusted accordingly.
- The project task was only very roughly outlined, so that the complexity of the project was wrongly estimated.
- The result of inadequate planning experience and a faulty planning is an unrealistically low estimate of expenses.

Characteristic of errors is that they occur suddenly and randomly. Usually, the occurrence of errors is considered to a certain extent in all operational planning to reduce the number of necessary control procedures and schedule changes. The reaction on errors varies depending on the gap between Actuals and Target and the gap exceeds a certain threshold.

The ability to solve a failure requires the analysis of their root causes. They can affect project staff, the employees affected by the project, the management, or also outside the project. If the root causes are known it must be decided whether or not to eliminate the cause through immediate action. You can try to either adjust/reduce the effects or to eliminate the root cause completely.

The team responsible for the relevant work package should suggest possible solutions to solve the issues. Possible control measures for this purpose are for example:

- A short-term redistribution of activities or work packages between the existing project staff
- The initiation of measures to reduce costs
- The use of previously scheduled time reserves
- A qualitative improvement of project results
- Conduct required education and training for project staff
- The short-term use of internal or external specialists
- The use of additional or alternative tools for project management,
- A change in the project organization of the project
- A new assessment of project risks and calculating preventive or restrictive measures.

If the errors cannot be eliminated by measures of project management, you need to change the plan. Temporal shifting of other activities can often compensate delays on activities. Therefore, a reaction on a deviation in an activity or a work package should not be hasty. But even if a change of plan does not eliminate the error, then check if a **new plan** is required. Drastic changes of the project planning usually require the approval of the Steering Committee.

21.10 Milestone Trend Analysis (MTA)

The milestone trend analysis is a very simple and convenient instrument to display the status of the project. Prerequisite for their application is a realistic schedule and carefully defined milestones.

The milestone trend analysis is a single chart that is updated during the entire project life cycle. The **horizontal** timeline marks the respective reporting date and the **vertical** axis the time planned for the individual report dates or updated milestone dates. Regularly (e.g. every 2 or 4 weeks) the milestone responsible person will be asked when the millstone will be fully achieved. This date is entered accordingly in the MTA diagram (Fig. 21.4). If there are changes in millstone dates or millstone objectives, then this must be documented. Using this tool in this way, major plan changes and their causes are documented basically automatically.

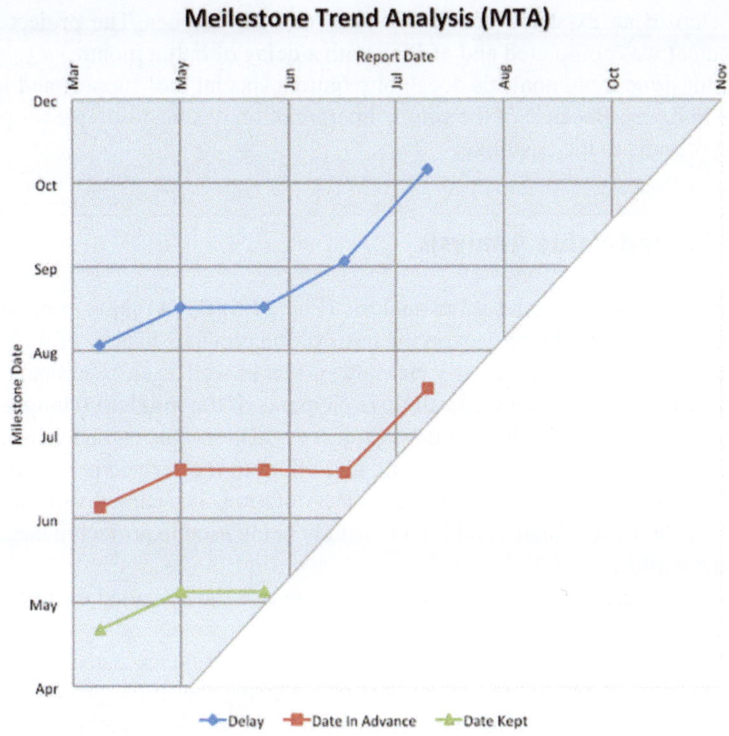

Fig. 21.4 Milestone trend analysis (MTA) example

Milestone trend analysis is a simple method for analysing the dates in a project and comparing them with planned data. You use it to recognize trends and deviations from the planned schedule quickly.

The scheduled dates of the milestones, which are relevant for the course of the project, are compared at various points in time. Deviations from the planned schedule are made apparent. In the graphical form an MTA chart is used, which is triangular where the sides are the times axes. The milestone dates are plotted against the report dates.

Over time, a curve is created for each millstone where you can see the trend of the project:

- If the curve is pointing up, a time delay exists.
- If the curve remains horizontal, the schedules are on track.
- If the curve is pointing downwards, an earlier completion than planned to be expected.

The example (Fig. 21.4) shows that in April the completion of the system concept was planned for the end of August. This milestone however moved backwards step by step to an expected completion date mid of October. The project status measurement was completed end of May with a delay of half a month.

The milestone trend analysis does not require a special tool support and is easy to create in Excel. Because of the simple interpretation it is also suitable for project status report outs to the customer.

21.11 Earned-Value Analysis

The instrument of the earned value analysis (Fig. 21.5) (EVA) aims to predict the future development of the project on the basis of the previous history of the project and to create a numbers-based early warning system as well as an assessment of the project situation. It tries to include all three elements of the **magical triangle** at the same time and incorporate them into the project evaluation. The earned value analysis is based on the thought of the costing and refers to the service provided in the form of planned and actual costs on the project duration. The earned value analysis comes from the United States and is increasingly being used in project management around the world.

Basis for the creation of an earned value analysis is the so-called **earned value**; the project (or even a work package) earns a specific percentage rating of the degree of progress. This is calculated by assessing actual performance with planned cost and therefore has the character of target costs. Meaning that if the project is 100% completed the project end value and the planned costs should be identical.

The earned value analysis requires a complete planning of the project and is based on the following statements:

- The **Schedule at Completion** (SAC) is the planned duration of the project.
- The **Budgeted Cost at Completion** (BAC) is the planned total cost for the project; they basically refer to the end of a project and a full completion of the project task point of closure (POC = 100%).
- **Plan Completion Grade** shows the progress represented at a project point in the time; they are usually defined as a percentage value. Based on the assumption that there is an affinity between the POC and the cumulative planned costs, a plan cost curve can be derived.

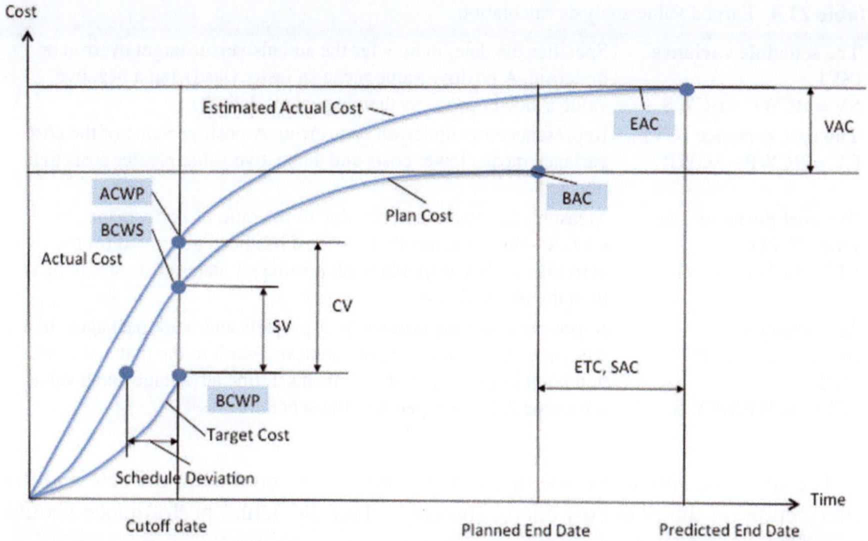

Fig. 21.5 Earned value analysis diagram

To assess the progress of the project the actual project situation needs to be acquired first. This captures the actual and the target costs. Earned value analysis calculations are based on three metrics which are to be determined in relation to the respective review date:

- The **Budgeted Cost of Work Scheduled** (BCWS) is budgeted planned costs for the activities planned at a point in time.
- The **Actual Cost of Work Performed** (ACWP) includes all actual costs or all costs that have been produced since the start of the project.
- The **Budgeted Cost of Work Performed** (BCWP) is determined as completion costs for the finished and signed-off activities, by evaluating these with the appropriate plan cost. They represent the target costs and work progress (**earned value**) of all project's achievements.

The values are then entered into a diagram showing then the cost curves based on early collected data (Fig. 21.5). For project controlling the three metrics BCWP, BCWS, and ACWP deliver meaningful numbers. The variances represent the absolute and the indices the relative actual status deviation from plan. Moderate cost differences between plan and actuals are described by the cost variance and the time deviation is described by the schedule variance (Table 21.4):

Table 21.4 Earned value analysis calculation

The schedule variance (SV) SV = BCWP – BCWS	Specifies the date, in how far the actuals versus target overrun or underrun. A positive value means a faster (lead) and a negative value a slower progress than expected (default)
The cost variance (CV) CV = BCWP - ACWP	Represents costs underrun or overrun. A positive value of the cost variance means lower costs and a negative value greater costs than planned
The cost performance index (CPI) CPI = BCWP/ACWP	Measures the cost efficiency due to the ratio of performance to cost. A value >1 states that less cost has been generated for the activities as they were planned; a value <1 states costs are more than the planned costs
The schedule performance index (SPI) SPI = BCWP/BCWS	Represents the time efficiency of projects and work packages. It calculates the ratio of already achieved work to the planned work at a point in time. A value >1 means a time advantage and a value <1 a time delay compared to the schedule

The schedule variance is the difference in time between the cut-off date and the intersection on the plan cost curve, showing when the actual performance should have been provided.

The variation can be linear projecting up to the completion date assuming that the performance continues at the same level after the cut-off date and irrespective of whether the variance is positive or negative.

The cost performance index can be used for predictions of future costs. A linear forecast of total costs (estimated cost at completion - EAC) results in a linear cost distribution of

$$\text{EAC} = \text{BAC}/\text{CPI} = \text{BAC} \times (\text{ACWP}/\text{BCWP}).$$

The **variance of completion** (VAC) then indicates how far does the total cost exceed the planned overall costs.

The **estimated time to completion** (ETC) can be analogous to

$$\text{ETC} = \text{SAC}/\text{SPI}\,\text{SAC}\times = (\text{BCWS}/\text{BCWP}).$$

If, however, the deviation is caused by a clearly identified and analysed problem and this problem has no further impact, this would result in the total cost forecast of:

$$\text{EAC} = \text{BAC} + (\text{BCWP} - \text{ACWP}).$$

There is no linear but an additive project end forecast in this case.

The example (Table 21.5) follows possible statements such as:

Table 21.5 Example of the earned value analysis

Case	BCWP	BCWS	ACWP	SPI	CPI
1	36	40	48	90%	75%
2	36	36	40	100%	90%
3	36	40	36	90%	100%
4	40	36	40	111%	100%

Case 1: Yet more costs have been encountered for less performance than planned. If the project continues without change it is expected to be 10% behind the planned date and cost 25% more.

Case 2: The project work was done in time related to the plan; however, the project is expected to be 10% more expensive than originally planned.

Case 3: Work is progressing more slowly than planned, but is within the planned cost budget.

Case 4: It was worked faster than planned; the project is expected to finish earlier and the planned project costs will not overrun.

The example illustrated shows in particular that the **earned value analysis** provides a much better statement than a pure target to actual comparison.

References

Michael Gessler. (2011). Kompetenzbasiertes Projektmanagement (PM3) Handbuch für die Projektarbeit, Qualifizierung und Zertifizierung auf Basis der IPMA Competence Baseline Version 3.0 / unter Mitwirkung der spm swiss project management association (4. Auflage ed., Vol. 1). Nürnberg: GPM Deutsche Gesellschaft für Projektmanagement.

Prof Dr. Shulte Zurhausen, M. (2010). Project-/Change Management/Organisation Lerneinheit 1. Hagen: Institut für Verbundstudien der Fachhochschule NRW.

22 Information and Documentation

Maintaining a clear record of project changes is essential for effective management. While a simple email may suffice for straightforward projects, larger projects typically employ standardized forms for documentation. The following steps outline the essential components of a change documentation process:

- Ensure all project stakeholders are informed about the change request process.
- Require that all change requests be submitted in writing, including a clear explanation of the business value they bring to the project.
- Log each change request into a scope change log, maintaining a comprehensive record ("Document, document, document!").
- Estimate the time required to evaluate the change. If the evaluation process is resource-intensive and could impact activity timelines, seek approval from the project sponsor to proceed. Record the decision in the scope change log if evaluation is declined.
- Evaluate the change thoroughly, assessing its implications on schedule and budget if approved. Present the change request to the project sponsor for final approval, documenting the decision and recommended actions in the scope change log.
- Regularly distribute the scope change log to team members to keep them informed about proposed changes and their status.
- Upon approval, update the project charter or other initiation documents as necessary.
- Adjust the work plan accordingly and distribute the revised version to stakeholders and team members.

P. Bauer, *A Comprehensive Project Management Guide*, Management for Professionals, https://doi.org/10.1007/978-3-031-68252-0_22

References

Accettura, A., Bergsma, K., Boszak, T., Callaway, J.L., Cote, N. Doepker, C. Harbidge, M., Her, S., Hlushko, T., Holmes, J., Knight, M., MacDowell, P., Marshall, C., McDougall, L., Prima, A., & Story, T. (2021). Project Management for Instructional Designers, First Canadian Edition. Retrieved from http://pm4id.ca. Licensed under a Creative Commons Attribution NonCommercial ShareAlike (BY-NC-SA) license.

Michael Gessler. (2011). Kompetenzbasiertes Projektmanagement (PM3) Handbuch für die Projektarbeit, Qualifizierung und Zertifizierung auf Basis der IPMA Competence Baseline Version 3.0 / unter Mitwirkung der spm swiss project management association (4. Auflage ed., Vol. 1). Nürnberg: GPM Deutsche Gesellschaft für Projektmanagement.

Prof Dr. Shulte Zurhausen, M. (2010). Project-/Change Management/Organisation Lerneinheit 1. Hagen: Institut für Verbundstudien der Fachhochschule NRW.

23 Communication

Projects inherently rely on collaboration, necessitating effective communication among team members through various means. For instance, regular updates on progress can be shared using tools such as email, project management software, or even social media platforms. Leveraging available technology greatly enhances these interactions, ensuring communication is both timely and accurate.

When team members are co-located in the same building, they can organize routine meetings, quickly seek answers by dropping by each other's offices, or casually discuss project matters during informal office gatherings. However, many projects are executed by virtual teams who primarily communicate electronically. To prevent misunderstandings that can undermine trust and to foster a cohesive project culture, it is essential for the project team to establish a robust communication plan.

Please note, this book does not delve into *communication* topics in depth. For a more comprehensive understanding, please refer to (Michael Gessler, 2011) chapter 1.18.

References

Accettura, A., Bergsma, K., Boszak, T., Callaway, J.L., Cote, N. Doepker, C. Harbidge, M., Her, S., Hlushko, T., Holmes, J., Knight, M., MacDowell, P., Marshall, C., McDougall, L., Prima, A., & Story, T. (2021). Project Management for Instructional Designers, First Canadian Edition. Retrieved from http://pm4id.ca. Licensed under a Creative Commons Attribution NonCommercial ShareAlike (BY-NC-SA) license.

Michael Gessler. (2011). Kompetenzbasiertes Projektmanagement (PM3) Handbuch für die Projektarbeit, Qualifizierung und Zertifizierung auf Basis der IPMA Competence Baseline Version 3.0 / unter Mitwirkung der spm swiss project management association (4. Auflage ed., Vol. 1). Nürnberg: GPM Deutsche Gesellschaft für Projektmanagement.

Prof Dr. Shulte Zurhausen, M. (2010). Project-/Change Management/Organisation Lerneinheit 1. Hagen: Institut für Verbundstudien der Fachhochschule NRW.

P. Bauer, *A Comprehensive Project Management Guide*, Management for Professionals, https://doi.org/10.1007/978-3-031-68252-0_23

Project Start

24

24.1 Model For the Start Process

The following illustration shows a possible start-up process that is split into two main paths:

1. Project preparation, which is still not solution-oriented—in this phase often, significant technical gate settings are done.
2. The following early, conceptual project phase where significant gate settings are developed and technical work is being done.

Figure 24.1 shows this concept of a possible project phase start model. The entire start-up process including the early conceptual stages can be described as starting process in the broader sense.

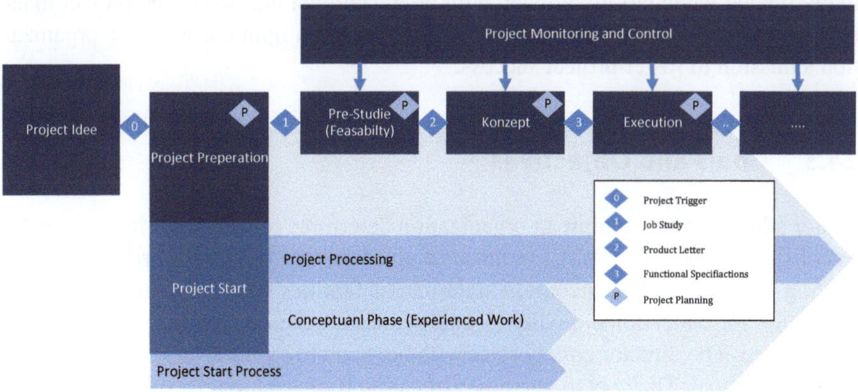

Fig. 24.1 Project phase start mode

P. Bauer, *A Comprehensive Project Management Guide*, Management for Professionals, https://doi.org/10.1007/978-3-031-68252-0_24

24.2 Project Selection

Projects are selected for a multitude of reasons, many of which may not be immediately obvious. It is crucial for the project manager to grasp why a particular project was chosen over other options, enabling them to rally the team around justifying this decision made by senior management.

An organization's mission serves as a declaration of its raison d'être. For instance, a police department may inscribe its mission on patrol car doors—such as "to protect and serve". A well-crafted mission statement is concise and typically includes:

- The organization's purpose
- Primary stakeholders
- Responsibilities towards stakeholders
- Products or services offered

The Department of Instructional Psychology and Technology, for instance, aims to enhance learning through improved instruction and teaching. Collaborating with partners, the (1) department pursues knowledge to enhance instruction, (2) applies technology to solve instructional challenges, and (3) empowers students with skills in instructional development, research, evaluation, and measurement.

Organizations broadly fall into categories such as profit-driven, not-for-profit, and governmental. A profit-driven business aims to generate profits for owners and shareholders; thus, it carefully evaluates project costs and potential profitability. In contrast, a not-for-profit organization, such as a charity, emphasizes the services it provides whilst managing costs to align with available funding. Seeking donations competitively with other non-profits, it strives to avoid exceeding its financial resources. Governmental agencies, funded by taxes and fees, serve citizens, with missions reflecting their responsibilities towards the public. Government entities compete for funding from higher levels of government, with project proposals more likely funded when closely aligned with organizational missions. The project manager plays a pivotal role in team building, ensuring alignment with the organization's mission to foster project success.

24.3 Goals and Objectives

Senior administrators within an organization determine how to fulfil its mission by establishing goals (Fig. 24.2). For instance, the director of a not-for-profit preschool serving children of low-income, single-parent families might aim to enhance its reputation for educational quality. A goal represents the end towards which efforts are directed. The director collaborates with her team to explore various strategies to achieve this goal. They opt to pursue certification from a nationally recognized body that assesses preschool program quality. Achieving this certification constitutes an objective.

Here, we clarify the distinction between goals and objectives. An objective must yield a measurable outcome. In this scenario, the attainment of certification serves as a measurable benchmark, distinguishing it as an objective. Whilst industry and business may vary in the usage of these terms, our approach in this text remains consistent. To discern whether a statement pertains to a goal or an objective, consider whether there exists a measurable outcome. Pursuing certification is an objective, treated as a project with a specific measurable outcome within a defined time frame.

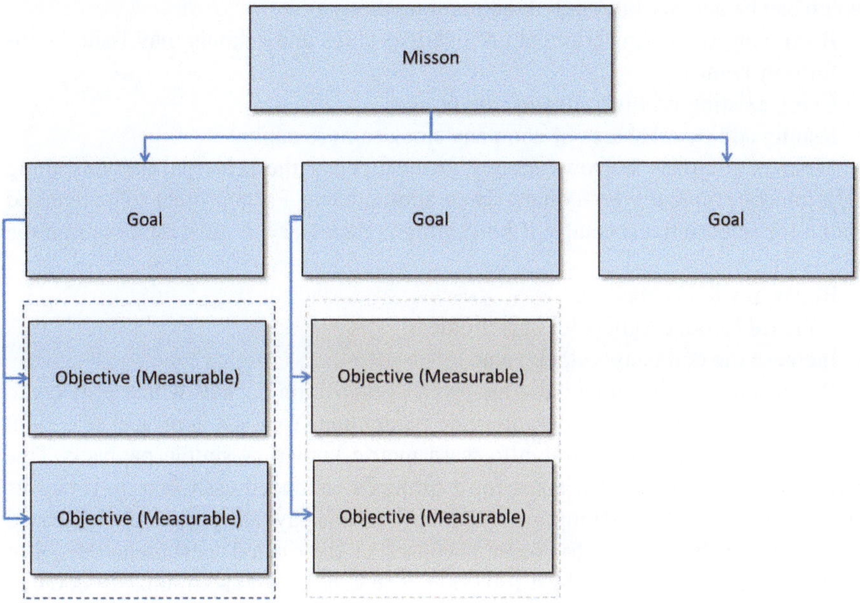

Fig. 24.2 Relationships between mission, goals, and objectives

If an organization's primary mission is profitability, it aims to maximize its earnings by either increasing revenue or reducing expenses. The movement of money within a project is known as cash flow, where incoming funds represent positive cash flow, and outgoing funds represent negative cash flow. Companies enhance profitability through operational efficiency improvements or by executing projects that generate returns. However, funding these projects requires financial resources, which can be acquired through three main methods:

- Borrowing funds (government entities like cities and schools may issue bonds for borrowing)
- Using existing profits to finance the project.
- Issuing additional shares of company stock to raise capital

When a company borrows money, it must repay the principal amount along with interest, typically on a quarterly or annual basis. For a project to be deemed viable for selection, especially if borrowing is necessary, it must demonstrate the ability to:

- Repay any loans obtained
- Enhance future earnings for shareholders
- Increase the company's stock value

When senior management at a for-profit organization decides which projects to finance, these financial considerations are paramount. To assist in project selection, managers often employ a straightforward metric known as simple payback. This metric assesses how long it takes for a project's enhanced cash flow to repay its initial investment. The assumption is that beyond this payback period, the increased cash flow can be utilized for other purposes or distributed to shareholders. For example, if a project funded by a 100,000 € loan generates an additional 20,000 € in cash flow annually, it would achieve a simple payback period of 5 years (Table 24.1).

Table 24.1 Simple payback

Year	0	1	2	3	4	5	6
Equipment Cost Maintenabce Salvage	($1.000.000)						$10.000
Income/Savings		$20.000	$20.000	$20.000	$20.000	$20.000	$20.000
Annual Cash Flow	($100.000)	$20.000	$20.000	$20.000	$20.000	$20.000	$20.000
Cumulative Cash Flow	($100.000)	($80.000)	($60.000)	($40.000)	($20.000)	$0	$30.000

The cumulative cash flow aggregates the annual cash flows over time. When the cumulative cash flow reaches zero or turns positive, it indicates that the initial investment has been recovered through the increased income or savings generated by the investment.

In corporate decision-making, companies often employ simple payback as a criterion to set a threshold for project evaluation. For instance, management might stipulate that only projects with a payback period of less than 3 years will be considered. Projects meeting this requirement would be prioritized over those with longer payback periods. In contrast, not-for-profit or government organizations may be more inclined to approve projects with longer payback periods, as their assessment criteria differ from those based solely on profitability comparisons among similar entities.

24.4 Internal Rate of Return

Companies driven by profit aim not only to repay loans but also to outperform competitors. When evaluating projects that involve purchasing and installing equipment for profit generation, executives often turn to another metric known as the internal rate of return (IRR). The IRR functions akin to an internal interest rate and serves to compare the profitability of different projects.

To calculate the IRR, the company assesses the annual cash flows expected over the project's lifespan. These cash flows may fluctuate yearly due to various factors like downtime during upgrades, periodic maintenance, or the eventual sale of used equipment. For example, suppose a company decides to upgrade its manufacturing line with state-of-the-art equipment. Initially, there will be negative cash flow (shown as year zero) due to conversion expenses. The new equipment is anticipated to remain competitive for 6 years before becoming obsolete, at which point it can be sold for a specified salvage value.

The IRR calculation requires inputting these net cash flows across the project's duration, ensuring there is at least one negative and one positive cash flow. The outcome is expressed as a percentage, indicating the project's investment performance (see Table 24.2).

Table 24.2 The internal rate of return measures the profitability of an investment

Year	0	1	2	3	4	5	6
Equipment Cost Maintenabce Salvage	($1.000.000)						$10.000
Income/Savings		$20.000	$20.000	$20.000	$20.000	$20.000	$20.000
Annual Cash Flow	($100.000)	$20.000	$20.000	$20.000	$20.000	$20.000	$20.000
Cumulative Cash Flow	($100.000)	($80.000)	($60.000)	($40.000)	($20.000)	$0	$30.000
Internal Rate of Return (IRR)	$0						

The anticipated equipment lifespan plays a crucial role in the IRR calculation. When project managers are aware that senior management plans to sell the equipment within 6 years, it allows team members to make informed decisions that align with this strategic direction.

Apart from financial gain, projects are chosen for a variety of reasons, such as:

- Staying competitive with industry peers
- Meeting legal obligations, like safety or environmental regulations
- Enhancing the organization's public perception

Timing is often a critical factor in project selection. Projects may be initiated at specific times of the year for reasons including:

- Utilizing surplus budget at year-end
- Boosting executive bonuses for the year or quarter
- Meeting deadlines for funding or certification reviews

Understanding the project's timing rationale is valuable for project managers, especially when scheduling adjustments are necessary that could impact the project's completion date.

24.5 Project Champions and Opponents

Understanding the reasons behind a project's selection is essential, but it is equally important to know which senior executives supported or opposed it and where the project manager's supervisor stood on the decision. Most project teams comprise members who report to other unit managers rather than the project manager. These team members might be less available if their managers prioritize other projects. An executive who proposed and strongly advocated for the project could be a valuable ally if additional resources are needed when challenges arise. This influential individual, known as a project champion or executive sponsor, can leverage their influence to support the project's success.

To identify the project's advocates and opponents, review public documents such as meeting minutes where the project was approved. Additionally, engage with a trusted network of colleagues to gather informal opinions, recognizing that these insights might be inaccurate but still provide useful context about potential misunderstandings.

In a large organization, an instructional design team was hired to enhance employee performance. The year-long project encountered resistance from middle management. Department managers were frustrated by the disruptions caused by the project team's assessments, interviews, and test implementations. Some findings indicated a need for specialized training, further burdening individual departments. However, the organization director prioritized performance improvement and provided the project team with the necessary support and authority to continue. Without upper management's reinforcement, department managers would have significantly hindered the project. Ultimately, the project's success demonstrated that the temporary disruptions led to substantial long-term benefits for the organization.

24.6 Project Scope Start-up

Recall from Chap. 10 that the scope document (also known as the scope of work document) delineates the project scope—detailing the tasks the project team is expected to complete and, equally importantly, what falls outside the project's purview. Depending on the project's complexity, the scope document can range from a single page to several hundred pages. For more technical projects, the scope will include numerous technical specifications. The length and detail of the project scope document are directly related to the project's complexity.

24.7 Uses of a Scope Document

A well-crafted project scope statement equips the project team with the essential information needed to design and implement the project execution plan. It also ensures the team comprehends the project's purpose and establishes a clear foundation for defining project success.

☞ Example: An automotive company is establishing a new plant to produce electric passenger cars in the southeastern United States. As the plant approaches completion, the plant manager awards a contract to an instructional design firm to train the new plant workers. Training for workers maintaining the production equipment will be provided by the equipment suppliers and is not included in this training contract.

The training project scope encompasses identifying the knowledge, skills, and abilities required for each worker classification and developing effective delivery methods (online, classroom, hands-on) to teach these competencies. It also includes conducting the training, evaluating workers post-training, and maintaining training records. Excluded from the project scope are responsibilities that fall to the automotive company, such as selecting and hiring workers and providing the necessary tools and equipment for training. These exclusions are clearly specified in the scope document.

During the plant design phase, the company's Human Resources Division evaluated various workforce models. Insights from other plants showed that a team-based approach, paired with lean manufacturing principles, yielded the highest productivity. This information was incorporated into the documents provided to the team responsible for developing the training project's scope. The plant manager, human resources manager, and plant engineer reviewed and periodically revised the draft training scope. The training project's scope of work was formulated using a blend of expertise from seasoned professionals, documents reflecting the plant's operational philosophy, and input from selected managers in operations and human resources.

The automotive project team possessed all the necessary knowledge to develop the training scope. However, there are instances when external consultants are needed to create a comprehensive project scope. For example, if the team in our automotive training case lacked experience in starting up another automotive plant, hiring a consultant with such experience might have been necessary to fully grasp the scope of activities required for training the automotive workforce.

The automotive project mentioned earlier exemplifies the typical information and personnel involved in developing a project scope. Based on the project details, the team can create a comprehensive project scope document.

Typically, the project manager drafts the initial project scope and then seeks feedback from the team, client, and key vendors. The project manager aims to build consensus around the scope, but the final approval rests with the project client or sponsor. Depending on the project's complexity, developing the project scope document can range from a brief discussion between the project manager and the client to a process that spans weeks for larger, more intricate projects.

The project scope is a dynamic document, and changes are inevitable. Adjustments to the scope are necessary to incorporate new information and can also introduce new objectives that alter the project's final outcomes. In some cases, these new outcomes can provide additional benefits for the organization sponsoring the project.

24.8 Deviation Versus Change

If a minor change is made to the schedule that does not impact the project's completion date, it is considered a deviation from the schedule. As long as the project's end date or major objectives remain unaffected, a formal change request to the client is unnecessary. However, it is still crucial to record and communicate these schedule deviations to coordinate resources and keep the client informed of the project's progress.

For instance, the cost of educational materials for employee training was initially estimated at fifteen dollars per training packet. However, the winning bid for the printing contract quoted a cost of sixteen dollars per packet. This resulted in a cost deviation, not a scope change. The additional cost was covered by the project contingency reserves, and the budget was adjusted accordingly.

24.9 Project Start-Up

The parent organization's decision-making process significantly impacts the timing of the project's start-up activities. Typically, the transition from planning to project initiation is marked by the decision to fund the project and the selection of the project manager. However, the selection of the project manager is not always the defining event. In some organizations, the project manager is involved in the project evaluation activities, whilst in others, the manager is selected after the decision to fund the project has been made.

Involving the project manager in the evaluation process allows them to understand the selection criteria, which can be valuable for making decisions in later project phases. However, selecting a project manager before a complete evaluation also carries risks. The evaluation might reveal a need for specific skills and experiences that differ from those of the initially involved project manager.

Choosing the best project manager depends on how well their abilities align with the project's needs. These skills can be assessed using the Darnall-Preston Complexity Index (DPCI). For instance, if the project profile indicates high complexity for external factors and medium complexity for technology, a project manager with strong negotiation skills and a good understanding of external influences would be preferable. Additionally, due to the technological complexity, the project manager should be comfortable working with technical team members. Therefore, the project manager involved in the selection process might not always be the best fit for the project's execution.

During the initial stages of a project, the project manager focuses on establishing the necessary infrastructure to ensure project execution and achieving clarity on the project charter and scope. Setting up project infrastructure can vary greatly depending on the complexity of the project. For instance, managing a worker-training project for a training college in South Carolina may involve leveraging existing accounting, procurement, and IT systems within the college, making this aspect relatively straightforward.

However, for larger and more complex projects, such as those spanning multiple countries like the one in South America, establishing dedicated project offices across different locations—Canada, Chile, and Argentina—presents significant challenges. Coordinating IT, accounting, and procurement systems to ensure compatibility across these offices requires meticulous planning and execution. Securing office space, hiring administrative support, and arranging essential services like telecommunications in Argentina demand focused project management attention during the project's early phases.

Additionally, the project manager typically organizes kick-off meetings to initiate key planning activities:

- Establishing the project office
- Developing project-specific policies and procedures
- Refining the scope of work, schedule, budget, and project execution plan

Depending on the project's complexity, these initial meetings can range from extensive and rigorous. Tools like workflow diagrams and responsibility matrices, outlined in Sect. 5.9), prove invaluable in defining activities and enhancing clarity in project infrastructure during the project's inception.

Typically, project start-up entails investing significant hours into developing the initial plan, assembling the project team, and fostering both internal and external relationships. It's during this phase that the project manager sets the project's tone and establishes expectations for each team member. On complex projects, the start-up phase can be turbulent, demanding that the project manager not only navigate this chaos but also instil confidence in both clients and team members. Achieving this comfort level requires the use of effective alignment processes, underscoring why there's a high frequency of meetings during the start-up phase of projects characterized by high complexity.

24.10 Enhance Alignment Meetings

On a significant and intricate project, achieving alignment required an intensive 5-day process involving over twenty team members and client representatives. To foster a relaxed atmosphere conducive to open discussions, these alignment sessions were hosted at a horse ranch in the Eifel.

Several companies specialize in designing and facilitating alignment sessions tailored for large-scale projects. Whilst each session is customized to suit specific project needs, they typically include common agenda items:

- Developing a shared understanding of the project's purpose
- Agreeing on methodologies and approaches to achieve project objectives
- Establishing trust among team members

Creating a shared understanding does not imply unanimous agreement on every detail. Team members may hold differing views on certain aspects, but they share a fundamental grasp of the project's overarching goals. For a project plan to succeed, it requires sufficient commitment from key stakeholders, rather than absolute consensus. Thus, healthy disagreements can be constructive during the planning phase. Addressing these openly allows project leadership to navigate potential challenges proactively. Conversely, unresolved disagreements that remain hidden can escalate into significant issues later in the project life cycle.

Establishing a common understanding among key project stakeholders can range from a casual discussion lasting a few hours to a detailed and intricate process. The methods used depend directly on the project's complexity, with more complex projects necessitating deeper and more intensive discussions on issues that rate high on the complexity scale.

To achieve a shared understanding, the following steps are crucial for key project stakeholders:

- Defining what constitutes project success
- Identifying potential obstacles to achieving that success
- Establishing key milestones and deliverables
- Clarifying decision-makers and the decision-making process

Defining project success initially involves straightforward criteria such as meeting deadlines, staying within budget, and fulfilling specifications. However, deeper discussions delve into broader organizational missions, overarching goals, and considerations such as safety and public perception.

Once a consensus on project success criteria is reached, discussing potential barriers becomes essential. In complex projects, achieving project goals can appear daunting. Addressing potential obstacles openly allows team members to voice concerns and collaboratively devise strategies to mitigate risks. This proactive approach prevents these barriers from overshadowing project progress and performance.

24.11 Project Purpose

The project's purpose often finds expression in formal documents such as a charter, vision statement, or mission statement. These statements are crafted during the project initiation phase, fostering a shared understanding among stakeholders about the project's objectives. A purpose statement forged through consensus among key stakeholders can be deeply motivational, aligning individuals' personal commitment with a project's meaningful goals.

Such purpose statements—whether termed as a charter, vision, or mission—serve as a guiding compass for the project, providing clarity and focus. Often referred to as an anchor statement, they serve as a touchstone against which critical decisions can be evaluated. A purpose statement directs the project's efforts towards actions and choices that contribute positively to its overall success. For instance, a purpose statement declaring the creation of a free educational website for high-school students influences decisions on educational content, suitable design for cognitive development, budget allocations, and more. It serves as a pivotal criterion guiding choices between materials and instructional methods.

Establishing a shared understanding of the project's purpose involves intricate dialogue among stakeholders. Crafting mission and vision statements reflects fundamental values held by individuals and the organization they represent. These discussions can be challenging, necessitating a supportive environment where participants feel secure expressing diverse perspectives without concern for repercussions.

24.12 Goals

Goals serve to amplify and operationalize the essence captured in the anchor statement. They take the emotional essence articulated in the purpose statement and transform it into tangible actions or behaviours that are measurable. Whilst purpose statements reflect the identity and values of a project, goals shift the focus to achievable outcomes. They streamline discussions, guiding resource allocation and setting priorities aimed directly at fulfilling the project's purpose.

Setting goals involves making deliberate choices. During the alignment process, project goals are crafted to encompass broad objectives that span the entirety of the project. Ideally, every team member should contribute to achieving these goals.

Goals can vary widely in their nature and characteristics. The types of goals and the methodologies used to formulate them depend on factors such as the project's complexity level, the expertise of the project leadership team, and the ambitiousness of the project plan. Ambitiousness, or boldness, measures the extent of challenge for the team. The more ambitious the goals and the greater the distance from current status to the desired outcome, the bolder the plan and the higher the internal complexity rating.

24.13 Clarity of Objectives Saves Money

In Michigan, a pivotal online instructional resource project faced a crucial juncture. The project team identified that upgrading the software could accelerate the resource's development by a month. However, this upgrade came at a higher cost than originally budgeted. Earlier assessments highlighted that delays would incur costs exceeding €100,000 monthly. Given the project's clearly defined objectives, the decision to invest in the more expensive software was swift and straightforward.

24.14 Roles

Role clarity is pivotal in both the planning and execution phases of any project. Given the unique nature of projects, it's essential to define the roles of key stakeholders and project leaders right from the outset. Sometimes, these roles are explicitly outlined in contracts or other formal documents. However, even with written descriptions, how these roles translate into the project's decision-making processes often remains open to interpretation.

Clarifying roles typically begins with a discussion where each individual describes their responsibilities, followed by questions from other team members to ensure clarity and resolve any discrepancies in understanding. On simpler projects, this process is usually brief, with minimal conflicts and straightforward resolutions. Conversely, on more complex projects, achieving role clarity becomes more challenging, with greater potential for misunderstandings and conflicts.

In cases where the project complexity demands a more structured approach to role clarification, team members, client representatives, and project leaders might use a flip chart exercise. Each group divides the flip chart into two sections: one for the major roles of the client and another for the roles of the project leadership team. Each group then prioritizes these roles, and the two flip charts are compared to align perspectives and ensure a common understanding of responsibilities.

Processes like role clarification assist each member of the project team in gaining a thorough grasp of how the project will operate, their individual roles, and the critical aspects of those roles. This clarity is crucial for refining and establishing effective work processes and approval procedures. Moreover, role clarification enables the team to develop processes that span role boundaries, where multiple team members may share similar responsibilities.

Role clarification contributes to the development of various aspects within the project:

- Communication planning: Ensuring effective channels and methods for communication among team members and stakeholders
- Workflow organization: Structuring the sequence and coordination of tasks to optimize efficiency
- Approval processes: Establishing procedures for reviewing and approving project deliverables and decisions
- Role boundary spanning processes: Facilitating collaboration and coordination between team members who share roles or responsibilities
- Means and methods: Defining the strategies and approaches that will be employed to achieve project objectives.

Another critical area of consensus building during alignment sessions is determining how project work will be executed. This includes agreeing on project management methodologies and the expected outcomes for stakeholders. On smaller, less complex projects, this understanding is typically developed through a review of tools and work processes associated with the project tasks.

Conversely, on more complex projects, discussions may delve into the use of specialized project management software tools, such as Microsoft Project, to standardize planning and tracking processes. Teams often use flowcharts to visualize and refine key work processes collaboratively. Additionally, discussions cover the establishment of necessary policies that provide continuity in project execution. These policies can range from travel and human resources policies to authorization procedures for budget expenditures, ensuring consistent and transparent project management practices.

24.15 Trust

Trust within a project team plays a crucial role in how information flows and decisions are made. It acts as a filter through which team members evaluate the information they receive. When trust levels are high, team members are more likely to share information freely and act on it without hesitation. Conversely, low trust can lead to scepticism, delays in decision-making, and reluctance to share critical information.

Communication levels within a project are directly influenced by the level of trust among team members. When trust is strong, communication tends to be open, clear, and frequent, enhancing overall project effectiveness.

Moreover, trust contributes significantly to team commitment and performance. When team members trust the project leadership and believe in the project's goals, they are more motivated and committed to achieving success. In contrast, when trust is lacking, energy and time are diverted towards verifying information and resolving misunderstandings, rather than focusing on productive project activities.

Establishing trust begins early in the project initiation phase, often during the kick-off meeting. Many projects incorporate team-building exercises or social activities into these initial meetings to foster trust and camaraderie among team members. For instance, some complex projects organize outings or events like spelunking in Puerto Rico's lime caves or chartered boat cruises off Charleston's coast. These informal gatherings create opportunities for team members to build personal relationships that strengthen collaboration and cooperation during project execution.

24.16 Key Takeaways

1. Scope defines the core tasks included in a project and specifies what tasks are excluded. Complex projects necessitate more detailed scope documents.
2. A scope document serves to equip the project team with essential information to devise and execute the project plan. It clarifies the project's purpose and defines criteria for achieving success.
3. Initially, the scope document is drafted and circulated for input from the team, client, and sometimes key vendors. The final draft is approved by the client or sponsor, and any changes must undergo approval using standardized forms and processes.
4. A mission statement articulates an organization's purpose, identifying primary stakeholders, products/services, and responsibilities. Goals provide directional statements, whilst objectives are measurable actions aimed at achieving these goals.
5. For-profit organizations aim to generate profits whilst competing with others. Non-profit organizations focus on serving specific groups. Government agencies, akin to non-profits, fund activities via taxes, fees, and government allocations, serving citizens' interests.
6. Economic tools like simple payback and internal rate of return assess and compare project viability. Simple payback determines when project income or savings offset initial costs. Internal rate of return calculates the average percentage increase in cash flow over a project's lifespan.
7. Project selection hinges on funding availability, influenced by how organizations acquire project funds. Projects are timed to capitalize on funding opportunities, sometimes initiated for undisclosed reasons. Understanding funding sources and project champions' motivations enhances project success prospects.
8. A project champion wields influence to support project success. Knowing their motivation, whether explicit or implicit, ensures project alignment with their goals.

9. The alignment process aims to foster a shared understanding of purpose, agree on methodologies, and build trust.
10. Key components of alignment include discussions on purpose, goals, roles, progress tracking, cost management, change management, and trust-building. Lack of trust leads to delays due to fact-checking and withheld information deemed sensitive or mishandled.

References

Michael Gessler. (2011). Kompetenzbasiertes Projektmanagement (PM3) Handbuch für die Projektarbeit, Qualifizierung und Zertifizierung auf Basis der IPMA Competence Baseline Version 3.0 / unter Mitwirkung der spm swiss project management association (4. Auflage ed., Vol. 1). Nürnberg: GPM Deutsche Gesellschaft für Projektmanagement.

Prof Dr. Shulte Zurhausen, M. (2010). Project-/Change Management/Organisation Lerneinheit 1. Hagen: Institut für Verbundstudien der Fachhochschule NRW.

Accettura, A., Bergsma, K., Boszak, T., Callaway, J.L., Cote, N. Doepker, C. Harbidge, M., Her, S., Hlushko, T., Holmes, J., Knight, M., MacDowell, P., Marshall, C., McDougall, L., Prima, A., & Story, T. (2021). Project Management for Instructional Designers, First Canadian Edition. Retrieved from http://pm4id.ca. Licensed under a Creative Commons Attribution NonCommercial ShareAlike (BY-NC-SA) license.

Projects Close-out

25

Team members who were excited by the project in its early stages may find it difficult to maintain their focus to complete the project. They might already be looking forward to the next project. Bringing a project to an end requires a different management style that focuses on details as well as an analysis of the decisions that were made.

25.1 Closing Out Contracts

In the final phase of the project procurement cycle, the project concludes by settling invoices and formally closing procurement contracts. Suppliers deliver goods that are expected to meet predefined quality standards. The project team meticulously reviews delivery records to verify adherence to these standards. Adjustments to final payments are made if any items are rejected due to substandard quality or non-delivery.

25.2 Punch Lists and Performance Tests

When a vendor is providing a service or constructing something for a project, it's common to encounter necessary adjustments or corrections before finalizing the contract. In software projects, performance tests are conducted by the end-users to assess whether the software meets specified performance criteria. If these expectations weren't originally outlined in the project scope, or if the software fails to meet agreed-upon standards, adjustments may be required.

If the expectations weren't initially included in the scope of work and the owner desires additional work, they typically issue a change order. Conversely, if the expectations were outlined in the scope, it remains the contractor's responsibility to fulfil them. Before concluding the contract, any outstanding minor tasks are

P. Bauer, *A Comprehensive Project Management Guide*, Management for Professionals, https://doi.org/10.1007/978-3-031-68252-0_25

compiled into a punch list—a comprehensive roster of items that still need attention as identified by the client, team, or manager.

The project team then addresses each item on the punch list, devising a schedule to complete the remaining work. If the punch list is extensive or the tasks substantial, the project team continues operations until it diminishes to a manageable size. As the punch list shrinks, the project manager gradually scales down resources, retaining only what is necessary to support the team addressing the remaining tasks.

25.3 Transfer to Customer or Sponsor

When the project deliverable is a software system or any other product that requires on-going operation and maintenance, it must be handed over to the designated individuals or teams responsible for its future management once the project concludes. These stakeholders often conduct their own assessments to ensure that the project team has achieved the desired quality standards and that all project components are fully implemented.

These performance evaluations are usually specified within the initial project contract.

25.4 Final Payments

The final payment isn't just a simple fraction of the remaining work. It often involves resolving the most challenging issues, which are typically more costly to address. Therefore, the final payment needs to be substantial enough to incentivize the supplier to prioritize and swiftly resolve these issues, ensuring the project meets its deadlines.

Once the supplier has fulfilled all contractual obligations, including rectifying issues and completing repairs identified in the punch list, the project team approves the contract and forwards it to the accounting department for the final payment. The supplier is informed that this last payment marks the conclusion of the contractual agreement between them and the project.

25.5 Post-project Evaluations

Before disbanding the team and shifting focus to future projects, a comprehensive review known as a lessons learned meeting or document is conducted. This review is aimed at identifying valuable insights from the project. The team examines successful aspects, capturing the underlying processes that contributed to their success and assessing their applicability to other projects. Similarly, the team analyse shortcomings, focusing on lessons learned and improvements gained from these experiences. The objective is not to assign blame but rather to foster learning and growth.

Quality management entails a continuous improvement process that includes leveraging insights from past projects to enhance subsequent endeavours. These insights serve as documented evidence of employing effective quality management practices. Some organizations formalize this process by instituting structured methods for refining work processes and integrating lessons learned across projects for collective benefit. Conversely, other organizations adopt a more informal approach, relying on individuals to internalize and share their project experiences informally with others. Regardless of the approach, the evaluation of the following elements is essential, and the findings from post-project assessments are consolidated into reports for both internal and external use.

25.6 Project Profile

One of the initial tasks involved creating a project profile to anticipate potential challenges. If the Darnall-Preston Complexity Index (DPCI) was employed, each complexity assessment is reviewed and compared against the actual events encountered throughout the project's duration. The team examines how the complexity evolved over time and assesses their strategies for managing it effectively. Insights gained from this exercise contribute to refining expertise that informs the development of future project profiles. If needed, adjustments are made to the DPCI rating for future reference in subsequent projects.

25.7 Trust and Alignment Effectiveness

The project leadership evaluates how trust, or the absence thereof, influenced the project and assesses how effectively alignment meetings contributed to fostering trust. They analyse which issues could have been anticipated and mitigated, and which were unforeseeable. They reflect on cues that may have been overlooked, signalling emerging problems. Additionally, they explore strategies the team could have employed to predict and prevent trust-related issues more effectively.

25.8 Schedule and Budget Management

The project team conducts a thorough analysis by comparing the original schedule and network diagram with the actual events that occurred. They examine the events that necessitated schedule changes and evaluate how effectively contingency reserves and float mitigated disruptions caused by these events. The adequacy of the original contingency time estimates is assessed, along with the accuracy of duration estimates and float calculations. These activities are crucial for the team to enhance their proficiency in estimating schedule components for future projects, focusing on improvement rather than assigning blame.

Similarly, a comprehensive review is conducted on budget estimates versus actual costs incurred. If discrepancies between estimated and actual costs are identified consistently, the team re-evaluates the choice of estimating methods employed.

25.9 Risk Mitigation

Following the completion of the project, the team conducts a thorough review of risk estimates in comparison with the actual events that transpired. They analyse whether any unforeseen events occurred and explore potential indicators that could have enabled the team to predict these events beforehand. An assessment is made regarding whether the project's contingency planning was adequate to handle unforeseen risks.

Even in cases where the project proceeds without any major issues, it remains important to evaluate whether the investment in risk mitigation was justified. This analysis helps in understanding the comparative costs between mitigating risks proactively and dealing with unexpected events as they arise. It provides valuable insights into the effectiveness of risk management strategies employed during the project.

25.10 Procurement Contracts

The project team conducts a thorough evaluation of suppliers and vendors to assess their performance and determine whether they should remain on the list of approved suppliers or vendors. They review the contractual arrangements with each supplier to evaluate the effectiveness of risk-sharing decisions and the impact of incentives chosen.

This assessment helps in making informed decisions about continuing partnerships with suppliers and vendors based on their performance and the alignment of contractual terms with project objectives. It also provides insights into refining future contracting strategies to enhance project outcomes.

25.11 Customer Satisfaction

The project team conducts a comprehensive evaluation of its relationship with the client, discussing whether the client should be involved in project decisions and alignment meetings. The team seeks feedback from the client to gauge satisfaction and pinpoint areas for improvement. Senior managers often interview the client to gather insights into the performance of the project team.

A detailed project report is compiled to offer stakeholders a comprehensive overview of the project. This report outlines the original goals and objectives and highlights how the project successfully achieved these milestones. It provides a concise summary of the project's performance in terms of schedule adherence and budget management. Additionally, the report includes an evaluation of client satisfaction. A version of this report is shared with the client to solicit their feedback and perspectives.

25.12 Senior Management

The executive summary presented to senior management encapsulates all pertinent information shared with stakeholders. It identifies areas where practices and processes could be enhanced, highlighting valuable lessons learned that can be applied to future projects.

25.13 Document Archival

Project documents must be securely stored in a location that ensures accessibility for future reference. This includes signed contracts and other critical documents that may be required for tax audits or legal proceedings. Organizational policies for document storage and retrieval, especially those concerning legal documents, must be strictly adhered to. Many project documents can be stored electronically, provided they are maintained in a format that facilitates easy recovery.

It is essential to implement standard naming conventions for electronically stored documents to facilitate sorting and grouping by name. For paper documents, determining their expiration date enables timely destruction when no longer needed. Typical documents that are archived include:

- Project charter documents
- Scope statement
- Original budget
- Change documents
- Darnall-Preston Complexity Index (DPCI) ratings
- Manager's summary of lessons learned
- Final DPCI rating

Maintaining organized and secure document storage ensures that project records are readily accessible while adhering to legal and organizational requirements.

25.14 Project Celebration

Final celebration marks the symbolic conclusion of a project and often signifies the disbanding of the team. It's a moment of reflection following the completion of a significant effort. Project team members and stakeholders typically invest considerable time and emotional energy into the project's success. The close bonds formed during this journey often make project closure bittersweet. However, it also presents an opportunity to enhance satisfaction among clients and team members.

Reflecting on the challenges overcome and successes achieved cultivates a positive recollection of the project and reinforces valuable lessons for future efforts. Recognitions, such as awards or plaques, may be presented to individuals who made exceptional contributions. Teams or groups that exemplified trust and collaboration might also be acknowledged for their positive impact. Celebrating the project's accomplishments fosters a sense of achievement and closure, instilling pride in a job well done.

25.15 Key Takeaways

1. To finalize contracts, rigorous testing of systems, meticulous inspection of materials, and compiling punch lists of remaining tasks are essential steps.
2. The post-project review serves several critical purposes: it analyses decisions made with limited information against actual project outcomes to extract lessons and enhance future decision-making. Moreover, it identifies opportunities for refining processes.
3. All original project documents, such as the charter, scope statement, and budget, are securely archived. Additionally, documents generated during the project, such as change agreements, are meticulously stored. Post-project reviews, including comprehensive summaries of lessons learned and the final project profile with its DPCI rating, are carefully preserved.
4. During the project close-out celebration, outstanding individual and group contributions are recognized through awards, fostering a positive atmosphere. The client or sponsor is also invited to share remarks, reinforcing a sense of fulfilment and achievement.

References

Accettura, A., Bergsma, K., Boszak, T., Callaway, J.L., Cote, N. Doepker, C. Harbidge, M., Her, S., Hlushko, T., Holmes, J., Knight, M., MacDowell, P., Marshall, C., McDougall, L., Prima, A., & Story, T. (2021). Project Management for Instructional Designers, First Canadian Edition. Retrieved from http://pm4id.ca. Licensed under a Creative Commons Attribution NonCommercial ShareAlike (BY-NC-SA) license.

Michael Gessler. (2011). Kompetenzbasiertes Projektmanagement (PM3) Handbuch für die Projektarbeit, Qualifizierung und Zertifizierung auf Basis der IPMA Competence Baseline Version 3.0 / unter Mitwirkung der spm swiss project management association (4. Auflage ed., Vol. 1). Nürnberg: GPM Deutsche Gesellschaft für Projektmanagement.

Prof Dr. Shulte Zurhausen, M. (2010). Project-/Change Management/Organisation Lerneinheit 1. Hagen: Institut für Verbundstudien der Fachhochschule NRW.

Questioner

26

26.1 Questions on Project, Project Management, and PM Process

1. What are projects characteristics?
2. On what does it depend if an assignment is referred to as a "project"?
3. What criteria can be used to evaluate the worthiness of the project?
4. What functions does project management include?
5. What types of projects are there?
6. Name a typical application of project management!
7. What special requirements must be taken into account for in the management of organizational projects?
8. What is the "magic triangle of project management"?
9. What are the characteristics of a process model?
10. Are there four basic ideas underlying the process model of systems engineering?

26.2 Questions on Project Requirements and Objectives

11. Show examples to explain what objective functional elements of magical triangle should be met.
12. Why is it useful to distinguish between result and procedures objectives?
13. How can you identify target interactions and resolve them?
14. Describe an example of how to proceed to create a target hierarchy. Can you explain the difference between "SMART objectives" and define the ill-defined objectives, please use concrete examples.
15. What are the rules for the phrasing of good objectives are essential for the stakeholder opinion? Justify your opinion.
16. With what questions could you coach your client, so that statements of objectives are more precise?

P. Bauer, *A Comprehensive Project Management Guide*, Management for Professionals, https://doi.org/10.1007/978-3-031-68252-0_26

17. What is the role of the objective setting at the project start-up phase?

26.3 Questions on Risks and Opportunities

18. What are risks, what are the chances?
19. How do risks and opportunities mutually interact?
20. What is risk potential?
21. When should risk management begin, when does it end?
22. What are the steps of a systematic approach in risk management?
23. What are typical questions to ask to identify risks?
24. What are typical questions for the identification of opportunities?
25. What interactions can exist between individual risks?
26. Which risks are not tolerable, because they are elementary?
27. What is a qualified, what a quantified assessment?
28. What are the probability limits where risk management is considered necessary?
29. What are the statements of a risk portfolio?
30. How is the risk score calculated?
31. What triggers the evaluation of the risk situation?
32. How can the effect be measured?
33. What distinguishes effective efficient measures?
34. Which can trigger the risk control?
35. With what questions should the risk assessment start at the end of the project?

26.4 Questions on Quality

36. How is the term "Quality" defined?
37. How is the concept of Quality Management defined?
38. What is the QM-System?
39. What is Six Sigma?
40. Describe the QFD?
41. Who does Kano fit into Quality?
42. How does the model process-oriented quality management look like?
43. What product types do you know?
44. What does the management of product and process quality contain?
45. How does product and process quality link together?
46. With what method can you detain quality requirements for the product in the project?
47. Which analytical method can be used in a project for error prevention?
48. What is the difference between a verification and validation?
49. What meaning does the stakeholder management have for the quality of the project?
50. What kind of quality requirements should a project member fulfil?

51. What is to be considered in the control of a project team, from the point of view of quality management?
52. Why are project and project phase reviews essential for the quality of the project?
53. What are the most common quality tools and how can they be used in the project?
54. To what extent are quality planning, quality control, quality assurance, and quality improvement of importance in a project? Show exemplary individual aspects that should be included as part of the problem or work package in project planning.

26.5 Questions on Project Organization

55. What is project organization?
56. What main tasks does the project steering committee have?
57. Which organizational units of primary organization should he belong to it?
58. When should the project steering committee meet?
59. What tasks and responsibilities has the project staff and which the project manager?
60. When can it be useful that the project leader takes over project implementation task?
61. What basic types of project organization are there? What typical characteristic do they have?
62. What competencies does the project manager have based on the various types of project organizations?
63. On what criterion does the choice of an appropriate project organization depend on?

26.6 Questions on Teamwork

64. How can a team be defined?
65. What are the pros and cons for teamwork?
66. What is facilitation?
67. What phase does a team development by Tuckman run through?
68. Whereupon does the project manager need to pay attention on during team communication?
69. What are the requirements are there for delivering effective team results?
70. Does a team need networking and how is it used?
71. What are essential characteristics of a team?
72. When is a team, team-capable?
73. How can team and teamwork are defined?
74. How can team meetings be operated effectively?
75. What roles and responsibilities should team member have?

76. Is conflict good for team?

26.7 Questions on Project Structures

77. Explain purpose and importance of the project structure?
78. Explain the concepts of project structure, work breakdown structure, project structuring?
79. Explain the difference between project management phases and phases of the project—examples!
80. How is the process of the project structure in the project management processes classified?
81. Name various aspects of structuring and explain the structural aspects of the matrix?
82. Explain the basic structure of a work breakdown of structure according to DIN 69901!
83. Which characteristically principles of work breakdown structures do you know? Explain these examples!
84. Name the principles of making of work packages and name essential features!
85. What information must a description of the work package contain?

26.8 Questions on Project Scope and Deliverables

86. What is the purpose of defining project scope, and why is it important for project success?
87. How do you gather and analyse requirements to define the scope of a project accurately?
88. What techniques can be used to document project scope effectively, and how do you ensure alignment with stakeholder expectations?
89. How do you manage scope changes or additions during the project lifecycle, and what impact do they have on project timelines and budgets?
90. What are the key components of project deliverables, and how do you ensure they are defined, documented, and approved by stakeholders?
91. How do you prioritize project deliverables to ensure that essential requirements are met within project constraints?
92. What measures should be taken to ensure that project deliverables meet quality standards and specifications?
93. How do you track and monitor progress against project deliverables throughout the project lifecycle, and what tools or techniques can be used for this purpose?
94. What role does scope verification play in ensuring that project deliverables meet stakeholder expectations, and how is it conducted?
95. What steps should be taken to formally close out project deliverables and obtain acceptance from stakeholders at the end of the project?

26.9 Questions on Project Phases

96. Describe an example of a typical project management application!
97. Decribe characteristics of a proces modelss model
98. What are the four basic ideas that the process model of systems engineering based on?
99. What objective is associated with the principle "From the Rough to Detail"?
100. What objective is associated with the action principle of progressive alternative education and removal?
101. What should a first rough phase plan include?
102. Name examples of project types specific phase models.
103. What advantages and disadvantages does the phase analysis have?
104. What are similarities and differences of milestones and gates?
105. What advantage and disadvantages if a process model is used?
106. How would you proceed to develop a company-specific process model?

26.10 Questions on Agile Project Management

107. What are the core principles of Agile Project Management, and how do they differ from traditional project management approaches?
108. What are the key roles and responsibilities of team members in Agile Project Management, and how do they contribute to project success?
109. How does Agile Project Management facilitate adaptive planning and continuous improvement throughout the project lifecycle?
110. What are the primary Agile methodologies used in project management, and how do they differ in their approaches and practices?
111. How does Agile Project Management foster collaboration, transparency, and accountability within project teams?
112. What techniques and tools are commonly used in Agile Project Management for task prioritization, tracking progress, and managing dependencies?
113. How does Agile Project Management address uncertainties and changes in project requirements, and what strategies are employed to mitigate risks?
114. What are the benefits and challenges of scaling Agile practices to large or distributed teams and complex projects?
115. How does Agile Project Management promote customer satisfaction and value delivery through iterative development and frequent feedback?
116. What organizational changes are required to adopt Agile Project Management effectively, and how can organizations overcome resistance to change and cultural barriers?

26.11 Questions on Scheduling

117. In what order should the process and scheduling planning be performed?

118. What is a network diagram?
119. What types of relationships are there in the precedence diagram?
120. What is the difference between minimum and maximum intervals for issuing relationships?
121. What are the result of a forward and a reverse calculation in a network?
122. What buffer types are there?
123. What is a "Critical Path"?
124. What impact does a "negative buffer" have?
125. With what steps and what techniques are used to create a network diagram?
126. According on what criteria should the level of detail be selected in the scheduling plan?
127. What simple techniques do you know of for use on scheduling and process planning?

26.12 Questions on Resources

128. What are the two organizational dimensions that are taken into account in resource planning?
129. Create a typical capacity and load diagram and list for a project-oriented working staff (values on an annual basis).
130. What is the processing time for an operation in days, which requires a processing time of 20 days, if two employees with a capacity of 50% and 30% work on this process?
131. Explain the terms capacity.
132. Name five nominal reasons why then mathematical load calculations can hardly meet reality.
133. What is a resource bar chart?
134. What opportunities are there to increase the capacity for a project?
135. What measures reduce the processing time for a work package or process?

26.13 Questions on Cost and Finance

136. What are the key components of project cost management, and how do they contribute to project success?
137. How do you develop a project budget, and what factors should be considered during the budgeting process?
138. What techniques can be used to estimate project costs accurately at different stages of the project lifecycle?
139. How do you monitor and control project costs to ensure adherence to the budget and prevent cost overruns?
140. What are the implications of cost variance and earned value analysis for project performance assessment and forecasting?

141. How do you manage cash flow in projects to ensure adequate funding for ongoing activities and avoid financial bottlenecks?
142. What role does risk management play in identifying and mitigating financial risks that may impact project costs?
143. How do you assess the financial viability of project alternatives and make informed investment decisions?
144. What are the best practices for reporting project financials to stakeholders and maintaining transparency in cost management?
145. How do you conduct post-project financial analysis to evaluate the actual costs incurred against the budget and identify lessons learned for future projects?

26.14 Questions on Procurement

146. What is procurement management, and why is it important in project management?
147. What are the key steps involved in the procurement process, from identifying needs to contract closure?
148. How do you select appropriate procurement strategies based on project requirements and organizational objectives?
149. What criteria should be considered when evaluating potential suppliers or vendors for a project?
150. How do you negotiate contracts and terms with suppliers to ensure favourable outcomes for the project?
151. What measures can be taken to mitigate risks associated with procurement, such as supplier failure or quality issues?
152. How do you ensure compliance with procurement policies, regulations, and ethical standards throughout the procurement process?
153. What role does procurement planning play in optimizing project outcomes and minimizing procurement-related delays or disruptions?
154. How do you manage relationships with suppliers and vendors to foster collaboration and achieve mutual goals?
155. What strategies can be employed to monitor and evaluate supplier performance to ensure adherence to contract terms and project requirements?

26.15 Questions on Contracts

156. What is the purpose of contracts in project management, and why are they essential for project success?
157. What are the key elements that should be included in a project contract to ensure clarity and enforceability?
158. How do you negotiate contract terms and conditions to protect the interests of all parties involved in the project?

159. What are the different types of contracts commonly used in project management, and when is each type most appropriate?
160. What steps should be taken to manage contract risks effectively throughout the project lifecycle?
161. How do you handle contract changes or modifications while ensuring compliance with contractual obligations and project requirements?
162. What are the consequences of contract breaches, and what measures can be taken to resolve disputes or conflicts arising from contractual non-compliance?
163. How do you ensure that contracts are administered and executed in accordance with relevant laws, regulations, and organizational policies?
164. What role does contract close-out play in ensuring that all contractual obligations have been fulfilled and project deliverables have been accepted?
165. How do you document and communicate contract-related information to stakeholders to maintain transparency and accountability in project management?

26.16 Questions on Contractual Law in Projects

166. What is the legal framework that governs contracts in project management, and why is it important for project stakeholders to understand it?
167. How do project managers navigate issues of contract interpretation and ambiguity to prevent disputes and ensure contract compliance?

26.17 Questions on Organization and Change Management

What is the role of organizational structure in facilitating or hindering change initiatives within a company?

168. How do organizational culture and values influence the success of change management efforts?
169. What are the key steps involved in creating a change management plan, and how do you ensure alignment with organizational goals and objectives?
170. How can leaders effectively communicate the need for change and rally support from employees at all levels of the organization?
171. What strategies can organizations employ to mitigate resistance to change and foster a culture of innovation and adaptability?
172. How do you measure the success of change management initiatives, and what metrics can be used to evaluate their effectiveness?
173. What role does employee training and development play in facilitating successful organizational change?
174. How do you identify and leverage change agents within the organization to drive change initiatives forward?

175. What are the ethical considerations that organizations should take into account when implementing change management strategies?
176. How do external factors such as market trends, regulatory changes, and technological advancements impact organizational change efforts, and how can organizations adapt to these external influences?

26.18 Questions on Claim Management

177. What is the purpose of claim management in project management?
178. How do you identify potential claims within a project?
179. What are the common causes of claims in project management?
180. What steps should be taken to document and substantiate a claim effectively?
181. How do you assess the validity and merit of a claim?
182. What strategies can be employed to resolve claims amicably and efficiently?
183. How do you mitigate the risks associated with claims during project execution?
184. What role does contract management play in claim resolution?
185. How do you communicate and negotiate claims with project stakeholders, including clients, contractors, and suppliers?
186. What measures should be taken to prevent future claims and disputes in similar projects?

26.19 Questions on Project Controlling: Control and Reports

187. In what relation are project management and control?
188. Which factors determine an effective project management and control?
189. What are the functions of project control?
190. How can the project progress be visualized?
191. To what extent have errors in early project stages greater impact in late stages of the project?
192. What are the tasks of project management?
193. What is the aim with the reactive project management? What control measures are possible within the framework of the reactive project management?
194. What actions are to be taken, if errors can no longer be eliminated by project control?
195. What statements contain a schedule list?
196. What interaction is there between buffer time and the critical path?
197. Which statements are derived from a milestone trend analysis?
198. What is the purpose of an earned value analysis? What statements can be derived?

26.20 Questions on Communication

199. Why is effective communication crucial for project success, and what are the consequences of poor communication within project teams?
200. What are the key elements of a communication plan, and how do you tailor communication strategies to different stakeholders and project phases?
201. How does active listening contribute to effective communication, and what techniques can be used to improve listening skills within project teams?
202. What role does feedback play in communication, and how can constructive feedback be delivered and received effectively?
203. How do cultural differences and language barriers impact communication within multicultural project teams, and what strategies can be employed to overcome these challenges?
204. How do you ensure clarity and transparency in project communications, particularly when conveying complex information or discussing sensitive topics?
205. What communication channels and technologies are commonly used in project management, and how do you select the most appropriate ones for different communication needs?
206. What are the best practices for conducting meetings, presentations, and status updates to maximize engagement and comprehension among project stakeholders?
207. How do you manage communication during times of crisis or conflict within the project team or with external stakeholders?
208. What measures should be taken to document and archive project communications for future reference and audit purposes?

26.21 Questions on Project Start

209. What are the key activities involved in project initiation, and why is this phase crucial for project success?
210. What is the purpose of a project charter, and what information should it typically include?
211. How do you define project objectives and scope during project initiation, and what techniques can be used to ensure clarity and alignment with stakeholder expectations?
212. What are the primary stakeholders involved in a project, and how do you identify and engage them during project initiation?
213. What role does project sponsorship play in project initiation, and how do you secure executive support for the project?
214. How do you assess project feasibility and determine its alignment with organizational goals and strategic priorities during project initiation?
215. What are the risks associated with starting a new project, and how do you conduct a preliminary risk assessment during project initiation?

216. How do you assemble and mobilize a project team during project initiation, and what considerations should be taken into account when selecting team members?
217. What are the deliverables of the project initiation phase, and how do you ensure they are completed effectively before proceeding to project planning and execution?
218. How do you establish project governance structures and establish communication channels to facilitate effective project management from the outset?

26.22 Questions on Project Close-out

219. What is the purpose of project close-out, and why is it essential for project management?
220. What are the key activities involved in project close-out, and how do they differ from activities in other project phases?
221. How do you ensure that all project deliverables have been completed to the satisfaction of stakeholders during project close-out?
222. What steps should be taken to formally hand over project deliverables to the client or end-users at the close of the project?
223. How do you conduct a lesson learned session or post-project review to capture insights and identify areas for improvement during project close-out?
224. What documentation and records should be compiled and archived as part of the project close-out process, and why is this important?
225. What measures should be taken to formally terminate contracts, release project resources, and close financial accounts associated with the project?
226. How do you communicate project closure to stakeholders, including team members, clients, and other relevant parties?
227. What are the criteria for evaluating project success during project close-out, and how do you measure the achievement of project objectives and deliverables?
228. What are the final steps in the project close-out process, and how do you ensure a smooth transition to post-project activities, such as follow-up support or maintenance?

Reference

OpenAI's ChatGPT AI language model, P. C. (n.d.).

Index

P. Bauer, *A Comprehensive Project Management Guide*, Management for Professionals, https://doi.org/10.1007/978-3-031-68252-0

MIX
Papier aus verantwortungsvollen Quellen
Paper from responsible sources
FSC® C105338

If you have any concerns about our products,
you can contact us on
ProductSafety@springernature.com

In case Publisher is established outside the EU,
the EU authorized representative is:
Springer Nature Customer Service Center GmbH
Europaplatz 3, 69115 Heidelberg, Germany

Printed by Libri Plureos GmbH
in Hamburg, Germany